WEAKNESS IS A CRIME

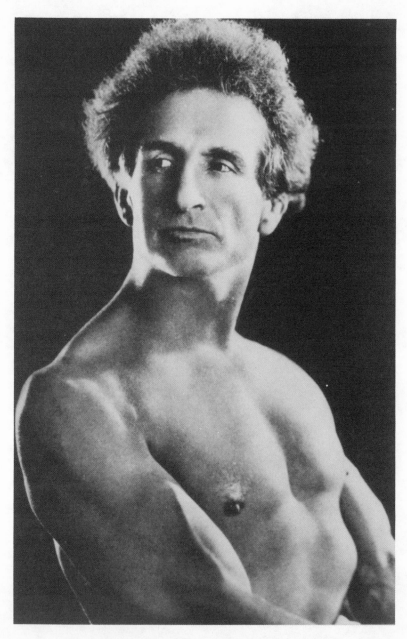

Bernarr Macfadden in 1931. Courtesy of Fulton Oursler, Jr.

WEAKNESS IS A CRIME

The Life of Bernarr Macfadden

Robert Ernst

SYRACUSE UNIVERSITY PRESS

First Edition 1991
91 92 93 94 95 96 97 98 99   6 5 4 3 2

Publication of this book was made possible by a contribution from the office of the Dean of the College of Arts and Sciences, Adelphi University, Garden City, New York 11530.

The paper used in this publication meets the minimum requirements of American National Standard for Information Sciences—Permanence of Paper for Printed Library Materials, ANSI Z39.48-1984. ∞™

Library of Congress Cataloging-in-Publication Data

Ernst, Robert, 1915–
    Weakness is a crime : the life of Bernarr Macfadden / Robert Ernst. — 1st ed.
        p.   cm.
    Includes bibliographical references.
    ISBN 0-8156-2512-X (alk. paper). — ISBN 0-8156-0252-9 (pbk. : alk. paper)
        1. Macfadden, Bernarr, 1868–1955.   2. Physical fitness—United States.   I. Title.
    GV333.M3E76   1990
    613.7'092—dc20
        [B]   90-38194
                                                                              CIP

Manufactured in the United States of America

For Esther

ROBERT ERNST is Professor of History Emeritus at Adelphi University. He is the author of *Immigrant Life in New York City, 1825–1863* (1947), *Rufus King, American Federalist* (1968), and various articles and reviews. He is married and has two adult sons.

Contents

Illustrations

Preface

IN THE NINETEENTH CENTURY P. T. Barnum was the supreme American showman—in the twentieth, Bernarr Macfadden. Like Barnum he was a genius at self-advertisement, but whatever others may have claimed, he sincerely promoted his ideas on health. Spectacular promotions were his specialty: exhibitions of bodily beauty and strength, group hikes for hundreds of miles, and celebration of his youthful eighties by dropping from the sky in a parachute.

The sickly son of impoverished Ozark farmers, he embraced, like Theodore Roosevelt, "the strenuous life," and dedicated a long career to everybody's physical well-being, which he believed led to mental health and happiness. He gloried in his attainment of a firm physique, rippling muscles, and boundless energy. He anticipated today's enthusiasm for walking, running, and jogging. Like many men of his generation he encouraged sports for all people of all ages. He championed whole grains, raw vegetables, salads, fruit and nuts, rejected alcohol, and denounced tobacco. To him, drugs were poison; *all* drugs were to be avoided. He trusted to the healing power of Nature; when afflicted, the human body recuperated naturally if properly cared for. Accordingly, he established health homes where his notions could be applied. Doctors called him a quack, which aroused his combative streak, and he assaulted organized medicine as a dangerous monopoly more alert to protecting its interests than curing the ill.

Sex was good and beautiful, Macfadden believed. He preached the naturalness of sexual expression and, when accused of flaunting the flesh in public, he crusaded against the moral censors. In private life, however, his intimate relations suffered from his volatile temper and philandering. Tender at times, tempestuous at others, he was attractive to women and married four times. All four marriages foundered.

The most colorful publisher of the twenties and thirties, Macfadden sensed the potential of a mass market of nonliterary readers. His tabloid newspaper, the *Graphic*, featured sex and sensation, crime and calamity. His magazines drew upon the yearnings of ordinary men and women. *Physical Culture* appealed to males eager for bodily fitness or cures of infirmities. *True Story* drew young, single women thirsting for the thrills of romance. The first of the confession magazines, it was a top money-maker and widely imitated.

Macfadden's ego was overwhelming. He craved publicity and reveled in adulation. Charmingly naïve, iron-willed and stubborn, he rarely expressed doubts about anything. Amusing to many, ridiculed by the press, frustrated in politics, he persevered on his lonely path, a scrappy fighter to the end, supremely confident in the rightness of his causes.

Acknowledgments

TO MY KNOWLEDGE no collection of Bernarr Macfadden's personal or business papers exists, and I found it necessary to use materials from a wide variety of sources. Information about Macfadden's early life was provided mainly by Macfadden himself to Fulton Oursler and Clement Wood, who wrote authorized biographies of him. Chapter 4 of the present work is based substantially on *Dumbbells and Carrot Strips,* by Mary Macfadden and Emile Gauvreau, which contains the only detailed account of Macfadden's early experiences with Mary, his third wife. Written after she became estranged from her husband, it is biased against him, a fact that the reader should take into account. Chapter 7 depends considerably on material made available to me by the American Medical Association.

This biography would have been impossible to write without the cooperation of Macfadden's widow, Johnnie Lee Macfadden, with whom I had many conferences and who generously permitted me to use material from her unpublished memoir of her life with Macfadden; without the illuminating luncheon conferences with S. O. Shapiro, formerly circulation manager for Macfadden magazines, who provided anecdotes and essential inside information; and without the insights of Fulton Oursler (Jr.), former deputy editor-in-chief of the *Reader's Digest,* who gave me access to uncataloged papers of his father, which are in the annex of the Fordham University Library.

The American Medical Association provided access to its Bernarr Macfadden file. The Special Collections Division of the University of Oregon Library, Eugene, Oregon, made available the Sydney and Marjorie Greenbie and the William Jourdan Rapp papers. David Sinclair gave me permission to use two letters from Upton Sinclair to Macfadden, and Mildred Mott Wedel allowed me to use certain items in the Frank Luther Mott Papers in the Ellis Library, University of Missouri, Columbia. Henry Holt and Company granted permission to reprint quotations from Mary Macfadden and Emile Gauvreau, *Dumbbells and Carrot Strips: The Story of Bernarr Macfadden* (copyright 1953). The first ten illustrations of my book have been reproduced from Fulton Oursler's *True Story of Bernarr Macfadden* (New York: Copeland, 1929) with the permission of Fulton Oursler (Jr.). The remaining illustrations (including that on p. 177 with the permission of Wide World Photos) have been supplied by Johnnie Lee Macfadden.

Among the many others who gave valuable assistance I wish to mention in particular Edward L. Bernays, Elsa W. Branden, Beatrice L. Cole, Thomas J. Crage (assistant director for Technical Services at the Fordham University Library, Bronx, New York), George B. Davis, George T. Delacorte, Norman Fine, Thomas J. Fleming, Bennett Garner, Tom Holloway, Beulah Keenan, Julia Flitner Lamb, Mrs. George R. Leslie, Jr., Campbell Norsgaard, Wilfred J. Rauber (historian of the town of North Dansville, N.Y.), Carroll Rheinstrom, Robert Rodale, Cindy Stewart (senior manuscript specialist, Joint Collection, Ellis Library, University of Missouri, Columbia), Micaela Sullivan (public medical historian, American Medical Association), Martha Rice Turnbow, Clifford J. Waugh (who wrote a thorough doctoral dissertation on Macfadden and who answered specific questions), Beverly McFadden Weiner, Robert F. Wesser, Lucia Temple Woolf, and Anna T. Zakarija (researcher/processor, Special Collections Division, Georgetown University Library). I acknowledge with appreciation a subvention by Adelphi University in support of this book. I wish to thank my Adelphi University associates, particularly Professors Wesley D. Camp, Robert Devlin, Donald N. Koster, and J. Lee Shneidman, for criticizing one or more chapters. Finally I am grateful to my wife, Esther Boyden Ernst, for her sympathetic listening and intelligent suggestions.

WEAKNESS IS A CRIME

Out of the Ozarks

WITH HIS WIFE AND SIX CHILDREN, millionaire Bernarr Macfadden stepped into a private railroad car in New York to make speeches in the midwest and to visit his birthplace in the eastern Ozarks. It was 1928, and the times were prosperous. Herbert Hoover had just been nominated by the Republicans for the presidency and Al Smith by the Democrats. In St. Louis, after lecturing to a group of businessmen, Macfadden met relatives and took them out to dinner, spending enough money to feed a family for a week. At Piedmont, a small town in Missouri somewhat more than a hundred miles south, 1,400 curious admirers and relatives crowded around him as he stepped off the train and addressed them. He paid the bill for a barbecue in the park, and while the children were shown movies the adults talked. After the festivities a cousin Jud McFadden drove the visitors seven or eight miles to the modest farm near Mill Spring, where sixty years earlier Bernarr Macfadden was born. One report had it that he wanted to buy the place but refused to pay what the owner demanded, probably a huge amount, if the owner considered the publisher's wealth and reputation.[1]

When Macfadden was born, Missouri had not quite recovered from the devastation of the Civil War. In the southeastern part of the state, violence had erupted early in the conflict. Greenville, already half burned, was evacuated in 1864 when Confederates under General Sterling Price raided the region, pushing north and west until, pursued by Union forces, they turned south and escaped into Arkansas. Union and Confederate scouting and raiding parties scoured the eastern Ozarks, burning houses, tearing down fences, pillaging, foraging, seizing horses, cattle, and hogs. The rampant lawlessness continued to plague Missouri for years as guerrilla bands roamed the countryside.

1

Two months before Bernarr was born, Dr. Sylvester Miller of Patterson was murdered in Creath's old saloon at Greenville. Missouri's first train robbery was staged in 1874 at Gad's Hill on the Iron Mountain Railroad. Petty crime became commonplace as logging operations, sawmills, and busy railroad towns of the 1870s attracted toughs and drunks.[2]

During and after the war, many farmers lost their land. Buildings, farm equipment, crops, and orchards were destroyed. Property values plunged. The state's taxable wealth was less three years after the war than it had been in 1860. The roads of the Southeast, never adequate, had deteriorated from the tramping of armies, and deepened ruts and weakened bridges kept the country folk isolated until a new post route was opened from Patterson to Doniphan in 1868. As people migrated from rural areas, the farm population dropped from 51 percent in 1860 to 44 percent twenty years later.

Most southeastern Missourians, whose families had originated in the southern states, supported the Democrats before the war. In 1860, only three of Wayne County's 732 votes for president had been cast for Lincoln, although during the war men and boys enlisted on both sides. A year after the Emancipation Proclamation freed the few blacks in this region, the Radical Republicans gained control of the state, and a constitutional convention in 1865 disfranchised Confederate sympathizers. Nine-tenths of Wayne County's electorate lost the right to vote, and the few who did vote were almost unanimously against the new constitution. While the state was in political turmoil, its economy gradually recovered. Mines of Pilot Knob and Iron Mountain shared in the statewide mineral boom, but the resources in abundant timberlands awaited better transportation. When the Iron Mountain Railroad was completed in 1873, healthy stands of oak, maple, walnut, and pine were turned into railroad ties, bridges, houses, furniture, wagon wheels, barrels, and tool handles in an ever-widening market.

The people of the eastern Ozarks were cautious, conservative, deeply religious, and usually poor. The men were *macho* and looked upon daily drudgery as women's work. They admired their horses. During the war, no horse had been safe from soldiers; some parents sent their children to herd horses in the swamps or mountains, and one woman sat up all night holding her horse's bridle rein while troops occupied her house. As before the war, racing was popular, track competitions were advertised at county fairs, and impromptu races could be seen on any stretch of rural road on a Saturday or Sunday afternoon.

Bernarr Macfadden's father, William R. McFadden, was born about 1833, one of a large clan of Scots-Irish McFaddins (as they spelled the name before the war) living in a southeastern area of Missouri they called Greenwood because of its tall virgin yellow pines. Here the first McFaddins had come from Virginia by way of Kentucky before 1815. They were pioneers who felled trees to build cabins and furniture and erect split rail fences. Although some of the later immigrants were substantial slave-holding planters, subsistence farmers predominated in this sparsely settled country. Some fortunate McFaddins prospered, however; Samuel McFaddin owned seven slaves in 1840. His son James had several children, one of whom was William.[3]

A large, broad-shouldered, and deep-chested man who had enlisted in the Union forces during the war, William had only a cursory interest in the daily routine of farm life. He liked to hunt and was passionately addicted to horse racing. With his brother Pennington, who was eighteen years older, he cut and burned pines to clear a training area for the racehorses they bred and sold as far away as New Orleans. Ordinarily sociable, he quickly flew into violent rages and, like other Missouri racing fans, drank heavily. He would buy a jug of whiskey at the track, get drunk, squander his money on losing horses, then stagger home and beat up his family.[4]

McFadden's run-down farm lay at the foot of a hill along the Black River, a rapid-flowing stream about two hundred yards wide, which coursed through the flood plain that gradually yielded to gently rolling hills of iron-rich soil and tempting timberland. At the farm, the river could be crossed on a small ferry held to its course by a rope tied to huge trees on both banks. Two miles downriver was the village of Mill Spring, an oasis of saloons, and gambling and boarding houses on the State Military Road.[5]

Late in the summer of 1867, William McFadden checked in at the Ironton House in Ironton, forty miles to the north, and on September 17 he married Mary Elizabeth, daughter of George and Mary J. Miller at their farmhouse in Ironton. An ecstatic young Mary sent a cake to the *Iron Country Register,* which responded with congratulations to the bride and groom in words that proved ironic: "May neither ever have cause to regret the important step so recently taken. Peace and happiness and prosperity attend them throughout the journey of life."[6]

When Mary first saw her new home at McFadden's Mill Spring farm, she was twenty-one, thirteen years younger than her husband. Eleven months later, on August 16, 1868, Bernard Adolphus was born, and in May or June 1870, a daughter Mary.[7] The modest McFadden farmhouse was a hive of activity, judging from its flock of inhabitants. Living with the family were two young male McFadden relatives, a domestic servant and her three children, two farm laborers, and an eight-year-old boy who may have been William McFadden's son by an earlier marriage. With so many crowded together under one roof, life was exciting if not always pleasant. For Mary Miller McFadden it was hard to manage a husband who gambled irresponsibly and was often drunk. When sober he was easy-going and convivial, but when he reeked of alcohol, turned violent, and ordered her about, she worried about the future of their marriage.

After one of William's drunken tantrums, she finally decided to escape to her parents' home in Ironton and took her two small children with her. Her contrite husband turned up at the Miller farm from time to time, skulked in a weed patch beyond the log fence in front of the house, and pleaded with her to rejoin him. He eventually coaxed her back to the neglected Mill Spring farm, but after he resumed his alcoholic ways, Mary and the children again found asylum with the Millers, probably in 1872. This time the separation was permanent, despite her pregnancy. A second daughter, Alma, was born shortly afterward,[8] and in 1873 Mary obtained a divorce.

The Millers' farm lay across the valley from the foot of Shepherd Mountain, a prominent hill whose approaches became a playground for Bernard and his sisters. The boy watched with fascination the lively baptismal immersion of black people in the stream flowing from the mountain, a joyful event in sharp contrast to the austerity of his Presbyterian Sunday school. But Bernard feared the water; according to family legend, as an infant he fell into a tub of boiling water on laundry day. He refused to dive and swim, which provoked the older boys to dunk him without mercy.[9] To his later embarrassment, he never learned to swim well.

A weak and sickly boy, he contracted a variety of childhood diseases from which he recovered slowly. When he was seven or eight, he was vaccinated for smallpox by the customary arm-to-arm method — the scab from a victim's arm was applied to the arm of the patient — and it took him six months to recuperate.[10] This painful experience deeply affected him, and he became a lifelong enemy of compulsory vaccination.

Bernard was five and one-half years old when in 1874 his father died of delirium tremens. Whatever he may have remembered of his father, his sense of loss was more bearable than the separation from his mother three years later. Mary McFadden hoped to relieve the burden of her three young children on her parents, so she took Bernard to the docks at St. Louis, where she turned him over to an agent of an orphan school down the Mississippi. The boy sobbed, protested, and tried to wriggle away, but he was led off, carried down the river, and placed among the overdisciplined, underfed pupils who told him: "You'll find out. They never feed us *nothin'*. Why, no boy *ever* grew any bigger, while they kep' him in *this place*." Recalling those hungry-eyed urchins, he later declared that Oliver Twist with a bowl of watered gruel was overstuffed when compared to himself at the orphan school.[11] He did remember the peanuts:

> Upon occasions the boys would have a nickel to spend, and when they bought peanuts they never shelled them—they ate them shells and all. And whenever a boy was fortunate enough to get an apple, no boy ever asked for the core, for there was no core—to give away.
>
> When the directors of this school visited the institution, a feast would be placed before the boys. . . . But if the writer lives a thousand years he will never forget the starvation diet furnished at that school.[12]

Peanuts were cheap in the 1870s, long before George Washington Carver's research, and sold as hog feed for about a dollar a ton. Noticing that Bernard coughed a lot and often ran a temperature, the headmaster attributed his malady to peanut deficiency and increased his fibrous rations.[13] Miserable, frightened, homesick, and subject to floggings, Bernard cried out for affection.

Meanwhile, Mary McFadden farmed out her little daughters to be raised by relatives. Young Mary eventually went to Kansas, married Roland R. Conklin, a Kansas City banker, moved with him to New York, and died some time before 1915. Alma was adopted by a couple in Doniphan and later married Thomas W. Mabrey, a prominent politician, who at the age of thirty was elected speaker of the Missouri House of Representatives. The Mabreys finally settled in St. Louis, where he got a position in the customs office. She died in 1902 when only twenty-nine.[14]

With her daughters off her hands, Mary McFadden retrieved Bernard from the orphan school. Free at last! but not for long. Soon after his ninth birthday, his mother sent him to relatives who ran a small hotel in Mount Sterling, Illinois, about one hundred miles north of St. Louis. "He ain't so much to look at, but there's likely work in him,"

Macfadden as a boy. Courtesy of Fulton Oursler, Jr.

the woman said after examining him like a slave. "If there's work in him, we'll get it out," her husband added, and the boy was put to work sweeping and scrubbing floors, emptying slops, doing laundry, carrying luggage, blacking shoes, and helping drunks to bed. Physically weak and scrawny, he was worn out most of the time. On rare occasions he was sent to school to satisfy the village truant officer.[15]

The hotel owner's wife, although doting on her two daughters, showed little love for the lonely Bernard. When a guest reported the loss of a pencil from his room, the woman blamed the boy for stealing it. He had, in fact, taken it, but blurted, "I ain't seen it." Interrupting him, grasping him by the collar and shaking him like a fruit tree, she scolded, "Don't you lie to me, you little thief, you!" After he finally admitted the theft, she beat him furiously. Sore and sobbing, he slunk away to his tiny upper-story room and concluded that honesty might have prevented the whipping. From his window he watched the trains at the railroad station, hoping his mother would arrive on one, but apparently she never came. She died of tuberculosis in 1879.[16]

When the proprietor told Bernard, "Boy, I've got news for you—your mother's dead," his wife chimed in, "And if you ask me, this one's going the same way soon. He's got all the symptoms. Consumption runs in the family." Bernard never forgot the predictions of his early death. With hotel profits falling, the hotelkeepers, anxious to avert burial costs, shipped him off to a farmer in nearby Macomb as a "bound boy" in exchange for a little money and produce.

His new master was Robert Hunter, said to be "the stingiest son of a bitch east of the Mississippi River," who lived with his wife, Ella, their baby of six months, and two of Hunter's sisters. Before carting him away in the wagon, Hunter looked him over dubiously. "He might be wuss, we'll take him, eh, Ella? Mebbe we kin make somthin' out o' him."[17] At Hunter's farm the weakling Bernard was set to work cleaning lamps, chopping wood, feeding and tending stock, and performing many other chores. He often thought of running away, but stuck it out for two years. In time, Bernard gradually experienced bodily changes and gained vitality (which he later explained as a powerful magnetic force coming out of the earth and sweeping through him). He now moved like a jackrabbit and worked uncomplainingly at even the heaviest task. He drove a team, plowed, planted, harvested, chopped trees and split logs, butchered hogs, fed and milked a dozen cows morning and night, churned butter, and washed dishes. Relieved of work, Hunter lay in bed reading the *Farmer's Almanac* while Bernard gained in strength and weight.[18]

The boy attended school sporadically in winter, trudging miles to the schoolhouse. A whiz kid at arithmetic, he was a dunce at grammar. He read mostly sentimental novels, devoured *Peck's Bad Boy*, and acquired copies of farm magazines. On Sundays he went with the Hunters to church and heard sermons promising hellfire and damnation to all but a select few. Instead of being scared he wondered, If even good people go to hell, why not relax? He spied a jug of Hunter's applejack in a corncrib, bought a plug of tobacco, and hid in a swamp, chewing most of the morning and swigging applejack all afternoon. For two days he was so dreadfully sick that for the rest of his life he opposed tobacco and alcohol.[19]

To Hunter's growing dissatisfaction, Bernard developed an independent spirit. When he wanted to buy shoes, the parsimonious farmer objected to the cost and later made no effort to have the boy's worn high boots repaired. Bernard then spent seventy-five cents, more than half his meager savings, for the cobbling. Convinced that he was unappreciated and being worked too hard, the lad determined to escape. Having inquired of a credit bureau about the finances of an uncle in southern Illinois, he learned that the man was generally known as a horse thief with a credit rating of zero, so he decided to return to his hotelkeeping relatives. Tying up his few belongings in a bandanna, he slipped out of Hunter's house, hiked two miles to town, and boarded a train for Mount Sterling.[20] He found on arriving that the man had died, his daughters had married and moved away, and his wife was operating another small hotel. Because she could not find work for him, she arranged for relatives in St. Louis to take him in.

He was twelve years old in 1880 when he boarded a train for St. Louis. Penniless, sitting behind a discarded newspaper, hoping for a free ride, he was forced to take more than one train. Occasionally, a conductor allowed him to reach the next station, but more often he was dumped out along the tracks. Eventually, by walking and riding, he reached his destination. He stayed with Uncle Harvey Miller and Grandma Mary Miller, with whom his sister Mary was living, and found work at $12 per month as a delivery boy for another uncle, Crume K. Miller, owner of a general store. After nearly a year, he quit to become an office boy in a produce brokerage house and later a clerk at $4 per week in the general store (or wholesale grocery business) where his Uncle Harvey was bookkeeper.[21]

Accustomed to outdoor activity and physical labor, Bernard found sedentary work irksome. Severe headaches tortured him. His body weakened, his muscles wasted away, and he weighed little more than

Macfadden as a delivery boy, with Uncle Crume K. Miller. Courtesy of Fulton Oursler, Jr.

a hundred pounds. He had one cold after another and a hacking cough that often kept him awake at night, while he remembered the prediction that he would die of tuberculosis. Patent medicines gave no relief. Doctors advised him, but he grew worse. While walking with his Uncle Harvey, he spied some posters advertising muscle building at the Missouri Gymnasium. He had no money for the initial fee of $15, and when he tried to borrow it, Uncle Harvey dragged him off to the zoo.[22]

Gymnastics and calisthenics were part of a growing physical fitness movement. Among German immigrants, the *Turnvereine* (gymnastic societies) had encouraged body building in America since the 1850s. Weight lifting was popularized by strongmen like George Windship, the "Roxbury Hercules." Light stretching, using exercise rings, and the tossing and catching of balls and beanbags were promoted by Dio Lewis, and S. D. Kehoe, and Samuel F. Wheelwright generated interest in using Indian clubs and wooden dumbbells.[23]

Bernard bought a pair of dumbbells for fifty cents and rising in his room at dawn, threw open the windows and frantically manipulated his purchase. When the Ringling Brothers & Barnum and Bailey Circus came to town, he watched with dreams of becoming a circus acrobat and almost killed himself practicing on a tightrope. His uncle permitted him to rig a gymnasium in the cellar, where he chinned himself on a horizontal bar and swung on two trapezes he set up with friends. Every day he walked a total of six miles to and from work. For long hikes he borrowed a ten-pound lead bar from a printer and carried it inside his shirt, to the astonishment of his grandmother. "You born idiot!" she declared, "You'll be in the lunatic asylum yet, you mark my words."[24]

Every day en route to his job he stopped to examine the high-wheeled bicycles in the window of a bicycle shop. For $10 down and $1 per week he bought a used bicycle and even dreamed of joining a man who had announced his intention of cycling around the world, but Bernard was a dud at cycling. He smashed into a telephone pole. He plowed into a pile of planks at a curb. While showing off in front of some girls, he suddenly took a header on the wet pavement. Although he soon lost interest, the vivid memory of his tumbles no doubt influenced his tepid recommendation of bicycling in later years.[25]

Gradually, his muscles improved with methodical exercise. He worked out by candlelight at night in his basement gym, making such a racket that his relatives thumped the floor with a broom handle. While on the job in the store, he slipped into a deserted workroom during lunch breaks and did dumbbell drills for half an hour. Dumb-bells or Indian clubs of various weights and shapes were to be his lifelong companions. Searching for books on the development of the body, he found William Blaikie's *How to Get Strong and How to Stay So*, a popular volume published in 1879. Blaikie propagated the ideas and programs of Dudley A. Sargent, former acrobat and weight lifter, who taught gymnastics at Yale and Harvard using weights, pulleys, and body-building exercises in his teacher training programs. Bernard was deeply stirred by Blaikie, who systematically expounded the bene-fits of daily exercise for boys, girls, men, and women who apportioned their time to the simple routines he described. The book confirmed his own experiences; no matter that he was the target of jokes and teased as a physical culture nut.[26]

Clerking in a store enabled him, in time, to pay for his board and clothing without help from relatives, but it offered little satisfaction to a restless fourteen-year-old boy. His body craved exertion, and he took to the road. Carrying a pair of Indian clubs, he bummed around on foot and by freight car, sleeping in haystacks and hobo camps, rarely

OUT OF THE OZARKS

holding a job more than a month. He found work on farms, chopped wood, and carried water for a construction gang. Between jobs he exercised in freight cars, singing all the while to give his flat voice more resonance, which provoked other hoboes to fling small pieces of freight at him.

He dropped in on relatives, most of whom could ill afford to take him in. An exception was his cousin, E. F. Medearis, a dentist in McCune, Kansas, who made him an assistant. He helped Medearis make false teeth, and he held patients' heads while the dentist drilled, becoming proficient, if not popular, with the victims. Renting a stable for use in his off-hours, he opened a boxing school, but unfortunately it attracted more loafers looking for fistfights than paying patrons, so he sublet it to a showman, who drew a crowd with a two-headed calf. When the dentist started a weekly paper, the *McCune Brick*, "intended to hurl advice at the community," Bernard became a printer's devil. He swept floors, helped run the hand press, and learned to set and distribute type. It was his first exposure to printer's ink in a job that had given writers like Mark Twain their start in the literary world, but the *Brick* soon crumbled. Medearis returned to tooth pulling, and young McFadden again took to the open trail. Hungry and desperate, he found work on the night shift in a Missouri coal mine, where he sweated in the grime, inhaled coal dust, and felt sharp pains shooting through his body. This was no way to achieve health, so he quit and returned to St. Louis.[27]

In the city, he shifted from one job to another: as a drayman he delivered canned goods, sacks of beans, and fancy groceries; as a bill collector he visited stores and saloons (one advised its customers "If drink interferes with your business, give up your business"). He worked as a bookkeeper for a wholesale grocery house. He ate in cheap hash houses, saved what he could, and joined a gymnasium, which functioned in a converted church.[28]

Overcoming an initial shyness on wearing his first pair of gym tights, he worked out on the horizontal bars, swinging forward and backward, and mastering flipflops and somersets. Within a year, he had whipped his body into such fine condition that he drew the respect of the other gymnasts. He learned wrestling from a friend, George Baptiste, an older, heavyset Greek-American, who told him, "Bernie, life is not all parallel bars, horizontal bars, and side horse." Bernard soon mastered the Cumberland, the Cornwall and Devon, the Lancashire (or catch-as-catch-can), and the Greco-Roman styles, and although ten pounds lighter, after a few months he was able to pin Baptiste. They were permitted by the gym manager to stage a wrestling tournament, which Bernard zealously promoted. Baptiste had matched him with a local favorite, and instead of the expected two-hour contest, McFadden got an overshoulder arm hold in the first minute, swung his opponent clear across the ring, and won the match before many spectators had taken their seats. He was a sensation![29]

Wrestling brought recognition and welcome cash. Bernard, now eighteen, had saved $300 and decided to go into business with Hilary Updike, a young man he had met at the gym. They became partners in the St. Louis Cleaning Company, a lace curtain laundry, but the two did not get along well. Updike carelessly wrecked a wringer, and Bernard, who later called him "a lazy snake in the grass," bought him out. For a time, he hoped to branch out and gain a monopoly of steam laundries under the slogan, "You're Not Clean Till You're Washed by McFadden," but soon afterward he sold out, determined to devote his life to physical education.[30]

He continued to wrestle and earn an income from promoting wrestling, mainly to build a reputation useful to him as a physical culturist, teacher, writer, and lecturer. His most important match was with Frank Whitmore, the heavyweight champion of Chicago, whom he boldly challenged and defeated after one and one-half hours of indecisive grappling. Then he opened his first studio. From his apartment window, he hung out a gold and black lettered sign:

BERNARD MCFADDEN
KINISTHERAPIST
TEACHER OF HIGHER PHYSICAL CULTURE

St. Louisans had never heard of a kinistherapist, nor had McFadden. Having carried a dictionary with him and spent time reading in the public library, he appreciated the Greek origins of something that suggested healing diseases through body movements, and the word sounded impressive. His course of exercises heavily emphasized rotation of the spine, which he believed must be kept supple to achieve bodily vigor. He created a slogan repeated many times during his career: "Weakness is a crime; don't be a criminal," and he thought seriously about food. Believing that most people ate too much, he experimented with diet, taking a single meal of half-cooked vegetables. It seemed to work well, but after several weeks he nearly fainted on the street. His wrestling friend Baptiste persuaded him to eat more, and they had a big meal together, but for the rest of his life he fulminated against gluttony.[31]

Although enough patrons came to his studio to pay the rent, Bernard was lonely, and he found teaching monotonous. Each day, after hours, he wrote articles and letters-to-the-editor on health building, and when they were not printed he recognized the disadvantage of his lack of formal education. He had attended elementary school only briefly and irregularly. To overcome his educational deficiency, he became an athletic trainer at a military academy in Bunker Hill, Illinois, a school for boys with behavior problems, which permitted him to attend classes in English, history, and other subjects in return for board and tuition. He closed his studio, assumed the title of professor, and began to absorb large chunks of grammar, literature, and rhetoric. After his first speech, a harrowing experience, he lectured, led drills, trained a champion wrestling team, and coached football, playing quarterback himself—to only a few complaints from rival teams. Apparently, he was the most popular teacher at the academy.[32]

During his year at Bunker Hill Military Academy, probably 1889–1890, he tried various diets, fasted, and for the first time he felt a romantic stirring. On evening walks in the small community, he stopped to chat with a charming girl in her front yard and on her porch, but the conversations ended when her father, considering Bernard uncouth and socially unacceptable, denied him permission to continue the visits. Nevertheless, McFadden developed enough self-confidence to begin writing an 80,000-word novel, a blundering attempt to combine physical culture with romance. When he tried to publish it later in Chicago, the publisher called it "the crudest piece of junk I have ever read."[33]

After returning to St. Louis, he continued to wrestle. Training under Baptiste, he defeated many champions—as they were loosely termed—from lightweight to heavyweight, including the "lightweight champion of the West" in seven and one-half minutes and the "welterweight champion of Chicago" in four. He made some money and widened his physical culture reputation.[34]

"Professor B. A. McFadden, the champion wrestler," became well known in central and western Missouri. In 1892–1893, he taught physical culture and coached teams at the Marmaduke Military Academy in Sweet Springs, near Sedalia, where some St. Louis businessmen had recently spent $150,000 to convert an old hotel and health resort into a school that would fuse scholarship, morality, and physical fitness. McFadden had played on various St. Louis football teams and, despite his short stature, was well qualified to coach football. Under his vigorous guidance, the school's team toured the state without losing a game. Later, in the drenching rain at Columbia, the Marmaduke boys tied the University of Missouri B team, 6–6, to the cheers of the entire faculty and student body, which had come by special train from Sedalia. While at Marmaduke, McFadden's book, *The Athlete's Conquest*, was—by some miracle—published, and he had the satisfaction of selling a copy to nearly every student. One boy was punished after being caught in a hallway in the middle of the night reading *The Athlete's Conquest* by the light of a lantern.[35]

Apart from his duties at the academy, Bernard pursued his athletic promotions. With some friends, he organized a traveling wrestling and boxing show, offering prizes to anyone who could match his prowess with a 100-pound dumbbell. The sponsors sought out local strong men to meet McFadden, hoping to swell their gate receipts, but they discovered that many "local" champions were braggarts or bluffers who refused the invitation unless he agreed in advance not to be too rough with them. On many occasions, he tried to dignify these proceedings by addressing the spectators on the beauties and benefits of physical culture.[36]

At this time, he was developing ideas about health that he would publicize for much of his life. They were not original, and it is likely that he was influenced by several earlier health reformers. As early as the 1820s, followers of Samuel Thompson, who maintained that disease resulted from a "clogging of the system," favored empirical observation over formal medical education. Homeopathic medicine, which originated in Germany about 1800 and flourished in America in the middle of the century, taught that disease was as much mental as physical, emphasized moderate dosages, and favored personal interaction of patient and physician. By the 1850s, many critics of traditional or "heroic" medicine completely rejected formal scientific education.[37]

Lay health reformers found a ready audience among believers in Christ's second coming. Asserting that the millennium could not be expected until people knew and obeyed the divine laws governing the moral and physical nature of mankind, some reformers argued that good Christians were obliged to promote health through a knowledge of anatomy and physiology and that studying the principles of health was a morally binding duty.[38] To young Bernard McFadden, religion meant little, but he accepted the notion that one should observe the human body, live in accordance with nature, and learn the principles of health.

In the 1830s, other reformers began to attack conventional medicine. Dr. Isaac Jennings, William Alcott (a cousin of transcendentalist Bronson Alcott), and Sylvester Graham had convinced themselves that medicines were worthless and advocated natural healing without drugs. For Jennings, supplying the essentials of health was enough to prevent disease. Alcott, emphasizing the value of hygiene in daily life and the connection between health and morality, opposed the drinking of tea, coffee, and alcohol, and the resort to pornography and masturbation. He promoted daily washing to open the pores, exercise in the open air, and avoidance of tight lacing. Graham, an enthusiast for whole wheat flour and a fruit and vegetable diet, preached against overindulgence in rich food, warned against sexual excess, and advocated loose clothing, hard mattresses, adequate ventilation, and exercise.[39]

Water cure establishments were widely popular by midcentury. Emphasizing the therapeutic uses of water, hydropathists advocated drinking "pure" soft water, taking hot and cold baths, fresh air and exercise, and the assumption of personal responsibility for moderate habits and living in accordance with nature's beneficence. Among the most influential institutional practitioners were Dr. Joel Shew, Dr. Russel Trall, Mary Gove Nichols (who also championed autonomy for women) and Dr. James Caleb Jackson. Jackson, abolitionist editor and hydropathic physician who expounded on the way people killed themselves by overeating, became the most famous water cure specialist in the United States, particularly after developing a large sanitarium and resort he called "Our Home on the Hillside" in Dansville, New York. This center for the water cure, dietary reform, and eventually the treatment of tuberculosis, became one of America's great nineteenth-century spas and health resorts.[40] Many years later Bernarr Macfadden would buy Jackson's Dansville establishment.

An associate of Jackson, Dr. Harriet N. Austin, editor of a health magazine, *Laws of Life,* criticized women's clothing as barbaric, unaesthetic, and injurious to the body. An active dress reformer all her life, she was deeply involved in dress reform conventions in upstate New York during the 1850s and 1860s and was secretary of the National Dress Reform Association.[41] If, as seems likely, young McFadden was affected by Austin and the other health reformers, he did not specifically acknowledge it. Now, as later, he took the credit for his causes.

McFadden spent part of the summer of 1893 in Sedalia, teaching wrestling, promoting exhibitions, and keeping himself physically fit. He earned a good income, and some of his pupils became friends.[42] Although his local reputation was assured, he was restless and adventurous, and he decided to visit the Columbian Exposition in Chicago, where one of his friends was demonstrating an exerciser. He aspired to meet new and, perhaps, important people to call wider attention to himself and his work.

Launching a Crusade

LIKE YOUNG AMERICANS all over the country, Bernard was drawn in 1893 to the World's Columbian Exposition in Chicago. At first sight, he marveled at the displays of classical sculpture—"perfect specimens of human life carried out in stone"—for nothing was more beautiful to him than a graceful human body. He intended to spend a few weeks absorbing the splendor and excitement of the fair, but a friend, Alexander Whitely, who had invented an exerciser and rented a gaudy booth on the midway, asked him to demonstrate the device, and, jobless during the summer, he did so. While at the fair, he came under the influence of the promoter Florenz Ziegfeld, who was glorifying Eugen Sandow, the "strongest man in the world." Ziegfeld's lighting effects, which accentuated the German strongman's muscles in the contrast of highlights and black shadows, fascinated young McFadden, who donned tights and began imitating Sandow's poses as Hercules, Atlas, Ajax, and Samson.[1]

Bernard's behavior caused comment. People talked about a "crazy fellow who ran around Chicago streets in short pants and a sleeveless undershirt when no respectable man would step out of his front door without a hat, coat and starched collar." Converting an old clubhouse on Grand Boulevard into a "temple of body worship," McFadden preached the "sublimity to be achieved by the cultivation of muscles and the digestion of raw vegetables."[2]

After six months, he returned to St. Louis but dreamed of wider opportunities elsewhere. In late 1893 or early 1894, he boarded a train for the East, arrived in Jersey City, and ferried across the Hudson. As the boat neared New York, he was thrilled by the galaxy of sparkling lights and the fourteen-story spire of the World building, the city's tallest skyscraper. New York seemed to offer bright prospects for a

17

health-related business. With fifty dollars in his pocket, he rented two large furnished rooms at 24 East Twentieth Street near Broadway for living quarters and a studio. He placed in his doorway framed photographs of himself posing as Hercules, David, and Samson, among others, advertised a free "Physical Culture Matinée," invited the press, and ordered a thousand circulars announcing his courses in physical culture.[3]

Bernard Adolphus McFadden was a name that did not satisfy him. He had experimented with Bernard Adolphus, B. A. McFadden and B. Adolphus McFadden. Professor B. McFadden was not much of an improvement. Bernard sounded weak to him. If he accented the last syllable and substituted an R for the D, it would seem powerful, something like a lion's roar—Bernarr, a unique name that people would remember. He dropped the Adolphus and, probably because there were so many McFaddens, he chose the name Macfadden, much to the resentment of his relatives scattered across the Midwest.[4]

Macfadden advertised in the newspapers. One of the curious reporters attracted to his studio discovered a roomful of fat men blowing up balloons. When asked about it, the physical culturist explained that balloons cost fifteen cents a gross—"cheaper than dumbbells." He stripped down his patrons, made them exercise, warned them to eat sparingly, and forbade them to smoke or drink coffee, tea, or alcohol. Because his clientele remained small, he accepted his friend Whitely's offer of a job demonstrating his exerciser, and he taught wrestling at the Manhattan Athletic Club, but quit when he found it too much work for $15 a week.[5]

To raise the tone of his establishment, he moved to a more imposing address, 296 Fifth Avenue, and had a new booklet printed with better illustrations and a fuller description of his ideas on body building and natural healing. Impressed with the decrepit condition of the bankers, Wall Street operators, and professionals among his wealthy patrons, he was inspired to spread his message to the entire country. To promote his career, he participated in his last wrestling match at a benefit in Madison Square Garden.[6]

He wrote articles for the press, but all were rejected. After an editor told him, "Nobody cares about all this health stuff," he determined to become his own editor and publisher. He derived most of his writing from his personal experience. Every time he "cured" himself of some malady he wrote a book about it. Perhaps from the stress of his new life in the metropolis, he lost his hair and was nearly bald at the age of twenty-six. When his hair grew back he pulled it rhythmically to stimulate the roots, a treatment he advocated in *Macfadden's New Hair Culture*, first a pamphlet, then a book published seven years later.[7]

Macfadden's income depended not on writing but on his physical culture courses until he invented and patented an improved exercise apparatus, a combination of rubber and cords running over pulleys. He stopped teaching, closed his studio, and gave full time to selling and demonstrating the device for a large sporting goods company. After the company failed, he opened his own shop to make and sell it, but grew restless and bored with record keeping and maintenance.[8]

England, he figured, would be a good market for the exerciser, and so he took second class passage on a Cunard liner in 1897 and was seasick the entire voyage. In Liverpool, he struck a deal with a sporting goods firm to supply dealers throughout England with his exerciser and to send him around the country to push it. Macfadden's tour attracted health enthusiasts and curious entertainment seekers. England went muscle-mad, as men and women crowded to the performances of this American showman, who traveled the countryside for two years, charging two shillings (about fifty cents) a lecture. He hired a box office man and ticket taker, and bought a cabinet with a black velvet backdrop. Against this black cloth he posed in a leopard skin as strong men such as Achilles or Atlas upholding the world. After these "living statues," inspired by Sandow's poses in Chicago, he lectured, demonstrated, and sold his exercisers, and he distributed a low-priced, four-page folder of his health articles (including an ad for his apparatus). People thought it was a periodical and asked about subscriptions. Macfadden sensed at once the possibilities of a magazine.[9]

When he learned from the man to whom he had turned over his New York shop that business had fallen off in his absence, he returned to America and resumed his exerciser sales. Accounts differ on what happened next; while manipulating physical culture (or bicycle) equipment in a Brooklyn (or New York) department store he met Tillie Fontain, a clever girl who was demonstrating cold cream (or body-building equipment). They got married, probably in 1898 or 1899, but it was a brief fling, and the marriage soon ended in annulment. Bernarr wanted to forget Tillie and in later years cultivated the impression that his subsequent marriages were the only ones. Some thirty years later Tillie would briefly flutter across his life, talking in Los Angeles with George Davis, western sales manager for Macfadden Publications, who told his boss about her. The physical culturist claimed not to remember her, but when Davis informed him that she needed

Macfadden at about thirty years of age. Courtesy of Fulton Oursler, Jr.

money, Macfadden authorized him to give her $150 a week and charge
it to his expense account. Thus, at least for several years, with Davis
as a conduit, a quiet transfer of money prevented her relationship with
Macfadden from being publicized.[10]

In 1898, Bernarr rented a small office at 88–90 Gold Street in
lower Manhattan and founded the Physical Culture Publishing Company as an outlet for his writings and to produce a new magazine,
Physical Culture. The first issue, which appeared in March 1899, sold
for five cents a copy. Like its English progenitor, it began mainly as
a circular for his exerciser, but it soon became much more. Its articles
were written by Macfadden under his own name or various pseudo-
nyms of both sexes. His youthful novel, *The Athlete's Conquest,* first
published in 1892, reappeared serially and was reissued as a book by
his company in 1901. Three years later he published a second novel,
A Strenuous Lover, a shallow, plodding romance of an invalid given
up as hopeless by the family physician who benefits from the natural
therapy of a friend who pours prescription drugs down the drain. The
hero is converted to fresh air, wholesome food, and pure water; he
gives up coffee, joins an athletic club, exercises in a gymnasium, becomes strong, and turns into an ardent lover.[11]

The time was ripe for *Physical Culture.* As athletics attracted
wide interest across the land and prosperity spawned country clubs
and golf courses, body building became less widely regarded as a silly
fad. Despite its drab appearance, Macfadden's new magazine was bold,
crusading, and sensational. Its first editorial was entitled "Weakness
Is a Crime," and beginning in February 1900, the cover of each issue
bore the legend, "Weakness is a Crime; don't be a Criminal." To Macfadden the human body was naturally healthy and strong except when
Nature's laws were grossly violated. The first duty in curing a disease,
he maintained, was to remove its cause. Drugs poisoned the system
and were useful only as antiseptics or antidotes. All disorders, he held,
could be cured or alleviated by physical culture, and vigorous health
was within everybody's reach. To become strong, one must regularly
exercise the entire muscular system.[12]

Countering the medically accepted germ theory, Macfadden taught
that when the blood became saturated with excessive by-products of
digestion and metabolism the body sickened. Only when the body
was run-down or undernourished did germs produce disease, which
he wrote was Nature's way of "housecleaning." He was ready to bet
his life against a five-cent bag of peanuts that he could eat all the ba-
cilli that might be sent to him, and they would have no effect. The

pros and cons of the germ theory were often argued in *Physical Culture*. Although the publisher did not assume responsibility for contributors' opinions, he opened his columns to writers with startling or bizarre ideas like "Why I Adopted Grass as a Diet," contributed by a Spanish grass eater who was photographed in a tuxedo and opera hat while grazing in a pasture.[13]

Vaccination, to Macfadden, was the deliberate poisoning of the body, a "crime" that could lead to cowpox, blood poisoning, or other dire perils. He never forgot his own painful experience as a boy. As the technique had not yet been perfected and sometimes resulted in injury or death, he eagerly reported cases of unsuccessful vaccinations. He printed articles by antivaccinationists and encouraged a bill in the New York legislature to investigate the practice of vaccination. When patients refused to be vaccinated, doctors resented Macfadden who, years later, charged the vaccine industry with magnifying epidemic scares in order to make more money.[14]

With the vivid memory of doctors' prescriptions that had not enabled him to surmount his boyhood weakness, Macfadden declared war against drugs and the doctors who prescribed them for every ailment. America, he contended, needed fewer societies for the prevention of cruelty to animals and more for the prevention of cruelty to human beings. Patients were not cured with drugs; they recovered in spite of such poison. A physician should help the body to heal naturally; if he neglected to cleanse the patient's lower bowel before treating an acute disease, he was a dangerous person.[15]

Macfadden chided doctors for bamboozling the public with ponderous terms they could not understand, like *icterus* for jaundice and *gastrodynia* for stomach cramps. "Do not be confused or befogged by mere names," he warned. Laymen had reformed the medical world, and the physicians followed along in a rut of their own making. When in 1911 Macfadden read in a medical journal that the common cold was one of the symptoms created by the nervous system to eliminate poisons and impurities from the body, he exulted in the thought that the medical profession was slowly discovering what he had advocated for years. "Medicine has had its day," he crowed. "It belongs to the ignorance of the distant past."[16]

The physical culturist passionately attacked organized medicine as a formidable, antisocial trust that controlled individual doctors, and was often commercially motivated, powerful as a lobby, and a hindrance to health. As the medical profession gradually took control of public health, the states began to require medical examining boards, graduate degrees, and licenses for doctors, which to Macfadden was the work of political physicians lobbying to put more money into their own pockets. To offset the American Medical Association (AMA), he proposed an association of nonmedical practitioners of natural healing methods. He even suggested that doctors be government employees who would offer free services and be promoted in proportion to their success in their localities. Their main duty would be to teach people how to avoid illness. Such a system would "revolutionize the medical world," treat causes rather than effects, and encourage competition among physicians.[17]

Macfadden waged a prolonged war against patent medicines, contending that they contained more alcohol than whiskey. He listed obituaries of prominent men who had praised such nostrums before they died, and he urged readers to register complaints with the post office. Favorite targets were *Liquizone, Duffy's Malt Whiskey, Lydia E. Pinkham's Vegetable Compound,* and *Peruna.* A best-selling soothing syrup, *Peruna* was 26 percent alcohol, according to Macfadden, enough for "a good noisy drunk" and more than enough to make alcoholic slaves of the women and children who used it. He denounced the patent medicine manufacturers as hyenas and jackals who sold false hope to the ignorant and poor. Condemning electric belts and other supposedly therapeutic devices, he vowed to stop the "conscienceless scoundrels" who peddled them. When the nostrum makers approached him to join them, he refused to respond.[18]

His claim that he alerted the public and awakened the conscience of other publishers to the evils of patent medicines was an obvious exaggeration. For thirty years before *Physical Culture,* a few American publishers had banned what they considered objectionable medical advertising, and the *Ladies Home Journal* announced in 1892 that it would not accept medical advertisements. Within two years, seven other publications followed suit. Edward Bok, the brilliant editor of the *Journal,* launched his battle against patent medicines in 1904, and *Collier's Weekly* soon joined the struggle with articles by Samuel Hopkins Adams and cartoons by Howard Kemble. As Macfadden put it, however, the *Journal, Collier's, Everybody's, Leslie's,* and others had "followed *Physical Culture*" in campaigning against pill peddlers, drug vendors and food adulterators.[19] That he was conspicuous in the fray is certain, but his role was less crucial than he insisted, and he ignored the efforts of the AMA.

In his crusade against quackery, he began a series of articles in December 1905 entitled "Rounding Up the Quacks," denouncing medical impostors as "infamous birds of prey" and a national disgrace. He named individuals, identified companies, and described their operations, encouraged victims to hire lawyers, and appealed to his readers to petition the president, the postmaster general, and the proprietors of newspapers to stop the iniquitous practice. He even wrote personally to President Theodore Roosevelt asking for the withdrawal of mailing privileges of newspapers that sold space to quacks.[20]

Despite his declaration that *Physical Culture* accepted no advertisements he could not conscientiously recommend, some of his magazine's many health-related advertisements made highly doubtful claims, such as the Page System of Hygiene, a course of instruction that taught "every known aid for the prevention of disease and sickness." He fired blasts at charlatans touting their cures for venereal diseases, yet he advertised his own treatments for gonorrhea, chancroid buboes, and syphilis, as set forth in his *Diseases of Men*, which offered prevention and cure by "rational, natural, unfailing methods." Such inconsistencies did not mark him as a hypocrite. Unlike many healers of the time, he sincerely believed in his health advice. Advertisements for health panaceas were common before federal regulation, it was difficult to snuff out all fraudulent claims, and publishers were reluctant to pare their advertising revenues.[21]

At the turn of the century, when health information was not readily found in most publications, the lively and hard-hitting *Physical Culture* proved phenomenally successful. Beginning at a single desk in a rented room of a real estate office, Macfadden moved after five months to larger quarters at Twenty-fifth Street and Broadway. By the end of the third year, he had fifty employees working in eight offices. Twenty-five thousand copies had been printed of the January issue and 40,000 of the April issue in 1900; by December, Macfadden claimed 550,000 readers, estimating five readers for every copy sold. In 1902, he doubled the size and price of the magazine. Nine years later, he declared that it had made a profit over the years of at least $250,000, nearly all of which he had applied to his various health projects. His combativeness, organizational efforts, and penchant for publicity won him a host of followers among the weak and the ill, the advocates of unorthodox therapies, the food faddists and reformers attracted by his proclaimed goal, "the physical emancipation of the human race."[22]

They were treated to columns of advice, articles on exercise and athletics, diagrams, cartoons, photographs, and diatribes against drugs, the "white bread curse," parental ignorance, the "criminal neglect of

An early issue of *Physical Culture*. Courtesy of Fulton Oursler, Jr.

our educational methods" and much else that raised Bernarr's adrenalin level. They read of his experiments upon himself and of persons allegedly cured by his methods. They flooded him with questions, and he personally handled his fan mail on a question and answer page. Most of his readers were men, but he cultivated women with articles on girls and babies, a women's column by Dr. Ella Jennings, and such pieces as Amy Hardwicke's "A Woman's Idea of the Physical Culture Man" and Emily Hastings's "What Bicycling Can Do for Women."

For a few years Macfadden published a companion magazine for women. Beginning in 1900 as *Women's Physical Development*, it became *Beauty and Health* in 1903 and three years later absorbed *Physical Culture for Boys and Girls*, which Macfadden had published for ten months. *Beauty and Health* reached a circulation of 80,000, but Bernarr, who wrote most of the copy, was overburdened, and his difficulty in finding authors who could write for both magazines and the strain upon his advertising staff led him to combine the publications in 1906. Male-oriented *Physical Culture* sharpened its appeal to women with articles on female beauty and exercises for "womanly strength and symmetry."[23]

Some well-known persons wrote for *Physical Culture*, among them Charles W. Eliot of Harvard on the value of athletics, Yale football coach Walter Camp on the latest developments in football, prize fighter John L. Sullivan on physical culture, and Carrie Nation on the evils of the tobacco habit. Among the more obscure but steady contributors were diet reformers like the fruitarian Otto Carque, the vegetarian Eustace Miles, and the naturopath August F. Reinhold, M.D., Ph.D., who wrote most of the magazine's early attacks against standard medical practices. Macfadden's "editorial right arm," John R. Coryell, originator of the popular fiction character Nick Carter, specialized in serialized fiction that interwove intrigue, romance, and physical culture. As H. Mitchell Watchet he wrote about fasting, and in "A Liberal View of the Nude," he well summarized Macfadden's point of view that the naked human body was nothing to be ashamed of.[24]

In his first two years as a publisher, Macfadden worked six days a week, nights, and often Sundays, concocting editorials, articles, and health books. The Physical Culture Publishing Company issued a dozen of his books within seven years. The relentless pace affected his eyesight, but he worked out some eye exercises and recovered. He wrote a widely circulated book with the help of an eye specialist who had independently reached the same conclusion that exercises were the proper treatment, but the eye doctor soon was criticized for having collaborated with him. "My God, Mr. Macfadden," he howled, "You have got to take my name off that book or my career is over." Obligingly, his coauthor recalled the volume and in 1901 printed a new version with only himself as author: *Strong Eyes: How Weak Eyes May Be Strengthened and Spectacles Discarded.* To him, eyeglasses were "crutches" that healthy people should be ashamed to wear; their eyes would soon depend on them. If properly cared for, the eyes should function unaided throughout life.[25]

As a teenager, Macfadden had become interested in diet, and sometime in the 1890s he lived for several months on raw food, bread, and crackers. He commenced with a two-day fast; then ate twice a day, starting with whole wheat grains or occasionally rolled oats and kernels of pecans, almonds, and other nuts; then a salad of lettuce, raw vegetables, and potatoes, with a dressing of lemon juice, olive oil, and salt. For dessert he ate dates, figs, or other fruit. Although he lost weight, he claimed that he became stronger and less irritable.[26]

As a farm boy, he had eaten whole wheat bread. Later, the white bread he ate in small towns apparently made him ill. This reaction led to his long war against white bread, the "staff of death" and "the greatest humbug ever foisted upon a civilized people." The superfine white flour sold on the market had lost its minerals in the milling and was really a fake food, Macfadden proclaimed, an incomplete food that caused weakness, starved people to death, and was worse than no food. It might be better than sawdust but not much. For fifty years he carried on a vendetta against the milling industry.[27]

Macfadden was seventy years ahead of his time in advocating the natural foods so popular today. Before 1900, nutrition investigators knew little of the essentials of an adequate diet, were mainly concerned with calories, and recommended foods with high fuel value per ounce. Knowledge of vitamins and minerals was almost completely lacking, and the green vegetables and citrus fruits that Macfadden recommended were disapproved because of their low caloric content. Although never a 100 percent vegetarian, the physical culturist held that a vegetable or uncooked diet provided more energy in proportion to the energy used in digestion than an ordinary meat-and-potato diet. He liked meat but believed that it left more impurities in the body than vegetables, and when he overindulged this appetite, he fasted to counteract the effects. Eat meat sparingly, he advised.[28]

In the fight against rancid and adulterated meats, he stayed on the sideline, allowing Upton Sinclair to carry the ball with his muckraking *Jungle* in 1906. Even so, he declared that non-meat-eaters should be grateful to "Upton St. Clair" for exposing "the filthy secrets of the Meat Trust." He urged his readers to demand passage of the Pure Food and Drug bill of 1906 and denounced tampering with, or contamination of foods by manufacturers.[29]

Whatever their diet, Americans ate too much, and overeating, according to Macfadden, was a sin. He theorized that the body wasted energy in ridding itself of excess food, dulling the nervous system, weakening the vital organs, and shortening life. Moreover, people ate too fast. Before swallowing they should hasten the flow of digestive juices by chewing the food to a liquid; this enhanced the enjoyment of food, and "the more you enjoy a meal," he affirmed, "the more easily it is digested."[30]

Liquids were vital. Water helped to prevent constipation, Macfadden insisted, but he condemned ice water as an unsatisfactory thirst quencher and shocking to the stomach. Fruit juices were his favorite drinks, and he recommended apple juice for better digestion and proper liver function. Grape juice he considered especially beneficial to invalids and people with weak stomachs and almost as nourishing as milk. He himself drank a lot of milk and once claimed that he downed nearly a quart at each meal. He recommended an all-milk diet for indigestion, blood diseases, and even syphilis; and years later he would suggest four to six quarts a day for best results. Because the body needed no caffeine, he disapproved of coffee and tea. He objected to liquor not only because it harmed the body but because it sustained drinking saloons, which fed prostitution and crime, and he supported the Anti-Saloon League.[31]

To show that good meals could be cheap, Macfadden opened a modest "Physical Culture Restaurant" in 1902 at the corner of Pearl Street and City Hall Place. Here for a penny one could buy a bowl of pea soup, steamed hominy, oats, or barley. In the basement nothing cost more than one cent, but upstairs in a self-service area the top price was five cents a serving. Few people patronized the basement, but the street level did a rushing business from dawn to midnight. Macfadden intended the restaurant to serve as a source of editorials and to demonstrate that it could be run without financial loss. It was so successful that he organized a company to open more eating places; and by midsummer 1903, he had opened two more in downtown Manhattan and one in Brooklyn, catering not only to the poor but to Wall Street and upper-crust patrons. By October 1904, the company operated eight restaurants in New York, two in Philadelphia, and one in Chicago. They were profitable: 21 percent dividends to 600 stockholders in 1907, the year of a frightening financial panic. By 1911, there were twenty restaurants in various cities, but Macfadden was no longer personally involved.[32]

Fasting, practiced as a health measure since the sixteenth century, was as important to him as diet. The September 1900 *Physical Culture* showed two profiles of him naked, one taken before a fast, the other afterward. He conceived of fasting when he noticed that ailing dogs and cats cured themselves by not eating, came to believe that because the body's energies were largely concentrated on digesting unnecessary food, the less food consumed, the more energy would be available for vitality. Fasting, he claimed, helped rid the body of poisons by giving the digestive organs a needed rest and encouraging Nature to do its healing work.[33]

Fasting was a panacea that would alleviate and even cure practically any disease, which ranged from asthma to "youthful errors." Here they are:[34]

asthma	eye troubles
biliousness	headache
bladder disease	heart disease
bronchitis	insomnia
catarrh	impotency
constipation	kidney disease
coughs and colds	liver disease
diabetes	neurasthenia
diseases of the prostate	obesity
diseases of the rectum	paralysis
diseases of women	rheumatism
dispepsia	skin diseases
emaciation	stomach diseases
epilepsy	vital depletion
ear troubles	youthful errors

No wonder the American Medical Association pronounced Macfadden a charlatan!

Experimenting upon himself, Macfadden fasted for varying lengths of time, sometimes for five or six days. He gave credit to Upton Sinclair for publicizing the benefits of fasting and suggested to him that the best results could be obtained from twelve-day fasts. Many years later, he wrote to Sinclair that fasting usually relieved headaches, though drinking a lot of water was quicker.[35]

Macfadden held that enforced feeding of ill or injured persons prolonged their incapacity. He blamed the doctors, not the assassin's bullet for the death of President McKinley. A gunshot wound affected the body like an acute disease, like a sore in the process of healing, he maintained. "Day by day I closely watched the despatches . . . for an account of the feeding process that I believed would surely begin too soon." After six days the president was given solid food and on the day he died was fed toast saturated in beef juice. "May God forgive the fools!" the physical culturist exclaimed. "The cup of coffee and other nourishment and stimulants . . . had done their work. Another martyr to the cause of medical experimentation was added to the list that is already swelled by millions upon millions of names." Had McKinley been forced to fast, he would have lived. After Wilbur Wright died of typhoid fever, Macfadden noted that he was "fairly stuffed with foods until the very night of his death. . . . My experience has taught me that premature administration of food to a typhoid fever patient is equivalent to signing his death warrant." The body should be free of toxins before it ingested food.[36]

As proper diet and fasting were vital, so was sexual vigor. Macfadden gloried in sexual power, in the male and female figures, and in his own zest for physical love. "The instinct of sex," he maintained, was "nothing more than a part of the nervous system," which could be strengthened by exercise. A poorly sexed woman had no right to marry because she was as incapable of fulfilling the duties of wife and mother as a man who lost his virility would be incapable of fatherhood. Male energy, he believed, was produced in the genital area, which accounted for man's creative powers in business, the arts, and the army. His exercise equipment included a glass tube "somewhat larger than the average male organ" to be placed around the penis and connected with a vacuum tube that would remove air and draw blood down into the organ, enlarging and extending it "to its greatest possible size." Somewhat later, to restore the vitality and potency of tired and harassed businessmen, he invented an electrical device with a fan that drew fresh outdoor air through a long rubber tube applied to the penis. Apparently, he failed to patent his "peniscope," which he visualized as selling in exclusive stores for $14.98.[37]

Sex and interest in sex were natural. Why should people feel guilty when they discussed sex? The sexes were made for each other. A healthy interest in the subject did not mean promiscuity, however, and Macfadden condemned prostitution as degrading, demoralizing, and disease producing, and he denounced the "perverts" advocating free love as "breaking every law of God or Nature" and fully deserving of the degeneracy that "quickly takes their kind into oblivion."[38]

Marriage, he held, was a human necessity, and the fullest physical perfection could never be achieved unless one married before one's sexual power waned. Successful men nearly always married, he affirmed; the responsibility of home life, which strengthened the will and the power of persistence, was usually one of the first steps to fame and fortune. As he tried to impress upon his wife, Mary, marriage was fundamentally a physical union. Its only purpose was procreation and a home, and a man's love for a woman ideally required that he look upon her as the future mother of his children. His life with Mary was hardly what he had advocated in *Marriage a Lifelong Honeymoon: Life's Greatest Pleasures Secured by Observing the Highest Human Instincts*, published in 1903 when he was thirty-five. Here he had asserted that sexual excess endangered a marriage, that a wife should never let herself be used by her husband, that she maintain identity and self-respect but also learn the feelings and expectations of her husband before having sex with him. To ensure this he proposed separate bedrooms or at least separate beds.[39]

In the early twentieth century, Macfadden and other sex reformers advocated sexual purity, hygiene, and the eugenic improvement of the (white) race. They condemned masturbation, not for the conventional reason that it led to insanity or death, but because they thought it weakened the nervous system and injured health. Apparently, Macfadden was not involved in the work of the American Federation for Sex Hygiene, pioneer of the American sex reform movement, but he agreed with its teachings and, like other reformers, denounced sex for pleasure.[40] Always publicity-conscious, he was probably the most outspoken American writer on the sex life of man and woman.

In boldly endorsing sex education, Macfadden was one of the first to publicize the subject of venereal disease. He was delighted when Edward Bok supported the teaching of sex in the *Ladies' Home Journal* and in *McClure's Magazine*. Like Bok, he argued that ignorant and reticent parents were to blame. A mother should tell her daughter and a father should tell his son about sex well before the onset of puberty, he declared. If one parent held back, the other had a "divinely imposed" duty to instruct the child. He blamed prudes for the prevalence of immorality. "The time cannot be far distant," he predicted, "when these poor, misguided human beings who are attempting to impress the entire race with their vulgar and indecent conceptions of the most beautiful piece of Nature's handiwork, the human body, will be incarcerated in some institution where they will be as harmless as those other lunatics who are now confined." Sexual morality, he insisted, was based on absolute obedience to one's "highest instincts," but because of prudery "not one man in a hundred knows anything about sex morality." In a chatty book of advice for young women in 1904 he wrote that ignorance of sex prevented "that opulent development of girlhood which is Nature's obvious intention." Sexuality led to all kinds of creativity, practical, literary, or artistic; and if a girl was too sober-faced and unhappy, it probably resulted from the crushing of her sex instinct. That happened when she was deprived of male companionship.[41]

It was a mistake to separate the sexes at any time, Macfadden believed: life could be full and complete only when desire for association with the opposite sex was entirely satisfied. He deplored the separate education of boys and girls. Through companionship they would educate themselves in the physical, mental, and spiritual aspects of sex, but he warned against too ardent lovemaking or premarital sexual intercourse.[42]

Macfadden's notions about men and women were as laden with sexual stereotypes as tinsel on a Christmas tree: girls should not sacrifice their sexuality for "pedantic ambitions"; women were inclined to trust their impulses and emotions, whereas men trusted reason and judgment; women acted out of intuition, men out of deductions from experience. Although a man liked intelligence, mental alertness, refinement, and wit in a girl, he could not wholly love someone who lacked the "charm of physical magnetism." Men were drawn to helpful, thoughtful, sweet-tempered women, and women wanted physically strong, virile men with courage, stability, nobility, and generosity.[43]

To Macfadden a woman's beauty was inseparable from her physical well-being. "Real beauty," he held, was "nothing but the comeliness of health." To be healthy, a female body must move freely, unrestricted by corset or tight shoes. Cultivate a play spirit, he told his girl readers; be a tomboy, climb trees, jump fences, and run races, for "play will do more to keep you young than anything else." He even suggested wrestling for adolescent girls, and he considered housework as good exercise.[44]

Clothing that limited women's movement aroused his wrath. Like others before him, but with far greater intensity, he campaigned against corsets as the "curse of beauty." Tight lacing stunted the development of the sexual organs, injured or ruined the digestion, restricted lung development, destroyed the ability to breathe normally, and ultimately made "shapeless, flaccid and nerveless the flesh at the waist." It supported the bust in an abnormal position, was in most cases "the direct cause of weaknesses peculiar to women," greatly lessened sexual desire, caused tumors and inflammations, prevented return of the blood from below the waist, weakened and sometimes killed the fetus, and was a principal cause of marital misery and divorce. In many supercharged editorials, *Physical Culture* repeated these themes, and its cartoons displayed "lady tennis players" and "lady hockey players" gasping for air and a nude woman revealing her corset-distorted body.[45]

Macfadden disdained the fashionable garments of the day. For women he favored a skirt slit at the knees or calves to give their wearers a "taste of real freedom," and he denounced a New Jersey politician for introducing a bill forbidding women from wearing them. Shoes were an "abomination," especially if they had high heels. Manufacturers should produce foot-shaped shoes without heels "for those who have sufficient intelligence to wear them."[46]

By limiting direct contact with the air, clothing prevented a natural cleansing of the skin. The whole body should breathe, absorb oxygen, and let the sweat evaporate, yet "we shut up our bodies in cloth and leather boxes," wrote Macfadden, convinced that Scotsmen got their vigor largely because they wore kilts. Holding these opinions, he cared little about dressing fashionably and chose to expose himself to fresh air and sunshine whenever feasible, to walk barefoot, to be free. "Our clothing is used as a means of covering our individual characters," he asserted. "Our garments put us all in the same mould. To a certain extent, they make us think the same thoughts, walk and talk and act in the same way. And if humanity is ever to advance beyond its present money-grabbing, greed-developing standards, our wearing apparel will, first of all, have to be changed."[47]

As a champion of robust health, Macfadden advocated plenty of exercise, even Sunday athletic games, despite local blue laws. His first book, apart from his early novel, had been *Macfadden's Physical Training*, a 125-page manual published in 1900, including illustrations of men and women using his exerciser and of himself nude, or nearly so, depicting his muscularity. Addressed to people of all ages, this little booklet contained sensible advice on muscular activity, diet, weight, bathing, tooth care, and restrictive dress. In his wrestling days,

Macfadden had often been tired after walking eight or ten miles, but he boasted in 1904 of easily walking eighteen or twenty-five miles and an equal distance after an hour or two of rest. He experimented on himself to determine the effects of long walks. From five to ten miles per day, he extended his range to between fifteen and twenty miles in the morning before starting his business day. In these walks to the office, he usually went barefoot and carried his coat and shoes until he reached the city. It was said that he believed human beings originally walked on their knuckles, urged walking on all fours to strengthen the spine, and did so himself to show how easily it could be done. If it became popular, he remarked, business would be conducted on the floor, and the savings in office furniture would amount to millions.[48]

"Life is one long continuous athletic contest," he affirmed, and sports prepared one for life. He championed boxing as one of the best health-building exercises. To those who called it cruel, he asserted that football and "automobiling" were more dangerous. Wrestling was the most perfect form of physical training because it imparted "all-around muscular, nervous, and functional vigor," and as his own experience showed, this sport did the most to develop great physical power. He also praised hand wrestling. Football was the greatest of all games, a strenuous and exhilarating sport that developed men and instilled persistence, energy, manliness, and courage, all needed for success in the business or professional world. True enough, it was dangerous, but hard knocks bred character, self-confidence, stability, and manliness, and a football field was the place to acquire them.[49]

In these opinions Macfadden was not alone, nor was he unique in believing that physical decline lowered moral tone and that athletic exercises promoted morals. The best way to build up the morals of a community or nation, he held, was to develop physical fitness: "Morals are, after all, a matter of instinct. . . . Physical culturists, in nearly every case, lead cleanly lives. They have no desire to be otherwise than moral, because their every belief tends toward morality." Over the years, Macfadden continued to associate physical and moral strength, and in his seventies asserted that there were "only rare exceptions when a strong character can be developed in a frail body. Whether you are a minister of the gospel, a legal expert, or a business executive, the force that originates in the healthy body represents a tremendously important factor. . . . Character becomes a divine force when stabilized by religious ideals. It is vitalized and strengthened by a hardy physique." (Verbal precision was never a Macfadden strong point.] As early as 1899, he had considered his crusade for physical culture to be far more important than religion. Indeed, it *was* a religion. It was the foundation of perfection: health and strength not only contributed to character but to discipline of will, success in business and in marriage, to courage, morality, virility, and happiness.[50]

Although physical educators were convinced that strengthening the muscles improved the mind, Bernarr's early writings did not explicitly make that connection. He probably shared their view that regular exercise fostered circulation, which hastened excretion of toxins and prevented a sluggish mentality or stagnant brain. If in his thirties he did not assert, as did the educational philosopher G. Stanley Hall, that educating the muscles also educated the brain, he accepted that notion in his fifties. Out of his conviction that a physical culturist's vitality made his brain a supercharged battery that ignited flashes of original ideas came his magazine *Brain Power* in the early 1920s.[51]

Macfadden saw physical culture as important to politicians. Stamina and a robust physique, he claimed, made for effective oratory, and he rejoiced that golden-tongued Senator Albert Beveridge of Indiana was "a physical culturist in every sense of the word." Theodore Roosevelt's indefatigability was the result of a rugged constitution, built up in the open air of the western plains. The eloquence of William Jennings Bryan, whose "cross of gold" speech won him the Democratic nomination for president in 1896, reflected a physical endurance like Roosevelt's. Samuel "Golden Rule" Jones, the reform mayor of Toledo, who slept on an outdoor porch, delighted Macfadden with his lifestyle and advocacy of able-bodied fathers and mothers for the future of America.[52]

A strong population, Macfadden held, was essential to a nation's well-being. "Can any reasoning human being question the dependence of a Nation upon the physical power of its people?" he asked. "Weakness and degeneracy mean ruin, and ultimate oblivion in every case." Impressed by military strength, he asserted that the United States Army should be a "monumental physical culture school." To encourage enlistments, it should organize a physical culture regiment based on his theories, require simple war food and ban whiskey, beer, and prostitutes. So much for practicality! His fascination with armies led to *Physical Culture* articles on the practices and physical training of the British, German, French, and Egyptian armed forces.[53]

He became a propagandist for a cabinet-level Secretary of Health. In 1902, he had castigated the press for ridiculing a bill in Congress to create a National Physical Culture Department and a Commissioner of Physical Culture in each state. Over two decades he supported a campaign to establish a national health department that was thwarted not only by opponents of federal paternalism but also by those fearful of an AMA scheme to dominate American health care. Believing that the United States government should take responsibility for assuring that American children achieved optimum health and strength, he advocated government nurseries and training schools to care for every child who became motherless or fatherless.[54]

Macfadden's interest in education focused narrowly on body building. "If I had the control of the schools of this country," he asserted, "I would make each child spend at least one hour in playing active games for every hour spent in study." He was enthusiastic about joyful play, and he strongly favored competition. In 1902, *Physical Culture* offered prizes to public school districts for boys and girls winning their separate competitive events, and he urged school teachers to form an advance army of physical culturists to "sweep weakness from the earth."[55]

To train school and college health directors he founded the Bernarr Macfadden Institute of Physical Culture in New York in 1905, where young men and women attended its forty-week courses in anatomy, physiology, the theory and practice of physical education, and Macfadden's curative methods, which he called physcultopathy. Needy students were offered jobs at his physical culture restaurants. The institute, which he moved shortly afterward to New Jersey and in 1907 to Battle Creek, Michigan, ran into trouble. One of the managers was arrested for stealing diplomas, and Macfadden fired his successor for disloyalty. Six dissatisfied and possibly lazy students publicly complained about their contracts, which required work in return for tuition and board and quit the school when Macfadden refused to deal with them as a body. He sold the institute to its senior instructors but apparently maintained a connection with it. As the Physical Culture Training School it moved in 1909 to the same building in Chicago where he operated a sanitarium. He personally prepared an examination in anatomy, physiology, hygiene, and physcultopathy, and a student who passed it received a certificate authorizing use of the title "Doctor of Physcultopathy." In 1913, a reorganization produced two schools, the American College of Physical Education to teach and develop skills, and the Macfadden College of Physcultopathy, specializing in physical culture healing techniques, which in 1915, as the International College of Drugless Physicians, offered postgraduate studies in addition to its two-year basic course.[56]

Macfadden gave himself generous credit for the growing public awareness of physical training. *Physical Culture* had a devoted following, and its publisher penned treatises on diet, disease, muscles, marriage, *The Power and Beauty of Superb Womanhood*, and *Superb Virility in Manhood*. Many others, however, shared in the health movement of the early twentieth century. The National League for Improvement of Physical Culture had no link to Macfadden, and the American Physical Education Association rejected his repeated efforts to gain its approval. Unlike Macfadden, nearly all the philosophers of physical education were physicians. As early as the 1880s, Dr. Dudley Allen Sargent's system of weight machines, mimetic exercises, and teacher training program at Harvard gained great national influence and in 1885, when Macfadden was only seventeen, nearly fifty colleges and clubs had adopted the Sargent system. Sargent reported in 1902 that 270 colleges had adopted physical education, 300 city school systems required their pupils to exercise, 500 gymnasiums had been established by the YMCA, and another hundred by clubs, military bases, and hospitals. Doctors Edward Hartwell, William Anderson, Luther Gulick, R. Tait McKenzie, and their colleagues had transformed an earlier emphasis on simple gymnastics to broad programs of physical improvement that they believed would lead to mental and moral elevation. Scolding parents for neglecting the physical education of their children, the chairman of the Public School Athletic League typically warned that the United States was becoming a nation of mollycoddles.[57] Meanwhile, crowded and soulless cities, waves of immigrants in urban slums, and WASP fears of "race suicide" strengthened a growing conviction that American society was approaching a crisis. A regenerative crusade was needed for the country's physical and moral health, and Bernarr Macfadden was probably its most earnest propagandist.

Nudity, Prudery, and the Law

MACFADDEN VOWED TO ESTABLISH physical culture societies in every city and town in America. In 1902, after returning from England where he had fostered an English edition of *Physical Culture*, he promoted a "monster" physical culture meeting at the Grand Opera House in New York and offered free Sunday evening lectures, with the help of male and female models, at the Murray Hill Theater.[1] Later, he gave free lectures in Cincinnati, Dayton, Indianapolis, Chicago, Minneapolis, St. Paul, St. Louis, New Haven, Hartford, Providence, and Boston, and by the end of 1905 had set up nineteen clubs in various cities, including Toronto and Montreal. He offered free admission to mixed audiences on "The Cause and Cure of Weakness" and "Is Medicine the Science of Guessing?" and charged a fee to hear "The Complete Powers of Superb Manhood" (for men only) and "The Cultivation of Perfect Womanhood" (for women only). He recruited associates and started a lecture bureau to furnish speakers to churches and literary and social clubs. They were lieutenants in his "disciples of health" army, girding to annihilate the "six great curses" of the age: corsets that weakened women's bodies; sexual ignorance that degraded humanity; muscular inactivity that caused people to "droop and wither before their time"; overeating; drugs and alcohol that robbed men of their reason; and tobacco, "the vehicle of the great demon Nicotine."[2]

He continued to experiment on himself. He developed a combination of wheat, oats, and nuts that he called "strengthfude." He planned to live for a month on five cents a day to prove that by eating very modestly a man could maintain his strength and weight, but after eighteen days he tired of the Spartan regimen and soon gave it up. When testing the effects of long walks, he found that three to five hours of steady, rhythmic movement and deep breathing increased the activity of his entire system.[3]

He opened a sanitarium in 1900 at Hudson, fifty miles north of New York City, the first of numerous health homes that became a standard feature of his physical culture movement and offered practical applications of his methods, and he announced grandiose plans for cooperative health homes for men and women near every large population center. They were to be lively places where "no restraint, no style, no conventionality" would deprive his patients of "as much joy as can be crowded into life." "Leave your old-fogy ideas at home," he urged, and pursue "the one object of all our efforts—to develop the powers, the intensity and beauties of youth. All sorts of active games will be encouraged."[4]

The next Macfadden health home, on the shore of Lake Ronkonkoma, Long Island, accepted a number of patients free of charge in an effort to popularize Macfadden's methods. At one time, 125 persons slept in tents because the building could not accommodate half that many, and there were other troubles. The fees of $8 to $15 per week for paying guests did not cover operating costs; some patients expected to stay as long as three months without paying, and others remained two or three weeks, learned physical culture techniques, went home to complete the cure, and then insisted on partial refunds. Deeply disgusted, Macfadden refunded their money. Because he was frequently absent attending to his publishing business, their lack of appreciation and complaints about his staff were justified. Some of the attendants failed to administer the prescribed regimen, some got drunk, and others robbed the patients. Despite several changes of management, he could not find a capable administrator, and after less than two years he closed the Ronkonkoma home.[5]

Meanwhile, his publishing business prospered. By the summer of 1903 the combined American circulation of *Physical Culture* and its sister *Beauty and Health* was almost a quarter of a million, and nearly 70,000 copies were printed for British readers. Macfadden's were not the only periodicals devoted to health. At least eight magazines (published in New York; Boston; Battle Creek, Michigan; and Oakland, California) printed similar information, and several of their editors commended Bernarr's new methods of making an old field attractive. He enjoyed their attention and professed no ill-feeling toward his rivals.[6]

From the beginning, *Physical Culture* contained not only drawings, cartoons, and photographs but reproductions of nude paintings and sculpture. Nudity soon became an issue. Although *Munsey's* had regularly printed nude art studies since 1894, it remained for Macfadden to be accused of exploiting sex. Two subscribers predicted that nakedness would injure the magazine, but the publisher happily reported that at least a dozen readers had expressed an opposite opinion. After William J. Cromie, the physical director of the YMCA in Easton, Pennsylvania, submitted a petition with ninety-two signatures objecting to nude pictures, Macfadden exploded: "One of the principal causes of physical weakness and ugliness at the present time is lack of respect for the human body—this idea that it is something vulgar to be hid and despised. Why should we be ashamed of our bodies?" Theodore Voorhees, a vice-president of the Philadelphia and Reading Railway Company, in obvious disagreement, gave notice that he considered *Physical Culture* immoral and ordered its removal from all the railroad's newsstands. Unintimidated, Macfadden printed Voorhees's letter with an editorial blast against prudery, and the magazine continued to display generous portions of the human anatomy.[7]

The eye-luring pictures of nude or near-nude figures, including Bernarr himself, tame by modern standards, sometimes bore little or no relation to the physical culture articles surrounding them, which explains why the publisher was criticized for advancing his cult "by the unveiling of the human body." A shrewd promoter, he also sincerely believed that the naked body should be displayed as the perfect creation of nature. He was not a committed nudist, but he saw nothing wrong in men and women appearing together naked. As love for the human body was natural and wholesome, familiarity with nakedness, he argued, would eventually close the liquor stores, gambling dens, and whorehouses. By his definition, those who perceived nudity as vulgar and indecent were filthy minded prudes. They should send their "thinking mechanisms" to the laundry to be cleaned and disinfected with "a strong solution of common sense and a few ounces of purifying inner contemplation." Accused of sensationalism, he denounced newspapers that depicted every detail of the latest murder and groveled in human anguish and misfortune, yet would not show even partial nudes.[8]

While waging war against prudery, Macfadden was also thinking about marriage. His union with Tillie Fontain had been a failure, yet he believed that marriage was a natural necessity, that successful men nearly always married, and that creating a home was one of the first steps to fame and fortune. In 1903, he married Marguerite Kelly, a Canadian nurse with an attractive face and a large frame. A physical culture enthusiast herself, she shared his interest in the outdoors, and he saw in her an ideal personal and professional associate.[9]

During the summer of 1904, Bernarr and Marguerite rented a bungalow twenty miles from New York City where Marguerite gave birth to a daughter they named Byrne, probably because it suggested a diminutive feminine Bernarr. The next year they moved to Macfadden's community, Physical Culture City in New Jersey, where he named its lake in Marguerite's honor. According to rumors among the settlers there, Mrs. Macfadden was somewhat oversexed and hard to satisfy. She apparently interfered in other people's affairs, to their great annoyance, and it was said that she stole her husband's old clothing from a chair and replaced it with a new, nicely creased suit. She was a social climber who invited to her house persons she considered important and in their presence would patronize Bernarr. Behind his back, when talking to the cleaning women she demeaned her husband, but she was conspicuously devoted to her child. As one of the settlers recalled, the baby was "a little, red object like a boiled lobster—the mother used to bring it among us and coo and coo over it so ridiculously that we made her behaviour a joke among us."[10]

Although Marguerite Macfadden contributed articles on diet, motherhood, and infant care to *Physical Culture* and became assistant editor of *Beauty and Health*, her social pretensions and busybody behavior made an unhappy marriage. Bernarr and his wife separated before their second anniversary. Taking little Byrne with her, she went to live with her mother in Canada and later obtained a divorce. At the time of the separation Macfadden declared that every divorce had a physiological cause and that based on his personal experience as well as the knowledge of experts in the causes of marital misery, marriage under the right conditions would bring happiness even beyond "the wildest moments of prematrimonial imagery." He wrote to three hundred clergymen, lawyers, politicians, judges, and physicians, requesting responses to his view that divorces resulted from ignorance or "deliberate violation of what may be characterized as the physiological laws of marriage," but, because divorce was a delicate topic, nearly all the replies were noncommittal.[11] Undoubtedly he was disappointed. As a fighting journalist, he understood the benefits of controversy and enjoyed shocking people with unconventional opinions.

Macfadden was a talented showman. In 1904, he sponsored a week-long "Monster Physical Culture Exhibition" at Madison Square Garden. It featured contests for the most perfectly developed man and woman, wrestling matches, a three-day fast, followed by a go-as-you-please race, with contestants walking, running, or crawling. Newspapers, noting the array of scantily clad bodies, called the affair a "shape show" and a "beauty show," and this aspect of the performance actually was the forerunner of bathing beauty contests. Undaunted by what he called distorted reports, Macfadden planned another show for the next year.[12]

As he was about to open this second show in October 1905, an amused *New York Times*, observing the preliminaries, noted the abundance of "superfluous muscle." In an elimination contest "all the bow-legged men and hollow-chested women" were shown to the exit door, where "one man waited outside the Garden for revenge but was persuaded by the temptation of liquor to remove himself." The women, said the *Times*, did not seem abashed as they stood in a row to be examined. Some tied their sashes tighter, others fussed with their hair. "There was a Swedish woman, a well known artists' model; a black-eyed sylph with muscles of steel, a fighting eye, and a brogue; a chunk of a woman with muscles like those of a man, and many others; also an actress fully dressed, who on the entrance of the female contestants, arose in her wrath to tell the press agent of the exhibition that the invitation to her to compete was an outrage."[13]

The show was advertised by posters tacked up about the city with pictures of the previous year's contestants. One showed a dozen women in white union suits with sashes around their waists; another showed a man in a leopard-skin breechcloth and a pair of sandals.

Four days before the opening night, Anthony Comstock, secretary and driving spirit of the Society for the Suppression of Vice, obtained warrants for the arrest of Macfadden, his show manager, and the man in charge of the posters. Comstock, accompanied by policemen, stormed into the offices of *Physical Culture*, searched the premises, confiscated posters—500 pounds of them already had been seized and destroyed—arrested Macfadden and led him to the Tenderloin police station. Released after posting $1,000 bail, the showman was outraged; the purpose of the show, he insisted, was to demonstrate how the spread of physical culture had improved the human body, and "manifestly that cannot be done if the exhibitors are covered with clothing." Nobody had objected to the previous show, and as in that one, the men would be nude above their waists, the women would wear white tights or union suits with sashes around their waists, and for best effect, their poses would be highlighted in front of a black curtain. Why the fuss? Women in tights were seen in every circus and men in breechcloths appeared at all kinds of athletic exhibitions. Comstock may have meant well but he was going too far. "I shall fight this case through every court in the land before I'll let it drop. If he beats me in court to-morrow I'll modify the posters a little for the benefit of the coming show. If I beat him the same old poster will go up. The exhibition itself will come off on schedule time, and in the way we intended. More than 100 men and 35 young women will take part in the exhibition, and it is too late now to either call it off or change the rules governing it. The posing of contestants we consider one of the most beneficial parts of the exhibition. Contestants are coming from all parts of the country."[14]

Despite Macfadden's arrest and the destruction of some posters, the union-suited poster girls appeared in drug stores, barber shops, and other popular gathering places. This was entirely lawful, admitted Judge Wyatt in Special Sessions, but he believed it was "not needed in this city." The *Times* called Macfadden an honest fanatic, but considered plausible his claim that "the physical culture of a human body cannot be judged when it is wrapped in a horse blanket or overlaid with an ulster." The exhibition, however, was of great interest to fellow physical culture enthusiasts, but at least for the moment Comstock seemed to have the better of it: let Macfadden give private showings, not money-making public exhibitions that catered to the baser instincts.[15]

In its annual report, the Society for the Suppression of Vice described Macfadden's posters as exhibiting "the forms of young women denuded of their proper womanly apparel, for young men and others to look at, and pay." The promoter "sought to crowd the Hall the first night with 'scientific people,' as they pretended. A special effort was made to reach the 'scientists' by means of a handbill displaying a number of young women without any clothes upon them other than skin-fitting tights. These lewd pictures were sent with 'complimentary tickets' to the 'scientists' in saloons and barber shops especially, and to public offices."[16]

The advance publicity and the news of Macfadden's arrest drew a large and boisterous crowd of 20,000 to Madison Square Garden when the show opened on October 9. Police reserves were called out, and after 15,000 spectators had filled the house, the fire inspector ordered the doors closed. Highlights of the men's events were footraces, wrestling matches, high jumps, and weight throwing. Women contestants stood on pedestals behind a muslin curtain on a central moving stage

— silhouettes seemed prudent under the circumstances. Large crowds continued to attend on succeeding nights, many viewers having been attracted by the producer's arrest. Macfadden pronounced the show a huge success, evidence that the American people were awakening to the benefits of physical culture.[17] Eventually, on March 28, 1906, the court ruled that Macfadden was technically guilty of violating New York State law but imposed no penalties; in short, he got a suspended sentence.[18]

The events of October 1905 inspired Macfadden to launch a broadside against prudery and against Comstock as the enemy's commander. In an editorial, "Comstock, King of the Prudes," the physical culturist condemned the mind of his antagonist as "positively reeking with misconceptions of the human body." To Comstock, who dictated to the unthinking public, beautiful works of art, in human form or otherwise, were nothing but a reflection of "that vileness which his mentality has created." He had "arrogated to himself the authority to pass on all literature and art." As censor of public morals, his perverted imagination found "vulgar and depraved meanings in the most inspiring sentence" and transformed the most beautiful picture or statue into something vile, making "an obscene mystery" of all that pertained to sex. Macfadden promised to fight Comstockery "to the bitter end."[19]

Never shrinking from grandiose ideas, Macfadden dreamed of creating a health community within an hour's ride from New York City to benefit not only its participants but to serve as an example to the country, even the world. Perhaps inspired by the Battersea Co-Operative Community in London, which linked hygiene and brotherly cooperation, he signed a contract in April 1905 to buy 1,900 acres near New Brunswick in New Jersey for an experimental Physical Culture City. The tract, formerly owned by the Buckelew family estate, was five miles long and two miles wide, situated thirteen miles northeast of Princeton and halfway between Helmetta and Spotswood, in the hamlet of Outcalt. Included in the purchase were an artificial lake, part of the Manalapan River, and the tracks of the Amboy division of the Pennsylvania Railroad. New York was 39 miles to the northeast; Philadelphia, 51 miles to the southwest.[20]

To keep control of the community, Macfadden insisted on leasing rather than selling land to his settlers, and he retained the right to demand that a lessee abide by the terms or forfeit the lease. By June, lots of 50 by 100 feet were being laid out and went for $15, an acre or more for a minimum of $50, and lakefront land for $70 to $100.

The leases, which ran 99 years, prohibited saloons, tobacco and drug stores, opium joints, and whorehouses. No physician or drug user could lease land. No medicine, meat, corsets, or high-heel shoes could be sold in this "city" where every inhabitant would "be able to use his or her God-given intellect and live and act according to its unhampered dictates." Physical Culture City was for people whose alert minds would be sheltered in healthy bodies.[21]

Designed to protect the moral and physical welfare of its residents, the community was operated paternalistically. It reflected Macfadden's passionate assault on prudery, and clothing was minimal. Hats were rarely worn. Most of the settlers walked about in bare feet. Some men wore formal shirts and pants, but others were content with sleeveless shirts and shorts or swim trunks. Women wore bloomers and, when swimming, bathing suits without stockings and skirts. If customary dress entailed discomfort, why wear more than what felt good? As Bernarr put it, "We believe out here in the sacredness of the human body. . . . I am fully aware that many people think we are a lot of crazy fanatics, but if fanaticism builds the highest degree of mental and moral health, enables one to secure the best in life, and completely annihilates all evil and destructive influences, it is well worth cultivating."[22]

The local inhabitants were apprehensive about their new neighbors appearing in breechclouts and "men and women getting themselves arrested by rural constables." Rumors of nudism swept through the area. Sunday sightseers traveled past Physical Culture City, and when their train reached Outcalt popped their heads out of raised windows, the better to appraise the bodies beautiful.[23] Some were shocked to see scantily clad, barefooted men and women who, like Macfadden, were sun worshippers before sunbathing became popular in the United States. Although not thoroughgoing nudists like those in German and French nudist colonies twenty-five years later, Macfadden's people flaunted their unconventionality before the eyes of resentful old-timers in Outcalt.

Newspapers printed sensational stories about Physical Culture City. Macfadden's students flocked to the settlement only to find that they worked a ten-hour day, and healthy patients who paid $18 a week for meals objected to a required fast for one or two weeks. According to the New York *World*, some of the students' researches delved excessively into the personal and intimate, a titillating tidbit that incensed Bernarr, who saw nothing queer or amusing about a community of nondrinkers enjoying healthful exercise, fresh air, and sunshine.

Charging that the reports were imaginative, he sued the *World* for $50,000 for libel but failed to convince the jury.[24]

Physical Culture City attracted only 200 settlers, most of them in tents, although Macfadden had dreamed of 30,000. His grandiose plans included libraries, schoolhouses, and a restaurant that were never built. The plant manager, Maxwell B. Liebers, superintended the grounds and posed his little daughters for publicity pictures; Macfadden and Liebers sat on chairs blowing soap bubbles from funnels, then handed them to the girls to display in front of the photographers. For a time the physical directors were Pete and Winifred Schweikert of Chicago, graduates of Macfadden's institute. The first cook was a literary Scotsman who humorously discoursed on English poets while chopping vegetables.[25]

An assortment of health seekers drifted into the settlement. A millionaire sent his son there with a tutor. Freddy Walsh, an aspiring lightweight boxer, strengthened his muscles there, as did Samuel Olmstead, a young health purist who later directed several of Bernarr's sanitariums, lectured, and wrote for *Physical Culture*. Attracted by Macfadden's milk diet and ideas on fasting, Upton Sinclair found that his experience in the colony influenced his concern with food, which culminated in his muckraking novel, *The Jungle*. A youthful dissipator named Harry Kemp "staggered to Physical Culture City an ailing red-eyed wreck" from riotous living and recovered by eating cereals, nuts, and fruit. He received a dollar a day and a bed in a tent for helping to lay out streets in the woods. Although he observed that Macfadden did not "believe in giving overmuch money to his employees," Kemp owed his recovery to the physical culturist's influence and to "a summer of life, naked, in the open air." Not literally naked, though, except for morning dips in Lake Marguerite. Bernarr found him wearing a gee-string, called him aside and told him that although he did not mind, others objected.[26]

Never a master of English usage, Macfadden employed others to clothe his ideas in good grammar. One of these was Susie Wood, his beautiful reddish-blond, large-eyed, soft-voiced, gentle, and efficient secretary. She supplied him more than grammar, and she was a welcome contrast to the nagging and belittling of Marguerite Macfadden. Hand in hand, Susie and Bernarr took long walks through the pines, returning only at sunset. Susie got pregnant, and her mother moved in with them as "housekeeper" in the Macfadden cottage on the lake shore. As the affair became obvious, rumblings were heard throughout the colony, and many settlers, already critical of Macfadden, were alienated.[27]

Susie was athletic and agreed with Macfadden's approach to physical culture. She thought of him as a dedicated pioneer and became a devoted disciple, working on his various health projects and testing his diets on herself before he wrote them up. Bernarr recognized her business acumen and placed her in responsible positions during the next fifteen years.[28]

Physical Culture City was a brief triumph and then a disaster. From the beginning there were dissidents; some of the sick grumbled when their nature therapy did not work. Hotheads advised brazen defiance of the complaints of the neighboring community. Publicity and promotion schemers beguiled Bernarr and then vanished. A medical adviser was arrested for peddling fake diplomas; his successor turned out to be a heavy smoker who later killed himself with an overdose of laudanum.[29]

In addition to creating a community of earnest believers, Macfadden had planned to make it the headquarters of his Physical Culture Publishing Company. He built a printing plant to turn out *Physical Culture* and his books and pamphlets. When he tried to obtain and install a post office on the premises, the Spotswood postmaster objected to the loss of a flourishing postal business, which had already brought him a higher salary. Macfadden, believing that a lawsuit against him originating in Spotswood was an outgrowth of such petty politics, was stunned to learn the real nature of the prosecution.[30]

John R. Coryell, the most talented of Macfadden's writers, had taken his employer's idea and written a story to illustrate the perils of undisciplined youth. It was the confession of a sixteen-year-old son of wealthy syphilitic parents who had neglected to tell him the facts of life. Learning from gutter companions that sexual indulgence would make a man of him, he drank, read obscene books, wenched, got venereal disease, went insane and had himself cremated alive. Published serially in *Physical Culture*, the story was entitled "Growing to Manhood in Civilized (?) Society."

Only six installments, October 1906 to March 1907, had appeared when Macfadden was arrested for violating a federal obscenity law. Indicted by the Federal Grand Jury of New Jersey, he heard the court rule that the story contained obscene, lewd, and lascivious material. The jury considered some parts so offensive that it excluded them from the court record. Macfadden's lawyer argued that the law was vague, arbitrary, and in violation of the First and Fifth Amendments, and he himself called it "monstrous legislation of nasty-mindedness." After only a few minutes of deliberation, the jury found the publisher guilty. He was sentenced to two years of hard labor in the federal penitentiary and fined $2,000.[31]

Macfadden was dumfounded. Coryell's story aimed at the "elevation of mankind by shedding light upon the vicious conditions that existed practically everywhere," he protested. "It was not published to appeal to the erotic nature of the public with a view of increasing the sales of my magazine, but there were high moral purposes back of it." Parents ought to give sex information to their sons, and the best way to dissipate ignorance of sex was by "open attack and plain speaking."[32]

Pending an appeal, he went on a lecture tour to put his case before the people. Wherever he spoke, in Boston, Cincinnati, Baltimore, or other cities, great crowds gathered. In Washington, he visited the postal authorities and learned that the post office had received no complaints about Coryell's story.[33]

The United States Circuit Court of Appeals for the Third Circuit affirmed Macfadden's conviction. It held that "Growing to Manhood in Civilized (?) Society," if not *Physical Culture* itself, was suggestive and plainly catered to a prurient taste, which was the "thinly disguised object of the author." It was clear, the judges decided, that the publication was "of the obscene, lewd and lascivious character, which it was the object of Congress by the legislation in question to suppress." According to Macfadden, the judges had vented their personal bias. "If the Bible were to be taken up in this hurried manner by a man who never saw the book before, but was imbued with the conventional ideas of literature, it would be branded as an obscene book," he fumed. He decided to take the case to the Supreme Court. He would fight with every atom of energy: "I will give fair warning to one and all that there is only one way to stop me from doing my chosen work, and that is to put me under six feet of earth; and if this is done, on top of my grave will grow a monument . . . so mighty in influence that it will sweep every miserable prurient prude from the face of the earth, and then this country, cleansed of these vultures in human form, will be capable of reaching a civilization that will be greater and grander than the history of the world has known."[34]

The Supreme Court declined to hear Macfadden's appeal on the ground that no constitutional question was at stake. The publisher then mounted a campaign to secure a presidential pardon and printed for *Physical Culture* readers blank petitions to be signed with as many names as they could obtain. He encouraged a massive letter-writing effort, urging supporters to write to President Roosevelt or to their congressmen or state legislators to use their influence in effecting a pardon. A flood of letters poured into his office, and a Bernarr Macfadden defense fund netted more than $800. Some of his followers suspected that interested parties, including patent medicine producers, had conspired to ruin him. The *Kansas City Post* and the *Louisville Herald* sympathized with the physical culturist and protested against laws muzzling the press. Calling the conviction a miscarriage of justice, the *National Prohibitionist* described Coryell's story as "sweet and innocent as spring violets" when compared with much that appeared in the daily newspapers and the popular magazines.[35]

The White House was deluged with letters and telegrams urging a pardon. President Taft, elected in 1908 as Roosevelt's successor, referred the matter to Attorney General George W. Wickersham, who held that the story had a wholesome purpose despite certain objectionable passages. He advised the president that a pardon was justified because in this case the law had been stretched and perverted. Accordingly, on November 18, 1909, Taft signed Macfadden's application for pardon, which relieved him of the prison sentence but did not remit the $2,000 fine, which he had already paid. The publisher resented the inconsistency. Either he was guilty or he was not. How was it possible to be at once wholesome and obscene? He could only assume that the attorney general let the fine stand "in deference to the trial Judge." Thirty years later he sought complete vindication when Senator Robert R. Reynolds of South Carolina sponsored a bill for the repayment of the fine, but it failed to pass.[36]

Macfadden's prosecution was a disaster for Physical Culture City and for his pocketbook. Not only did it dash his hopes for the colony; it cost him a fortune—$60,000 to $75,000, he estimated, exclusive of legal fees. Others who had an interest in the settlement lost between $25,000 and $40,000. Because he had no postal facility in the community, the printing plant that he had installed for $50,000 had to be sold at a loss, and he resumed publishing in New York. Preoccupied with his trial, he neglected Physical Culture City, but he called a meeting in its gymnasium to respond to criticisms. He walked back and forth, weary, vexed, and resentful, lashing out at rumormongers and backbiters and condemning "traitors"; if they could not be loyal to him they should get out. His disciples gradually drifted away, and he disposed of his stock in the community. What he had visualized as a thriving settlement of five thousand nature lovers was reduced in a few months to a handful of inhabitants. The great experiment was abandoned.[37]

During the appeal of his conviction, he broadened his attack on prudery by organizing a "Sterling Purity League." At an open meeting at the Waldorf Astoria in New York he called for a "cleaner and nobler manhood and womanhood" to fight the degeneracy caused by "prurient prudery." As conventional as they were radical, the league's principles were pure minds and bodies; monogamy; a single standard of morals for men and women; sex education; sexual intercourse only for procreation; vegetarianism; moderate eating habits; and abstinence from drugs and tobacco.[38] After his pardon, Macfadden allowed the league to fade away and concentrated on his third sanitarium.

In 1907, before his conviction, he had opened the Macfadden Health Home in Battle Creek, near the well known sanitarium of John Harvey Kellogg. Macfadden's building, the former Phelps Sanatorium, was a mansion with white columned rotunda and massive fireplace, swimming pools, Russian and Turkish baths, and recreational facilities. Only physicians committed to drugless healing were employed, and the medical staff was headed by a California naturopath. Manipulative therapy, deep breathing, exercise and dry friction bathing with stiff towels formed much of the routine. Every Friday evening Macfadden lectured and posed "living statues" in front of a black velvet curtain.[39]

The physical culturist had expected to compete successfully with the Kellogg brothers, but his prosecution had drained his finances, and apparently he grew sour on Battle Creek, where his quaint ways raised eyebrows. One cold winter night he showed up in a Davy Crockett cap, bearskin cutaway, wristlets, and gauntlets, and carrying in each hand a hot China stove. The amused staff threw him out into a snowbank.[40]

In 1909, he moved his establishment to a large five-story structure, the former Lakeside Club, in Chicago's South Side and renamed it the Bernarr Macfadden Healthatorium. "The most complete establishment for drugless healing in the world," as one cultist called it, attracted patients from all over the United States. Unlike the slipshod management of his earlier sanitariums, this health center was efficiently supervised by Susie, Macfadden's "right arm" and probable mother of his daughter Helen. Susie was married not to Bernarr but to Morrie Wood, a mild-mannered man she dominated. Although in

1911 Macfadden dropped his formal connection with what was re-named the International Healthatorium, Susie, his loyal friend, continued to operate it until after World War I.[41] His abrupt renunciation of this cherished project was a consequence of actions by the United States Post Office after his conviction for sending obscene literature through the mail.

Nine months after relinquishing the healthatorium he resigned as president of the Physical Culture Publishing Company. The post office had banned his books and now threatened to bar *Physical Culture* from the mails. This situation threatened to abort his most recent and ambitious publishing venture. In 1911, he had published the first volume of an elaborate five-volume illustrated compendium, *Macfadden's Encyclopedia of Physical Culture*. With the collaboration of numerous specialists in natural healing, he systematically set forth his "physcultopathy" principles of exercise, natural foods, avoidance of medicine, and emphasis on cleanliness, fresh air, and sunshine. Volume one dealt with anatomy, physiology, and the relation of diet to health; volume two treated physical training and sports, dancing as exercise and art, voice culture, and beauty care. The third volume covered fasting, hydrotherapy, first aid, and the "natural treatment" of diseases; the fourth volume listed fifty-nine diseases, their causes, effects, and treatment. Volume five dealt with sex, reproduction, parenthood, and child rearing. That this "bible of physical culture," as an admirer called it, would eventually go through many editions and enlargement to eight volumes in 1928 could not then be anticipated.[42] Macfadden was faced with the immediate need to keep his company alive.

To avert financial ruin, he transferred his stock in the Physical Culture Publishing Company in escrow to the company treasurer, Charles Desgrey, whom he named to succeed him as president, and directed him to send the dividends to Susie Wood. It was a temporary arrangement: Macfadden would go to England and on his return resume control of the company. As Desgrey later asserted, Bernarr put his arm around the interim president and said "I want you clearly to understand that when I come back you are to receive a one-third interest in my share of the business." Publicly, Macfadden merely announced that he was giving up control of *Physical Culture* to create "a world wide organization for the advancement of physical culture principles."[43]

As he fled across the Atlantic in 1912, he hoped that by lecturing and selling his publications in England he might earn enough to emerge from debt and rebuild his crippled career. What he could not foresee was the chain of events over the next two years that would have a lasting impact on his life.

The Perfect Woman

A BEAUTY CONTEST of athletic and shapely girls was Macfadden's big publicity gimmick for his British lecture tour. In his two magazines published in England, *Physical Development* (for men) and *Beauty and Health* (for women) he announced a prize of £100 for "the most perfect specimen of English womanhood." It aroused intense popular interest among girls all over the country. To enter the competition, a girl had to submit a picture of herself in tights, and Macfadden's committee of judges—an artist, a doctor, a physical director, and a journalist, presided over by the publisher himself—was overwhelmed by an avalanche of photographs from nearly five hundred contestants. From the original entrants, twenty-five young women were finally selected to come to London, expenses paid, to appear personally before the judges, who would base their choice upon health, muscular development, and good looks. In an atmosphere of suspense built up by Macfadden headquarters, the press printed pictures of the finalists in tights awaiting the verdict. The judges, after carefully taking the girls' measurements, unanimously declared the winner to be Mary Williamson of Yorkshire, a Halifax carpet-mill worker. Mary had refused to pose in tights, wearing instead a form-fitting swimsuit with trunks down to her knees, but Macfadden was aware of her swimming prowess from newspaper accounts and exempted her from the requirements of tights and tape measurements.[1]

Mary Williamson was born July 13, 1892, a three-pound, premature baby, to a devout Baptist family that moved to Halifax, a city of 125,000, when she was eleven. Her father, a mechanical engineer with a literary bent, encouraged her to strengthen her puny body by vigorous exercise. Eventually, she could run faster than any of her boyfriends. Her school had a swimming pool, and in two years she was the champion swimmer of Halifax. By the age of fifteen, she had won twenty prizes and the Royal Life Saving Society's silver medal of merit for saving a life at the risk of her own. She twice completed a fifteen mile swim in the Thames. At nineteen she had won sixty swimming prizes. Apparently, she was the only athlete in her family; her two brothers worked at the Dean Clough carpet mills in Halifax, and her sister, thirteen years younger, remained at home. Passionately fond of children, Mary was dreaming of marriage to someone who had a definite purpose in life, and she hoped to have at least six children.[2] Macfadden was eligible.

A different but not inconsistent version of her meeting with the physical culturist was related fifty years later by a friend on her swimming team: "some man had put an ad. in the paper for a wife and she should be a good swimmer," so Mary Williamson answered the appeal. Whatever the truth, she first met Macfadden when he greeted her on January 9, 1913, at the London railroad terminal. He was wrapped in "a long rabbinical overcoat."[3]

Mary was elated to be chosen as Britain's "perfect woman" and regarded Bernarr Macfadden as a kindred soul, "a chaste Galahad who talked the tongue of nature, which was my language."[4] He admired her sturdy and supple physique, her pleasant looks, her vivid blue eyes and wavy golden hair. Her triumph over childhood weakness held special meaning for one who had also been a weakling and doggedly built up his strength. Lonely and seeking personal fulfillment, he was a serious suitor within a few weeks. Mary, laughing off her friends' insinuations that this health fanatic was considering her chiefly as a vehicle for his experiments, was enthralled by his masculine vigor and his crusading determination to rescue mankind from physical weakness. It was not exactly love at first sight, but their romance — if it can be called that — flourished in the excitement of two superb bodies and resolute minds with similar ideals.

Bernarr Macfadden and Mary Williamson were married on March 5, 1913, less than two months after they had met. He was forty-five. She was nineteen. Admiration of her middle-aged bridegroom could not hide her amusement at his unique behavior. For their honeymoon she gave him a pair of silk pajamas on sale at Selfridge's in London, and he promptly tossed the bottoms onto the chandelier above their bridal bed, delivering at the same time a tirade that pants in bed were an unnatural interference with procreation; he would never be caught wearing them to bed.[5]

Macfadden's colossal egotism dismayed Mary, particularly when he made demands upon her. During her pregnancy, which began soon after their marriage, he forbade her to eat roast beef and her beloved Yorkshire pudding. He prescribed oatmeal mush, stewed raisins, and vegetarian foods, though he assured her that the diet would end when the child was born. Much harder for her to accept were his requirements of her as his partner in a health lecture tour of Wales, England, Scotland, and Ireland, during which neither their marriage nor her pregnancy were divulged.[6]

Always a showman, Macfadden capitalized on the newspaper publicity Mary had won as "Great Britain's Perfect Woman," and they appeared together on the stage as "the world's healthiest man and woman." She opened her part of the act with classical poses in a flowing Greek robe until the lights went out. When they went on again, she was revealed in flesh-colored tights, engaging in vigorous exercise with a girl she had trained under her husband's demanding eye. Audiences were as much attracted to Mary as to Bernarr, much to his annoyance. Lines formed in several cities, lecture halls were filled, and gate receipts were overflowing. One-night stands were sometimes held over for his sessions on sex, one for men, another for women. His health books, hawked in theater lobbies, sold so well that new supplies had to be brought in from London. If Mary Macfadden was unhappy at the sale of glossy postcard photos of her in pink tights, she was positively repelled by having to jump on the man with the "iron stomach."[7]

To the beat of Chopin's funeral march on the fiddle and piano, she climbed from a chair to a high table, the spotlight playing upon her lithe body in the semidarkness. Macfadden lay nude, except for a breechcloth, below her.

"Announce your exact weight, please?" he demanded.

"One hundred and forty-two pounds."

"Are you ready? If so, proceed!"

To the gasps of the spectators, Mary jumped upon her husband's stomach and bounded swiftly to the floor. Leaping to his feet as the audience applauded, Macfadden took deep and protracted bows, the spotlight playing upon him, his long hair almost touching the stage.[8]

Rationalizing that he needed her, Mary yielded to his will. He did, in fact, need her. "He would not be able to get along without me [she wrote in a casual diary].[9] Today he said so again. He has to be the way he is to do what he is going to do. I must help him. It takes so much understanding. God knows I love him. . . . How can he be so pitiless when I tell him I am frightened to death? He is so sure. Every day I try to believe he is right. But I'm carrying the baby."

Macfadden's *macho* attitude alternated with moments of compassion. One night when his wife's legs were painfully bruised, he was full of kindly concern, smiled tenderly, and offered her a jar of Professor Bodenheim's Bag Balm to rub on her legs. He liked to take long walks with her in the country, unruffled by astonished onlookers staring at his bare feet and at his broad-toed brogans tied by their laces and slung around his neck.[10]

These times of tender solicitude did little to quiet her fears. In the fourth month of her pregnancy, she began to have nightmares. At least once a week she dreamed that she stood on the edge of a precipice and suddenly was pushed off. She held her baby in one arm as she hurtled through the air to the sharp red rocks below. Awakening, she could not bring herself to tell Macfadden, so she bottled up her anxiety. He often told her that nothing could be more natural than birth, and it was the duty of the mother of a perfect child to be vigorous and active almost until the time of delivery.[11]

Bernarr had insisted when they were married that she must fully exemplify his principles, that she must be a living example of all his teachings. "Doctors are taboo," he warned her. Their children would be delivered by midwives. They must never be vaccinated. If they were sick he would prescribe natural methods of healing. "You will bring them up," he told her, "but strictly under my regime of health."[12] She accepted his specifications but never overcame her qualms.

The Macfadden tour went on to Scotland and briefly to Ireland before winding up in London for a final engagement at Royal Albert Hall. Before this performance, in which she would make her last seven-foot jump, she awakened in a sweat from another nightmare. Momentarily, she thought of leaving Bernarr, but she shrank from the publicity and the humiliation she would have to endure. She smothered an impulse to commit suicide. Although scared and feeling trapped, she determined to do what he expected of her. After all, she loved him.[13]

From London the Macfaddens moved to Brighton, where they opened a health resort in a leased four-story building, No. 6 Eastern Terrace, Kemptown, where ex-president Grant had once been entertained. Bernarr's first English health home in Chesham had been a disappointment, and he had closed it after Mary won his contest, but the idea of a jointly operated health home appealed to her when he broached it after proposing marriage. She agreed to pool her prize money and her share of the income from the sale of her photographs in this ambitious Brighton enterprise. Owing to the Macfaddens' reputation in England, their new home soon did a thriving business. Heart patients were required to avoid the elevator and climb the stairs; special exercises were ordered for those unable to do so. Patients were given very little food, for Macfadden believed that overeating or the consumption of devitalized foods like white flour products, white sugar, pickles and salty foods were the chief causes of heart weakness.[14]

The belief that, in general, there was only one disease, impurity of the blood, was Macfadden's underlying principle. Distress and pain were warnings of poison within the body, hence what doctors called disease was really a natural process to rid the body of impurities. Fasting, Macfadden held, was the only cure. As he explained to the patients, a fast enabled the system to consume superfluous tissue, devouring useless fat and "the wasted portions where the symptoms of disease are ravaging the body. It actually and naturally selects the diseased portions first. That's common sense."[15] As Mary observed, her husband's explanations kept down the food bill.

From time to time, the physical culturist received messages from America. Bad news gave him fits of depression. He read the cables repeatedly, shook his head and then set them on fire. One afternoon he brightened at a particular message which he tore up, remarking "Oh, what a relief. Susie isn't dead. It's her baby." Some days later, after receiving another cable, he was unusually considerate of Mary and told her the best thing he ever did was to marry her. "You have superior understanding. I don't know of any other woman who could understand what I'm going to tell you. It takes a love of humanity, a feeling of charity for those in trouble. You've got those things in you. It's natural for you to relieve distress. I need your help." Then he told her a yarn about a penniless patient at Physical Culture City who on her deathbed had begged him to take care of her infant girl. He promised to do so. He then paid strangers to bring up the little girl. "She shouldn't live this way," he remarked. "I don't feel I'm keeping my promise. She's in her seventh year, tender, trusting—and parentless."[16]

"You want me to bring her up, don't you?" Mary responded. "Of course I'll do it. A motherless child! You're really a noble person. Few men would have taken that responsibility. I'll be a real mother to the little girl. I'll take her." Bending over to kiss her and heaving a deep sigh of relief, he murmured "I'll never forget this. I'll send a cable to have her brought over. We don't have to sign papers of adoption. We're not taking her from anybody. She's alone. A sweet little girl. Her hair is the color of *carrots*. We'll call her Helen Macfadden."[17]

Bernarr Macfadden never admitted that Helen might be his and Susie Wood's daughter. In September, the little girl arrived, lonely, bewildered, and withdrawn, and accompanied by the well-to-do old lady who had put up bail money for Macfadden when he was arrested for publishing Coryell's story in *Physical Culture*. The elderly chaperon soon left for America, much to the relief of Mary, who accepted Helen as her own.[18]

The Macfadden health home prospered, increased its fees and still had a waiting list. Newspapers reported debates by medical men over Macfadden's theories. At an office he retained in London to supervise his publications, the physical culturist basked in the warmth of new-found well-wishers. One of them, a bearded fanatic, entered the office announcing that he was Jesus Christ and offered to cooperate. Feeding him carrots and rainwater, Bernarr convinced the visitor that he himself was Jesus Christ and got the zealot to settle for Luke and, thereafter, preach physical culture as biblically inspired.[19]

When Mary's full-length picture appeared on the cover of *My Weekly*, England's equivalent of the *Ladies Home Journal*, and her advice on health and beauty graced its pages, she was inundated with letters from admirers. Her husband wanted to capitalize on this by having her dive sixty feet into the Channel from the top of Long West Pier. To her protest that she was nearly six months pregnant he declared, "That's just the point! It will show the world what a prospective mother can do if she follows my physical culture regime. It'll be a finishing stroke to the age-old medical nonsense that a pregnant woman must be coddled. It'll be a sensational proof that she can stand any amount of exercise and will have a better baby for it."[20]

He assured her that she had nothing to fear, that she was an aquatic expert who knew how to dive. It would be a spectacle, and he would arrange for crowds, reporters, and photographers. She gave in. On the appointed day Macfadden harangued the multitude as his wife perched on the top platform of the pier. He fired a pistol, and she performed a sensational swan dive, emerging to cheers and a trumpet fanfare.[21]

Her aquatic prowess soon saved Macfadden's life — or so she later claimed. They were playing with a medicine ball on the beach with some of their more vigorous guests when, flouting her warning, he suddenly plunged into the Channel. The water was roughly whipped by a brisk southwest wind, the tide reached thirty feet at that spot, and the undertow was strong. A poor swimmer, Bernarr cried for help. Mary swam out to her frantically thrashing, gasping, choking husband, grabbed him, subdued him, and with the help of a giant wave, brought him to shore. Embarrassed, he ordered the patients on the beach not to say a word about the incident.

Mary's labor began late in December, and two brawny midwives arrived at the health home. When Macfadden tried to take charge and warned them not to summon a doctor if needed, they hustled him out of Mary's room and locked the door. Hours later he knocked furiously and was allowed to enter. Stern-faced, his jaw set firmly, he ordered the women to keep the door unlocked, bent over his wife's bed and assured her that all would be well: "All we have to do is work with nature." He left and returned twice until he was locked out again by the midwives, who were incensed at his meddling. Later, at his imperious insistence, they opened the door slightly. He forced it wide open and scuffled with the two Amazons, who lifted him up and threw him out of the room.[22]

The day after Christmas, after prolonged and arduous labor, Mary gave birth to a daughter, whom they named Byrnece. The infant weighed only a bit more than five pounds—a disappointment to the physical culturist, who added three pounds to the public announcement of the birth. Three days after Byrnece was born, Macfadden fired the midwives. Postnatal care was another money-making scheme of doctors and contrary to physical culture principles. Indian women, he insisted, were up and about with their day-old papooses on their backs. He demanded that Mary get back to work.

When the baby was four days old, Macfadden took it from her breast and immersed it in cold water up to its nose and mouth in the bathroom basin. Aghast, she struggled with him for the infant, screaming, "Bern! For the love of Christ! Have you gone mad!" He let her have the shivering child, which she snatched and snuggled in the warmth of her bed. He reproved her severely for violating the tenets of physical culture. "The baby should be dipped in very cold water every morning. *It's going to be.* It will become used to it and enjoy it. Nature will habituate it to the low temperature. That's the way to work with nature. . . . Your baby-doll coddling and cooing isn't helping it. You're like every other woman who's been hoodooed by medical fools. . . . You're acting like a sentimental adolescent about that baby. You're not going to interfere with my teachings and practices! You know what

I've *lived* for. You agreed to everything. You agreed in writing! You signed up!"

Mary's temper flared. A long and bitter argument broke out, neither she nor her husband sparing their verbal punches. A polar bear would not do to a four-day old cub what he had done, she declared; animals knew more about nature than he did! This was her child, and she had to save it from *him*. Frozen-faced and trembling, Bernarr finally shouted, "Enough! So long as you're my wife you'll do what I say! You signed up!" Mary gave in. Both were sorry they had lost their tempers, and they agreed that she should perform the baby-dipping every morning. When he was not present she merely dunked Byrnece's bottom into the water for a fraction of a second.[23]

They drank in the New Year with beet juice, and before the end of January she was pregnant again. Underweight and undernourished, she resumed her prescribed vegetarian diet. Macfadden, who spent much of his time in London, returned later one night to announce that they were going to France, and that he had arranged for Helen, then attending a Brighton private school, to go with them. Three days later they crossed the channel, taking along five sizes of dumbbells, Indian clubs, and steel spring exercisers.

In Paris they took lodgings in a pension, where Bernarr carried their luggage up four flights of stairs. Knowing almost no French, he relied on John R. Coryell, the *Physical Culture* writer who had been one of the judges in Macfadden's English "perfect girl" contest and who was now in Paris consuming sumptuous meals and fine wines. To convert the French to physical culture Bernarr bought a large enclosed wagon for touring the country, but when he discovered that fully loaded with family, baggage, and equipment it was too heavy to be hauled either by automobile or a team of less than four horses, he abandoned the project. Meanwhile, Mary overcame a ten-day bout with pneumonia with the help of copious drafts of honey-sweetened water. After seven weeks in the French capital, Macfadden and his family moved to a cozy cottage he rented in the tiny town of Winnereux near Boulogne on the northern coast.[24]

While his wife gazed longingly at the Dover cliffs in the distance, he dictated memoirs of his childhood and learned a smattering of French from an English secretary, searched the Bible for phrases justifying vegetarianism, and crossed to England two or three times a week to attend to his publications and health home. "Jesus Christ was a healer because he was the first physical culturist," he told Mary. "My teachings are those of the early prophets. I live as they did. It is my duty to influence the world to live that way." As a start, he set down words to convert secular songs into physical culture hymns for a world-wide religion based on Scripture.[25]

Physical fitness involved more than words and phrases, no matter how inspired. He prescribed more gymnastics for his pregnant wife, but exercise with a medicine ball only contributed to a miscarriage. During the summer she again became pregnant, and for months thereafter he insisted that she do two hundred knee bends every morning.[26]

War suddenly disrupted the Macfaddens' five-month seaside sojourn. The German invasion of Belgium in August and the imminent threat to France led them to recross the Strait of Calais. They headed for London, and after two months they rode south to their thriving Brighton health home, which had been capably managed in their absence by a graduate of the healthatorium in Chicago. Cables from America evidently convinced Macfadden that his difficulties in the United States had been overcome. After only a month in Brighton he decided to return to America, reclaim the stock he had placed in escrow and make a new start in the publishing business, once again in his own name.[27]

Leaving the Brighton home in the hands of his protégé, Macfadden booked passage for himself and family on the *Lusitania*, which less than seven months later would be sunk by a German submarine with the loss of nearly 1,200 lives. The Cunard liner steamed out of Liverpool late at night on October 3, its curtains tightly drawn, hugging the British coast until it zigzagged its way across the Atlantic. En route, despite his seasickness, Bernarr composed a public relations article announcing his triumphant arrival: "The return of Bernarr Macfadden to America signalizes the extraordinary progress of the world physical culture movement since he has been abroad." Despite the public's tendency to label reform leaders as fanatics, he went on, much of what they preached was becoming accepted. His British lecture tour had produced great enthusiasm, he reported, though the French lagged behind in knowledge of practical health building. His faith in a world movement for physical culture was greater than ever, and his reform proposals were "uppermost in the public minds. *The force of our propaganda will be felt more and more every year.*" He even hinted at carrying physical culture into politics, with the ultimate goal of having his principles taught in every home and school in the world.[28]

After six days, the *Lusitania* reached the Narrows safely, glided past the Statue of Liberty and docked at New York. That sunny morning was brighter than Macfadden's immediate business prospect. Off the gangplank and onto the street, Macfadden hailed a taxi, and the family was driven to the Yonkers home of his magazine manager, Charles Desgrey, whose wife was a sister of Susie Wood, then managing the Chicago "International Healthatorium." Bernarr informed Desgrey that, inasmuch as he had made Mary a partner in the business, he could no longer honor his earlier agreement to turn over to Desgrey one-third of his stock in the enterprise. Although Desgrey would work out his contract on *Physical Culture* until the end of 1917, he was no doubt embittered by what seemed a betrayal. As a partner, Mary had a double duty: to read manuscripts at the company's nineteenth floor offices in the Flatiron Building, and to play her maternal part in the physical culture family that Bernarr hoped would be an example to Americans, if not all mankind.[29] For years, she would be continually pregnant.

In November, after their brief stay at the Desgrey's, the Macfaddens rented "Balmy Breezes," a flimsy summer cottage in Far Rockaway, Long Island, for forty dollars a week. The mattresses were of straw, the furnishings run-down, the furnace balky, and the freezing winter air pushed up through cracks in the floorboards. Bernarr, who always suffered in the cold, tried to keep warm by standing on his head and wiggling his legs. At night he slept in long, thick red underwear over which he wore a flannel nightgown, his legs in bed socks, his hands in gloves and wristlets, his head in a fur-lined Daniel Boone cap with long earpieces. Mary, meanwhile, placed her fur coat under the cheap mattress and curled around Baby Byrnece, and in the daytime did her household chores in that coat and a sunbonnet to warm her ears.[30]

After four weeks of shivering, Bernarr and Mary went to visit the healthatorium in Chicago, leaving Helen with the Desgreys in Yonkers. Susie Wood, probably Helen's mother—although Mary did not know it—greeted them warmly and embraced the "perfect woman." "I'll call you Mary right off," she purred. "Call me Susie. We're going to be friends for life." Bernarr smiled happily and danced about. In the dining room, they ate a sumptuous yet vegetarian luncheon and drank experimental tea brewed from grass, alfalfa, and clover leaves. Susie's guests were accommodated in her apartment and remained at the health home until early in 1915, though Bernarr took three or four business trips to New York.

He arranged for his family to return not to the decrepit cottage but to a twenty-room residence he rented for a thousand dollars a month, staffed by the same housekeeper and help he had employed at the Brighton health home. To make it easier to pay the rent he planned to take in boarders who would share the raw cabbage, greens, carrots, beet juice, and honey-sweetened water. When Mary, who was otherwise thrilled with the palatial facilities, demurred at maintaining a boarding house while she raised her little children, he argued that more children required more money. "We need more money right now," he said. "This is the way to make it quickly. You know what we did at Brighton." The lease forbade boarders, but he reassured his hesitant wife by declaring that he had "toned down" landlords before. "Why should all these rooms go to waste!" Without admitting that the vegetarian diet he had ordered Mary to follow while carrying Byrnece was too Spartan, he now mollified her by letting her eat meat. Once in a while, he told her, the body needed some red meat, so they sat down to devour three servings of savory roast beef.

Macfadden bought a car. Steering it into their driveway, he pressed the horn, which blared the first seven notes of "In the Good Old Summer Time." It was a 1903 Palmer-Singer with a floppy canvas top. He had just driven it out from Brooklyn and, he beamed, "You should have seen me beat out those horses through Jamaica." To save money, he drove on worn secondhand tires which blew with alarming frequency. In this "ambulatory piece of junk," as Mary later called it, he brought midwife Bridget McGoorty for the delivery of Mary's second baby on April 19, 1915, a nine-pound girl with blonde hair.[31] As Bernarr demanded that his children's names begin with "B," Mary chose Beulah, an Old Testament name that intrigued her husband. He publicized the health home as "Beulah Vista."

Macfadden needed an immediate income to pay off substantial debts, chief of which was $16,000 owed to the New York and Pennsylvania Paper Company, *Physical Culture*'s principal creditor. Moreover, before leaving the United States in 1912 he had incurred a $19,000 deficit from a nationwide lecture tour. Beulah Vista was his salvation. It soon attracted enough boarders to enable Macfadden to sock away some savings. It also brought a visit from the irate landlord, who threatened to break the lease unless all the "interlopers got the hell out." Miraculously, after a furious argument on the staircase, Bernarr persuaded him to allow boarders until autumn.[32]

A small income from boarders did little to solve Macfadden's financial difficulties. Although he resumed the presidency of his company and the editorial direction of *Physical Culture*, the firm's funds drained away. The magazine could not attract big money advertisers, particularly as Macfadden disapproved of tobacco, cigarettes, pipes, liquor, coffee, tea, hats, high-heeled shoes, or other body-contorting apparel. Its advertisements were mainly for specialized products with a limited market, such as automatic exercisers, punching bags, dumb-bells, gadgets for measuring lung capacity, arch supporters, the Miz-pah jock strap, the hand-pumping shower (a favorite with Bernarr), and concentrated carrot juice or powder. Because of his conviction for sending obscene matter in the mails, Macfadden could not advertise his own books, so his royalties shrank. He tried to patent a number of devices ranging from an air purifier to a double-deck subway car and a narrow gauge railroad to pull shoppers past the counters of depart-ment stores. For sedentary business and professional men in over-heated, stuffy offices he invented a contrivance to conduct invigorat-ing air directly to the penis, thus aiding vitality and potency. These contraptions produced no income, and his "Washed Air Company," legally known as the Vitalized Air Corporation, failed. His health crusade was confronted with bankruptcy. To save money he furnished living quarters without looking for a permanent home, much to his wife's uneasiness. The Macfaddens moved into the city after the pipes burst at Beulah Vista and water cascaded into the kitchen. They spent most of the winter in a Riverside Drive apartment, not exactly in a low rent area, but Bernarr wanted to keep up appearances.

In the spring of 1916, the family rented a house in Port Washing-ton, where their third daughter was born on October 6. The infant was huge and weighed thirteen pounds. Mary had proposed naming it Brenda, but her husband objected. "Brenda is no name for this true physical culture baby," he sniffed. "It doesn't have the ring of strength and *brawn*, which fills her body. *Brawn!* That's it! I'll call her *Brawnda.*" After a hot argument, the best that Mary could do was to change the spelling to *Braunda.*

The next year, the Macfaddens occupied a house in Douglaston on Little Neck Bay, somewhat closer to Manhattan. In December, an-ticipating the worldwide epidemic that took a toll of ten million lives, influenza struck Mary and her three daughters. Bernarr ordered them to fast but allowed them orange juice or milk and honey, attended to them personally when at home, but would permit no physician to enter the premises. Whether from his ministrations or not, all four patients recovered in three weeks. Weak and exhausted, Mary gave birth to her fourth *B*, a nine-pound girl, on January 26, 1918. The Mac-faddens were living on Beverly Road, and so Bernarr named the in-fant Beverly. He made no secret of his disappointment at having only daughters. "We're going to see what we can do about having some boys," he announced. "I want sons to carry on my torch."

Mary herself decided that she would have no more children if she could not produce a son, but she gave first priority to finding a permanent residence instead of migrating like birds every season. The Macfaddens lived briefly in Long Beach and Great Neck, but in 1920 bought a ten-room house on twenty-two acres that included a stream with a waterfall in Nyack on the west shore of the Hudson and north of New York City. For $10,000 it was a bargain. The hills and woods delighted them, and they built a swimming pool beside their private brook. The Nyack home was the site of Bernarr's and Mary's conscious efforts to bring into the world a boy.[33]

Among their visitors was a Dr. David M. Reeder of La Porte, Indiana, who had chatted with Macfadden in his New York office and who had studied sex determination. Mary encouraged him to elaborate on his study of more than two thousand cases of childbirth for which he usually was able to determine the date of conception. He concluded that if conception occurred within three days after the end of the menstrual period, a girl would be born; if conception took place from the fourth to the seventh day, either a girl or boy would result; if it happened from the eighth to the twentieth day, the issue would be a boy, and more certainly so as the twentieth day approached.

Fascinated, Bernarr proceeded to apply the Reeder theory. He later claimed as his own the rule of sex predetermination, and he set forth the technique in two *Physical Culture* articles, "Determining the Sex of Your Child," in March 1922, and "A Boy or a Girl—Take Your Pick," in March 1925. In a publicity release to doctors his Physical Culture Corporation took credit for this "absolutely dependable solution of the sex determination problem," the facts of which physicians and osteopaths had "verified . . . beyond all possible doubt." To inquiries from physicans who had read the 1922 article, the American Medical Association replied that it knew of no scientific evidence for Macfadden's claim and it added "as you probably know Macfadden apparently rejects even the most axiomatic facts of science and persistently blackguards the medical profession. Some years ago when he was running a so-called 'Health Home' in Battle Creek, Mich., he attempted to appeal to the venal members of the medical profession by offering to any physician, who might send him a patient, one-half of all the fees he obtained from the victim."[34]

Spectacular publishing profits, mainly from their confession maga-

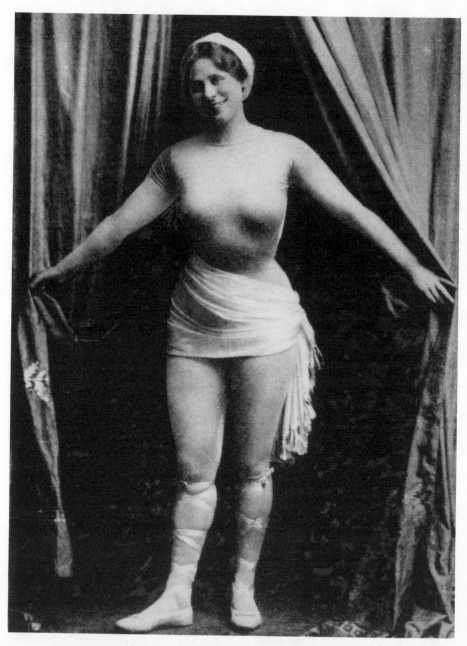

Mary Williamson Macfadden. Courtesy of Fulton Oursler, Jr.

zine, *True Story*, brought wealth to the Macfaddens almost overnight in the early 1920s. They spent the winters in a comfortable apartment on Riverside Drive in the city, where their first son was born. Mary named him Byron, whose poetry she loved, but Bernarr, whose mid-American taste did not run to romantic figures, called him Billy.[35]

When Billy was eleven months old, in December 1922, he suddenly went into a convulsion. Bernarr ordered a hot sitz bath, told Mary to strip the baby naked, grasped the little creature and plunged it into the water up to its neck. Shocked, Mary lifted the infant to her breast. "Bern!" she shrieked. "For the love of Christ, call a doctor!" but Macfadden was immovable. Byron died in his mother's arms.[36]

To overcome their grief, Macfadden proposed vigorous exercise. "We will walk it off. I'll walk with you for a week until you all get a good, healthy, tired feeling," he told his family. They slipped off quietly to Atlantic City, where he paced his wife and four daughters in marching back and forth on the boardwalk. Embarrassed because he had publicized his family as paragons of health and his son Byron as a successful demonstration of predetermined sex, he snatched up newspapers for possible accounts of Byron's death.

Soon after they returned to the Riverside Drive apartment he received an anonymous telephone threat. "That's what happens to a rich man," he sighed as he hung up the phone. He was worried about the family's safety. Turning over the direction of his publishing business to Fulton Oursler, his managing editor, he and his family took a night train to Athol, a small town in Massachusetts near the New Hampshire border, where his daughter Helen had been placed in the Reverend Ezekiel Parslow's farm school for teenaged girls. The retired clergyman welcomed the Macfaddens and tried to console the despairing Mary. Bernarr sought to comfort her, saying that another boy would make her forget her grief, and he decided that only continuous daily exercise would lift her from black despondency. He persuaded her to walk with him to New York, two hundred miles away!

Entrusting their daughters to Parslow's care, Bernarr and Mary, their light luggage slung over his back, trudged south in the snow. At night they stopped at inns along the way. After leaving Springfield they braved a blizzard, icy winds, and snowdrifts, and reached Windsor Locks at midnight on New Year's eve. They were in Hartford the next day, and after fourteen days afoot they arrived at Greenwich.

Leaning over their hotel bed, Macfadden caressed his wife. "Look, sweetie, let's pick up where we were before Billy—" he stopped as he saw her anguished look. "I never saw such a look of pain in a pair of beautiful eyes," he resumed. She repelled his overture and asked him to promise never again to discuss Byron's death. "Well, that's a hard thing to ask," he replied. "I can promise you this much. I will never talk to you personally about it again. But my public must have an explanation. They still think all over the country there are five children in the physical culture family." She remained unconsolable. He pleaded, "Why keep tearing yourself to pieces? The family depends on you. The girls live for you. They will need brothers to protect them—A home that's completely feminized isn't normal. Penalties devolve on girls that have no brothers. We need sons as safeguards for us in our old age—and for our fortune. *We're going to be worth millions!"*

That night, the tenth after Mary's period, Bernarr made love to her while she sobbed uncontrollably. She cried out so loudly that the room clerk telephoned to inquire what was wrong. Walking away from the phone, Macfadden told his wife, "You won't have to walk the rest of the way home. You've *had* your cure!" The next morning they boarded the train for New York.

Macfadden did not consult her in preparing an editorial for the February 1923 issue of *Physical Culture* in which he accused himself of causing his son's death by letting his wife's sentimentality interfere with his own judgment about Byron's proper feeding and exercise. He also mentioned a serious fall, followed by a series of convulsions in the child's body. Before publishing the piece, he showed it to his chief editor, Fulton Oursler, who did not express his belief that Macfadden had failed to call a doctor in time. He urged his boss not to publish the editorial. It was bad taste, he said, to make the death of a child the subject of public discussion and a mistake to blame his wife publicly. However, Macfadden insisted on publishing the statement without essential changes; silence would benefit his enemies and alienate his followers. Thousands of readers wrote to praise him for his courage in expressing his convictions.[37]

Twenty years later, Mary Macfadden recalled that her husband's public account of Byron's death was "the beginning of the end between Bernarr and me." She not only denied the truth of his explanation but was appalled at her husband's public airing of what was to her an intensely painful, private matter. In the months after the tragedy, her despondency turned into despair. Between the births of her last two children, both boys—Berwyn in 1923 and Brewster in 1925—she contemplated suicide.[38]

Reunited at their Nyack home in 1923, the Macfadden family followed Bernarr's intensely regimented routine. The four girls were drafted for gymnastic performances at radio station WOR, where Macfadden was publicizing his physical culture family and soon inspired John Gambling to broadcast his popular morning musical exercises. When the Macfadden children caught the whooping cough, Bernarr ordered them on a complete fast for three weeks except for orange juice. Ignoring Mary's appeals to relent, he insisted that he was practicing what he preached, and the children accepted his authority. During the summer, he insisted that Mary, who was pregnant again, do daily knee bends before breakfast, join in fast sets of tennis, swim in the pool, and take brisk five-mile walks until almost immediately before the baby was due. During Mary's agonizing delivery of a baby boy almost strangled by the umbilical cord, he watched at the foot of the bed and refused to summon a doctor, despite the frantic pleas of their Austrian midwife. Berwyn seemed to be living proof of Dr. Reeder's (and Macfadden's) theory of sex determination. It is not known whether the sex of their last child, Brewster, a thirteen-pound son born in 1925, was similarly predetermined. Mary wanted to call him Bruce, after her father's Scottish ancestors, but Bernarr considered the name weak and demanded that the boy be called Brewster, which rhymed with rooster and suggested the combativeness of a fighting cock.[39]

Macfadden, at the age of fifty-seven, had fathered nine children. Seven were Mary's, including the short-lived Byron. Friendly, freckled, red-headed Helen was brought up as a sister to Mary's daughters. When she was in her late teens, as a physical culture girl under her father's tutelage, she walked more than three miles from their Riverside Drive apartment at 137th Street to her office job at Macfadden Publications and trudged home in the evening unless offered a ride, which she always promptly accepted. In 1929, Macfadden arranged for her to be featured in a stage presentation of "The Perfect Girl," part of a physical culture movie, *Rampant Youth at Sixty*, and once a week she led a dozen chorus girls in a physical culture drill for women. On the editorial staff of *Physical Culture* in the 1930s, she wrote monthly articles of health advice for girls. Advertised as "one of the late Florenz Ziegfelds's glamour girls," she wrote *Help Yourself to Beauty*, which the Macfadden Book Company published and sold at a dollar a copy. She married Joe Wiegers, Macfadden's publicity director, and of all the Macfadden girls, she was the most closely associated with her father's publishing business.[40]

Least known of Macfadden's children was Byrne, his daughter by Marguerite Kelly, who after the breakup of their disastrous marriage,

lived with her mother in Canada. In the early twenties, Byrne joined
Macfadden Publications (formerly the Physical Culture Publishing
Company) as a reader, then a writer. Promoted to the staff of *Dance
Lovers*, she interviewed Broadway celebrities and wrote an article
describing how she had learned to "shimmy" from Gilda Grey. While
assisting Vera Caspary on *Dance Magazine*, she developed a bad cough,
but in spite of her colleagues' urging avoided medical treatment. She
was fun loving, wore lipstick, smoked, occasionally downed a highball,
and spent many nights on the dance floor, where she had a crush on
Vincent Lopez, the popular band leader. Her conduct was careless in
view of her weak heart. She often fainted. Believing that strenuous
exercise would strengthen her heart, Macfadden ordered her to attend
exclusive classes conducted by the governess of his other daughters,
who performed as the "Macfaddenettes."[41]

Byrne's anxious mother hastened to New York and put her daughter to bed in a one-room apartment on Seventy-ninth Street. There
the girl weakened and hemorrhaged. Macfadden stopped her salary
to prevent its being spent on doctors. He would not permit her to be
taken to the hospital, but he was willing to pay all her expenses if
she would submit to his physical culture treatment for pneumonia
or any chest or lung ailment: immersion in a tub of ice water. No physician got near her, and Byrne died at the age of twenty-two on June 20,
1926. Her father did not attend the funeral, and he forbade his employees to discuss her death. According to dance editor Vera Caspary,
who had befriended Byrne, he was irritated when his younger daughters wept at the undertaker's and hurried them along for an appointment with a photographer. To his daughters' dismay, he declared, "It's
better she's gone. She'd have disgraced me."[42]

It was typical of Macfadden to consider first his public image. On
occasion he could be tender, and he had a certain magnetic attraction
for women, but fundamentally, his wife and children were instruments
in the sincere, humorless, and sometimes cruel application of his
health doctrines. He considered them as the means to an end, an example to his followers, an object lesson to the nation and the world.
The outward success of the physical culture family served as well to
satisfy his craving for popular approval, to gratify his monumental
ego. What was revealed to the public was a smiling, model family,
strong and healthy from living in accordance with nature's beneficence. For twenty years, the public had no inkling of the turmoil in
the physical culture family and of Macfadden's discovery that the "Perfect Woman" was less than perfect. The flamboyant physical culturist
was making millions at the helm of Macfadden Publications.

Confessions Make Millions

IN THE MID-1920s at precisely 3:00 P.M., a chord on the piano summoned employees to leave their desks on the top floor of the Macfadden Building, Broadway and Sixty-fifth Street, for fifteen minutes of calisthenics. Although office workers of at least one other company had performed calisthenics in 1919, physical exercise was not the custom in the business world of the 1920s. But Macfadden was an evangelist determined to set examples of body building.

The office staff of the former Physical Culture Publishing Company, reorganized in 1924 as Macfadden Publications, bent and stretched in the middle of the desk area as Dr. Paul J. Veatch, a *Physical Culture* writer and health consultant, pounded the piano. On hot days the pungent odor of sweat permeated the area. For about two years, the exercises were conducted from a desk top by Ruth ("Curves") Cohen, a shapely and dazzlingly delightful girl, who later married Lyon Mearson, editor of Macfadden's *True Romances*. Apparently these calisthenics were tolerated good-naturedly even by those who hated exercise, although former employees disagree on whether they were compulsory. One of them recalls that they were mandatory and that no one was excused, but Emile Gauvreau believed otherwise. Immediately after he was hired in 1924 to edit the *Evening Graphic*, Macfadden's tabloid newspaper, he was astonished to see the windows being opened to a cold and windy April afternoon and "a tanned athletic creature attired in sandals and a leopard skin" springing upon a desk and commanding everyone to rise. "The entire department was set off into violent calisthenics, swimming in the air, inhaling, exhaling and legs kicking back while the leopard man exhorted the limb swingers into a furious tempo." Gauvreau sneaked out to the fire escape, where nonconformists smoking cigarettes told him that the exercises were not compulsory.[1]

The leopard man was not Macfadden. Although the boss usually was on the premises every day, he had neither the time nor the inclination to mingle with the employees, but they were aware of his presence. No liquor or tobacco could be seen in the vast, open desk area, although there was furtive smoking in the toilets. Some staff members even displayed milk bottles on their desks. Macfadden's sexuality was common gossip. Late one afternoon, when a newly hired executive asked what time it was, an old-timer replied, "It's always sex o'clock here."[2]

Macfadden employees were alert to the many good-looking females entering and leaving the offices. Rumors abounded. Bernarr "had lots of women," one high-level staff member recalled, but he was discreet in public and "nobody in the company fooled with his women." Except at the top level, there was no gender gap at Macfadden Publications. During the 1930s, a certain Miss Harvey, tall and attractive, an "efficiency agent" with a talent for observing operations, reported directly to Macfadden. One trusted official suspected that she really was a detective employed in a surveillance system throughout the company.[3]

At Macfadden Publications, people were always coming and going. The editors brought in celebrities, experienced theater folk, and aspiring movie stars of both sexes. *Physical Culture* attracted the muscle boys. Other visitors were job-seekers or their relatives, among them a former model and chorus girl with legs said to be the prettiest in the world, shepherded by a wrinkled woman who claimed to be her mother. Another applicant was Mother Millikin, who brought in pictures of her girls in the nude, hoping they would be allowed to pose for magazine covers or to illustrate the exercises in *Physical Culture*.[4] A mecca of "the world's oddest pilgrims" was a former editor's piquant appraisal of the Macfadden offices. "The boss collected freaks as a museum collects masterpieces. Opportunists as well as true believers came—along with disciples of various musical cults, apostles of sex freedom, whores of literature, saints of digestion. A modern Samson held iron weights suspended by his hair. A hero of the alimentary canal swallowed screws and nuts and could on command bring up a bolt or pecan. The great crusader sponsored all of these fanatics, and may even have believed in some."[5]

Over it all presided Bernarr Macfadden, proud of the famous names enlivening his office and tolerant of eager people on the make, health enthusiasts, and champions of odd causes.

The key figure, a sort of prime minister, in the Macfadden publishing empire was the chief editor, Charles Fulton Oursler. He was known as Charlie by his friends, but dropped the Charles once his reputation was made. Tall, intense, scholarly in appearance, with oak brown eyes and a long nose, he downed quarts of milk, which pleased Macfadden. But he was a chain smoker. Not feeling bound by Bernarr's antismoking rules, he filled his private office with clouds of cigarette smoke and even struck matches on no smoking signs.[6]

Oursler had been managing editor of *Music Trades* and in 1921 had contributed four articles to the first issue of a new Macfadden magazine, all of which were accepted. Seeing four checks made out to the same author, Macfadden asked to meet him, and the next day Oursler walked into the publisher's tiny, cramped, noisy office, then at 119 West Fortieth Street, where the business occupied an entire floor crowded with employees. To save space Bernarr had installed a double-deck tier of offices, with salaried writers and minor editors in the upper level, reached by stepladders, and various guest writers in the lower level.[7]

"I like to know the men I am doing business with," Macfadden opened. "Tell me about yourself." The talk flowed all afternoon— politics, food, Freud, and the jazz age—which impressed BM, as he was known by his associates. By Christmas he offered Oursler a job. The youthful editor, not yet twenty-nine, declined but agreed to Macfadden's proposal that he spend the noon hour with him five days a week for $100 a week.[8] For six months he chatted with Macfadden at lunchtime and improved the edited manuscripts by altering a heading, a box, or a blurb. In June 1922, Macfadden finally induced him to join the company. He was given an office and a secretary but no duties until a week later he found two envelopes on his desk. The first enclosed a note from BM:

Dear Mr. Oursler:

I am going away on a trip and am leaving you in complete editorial charge of my properties. You know what I want. Give them their orders. I will back you up. You are herewith appointed supervising editor of the Macfadden Publications.

The second contained the boss's memorandum to all the editorial staff announcing Oursler's appointment. It was signed by every recipient.[9]

Macfadden and Oursler had an extraordinary friendship. Although

their interests were different and they frequently disagreed on editorial policy, they trusted each other and their relations were always
cordial. "He never reproached me," Oursler reminisced; "he never spoke
an uncivil word to me; we never even had the shadow of a quarrel.
. . . No man has ever had a better friend than I was to find in Bernarr
Macfadden."[10]

The new chief editor was an amateur magician and a friend of
Howard Thurston and Harry Houdini. At Macfadden Publications,
where he was called "Svengali," he sometimes wore a Sherlock Holmes
hat and performed magic tricks at sales meetings. Out of his hobby
evolved an interest in spiritualism and a friendship with Sir Arthur
Conan Doyle, an ardent spiritualist devotee. He worked with Houdini
to expose fake mediums, and he organized a committee to offer $10,000
to anyone who could demonstrate a supernatural phenomenon.[11]

Enigmatic, charming, and magnetic, he won friendships by showing concern for the topics dear to those he talked to. He was loved,
hated, admired, and despised by the editors and assistants he supervised. Editor Lyon Mearson's wife, whom Oursler hired, fired, and re-
hired, called him a son-of-a-bitch to work for, but despite his merciless criticism of her found him exciting and dynamic and remained
loyal to him. Some of the staff were enemies behind his back. As one
remarked, "I guide my life by five words—Dare, do, and keep silent."
A trusted executive considered Oursler "the biggest con man that ever
lived." Another called him one of the greatest editors in the country,
but others were turned off by his vanity and pretentiousness. Fresh
out of college, one young editor who watched him swagger and order
his secretary about, found his criticisms hard to take. A member of
the art staff thought him "a big phony" who had contempt for the whole
Macfadden enterprise.[12]

Next to the publisher, Oursler was the dominant figure in Macfadden Publications. Even before he became editor of *Liberty* in 1931,
he wrote cover blurbs for every Macfadden magazine and exercised
general supervision over their editorial policies, sometimes by remote
control. In the summer months, beginning in 1931, he appeared at
his New York office only for a few days, for BM permitted him to edit
magazines by teletype from "Sandalwood," his large shingled house
at West Falmouth on Cape Cod, where writers converged on week-
ends. Eventually, the rambling structure had nearly thirty rooms, seven
bathrooms, three fireplaces, a cellar darkroom, four porches, playhouse,
two-car garage with an apartment for the help, sheds, wine press, and
pump house. Here Oursler and his wife, writer Grace Perkins, hosted

Heywood Broun, Sinclair Lewis, Sylvester Viereck, mystery writer S. S. Van Dine, Eleanor Roosevelt, Thomas E. Dewey, and hundreds of other celebrities, literary and otherwise. Here Macfadden came, flying his own airplane over the house, landing at an airfield over ten miles away, and alternately walking and running barefoot behind the car his host invariably sent to fetch him. At New York headquarters subordinate editors gathered at noon around the teletype receiver to read Oursler's messages.[13]

Two years before the talented and ambitious Oursler initially fascinated Macfadden, the foundation of a flourishing publishing empire had been laid. *Physical Culture* had been in existence since 1899, capably edited by Carl Williams from 1916 to 1923 and selling well, but the financial power of Macfadden Publications was produced by a new monthly magazine that would revolutionize popular periodicals.

True Story hit the newsstands in May 1919. Tales of its origin are conflicting. After her relations with Bernarr soured, Mary Macfadden claimed it as her own idea. According to her account, Bernarr worried aloud while walking with her in the sunset. Lacking capital and credit to start more vegetarian restaurants or health homes, with a wife and four children to support, he hoped it was not the sunset of his life. "Can't you dig up an idea from your mind to pull us out of this hole?" he asked. She advised branching out. As manuscripts and letters submitted to *Physical Culture* showed, muscle-bound and emotionally frustrated men wished to share intimate personal experiences, she explained, and broken-hearted women had written to confess their sexual mistakes until their conversion to physical culture had led them to love and a happy marriage. "These are true stories," Mary affirmed. "Let's get out a magazine to be called *True Story*, written by its own readers in the first person." It had never been done before, and a new wide readership might lead to other similar publications. At dinner that night Bernarr slowly chewed carrots, announced that he would discuss the matter with his associates, and pledged all at the table to silence.[14]

Macfadden insisted that he alone was the first to conceive *True Story* and refused to give his wife any credit for the idea. She could not tell a verb from a noun, he sneered, yet she embarrassed him by repeating her version. His own account was simple and unembroidered. He had been considering a mounting pile of letters from *Physical Culture* readers who unburdened themselves and sought his counsel, and his advice column for women took far too much of his time. As he sat barefooted for long hours reading confessional letters, he became convinced that he had the makings of a promising magazine.[15]

Harold Hersey, a pulpwood editor who briefly worked for Macfadden Publications, tells another story. Macfadden returned from a publishers' conference envious of pulp magazine profits and announced to his business manager, Orr J. Elder, a plan to issue a pulp magazine, call it *True Story*, illustrate it, and print it in larger format than the usual seven-by-ten size. The dramatic life stories of contributors would be printed with as few editorial changes as possible. Although everyone on Macfadden's staff except Elder and one or two others discouraged the scheme, BM, buoyed by an intense faith in himself, persisted, borrowed a million dollars, and launched the project.[16]

Macfadden's authorized biographers do not mention his wife either as inspiration for, or collaborator on, *True Story*, probably because Bernarr wanted it that way. Oursler stated baldly that the publisher first broached the notion to his English bride before bringing her to the United States in 1914, and five years later was selecting stories, proposing illustrations, and editing every sheet that went to the printer. The position of editor he offered to John Brennan, who had been an associate on *Physical Culture* since 1905, on condition that he have "nothing whatsoever to do with the selection of stories." When the astonished Brennan asked what the editor would do, BM barked, "Get the book out—on *time.*"[17] The accommodating old associate accepted.

A magazine with a special appeal to girls, featuring romance, sex, and adventure, was well suited to the twenties. Postwar rebellion against Victorian attitudes, the vogue of Freudian psychology, and the open discussion of sexuality created a popular receptiveness to BM's enterprise. The titillation of forbidden encounters, the emotional turmoil, and the moral dilemmas of fundamentally good heroines afforded escape from the humdrum lives of the semiliterate. Usually Plain Janes caught in stock situations and encountering stock characters, the narrators told their stories in their own clear and simple way, recounting events of young love, betrayal, good or bad fortune, marriage, motherhood and family, and countless challenges to innocence. In the end, they generally emerged chastened and comparatively serene. "Trapped by Destiny," "Did I do Right?," "He Wanted Children," "I Wanted Love and So—," "Things Wives Tell," "My Dangerous Paradise," and "Ignorant of Life" were typical *True Story* titles.[18]

The first issue, displaying on its cover a man and a woman with the caption "and their love turned to hatred," offered $1,000 for the reader's "life romance." Priced at twenty cents, it sold 60,000 copies, about par at that time for a new magazine. For the first year there was no hint of great success, but suddenly the circulation rose phenomenally to nearly 100,000 and in four years to three-quarters of a million. Originally a pulp, *True Story* was so successful that Macfadden raised its price and converted it into a smooth paper publication to attract the loyalty of big advertisers. In time, a single issue carried half a million dollars in advertising. By 1924, the magazine had 848,000 readers, by 1925 more than a million and a half, and after 1926 more than two million.[19]

To handle the thousands of stories submitted for publication, Macfadden set up a "manuscript department" headed by Susie Wood, once his secretary. This department comprised numerous girl readers, including stenographers, dancing teachers, and even wrestlers, who were instructed to read not for style or good taste, but "for interest," and to rate a manuscript on a scale of 90 to 100, depending upon how they felt while reading it. Stories rated 95 and better were read by Macfadden himself and his wife, and later by others in the editorial hierarchy. In this cumbersome and time-consuming method, Macfadden was the ultimate judge. An article selected by him reflected his optimistic faith that one could overcome the pitfalls of life, win redemption, and achieve happiness.[20] It also reflected the fact that sex sold magazines.

Ministers and church leaders denounced *True Story* as lewd, licentious, and pornographic. They organized boycotts, which together with hastily passed local laws forced newsstands to stop selling Macfadden publications. When BM protested that the stories in the magazine had a moral purpose, Oursler suggested that he hire a clergyman as an associate editor to read all stories selected for an issue and reject any he thought objectionable. The publisher accepted the proposal and promised to abide by the results. A former Baptist minister visited Oursler at the time and got the job.

Not long afterward, Macfadden expanded the idea by creating a "ministerial advisory board." In telegrams to some well-known clergymen, he explained that *True Story's* purpose was "to teach the lessons of life in story form," which required the portrayal of human transgressions. "I want to be sure that I am doing this in the best spirit of service," he continued, "and I am asking you to help me make my magazine one of real helpfulness. Will you accept a place on a ministerial advisory board?" Macfadden promised that the clergymen's advice would be taken and anything, even an entire story, found objectionable would be rejected.[21] As a result of this appeal, he and Oursler created a board of clergymen: a rabbi, a Roman Catholic priest (who resigned when his bishop learned of it), a Methodist, a Presbyterian, and a Congregationalist. All four, working in their off-hours, received copies of the stories, changed phrases, and deleted what they thought improper for a mass circulation periodical. If a story was rejected by a single board member, it was returned to the author.

The method worked. One suspicious editor, despite his aversion to censorship, attended a luncheon with Macfadden's ministerial board and found himself agreeing with the "peculiarly American method." As Oursler exulted, the plan made *True Story* and three other Macfadden magazines, *True Romances, Dream World,* and *True Experiences,* "immune from the reformers." To another editor the board's approval of an article was "practically as good as the word *kosher* on a salami." Use of "literary laundrymen" to save Macfadden from prosecution, and written endorsements by three thousand clergymen did not, however, squelch criticism of the magazine.[22]

Not every contribution to *True Story* arrived in the mail. Some staff members turned out stories under fictitious names, and one valued editor won first prize for her entry in a *True Story* contest under an assumed name. Troubled by her conscience, she confessed to BM. He did not fire her. "Of course you mean to give the money back," he said, and when she assented he gave her a new, better contract and a large bonus.[23] The incident illustrated his ability to mix shrewdness with kindliness.

After the writer of "The Revealing Kiss," in the January 1927 issue, had used the actual names of eight people and described them as boozehounds and illicit love-makers, Macfadden Publications was sued for half a million dollars. As a result, the publisher required every contributor to submit character references and sign an affidavit that the incidents depicted had occurred in his or her own experience, or that of a personal acquaintance, and that all names and places had been changed. To encourage honest writing BM published a manual describing the technique best suited for *True Story.* Warnings appeared in each issue of the magazine that plagiarizers would be prosecuted to the limit of the law, but there is no evidence of such prosecutions.[24]

To enhance the appeal of each story, a blurb—an attention-getting explanatory lure—was added below or above the title. Thus, for "Under Cover of Marriage," the blurb stated: "He had been willing to risk anything to possess completely this woman he loved. But never, in his wildest dreams, did he imagine that it would all end in—." And for "I Was a Child Wife" the blurb read, "She was nothing but a gangling, awkward girl, yet they pushed her headlong into the amorous arms of this man who was not fit to marry any woman."[25] Oursler was a master of such come-ons, and Macfadden gave him a free hand.

Macfadden liked serials, but because few amateurs could fashion suspenseful endings for each installment, the serials were reworked by editors who moulded the amateur stories into suitable lengths.[26] Eventually, some well-known individuals wrote for *True Story,* among them Warden Lewis B. Lawes of Sing Sing prison, Daniel Carter Beard, National Commissioner of the Boy Scouts of America, Governor Wilbur L. Cross of Connecticut, and Madam Ernestine Schuman-Heink, the opera star, but ordinary folk continued to contribute most of the articles.

True Story changed with the times. In the late twenties it printed stories of high school and college life, reflecting the living styles of more prosperous and better-educated people. Even so, it still appealed to its vast traditional audience and boasted that it was "practically the sole representative of more than two millions of . . . wage-earning Americans."[27] As readers began to include more young married couples in the 1930s, the magazine introduced special departments catering to their interests. A Home Problems Forum featured emotion-laden dilemmas involving opposing viewpoints, and readers were invited to offer their own solutions. Prizes of ten to fifteen dollars were paid to those best resolving such problems as whether a father should open his daughter's mail, whether privacy was possible while one lived with in-laws in a two-family house, and whether a couple should buy life insurance or invest in a home. Introducing each problem was a blurb such as this: "Harry and Tess have been married almost a year. Tess who has always been emotionally close to her sister tells her all the personal details of married life. Harry objects. Tess claims he is trying to come between her and her sister. *What do you think?*"[28]

Regular features were the "True Story Homemaker" (directed by Professor Bristow Adams of Cornell University), "Helps to Happier and Healthier Homes," and a "Shopping Service." For the newly married a set of sixty booklets on homemaking was offered for a dollar, and a book of clothing styles and a cookbook could be had for ten cents. Letters from readers appeared in a "What Do You Think?" section, and contests were run from time to time. Monthly manuscript contests tempted amateur writers—first prize was a lavish $1,500— and the winners' names were published. Macfadden's contests attracted as many as 50,000 homespun stories a year, enabling *True Story* to clear between three and four million dollars annually in its greatest period.[29]

Page sixteen was Macfadden's. His editorial themes were inspirational. "Is Your Life Balanced?" encouraged hobbies. "Build Your Life on Truth" warned against pretense and dishonesty. "The Source of Power and Beauty" praised sexual allure as a God-given mechanism to perpetuate the race. "You're As Good As Your Ideals" assured his readers that all dreamers were idealists and that dreams were "the creative force behind every achievement." "Don't Live Without Love" explained that love "of the right sort" inevitably led to success and helped one to dominate every situation and meet every emergency, "for only when you are obeying the laws of Nature, the demands of your highest instincts, can the fullness of life be yours." In "The One Thing That Matters," a male-oriented Macfadden touted the harmonious home: "You need a home with a sweetheart in it, and with happy voices resounding through its rooms, glad to your homecoming. When you have a wife and a home like this, then indeed you have a divine incentive for work." Upbeat, conventional, banal, these personal messages conveyed the simple intensity of a believer who had no fear of the obvious. Neither devout nor introspective, the publisher of *True Story* placed himself on the side of divine influences at work in the world.[30]

When *True Story* was launched, Macfadden often could not decide whether he liked an artist's drawing, but he knew what he liked in a photograph. Though not the first publisher to use photographs to illustrate fiction, he decided to do so in a big way. He continued to employ illustrators, but his literal-minded enthusiasm for photography resulted in his setting up a studio, and *True Story* was the first national publication to use photography successfully, thereby setting a trend in popular magazines. Fortunately for Macfadden, the movies were purveying mass entertainment all over the country. Aspiring starlets courted publicity, and *True Story* cooperated. Among the young actresses and actors who had not yet made it to Hollywood, Norma Shearer, Jean Arthur, Anita Louise, Madge Evans, and Fredric March gained exposure by posing for Macfadden's magazine, and in the thirties stars like Sylvia Sidney, Merle Oberon, Katharine Hepburn, and Maurice Chevalier appeared in its pages.[31]

If BM allowed Oursler freedom as supervising editor, he expected his other editors to conform to Oursler's direction, but essentially it was the boss who called the tune. This was acknowledged by the able and aggressive William Jourdan Rapp, who became editor of *True Story* two years after joining the company and serving briefly as editor of *True Romances*. When Macfadden offered him the editorship of *True*

Story in 1926, he accepted only if he got an immediate and hefty pay raise. Apparently, Macfadden met his terms, and Rapp remained as editor for sixteen years.[32]

His longevity was ensured by catering to Macfadden's inflated ego. "I realize," Rapp wrote his boss, "that this great magazine's good fortune is primarily due to your own genius which has established and controls its policy and which has built up the splendid organization to exploit all its possibilities." Nevertheless, the editor took credit for inspiring and helping to write many of the magazine's promotions, dominating an Ideal Marriage Contest and overseeing movie shorts to advertise the Court of Human Relations radio program, both designed to promote *True Story*, and initiating a radio hour that he supervised from its inception in 1928. Rapp denied that the magazine overemphasized sex. Linking morality and economics, he asserted that liquor and gambling destroyed incomes, and if wage-earner husbands ran around with other women the economic and emotional security of the home was at stake. "Security," he explained, "that's their chief concern, not sex." Eventually, *True Story* published pieces about sharecroppers, coal miners, milk strikers, and the plight of women in Nazi Germany.[33]

Under Rapp's guidance, *True Story* became less amateurish. He brought in important personages to write accounts of their lives, among them Henry Ford, Immigration Commissioner Edward Corsi, and Mrs. Frederick M. Paist, president of the national board of the YMCA. He deemphasized sexual escapades when he became convinced that readers were beginning to favor true love and virtue over seduction, that young couples wanted help in solving marital problems, and that the economic depression called for articles on social issues. To one Macfadden executive, however, less sex made *True Story* "a little prim."[34]

The magazine was distributed almost entirely on the newsstands, and its subscription list was small when compared with Hearst's *Cosmopolitan* and Crowell's *American Magazine*. Its direct retail sales far exceeded its competitors'. Whereas *True Story* won nearly two million readers in six years, it took twenty years for the *Ladies' Home Journal* to attain a circulation of a million and thirty years for the *Literary Digest* to reach two million. Even during the depression of the thirties, two million copies of *True Story*, distributed through wholesalers, sold on the stand every month. British and German editions appeared, and *True Story* supplements adorned two Scandinavian publications.[35]

Success attracted an array of imitators. Fawcett brought out *True Confessions* in 1922, which for years was second only to *True Story* in circulation. *True Marriage Stories* and *True Love Stories* were introduced two years later. *Modern Romances*, a very successful competitor, was launched in 1930 by George Delacorte, who started and suddenly dropped *My Story* in 1931 when Macfadden threatened to undercut it with a rival *Your Story*. *Secrets* appeared in 1936 and *Personal Romances* in 1937. Inspired by *True Story's* phenomenal growth, Macfadden himself sponsored several spin-offs: *True Romances* in 1923, which sold out its huge first issue and which, emphasizing beauty and charm, sold half a million copies within a year. It became the second largest of his magazines in circulation and profits. *Dream World* in 1924 was more fictional and featured Prince Charming motifs. *True Experiences* in 1925, a fortnightly, highlighted female vicissitudes on the job and in the big city.[36]

True Story and, to a small extent, *True Romances* were the power-houses of Macfadden Publications, and the income they produced enabled BM to experiment with other ventures and to continue *Physical Culture*, which had less than half the circulation of *True Romances* in the latter twenties. *Dream World*, featuring passionate love stories, gained a circulation of more than 300,000 in 1927, its fourth year, but it then declined in a fiercely competitive field. *Your Home*, described by Macfadden's publicity men as "a magazine of taste and refinement for people of moderate means who appreciate the better things of life," specialized in site selection, buying, construction, furnishing and decoration, maintenance, and insurance of homes valued at $10,000 to $25,000. *True Ghost Stories* stemmed from Oursler's enthusiasm for the occult and Macfadden's recognition of a growing public interest in psychic and supernatural phenomena. Ghosts, phantoms, and spiritual manifestations emanated from its pages. After a short period of prosperity, the magazine lost ground and gave up the ghost in 1931.[37]

In 1922 Macfadden introduced *Midnight*, later labeled "a cross between *True Story*, tabloid crime, and Edgar Allan Poe." At once a newsstand best-seller, it was dropped within a year because it ran afoul of John S. Sumner of the New York Society for the Suppression of Vice, who obtained summonses for everyone connected with the magazine. BM, bitterly remembering his arrest and conviction in 1905, conferred with Sumner and begged him to withdraw the summonses. In return for the immediate discontinuance of the magazine, Sumner relented. That night, editor Oursler and his staff burned bundles of copies in the office furnace, and others were thrown into the East River, in a

"massacre" likened to the wholesale assassination of French Hugue-
nots on St. Bartholomew's Day in 1572.[38]

Dance Lovers and Dance probably were encouraged, if not inspired,
by Mary Macfadden, who studied "nature dancing" and took dancing
lessons during her first two years in the United States. Bernarr wanted
his daughters to be expert dancers, although Vera Caspary, editor of
Dance, was not impressed with his appreciation of the aesthetic. His
taste in dance photos, she claimed, "ran to ladies with enormous
thighs." In the 1920s, when Macfadden published these periodicals,
the dance audience was tiny, the ballet at a low ebb, and modern
dance only in its experimental stage. Dance struggled for existence
until it expired in the great depression.[39]

Macfadden Publications sought to cash in on technological
changes in the twenties. As more Americans bought mass-produced
cars at affordable prices, BM launched Automotive Daily News in
1925, a trade paper for the auto and auto accessory industries, to which
executives and high-level employees subscribed. After a slow start it
made a profit in three years. Model Airplane News catered to the youth
market. Started in 1929, it appealed to boys' fascination with flying
and presented working plans for model airplanes and information
about aeronautics.[40]

The pioneer of factual crime magazines in the United States was
Bernarr Macfadden, who introduced True Detective Mysteries in 1924.
Except in its earliest issues, TDM's accounts of crimes and the capture of criminals were authentic; its writers were detectives or newspapermen who had solved or covered actual cases. Macfadden himself wrote many of the editorials in its first year. When he no longer
had time for them, they were contributed by commissioners and police
chiefs, senators and congressmen, governors, federal and state judges,
and district attorneys. Under managing editor John Shuttleworth, a
sophisticated and efficient former Macfadden reader, the magazine's
circulation doubled and redoubled. By its sixth year it was selling
221,000 copies, and its success brought on imitators like Walter An-
nenberg's Official Detective Stories. BM countered the rivals with a
spin-off in 1929, The Master Detective, placed on the stands every
month two weeks after its parent.[41]

Macfadden, like Oursler, was keenly interested in crime control,
and he shrewdly used his magazine to build a popular following. In
1931, True Detective Mysteries published "I am a Fugitive from a Geor-
gia Chain Gang," by Robert Elliot Burns, an escaped convict then being hunted for stealing a mere $5.80, for which he had been sentenced

to ten years at hard labor. BM claimed that Burns's story stirred the
public to demand a review of American penal practices. Later in 1931,
True Detective Mysteries inaugurated the "Line-Up," which publicized
the identifying physical characteristics of felons and murderers wanted
by the police. Attracting masses of loyal readers in the United States
and abroad, the magazine almost doubled its size in 1932. It printed
first-hand accounts of crime in England, Iceland, Scandinavia, and
Russia by police officials who were interviewed by a staff investiga-
tor, started a pictorial feature, "Crime Does Not Pay," and a department devoted to the problems of scientific crime detection. For an
article in 1936 on their war against crime, it obtained reports from
thirty-two governors. It printed a series on parole as practiced in the
United States, and it offered $1,000 rewards for information leading
to the solution of unsolved mystery cases.[42]

J. Edgar Hoover, the hard-boiled director of the FBI, was delighted
with the crusading journal. He commended Shuttleworth for his leadership in furthering law and order and thanked him for the "excellent
cooperation" of the Macfadden organization. Having followed the periodical since its inception, particularly in the 1930s, Hoover professed
to see in it the reflected idealism of Shuttleworth, Oursler, and Macfadden. To BM he wrote, "It can be truly said that TDM has done much
in the field of public education by portraying crime as it actually is,
without attempting to glamorize our more notorious criminals."[43]

Macfadden ably exploited his spectacular successes, but if a magazine showed little promise he soon abandoned it. One of these was
Brain Power, intended to supplement *Physical Culture* by fostering
self-improvement of the mind. Although mental health commanded
a ready audience in the 1920s, the new monthly was dropped because
the publisher and editors disagreed on ways to present the material
and because the title subjected readers to ridicule as feebleminded.
Brain Power's failure, Oursler lamented, was one of the real tragedies
of BM's career. A proposed *Macfadden's Magazine* never came to life,
and *Beautiful Womanhood*, according to Mary Macfadden who had
suggested and helped to develop it, collapsed as a result of her husband's impulsiveness. He saw a woman on the street whom he perceived as a "devitalized" spinster and at once decided that *Beautiful
Womanhood* should shame old maids out of existence. Oursler, who
was with him, agreed; the magazine printed an article attacking spin-
sters, yet strangely it won a reputation of appealing only to homely
women. They stopped buying it out of fear of ridicule. In any event,
BM did not want this magazine to impede the progress of *True Story*.

Some Macfadden magazines. Courtesy of Fulton Oursler, Jr.

Among other ventures that failed to take hold were *Metropolitan, Your Car, Sport Life,* and *Modern Marriage.* Macfadden's attempts at humor magazines flopped: *Mustard Plaster* in 1929 and *Star Comics* and *Star Rangers* in 1937. Religion got even shorter shrift. *Your Faith,* a 15 cent digest-sized monthly that appeared in March 1939, promised to print "true stories of the influence of prayer on human lives," but it never got off its knees.[44]

After lengthy negotiations with Louis Howe, friend and adviser of the Hyde Park Roosevelts, Macfadden and Oursler cleverly arranged for Eleanor Roosevelt to edit *Babies—Just Babies.* The contract, in April 1932, provided for Mrs. Roosevelt to receive $500 for each issue, but if at the time for renewal she were "living in the White House," her salary would be doubled. With her husband's approval and after considerable family discussion, she agreed to the contract. Later she was criticized for "commercializing her position" as wife of the president-elect. The venture was widely ridiculed, and even Mrs. Roosevelt's friends joked about it. Hurt by the derision, she withdrew, and *Babies—Just Babies,* the most expensive of Macfadden's magazines, died in a few months. Professing to understand her point of view, BM expressed to her his regret that she was "not able to continue with us." Twenty years later, Mary Macfadden alleged that her husband's true reason for approaching Eleanor Roosevelt was his hope that her influence might induce Franklin to make him secretary of health or otherwise facilitate his political ambitions.[45] She may well have been right.

Macfadden bought several existing magazines. At Oursler's suggestion he acquired the prestigious but almost moribund *Metropolitan* in 1923. Oursler planned to serialize Theodore Dreiser's *Genius,* which had been suppressed by its publisher, and make it the lead article in the first issue, but Macfadden preferred a confessional story about an artist's model. "I read this story myself," said BM, "I know what I am talking about." To which Oursler responded, "I wrote this story myself. I know what I'm talking about. It's awful." Having written it for *True Story,* he thought it inappropriate as a companion to Dreiser's novel, yet despite his protests Macfadden ordered him to run it alongside *The Genius* but praised him for his devotion to the magazine and humility about his own yarn. Under Oursler's general supervision, the editor of *True Romances,* Lyon Mearson, was made editor of the *Metropolitan.* Mearson desperately attempted to wed literary grace to physical culture, or, as he put it, "to cook the oil of carrots and the waters of truth in the same ten-cent-store pot." One of Macfadden's few humorists, he took note of the boss's interest in sex by proposing that the array of flags fluttering on the roof be topped by a huge banner flaunting a phallus.[46]

As radio networks spread across the land in the twenties and thirties, BM was the first publisher to advertise on the air, first promoting *True Story*, then *Physical Culture, True Detective Mysteries,* and *Liberty* (acquired in 1931). In 1928, *True Story* began its "Mary and Bob" series, a pioneer in human-interest programs. Others followed: A. L. Alexander's "Court of Human Relations," "Hollywood Interviews," "Heart Throbs of the Hills," and in 1937–1938, John J. Anthony's "Good Will Hour." A Bronx hustler who posed as an expert in human relations, Anthony claimed to have three university degrees but actually was a high school dropout. His opening question, "What is your problem, madam?" became well known, and his brief and simple replies invariably stressed fidelity and the Golden Rule. Despite the disapproval of most of his executives, Macfadden upheld the initiative and heavy financial commitment to this program by his circulation manager, S. O. Shapiro. "What I like about Shap is his guts," he told his associates. "He's got imagination." Although newspapers flayed the "Good Will Hour," it boosted *True Story*'s sales. BM was delighted with the program and thought it was great publicity. Although Macfadden magazines were aired on WOR and CBS networks, most programs were carried on NBC. In 1940, after several run-ins with that system involving what Oursler claimed to be censorship, *Liberty* switched to five Mutual stations with a series of fifteen-minute newscasts by Gabriel Heatter.[47]

Macfadden's movie ventures were expensive flops. His earliest were two films in 1915 and 1916 touting physical culture and pleading for bodily preparedness in anticipation of American entry into the great war. "Facts and Follies," a series of exercise films, was released in 1919. During the twenties, BM rented a studio and with the help of unemployed actors and actresses produced "Zongar," a sort of superman movie that stressed physical activity; "Wrongdoers," starring Lionel Barrymore; "Broken Homes"; "Wives at Auction," portraying the perils of marriages that ignored physical culture; and several film adaptations of *True Story* romances. These movies were stifled by a lack of proper distribution facilities and access to big theaters, and after losing millions of dollars, Macfadden gave up, although in the late twenties he featured himself in "Rampant Youth at Sixty" and a two-reeler, "Health Is the Greatest Wealth."[48]

Macfadden sensed a new market for magazines featuring photographs and intimate glimpses of film stars. His *Movie Weekly* in 1921–1924 was followed by *Movie Mirror* in 1931, which glamorized Hollywood personalities. In 1934, he bought *Photoplay* and *Shadowplay,* but by then his interest flagged and politics became his passion.

His most important purchase was *Liberty,* which enabled him to write freewheeling editorials on public affairs during the depths of the depression. Brilliantly edited by Fulton Oursler, each issue of this magazine had two editorials, one by Oursler, the other by Macfadden, and they almost never clashed. *Liberty,* which depended heavily on sales by boys along routes in their neighborhoods, was for ten years BM's political mouthpiece.

Bernarr Macfadden's numerous publications conveyed his opinions to a wider public than could be attracted by *Physical Culture* alone. They reached an immense audience. With a combined circulation of 7,355,000 in 1935, they exceeded the total circulation of Crowell or Hearst magazines. BM had accumulated a fortune of $30,000,000 by 1931, more than $600,000 of which he squandered in 1927 on a New Jersey real estate development that he lost for nonpayment of taxes.[49]

Although each Macfadden magazine had an editor under Oursler's supervision, it bore the imprint of BM himself. He wrote editorials — often urgent, often banal — on how to achieve health, strength, happiness, success, and the good life. In spreading the gospel of healthful living he sustained a missionary zeal, and it is significant that in *Who's Who* he listed his occupation not as publisher but as "physical culturist." Publishing was to him a means of striving for his ultimate goal of a physically strong and therefore, as he believed, happier and wiser American people.

The "Porno-Graphic"

"DON'T TELL MY MOTHER I'm working on the *Graphic*. She thinks I'm a piano player in a whorehouse." So went a popular quip in the magazine and newspaper trade. Newspapermen called it the "porno-Graphic," and to one journalist it was the country's "outstanding example of sleazy, vulgar journalism." *Time* said it set an all-time record for "sensational incoherence." Its only value, one writer charged, was that it "educated readers up to a point where they were able to understand the other tabloids." The New York Public Library refused to place it on the racks of its newspaper room.[1]

When Bernarr Macfadden started the *New York Evening Graphic* in September 1924, the *Daily News* was a thriving morning tabloid, five years old, with a daily circulation of 1,750,000, the largest in the United States. If McCormick and Patterson could do so well with a sensational formula of news, crime, and sex, why not Macfadden? The physical culturist publicly announced the *Graphic* through an advertisement in the New York newspapers showing a profile bust of himself and headlines proclaiming a paper with a "new idea"—"not a picture paper but a real newspaper with all the news in tabloid form." Above his large signature at the bottom he promised a paper that would "shatter precedent to smithereens" and differ with the average newspaper about what constituted news. William Randolph Hearst, who had learned that Macfadden would enter the tabloid field, moved faster and published the first issue of the *Daily Mirror* a step ahead of him in June. The *Mirror* and the *News*, the city's only tabloids, refused to carry the *Graphic*'s advertisement, and BM later claimed that all the New York publishers tried to hinder his paper's advertising and circulation.[2]

Already a fabulously successful magazine publisher, Macfadden eyed the newspaper field as offering new opportunities for his health crusade. A daily paper would reach many thousands of local readers and win converts to his preachings on exercise, proper diet, and natural healing, and his opposition to the medical establishment. It would also enable him to vent his outrage at puritanical censorship, for he had never forgotten his bouts with local censors and still resented his prosecution in federal court and $2,000 fine for sending "lewd" material in the mails. In an early issue of the *Graphic*, a cartoon would show a terrified couple menaced by long-nosed, high-hatted figures labeled "self-appointed censor" and a self-righteous "holier than thou bird" uttering "We'll save the world." Another portrayed a well-dressed doctor, with skull and crossbones on his vest, labeled MEDICAL TRUST and carrying a sign: "Compulsory Vaccination, Compulsory Medical Treatment, Laws Favoring Medical Trust," while in the background a menacing ogre labeled "Comstockery" threatened to "regulate your morals, your books, your pictures and plays."[3]

Flushed with political ambitions, Macfadden regarded newspapers as a means of kindling national publicity for himself, and the *Graphic* was the first of nearly a dozen papers he owned at one time or another, including the *Philadelphia Daily News*, the *Investment News*, the *Automotive Daily News*, three papers in Michigan cities and one in New Haven. In the rather exaggerated opinion of a *Graphic* staffer, all of them were intended to generate support for the notion that Macfadden should be president of the United States. BM's announced platform favored eradicating intolerance—"religious or otherwise"—abolishing government censorship, smashing graft and favoritism in business and politics, touting direct primaries for all elective officials, and amending "all prohibitory laws that infringe constitutional rights as originally interpreted by the framers of the American Constitution." For local voters he proposed a seat for every person in the city's subway and elevated trains and a bridge across the Hudson linking New York and New Jersey.[4]

Claiming that he was not in his new venture for the money, he confidently expected to make a few million dollars out of it, a gross miscalculation. Money and pretension, he professed, were of little value to him. "I can be just as comfortable in a cottage as I can in a luxurious palace. And I would not give three whoops in Hades for all the social honors of the universe." What he wanted was a paper with a popular appeal, one that would "throb with those life forces that fill life with joyous delight."[5]

One morning, Macfadden told Fulton Oursler, managing editor

Macfadden in a characteristic pose, about 1924. Courtesy of Fulton Oursler, Jr.

of his magazines, that with *True Story* earning net, after taxes, about ten thousand dollars a day, he was ready to put out a newspaper. He asked Oursler to find an editor. Hoping to control his boss's liking for lurid sensationalism, Oursler discussed the project with Macfadden Publications executives, who took a dim view of BM's proposal. Vice-president Orr J. Elder flatly opposed it, and other officials fretted at Macfadden's "draw poker" methods of starting new ventures, but they agreed to let Oursler bring in a conservative managing editor. He recommended Emile Gauvreau, who had resigned as managing editor of the sedate *Hartford Courant,* and for the city desk, Martin Weyrauch of the *Brooklyn Eagle,* a paper in Oursler's opinion second to the *Courant* among the vestal old maids of American dailies.[6]

He then introduced Gauvreau to BM. Brilliant, tough, and sardonic, of French-Canadian-Irish origin, the editor was a short man with a limp, the result of a childhood accident. As a boy, he had read *Physical Culture* and after his injury had used Macfadden's exercises to strengthen his leg enough to ride a bicycle. Years later, as a writer, he sold several love stories to *True Story* and exposed in the *Courant* a medical diploma mill operating under Connecticut's loose medical laws. BM, who had bought the old *Evening Mail* building with its presses and equipment, at City Hall Place, hired Gauvreau to organize the new tabloid. As Gauvreau began to install a staff, Macfadden told him he wanted a paper with a serious purpose, one that would play up physical culture. "I want you to editorialize the news, too," he instructed the new managing editor. "Don't stop with the bare skeleton of the facts. Point out the moral—the social lesson. A man's found dead, from an alcoholic spree. Don't stop with saying it—Drive it in! Influenza epidemic—play up the fact that the bodies of the victims are susceptible to the disease, because of a lack of bodily care."[7]

Gauvreau was not to be pushed around. Macfadden asked Oursler to spend mornings downtown at the *Graphic,* but the power-conscious editor resented Oursler's presence and regularly ignored his advice. The *Graphic* was the only unit of Macfadden Publications in which Oursler had almost no influence, and Gauvreau was permitted complete authority over its operations during his five years with the paper. At once, the new editor embarked on a public relations blitz, soliciting congratulatory messages from governors, senators, and cabinet members on the inauguration of the new tabloid.[8]

Macfadden himself took to the radio to publicize the *Graphic* through an early morning musical setting-up exercise program over

WOR. John A. Gambling remembers his father, John B. Gambling, telling him that when Macfadden failed to show up one morning the elder Gambling, then a technician, was ordered by the chief engineer to take over the program, which he did, and it remained popular for years.[9]

Under Gauvreau's direction, the *Graphic* employed capable journalists. John L. Spivak was a star reporter; Ryan Walker, a cartoonist who once worked on the *World* became art editor; Robert MacNamara, also from the *World*, was an effective rewrite man. John W. Vandercook was feature editor for a short time, Lester Cohen contest editor, Jack Coombs picture editor, and Irene Vandike editor of the woman's page. Tall and talented Grace Perkins, who worked in the city room, later married Fulton Oursler. At an old rolltop desk near the sports department sat Walter Winchell in his first job on a daily paper. He solicited theater advertisements, was nightclub editor and drama critic, and wrote an influential column, "Your Broadway and Mine." The *Graphic* was the making of Winchell.[10]

To Macfadden, Winchell's column was, as Gauvreau noted, "a mass of unintelligible jargon." In sprightly language, much of it coined by himself, Winchell's gossip of nightclubs and drawing rooms recorded "the biological events of the town, the new mistresses, babies, secret brides, separations, divorces, yearnings, fights, engagements." After Winchell left the paper his column of keyhole journalism was taken over by Louis Sobol, and when Sobol went over to the *Evening Journal,* he was succeeded by Ed Sullivan, who later achieved fame as a radio and television personality. Other notables who began their careers on the *Graphic* were Artie Auerbach, who became "Mr. Kitzel" on Jack Benny's radio show, Jerry Wald, who conducted a radio column, "Not on the Air," and later won an academy award for the movie script "Johnny Belinda," and John Huston, who went on to a great career as an actor and movie director.[11]

The *Graphic* reached out and embraced its readers. Won over by streamer headlines and news stories of the latest scandal, murder, or disaster, they were held loyal by romantic and mostly confessional fiction, vividly written special articles, and a Saturday magazine and rotogravure section managed by feature editor Joseph Applegate, masterful designer of colorful and sensational layouts. In a single issue[12] of the magazine one might choose from:

DATING BUREAUS FOR LONELY CO-EDS
TO SOLVE UNDERGRADUATE SEX PROBLEMS, by Frances Fink

WHAT HAPPENED
WHEN A LADY DIDN'T
TELL HER SECRET PAST, by Agnes Moore

LOVE—THE THEME SONG OF LIFE, SAYS
COMPOSER, by Freya Wyant

MODERN LAW TIGHTENED
TO MEET BRUTAL
CHALLENGE OF
UNDERWORLD CODE, by Lois Bull

WHY INSECTS BEHAVE LIKE
HUMAN BEINGS, by Jack Nye

WILL GARBO REALLY
GO HOME THIS
TIME, by Julia Shawell (who also conducted a column,
"Getting Personal.")

Fiction was embellished with dramatic and titillating pictures.
One journalist figured that an average rotogravure section had about
eighteen pictures, of which fifteen were "females in undress." This was
not far from the truth, and there would have been no *Graphic* without pictures. Among the scantily clad girls in the issue of January
1932 were stage and screen stars Claire Luce, Dorothy Gish, and Greta
Garbo. Some men made the grade, like actory Henry Hull and sports
achievers like Johnny Weissmuller, famed as Tarzan the ape man. In
appealing to the senses, the *Graphic* even experimented briefly with
perfumed ink.[13]

Easily found on the last pages was the sports news. Ed Sullivan
came from the old *Mail* to the *Graphic*'s sports department, wrote
"Sport Whirl," promoted strongman tournaments and dinners attended
by prominent guests, including Jack Dempsey, Gene Tunney, Babe
Ruth, Red Grange, Gene Sarazen, singers Rudy Vallee and Sophie
Tucker, and Mayor Jimmy Walker. Eventually, Sullivan became sports
editor until personnel changes led him to take over the Broadway column.[14] Even then the sports section remained lively, with abundant
news and pictures of athletes, and in the paper's last months, a com-
mentary, "Dave Walsh Speaks His Mind."

Cartoons, comics, puzzles, a children's page, columns of advice
on beauty, health, and self-improvement—the *Graphic* had them all.
A physical culture page kept readers aware of Macfadden's health doc-

trines with shortened versions of *Physical Culture* articles, nutrition information by Milo Hastings, director of the Physical Culture Food Research Laboratory, and Paul J. Veatch's question and answer column, "Vigorous Health." In the paper's early issues, Mary Macfadden, wife of the publisher, conducted a column that told women how to overcome the drabness of life by developing the ego and the physique, how to retain youthfulness by falling in love, and how to choose a husband for a happy marriage.[15]

The *Graphic* printed both truth and fiction that spotlighted human weakness or strength. Whether the story was about a wife beater, a criminal, a drunkard or drug addict, a vagrant, a divorcée, evangelist, actress, athlete, or business tycoon, the formula was simple. The successful explained how virtue had brought them fame or fortune, and the transgressors told why they had sinned. In its way, the paper stood for traditional morality. "I want the moral implications of a story emphasized," Macfadden told Gauvreau, "so that the *Graphic* will be put into the hands of son and daughter by any mother in New York." He said his young daughters read it every day, and he published their photos in it. It carried on his crusades. As iconoclast H. L. Mencken gleefully remarked, if it accomplished nothing else, at least it "made hundreds of thousands of New Yorkers privy to the crimes of the Medical Trust."[16]

As a purveyor of the news, the *Graphic,* although weaker than its rival tabloids, the *News* and the *Mirror,* outdid them in concentrating on sex, mayhem, and murder. One Macfadden executive was said to have remarked that BM was really interested in only two things, sex and money, in that order. If that stretched the truth, Macfadden certainly exploited sex and sensation. He believed that impersonal reporting made newspapers dull. His own paper would be a sort of daily *True Story.* At the outset he advised his staff that his paper would be "of the people, by the people, for the people. As you know, the people themselves will write a great deal of this paper, and the editors and reporters will help them write it." It followed that news items in the *Graphic* concentrated on what somebody said about an illegitimate baby, a robbery, a fire, a murder, or disaster. After a lurid headline, a short paragraph summarized the essential events, the names, and the dates, followed by a series of first-person stories bylined by participants but actually written by reporters, each conveying the heartache of a participant. Macfadden was charged with discarding "all pretense to the civic function of keeping the public informed of the progress of events," but he thrilled his readers with personal de-

tails, like those in the Hall-Mills murder case or the last days of Ruth
Snyder in the death house at Sing Sing.[17]

The *Daily News* had set the tabloid pattern of large, boldface headlines that fairly shouted at the newsstand buyer, and like the *Mirror*,
the *Graphic* would not be surpassed at concocting sensational come-
ons. In the sex and sadism category a few of the *Graphic's* streamer
headlines were:

SHACKLED GIRL FLEES
CHAINED, SHE CREEPS
MILES TO POLICE

"RUINED BY LOVE POTION!"
SAYS GIRL IN OWN STORY OF HER MAD REVELS

VICE COPS WHO STRIPPED,
BEAT WOMAN CONVICTED

BROOKLYN VICE BARONS
LURE INNOCENT GIRLS TO SIN DENS

MATE GIVES CHEATING WIFE
TO WHITE SLAVE TORTURERS[18]

In the wealth and poverty department were:

BROKER STOLE $1,000,000

FAMILY OF SIX STARVING
MOTHER AND 5 CHILDREN HOMELESS
FOUND SLEEPING IN CRUDE TENT IN YARD[19]

In the murder category:

FIVE SHOTS IN FLOATING BODY
BARE RICH JEWELER'S FATE

GUNMEN BUTCHER BABIES
IN SCHULTZ BEER BATTLE

KIDNAPPED SCHOOLGIRL, 12,
FEARED SLAIN BY FIEND[20]

Other featured stories were headed: "Boys Foil Death Chair, Mothers Weep as Governor Halts Execution," and "Wife Says Spyglass Parson Peeped at Girls Undressing." On March 20, 1931, three headlines announced: "Phony Lottery Raided," "Sinclair Lewis Socked by Dreiser," and "Soldiers Quell New Joliet Riot." After student editor Reed Harris was expelled from Columbia, the *Graphic* screamed: "Co-eds Hurt, Tear Gas Used, in Wild Riots at Columbia."[21]

The kidnaping of the Lindberghs' baby, Charles, Jr., in 1932 was widely covered by newspapers all over the United States, and the *Graphic* made the most of it on a daily basis. It printed countless pictures of "Lindy Baby" (many under the caption "Watch for Him"), of the family, their home in Hopewell, New Jersey, the surrounding woods and much more. Front page headlines reported each clue, many of them false, the activities of various publicity seekers, and the father's persistence in following every lead. On a false tip that the child was buried in a Trenton cemetery the paper sent out reporters one night with pick and shovel, but they dug up no story. Macfadden wrote an editorial opposing the death penalty for kidnaping on the ground that it would make kidnapers more reckless and more likely to kill their victims. Superseding its earlier offer to pay $1,000 for exclusive information leading to the arrest and conviction of the kidnaper or kidnapers, the *Graphic* printed a notice signed by Macfadden in which he personally offered to act as intermediary and to guarantee payment of any ransom, that he would not reveal anything that would lead to the arrest and conviction and would not testify against the kidnaper in court. It went unanswered. Seventy-three days after the kidnaping, the baby was found in a shallow grave in the woods near the Lindbergh home.[22]

The *Graphic* took certain liberties with the truth. It faked an interview with a Baptist minister's son, hinting that he was a religious fanatic because at a prayer meeting he had had a visitation from God. In a sermon to his large congregation, the minister denied that his son had given an interview and rebuked the newspaper. In another instance, a reporter concocted a story with Norman Carroll, brother of the theatrical producer. A chorus girl was told to go into hiding, and the *Graphic* spread on the front page: "Possessed by a mad and hopeless love for a young and beautiful Broadway dancer who extended him many kindnesses but rejected his frenzied wooing, an undignified young poet ended his life by inhaling gas. . . . In a farewell letter . . . he disclosed his infatuation for the charming 23-year-old member

of Earl Carroll's Vanities. Because of her coldness, the letter said, he
had decided to 'cash in his chips on this merry little game of life and
love.'"[23]

Better known than trumped up stories were the faked pictures
which the *Graphic* called "composographs." Composite arrangements
to simulate a single picture were not new in journalism—the *News*
had used one in 1925 to dramatize an earthquake—but they had been
used sparingly. The *Graphic's* ingenious camerawork produced composite photographs of posed models and drawings often grafted onto
the faces of well-known persons. When in 1926 Leonard Kip Rhinelander, a wealthy socialite, sued for an annulment of his marriage because his bride Alice failed to tell him that she was part Negro, she
contended that it had been obvious that she was not pure white and,
to prove it, arranged to reveal herself to the court. The jury room was
cleared for the unveiling, so there was no chance for a cameraman
to snap a thriller, but this did not faze the resourceful *Graphic* art
department, which photographed a showgirl stripped to the waist, then
added pictures of Rhinelander, Alice's mother, the judge, a threatening lawyer, and others. This phony court scene, which took twenty
separate photographs to make, appeared on the *Graphic's* front page.
Except for a small disclaimer at the bottom of the page, the picture
looked like the real thing. This first "composograph" was said to have
boosted circulation by 100,000.[24]

In 1927, the *Graphic* made hay with the Browning-Heenan separation suit. Edward West Browning, an eccentric, middle-aged, millionaire real estate dealer with a passion for publicity, was married to
Frances Heenan, formerly a poor working girl who as a teenager had
met Browning in a dance hall. She called him Daddy, and he called
her Peaches. Shortly after their marriage, she left him, claiming that
he gave her nightmares instead of love; and Browning then accused
her of marrying him for his money and sued for a separation, but he
offered to forgive her if she would return. She sued for an annulment
of their marriage. For weeks, the *Graphic* featured stories about Daddy
and Peaches, serialized her "private diary," and ran composographs of
them in bizarre situations, one of them showing Daddy dressed as
a caliph amusing his bride, and another showing them frolicking about
their bed, with Daddy uttering "Woof! Woof! Don't be a Goof!" Browning accused Peaches's mother of eavesdropping while he was making love, so the *Graphic* obligingly printed a composograph supplying the imagined details. Weeks later, Peaches's annulment suit was
dismissed, but not before the Society for the Suppression of Vice, act-

ing on several complaints, obtained a summons for Macfadden, Gauvreau, and other *Graphic* staff members for violating the law on indecent publications. In White Plains and Princeton, efforts were made to ban the paper's distribution. Newsdealers refused to handle the *Graphic* and Hearst's *Mirror*, but backed down when agents of Macfadden and Hearst threatened to take their magazines off the dealers' shelves. The *Graphic* picked up a quarter of a million readers.[25]

When the notorious bandit Gerald Chapman was hanged in 1926, a *Graphic* employee nearly lost his life while being photographed "hanging" from a steampipe with his head masked and his hands and feet bound. Standing on a box, he accidentally kicked it away and was saved only by the director of the scene who nimbly caught and held him up. Thirteen photographs completed what appeared to be a vivid view of Chapman swinging from the ceiling.[26]

After printing a front page composite picture of Francis (Two Gun) Crowley, strapped in the electric chair at Sing Sing prison, the *Graphic* took note of the prison rule forbidding cameras and justified its creative camerawork "because of the lesson such a picture would carry to misguided youths for whom gangland holds a lure, for the warning it conveys to the rats of the underworld, an actual picture of the death chair was made and the picture of a man bound and masked placed in it—the grim lesson of the electric chair was held up for the perusal of those who are inclined to wander from the straight and narrow."[27]

Blending sensationalism and righteous moralism, the paper assured the public that it would always know when a picture was a composite because it would be labeled "composograph." It called attention to the legend under the picture: "Rats of the underworld, adventure-crazed youth, pay close attention to this composograph. It represents the only reward that can come of a life of crime. The electrodes are in place, the heart soon to be stilled is beating now. In another moment the current surges through the form, making it leap and twist and strain. And then the body falls back a lump of lifeless clay. Study it and understand that it still is society's way of dealing with those who kill."[28]

The *Graphic* published at least fifteen composographs within six years, and Macfadden stoutly defended them in an editorial shortly before his newspaper expired. To call them evil, he declared, amounted to hoaxing the public. A knowledgeable critic "would have to consider his listeners but little more than morons, if he tried to attach evil significance to such pictures."[29]

The *Graphic* left no aspect of a reader's daily life uncovered. Various departments dotted its pages, analyzing handwriting; giving information about dressmaking, fashion, and shopping; advising women how to become beautiful and charming and how to win husbands; and offering solutions to problems of marriage and motherhood. The paper paid a dollar for published contributions to "Why I Blushed," "The Cutest Thing Baby Ever Said," "The Hardest Question Baby Ever Asked," "What I Did to Reduce" (later called the "Fat Women's Club"), and "How I Won My Husband." For men it printed "Aviation News" and "Investment Bureau," and for children a "Junior Aviation Club."

At the outset, it invited friendless people to describe their lives and hopes for its "Lonely Hearts" department, and so many letters were received that it needed a separate staff to keep abreast of them. It sponsored its first "Lonely Hearts Ball" at Madison Square Garden, which was jammed with forlorn women and bashful bachelors. According to editor Gauvreau, the lonely hearts project ended after a woman brought in a baby, saying it happened after the ball, and after police identified as a "lonely heart" the victim of a torch murder.[30]

Contests were another way to entice readers. When the *Graphic* began, it ran a "Diana—Apollo" competition to find ten men and women, each of whom was a perfect physical specimen—a sort of re-run of Macfadden's contest in England that brought him a wife in 1913. It also accorded with his interest in eugenics, in the mating of healthy, attractive young people. The *News* had once had an Apollo contest without mentioning marriage, whereas the *Graphic* announced that its winners would be introduced at a dinner and that if an Apollo married a Diana the couple would receive a prize of $1,000. One hundred dollars was offered for each child born in the first five years of such a union. Eager applicants sent in pictures of themselves in swimsuits. After three months, winners were selected, but it seems that no marriages resulted and no money was awarded. The *Graphic* sponsored many other contests. It offered $1,000 for the best letters on capital punishment. It ran a limerick competition and awarded a dollar for accepted answers to "Why I wear a beard." "If you are broke, write us a joke" offered winners tickets to Loew's theaters, with their names announced on the screen, a promotion that delighted Macfadden. As the craze for crossword puzzles swept the country, the *Graphic* was the first paper to carry a contest, featuring $1,000 in prizes. BM told Gauvreau to see that the puzzles were easy. Later, another such contest offered 2,619 prizes worth $25,000. The winners were named at Madison Square Garden in the presence of Macfadden, Alfred Lunt, Lynne Fontanne, Fred Astaire, George Abbot, Joe E. Brown, and Lawrence Tibbett, as 25,000 fans cheered and 20,000 failed to get inside the gates.[31]

Then there were cartoons and comics. Unlike any other comic strips, except possibly Popeye, the spinach-eating sailor man, several comics in the *Graphic* emphasized physical culture. At Macfadden's suggestion, "Little Samson" showed a tiny man with bulging muscles performing incredible feats of strength and endurance. The "Antics of Arabella" presented painless physical culture in a sequence of pictures showing two girls, one exercising while the other watched, their conversation ending with a quip, usually about a boyfriend. Typical dialogue: "I got a heavy date with Bill tonight."—"Yeah! Who was the John I saw you with last night?"—"That wasn't John. That was Harry." By 1932 the paper had added many comic strips, among them "Meyer the Buyer" by Hershfeld, "Young Buffalo Bill," "Buck Rogers," and a serious strip, "Highlights of History."[32]

Macfadden pushed his health ideas in his tabloid. In the beginning he contributed short articles on keeping fit, offering recipes and hints on exercise, and during the almost eight years of the *Graphic* he wrote daily editorials, some on health topics. Among his titles were "High Heels and Shapeless Calves," "Shoes—Airtight Boxes," "Grapes— Food for the Gods," "Fat Is Fatal," "Athletes and Motherhood," "Sun for the Baby," and "Competition in the Healing Art," a fusillade against the medical establishment. In "Singing and Longevity" he praised singing as adding to vitality, vigor, and enjoyment of life. In "Bodily Influence on the Mind," he wrote "We hear so much about the influence of the mind on the body that few of us have ever given thought to the effect of the body on the mind."[33]

A prolific editorial writer, BM did not limit himself to physical culture. He was said to dictate a month's supply of newspaper editorials within a few days before dashing off on a business trip abroad. Many of his editorials dealt with love and marriage, some urged readers to be true to themselves, build their character, work hard, avoid overindulgence, and anticipate the bumps along the road of life. In "Religion and Divorce," he argued that divorce was a "God-given sanctuary" to those who needed it. He opposed laws prohibiting dissemination of birth control information and condemned the conviction of Mary Ware Dennett for sending through the mail her pamphlet on sex. "It is a shock to this fine grandmother," he declared, "to discover that the edicts of the obscenity law are in evil harmony with secrecy, uncleanliness and lasciviousness," and he cheered the reversal of her conviction.[34]

Whatever the topic, whether or not he knew much about it, the physical culturist never hesitated to dispense advice. His editorials often meandered through swamps of murky generalization and his reasoning was unsophisticated, but he was usually consistent in his point of view. Readers of the *Graphic* did not take to high-sounding words, and he recommended simple language. In "To the Cemetery with Dead Languages," written after Yale dropped its Latin requirement, he explained that the proper way to write effective English was to study the shades and meanings of commonly used words and avoid those that would drive an ordinary person to a dictionary.[35] So much for educating the masses in the art of communication.

Never reluctant to deliver opinions on public affairs, Macfadden, no coddler of Communists, upheld free speech for them: "Let them talk. What harm can their arguments do us? They may teach us something that is worth while." He opposed prohibition as a spawner of lawlessness and supported the investigation of President Hoover's Commission on Law Observance and Enforcement, headed by George Wickersham, which reported the difficulties in enforcing the Eighteenth Amendment. During the depths of the depression, he criticized the antitrust laws and federal tax policy, and to deal with unemployment he favored settling people on the land and instituting a six-hour day for workers. He advocated the abolition of the death penalty, a course which the *Graphic* maintained from the outset, favoring clemency for poor youthful murderers as unfair when rich killers like Leopold and Loeb got life imprisonment. Later he modified his stand on capital punishment by suggesting hanging or the electric chair for "graft and disloyalty," and he came to agree with H. L. Mencken that chronic, incurable criminals deserved death. He criticized gun control and approved a bill in the New York assembly permitting citizens to protect themselves with firearms. After the Seabury investigation of corruption in New York City's Tammany-controlled government disclosed huge fortunes whose owners had no idea of their source, Macfadden editorially suggested to Governor Roosevelt a law requiring confiscation of a person's wealth if he could not explain where he got it. For New York City he proposed a business manager instead of a mayor. In national politics he supported Calvin Coolidge as a level-headed disciplinarian, but because he also approved of Governor Alfred E. Smith, he did not take sides in the presidential election of 1928.[36] Four years later, he was for Herbert Hoover and in 1932 for FDR.

In world affairs he cautioned against "foreign entanglements" and opposed Secretary of State Harold Stimson's doctrine upholding the sovereignty and territorial integrity of China because it was "not our business to tell Japanese officials how far they may go or what they may do." To promote exports, he favored American recognition of the Soviet Union. He urged foreign travel as a means of broadening one's mental outlook. While upholding the separation of church and state, he praised Mussolini's concordat with the Pope in 1929. His fascination with Mussolini as a "governmental genius" reflected his own passion for law and order, strong leadership, and energetic action. He knew nothing about the true nature of Italian fascism, but he thought Italy's strongman had saved that country from chaos; not only that, Mussolini was the first head of state to have created an undersecretary of state for physical education.[37]

While traveling in Europe in 1930, surveying child health and welfare institutions for a White House Conference on Child Health and Protection, Macfadden visited Il Duce at the Palazzo Venezia in Rome. He was charmed when the dictator rose from his desk and briskly strode forward to greet him like an American executive. To the publisher "this amazing man" who showed "no unseemly egotism" had demonstrated his capacity for leadership. "As you talk with this great Italian personality," BM reflected, "you feel that there is a natural born emperor."[38]

"Your soldiers eat too much," said Macfadden, who had noticed fat and flabby men in uniform. "If I had a few of your men for three weeks, I guarantee you they'd be better soldiers." He invited the dictator to send to the United States, without charge, a group of young men for a course on physical development under Macfadden direction. Il Duce accepted the idea and dispatched forty cadets from the Fascist University of Rome to Macfadden's health hotel in Dansville, New York, for two months of physical conditioning followed by further training at the Castle Heights Military Academy in Lebanon, Tennessee, a Macfadden school. The *Graphic* printed a two-page spread, with pictures of Macfadden, Mussolini, and the cadets, all with extravagant captions. The headline boasted,

MUSSOLINI AND MACFADDEN TRY
A NOBLE EXPERIMENT TO PREVENT WAR

This curious announcement may have been suggested by the caption under Il Duce's portrait, stating his belief that physical perfection in a nation was not only vital but a powerful aid in keeping the peace.[39] Macfadden certainly believed it.

In another self-promoting experiment, the publisher arranged to strengthen the bodies of fifty weakling children from a Portuguese foundling asylum. At his expense they underwent a physical culture program for six months in 1931–1932, supervised by his American medical director in a government building near Lisbon.[40] BM's main interests, however, were in America, where he was preoccupied with health projects, family problems, political dreams, and the direction of a publishing business that involved him in many brushes with the law.

Macfadden's lawyers were kept busy with libel suits against the *Graphic*, which Gauvreau called "the most sued paper in American journalism."[41] Unruffled, BM was never willing to check its sensationalism and pointed proudly to its soaring circulation. The most spectacular suit, perhaps, was brought on by the tabloid's story about the Atlantic City beauty contest in 1925. Its headline proclaimed:

BEAUTY CONTEST EXPOSED
Frame-up in Atlantic City
Miss America Couldn't Lose

Although the article uncovered some irregularities, it did not support the conclusion that the contest was a racket. Nevertheless, Atlantic City officials sued the paper for $4,000,000, and one of the contest judges, Earl Carroll, best known as the producer of the spectacular "Vanities," sued for another million. John S. Sumner, head of the New York Society for the Suppression of Vice, brought charges against the *Graphic* for publishing pictures of "bloodshed, lust and crime," but the case was dismissed on the ground that no law had been broken. Sumner also sued the tabloid for $100,000 for stating that his society had "the rich privilege of splitting fifty-fifty on all fines collected through its instrumentality." During its eight-year career, the paper faced libel suits totalling $7,000,000, but it fared extraordinarily well in the courts: it lost only $5,290 in judgments and settlements.[42]

Macfadden achieved his aim of publishing a paper different from any other. In effect a daily magazine, it outdid its rivals and although as many as sixty editors and writers were on its staff, it always was ready to feature a celebrity like nightclub hostess Texas Guinan, who told the story of her life, and Fiorello LaGuardia, billed as "America's most liberal congressman," who wrote "I'm Telling You Confidentially." Except for periodic conferences with his editors, BM usually left the conduct of the *Graphic* to Gauvreau and his successors, taking a personal hand in its supervision only during its final six months.[43] The paper was unique in featuring physical culture. It influenced tabloid journalism by forcing rivals to mimic its successful innovations and to print more suggestive pictures, more colorful articles, more blatant headlines. By achieving notoriety, it acquainted more New Yorkers with the name of Bernarr Macfadden.

The *Graphic's* focus on amusement and excitement and its neglect of many serious issues at home and abroad reflected the lighthearted self-indulgence of Americans in the 1920s. In the words of one commentator, the paper's features were "less the result of a publisher's whim than a consistent, if somewhat extreme part of a larger pattern—the crazy-quilt of post-war America."[44] BM understood this and connived at winning the loyalty of working class New Yorkers, the same sort who read his magazines. According to Gauvreau, he often awakened the editor at 3:00 A.M. with a circulation idea. Once he told Gauvreau, "some convict was executed at Sing Sing last night. Run a full-page picture of his face on the front page and over it use a two-word headline, two inches high. 'ROASTED ALIVE!'"[45] This boosted by 30,000 the next day's run.

The *Graphic's* circulation was phenomenal. In its first week it sold 400,000, mostly to the curious, then lost ground, but after a year had nearly 100,000 steady readers. Circulation reached 200,000 in 1925, cutting deeply into Hearst's *Evening Journal*, a matter of keen interest to Macfadden. At its height, the *Graphic* had a circulation of 600,000, exceeded by only a few other American papers. It dropped to 350,000 at the onset of the depression, but when the paper folded, its circulation of 237,000 was the second highest of New York City's evening dailies.[46] Even in its good years, however, it lost money.

Macfadden owned ten daily papers, including four other tabloids in Philadelphia, Detroit, and New York, and full-sized newspapers in New Haven and in Lansing and three other Michigan communities, and all were unprofitable. The *Graphic* was the biggest money loser. Every year it ran into red ink, usually in six or seven figures. Although concerned about the financial drain in 1928, BM remarked hopefully, "If we can get the losses down to $10,000 a week we'll be sitting pretty." When Gauvreau told him that Hearst wanted to buy the *Graphic* for $2,000,000, Macfadden let it be known that he would sell it, but for twice that much. Hearst did not buy. To stem the *Graphic's* losses BM brought Lee Ellmaker, chief executive of the Philadelphia *Daily News*, to New York, and Ellmaker demanded such severe economies that Gauvreau resigned in 1929.[47]

In spite of Ellmaker's edicts, the paper continued to lose money. When Macfadden heard someone say that it had cost him two million dollars, he snapped, "The *Graphic* lost between seven and eight million dollars." Years later he crowed, "I damn near put the *Mirror* out of business. I would have, too, if my employees had been entirely loyal." He declined to explain why or how, but he probably was recalling that Walter Winchell and many other staffers, on learning that the paper had lost five million dollars in five years, had left for other jobs before it was too late. If one adds to its operating losses the costs of the old plant at City Hall Place and the eight-story building on Hudson Street, acquired in 1926, the *Graphic* lost as much as $11,000,000. As the depression deepened, advertising revenue dropped off, and BM recognized that the losses were too great. He tried to save the paper by selling its stock to his employees: by paying 10 percent of their salaries over a period of twelve and one-half years, the staff eventually could own it. The boss was unable to unload the white elephant; only a tiny sum was collected. Meanwhile, employees were laid off. When word got around that the *Graphic* would fold, Howard Swain, then managing editor, hired a security guard to prevent typewriters from disappearing. Macfadden summoned Swain to his uptown office, thanked him for years of service, and gave him a year's salary, $21,000 in hard cash. The *Graphic* filed for bankruptcy and with the issue of July 7, 1932 quietly died.[48]

Although Macfadden admitted to costly errors in operating the paper, he believed that its failure was caused entirely by the depression. He never acknowledged its shortcomings. Its contents dismayed some of his subordinates, and when they protested he was astonished that they thought anything wrong. Once, when a staffer brought in what he considered a particularly objectionable issue, Macfadden looked up from his desk, surprised and puzzled. "If you say its bad, all right," he responded, "but I don't see what's the matter with it."

BM's inability to establish for his paper a consistent editorial point of view, apart from physical culture, and his approval of contests and other gimmicks to win readers prevented the *Graphic* from taking a serious view of the news. Despite its articles and editorials on taxes, unions, and unemployment in the depression years of 1930–1932, its attempts to treat the grave economic issues of the time were too few and too late. It reported Japan's war on China, but its coverage of world events remained skimpy. Finally and most importantly, it had trouble with advertising, a paper's lifeblood. Potential advertisers shunned the *Graphic* because of its sensational excesses, so that it never brought in the revenue that its large circulation otherwise would have commanded, and during the lean years of the early thirties the paper's advertising plunged to a new low.[49]

Moralists of the day did not mourn the loss of the *Graphic*. "Out of the prevalent business gloom," the *Christian Century* observed, "comes at least one ray of sunshine—Mr. Bernarr Macfadden's New York tabloid newspaper, the *Evening Graphic*, has suspended publication!"[50]

"The Father of Physical Culture"

FANATIC, FAKER, FADDIST, and quack were terms doctors applied to Macfadden, a lifelong battler against conventional medicine. While he condemned the American Medical Association as an entrenched and intimidating monopoly, orthodox health specialists decried his publishing of *Physical Culture* and his simplistic solutions to complex medical questions. The medical director of the Life Extension Institute labeled him "one of the greatest obstacles to sound health education" in America, a "potential murderer" who catered to erotic impulses. "Under the guise of physical culture and hygiene, he is making a vicious sex appeal in his publications and undermining the faith of the people in scientific medicine and the true principles of hygiene and preventive medicine. He is jeopardizing life and unquestionably causing many deaths by influencing people to employ the wretched fakirs and quacks who advertise in his journal."[1]

The AMA first took action against cults, quacks, and nostrums about 1906, but its files did not mention Macfadden until 1911. In response to physicians who had inquired about a Macfadden rehabilitation center in Chicago, the association asserted privately that Macfadden was "medically speaking, grossly ignorant." It referred to his claims that drugs were useless for diphtheria, that antitoxin was dangerous, and that a child with that disease should be encouraged to move about instead of being put to bed. "We do not believe that any man who would promulgate such a lamentably dangerous doctrine is competent to give instruction in physical culture or any other subject affecting the health of a human being," wrote Arthur J. Cramp, head of the AMA's propaganda department. The association maintained a "fake file," which included criticisms of Macfadden, two of which appeared in medical journals in 1910 and 1912, but until 1924 it publicly ignored the physical culturist on the assumption that his followers would not be convinced by an open rebuttal.[2] Individuals, however, counterattacked. With evident glee, Macfadden printed this crude threat: "Macfaddens—You rascal will be put out of business with a lot of other faddist(s). You pretty near ruined our business. We, the members of the American Medical Association, are going to create a National Board of Health, and we shall have it our own way soon, and don't you forget it. We are after your scalp and a lot of other ilks of your kind. We will make it hot for you to exist. . . . You have killed our business, and we will make you sorry for that. Now the people have no use for surgeons."[3]

Late in 1924, the AMA published in its popular journal *Hygeia* two articles under the general title, "Exploiting the Health Interest," the first treating the advertising that made "physical culture" commercially profitable, and the second describing the literature on which "'physical culturists' and Macfaddenists" thrived. *Hygeia*'s editor, Morris Fishbein, a physician long associated with the AMA, published a highly successful popular book, *Medical Follies*, in 1925. Fishbein devoted a chapter to Macfadden who, he declared, had promoted dozens of discredited notions and attacked scientific medicine and its modern treatment of disease and its mod-ern treatment of disease and campaigns for disease prevention. According to Fishbein, the physical culturist had not only aligned himself with "borderline cultists" devoted to the "promotion of some single conception of disease causation, prevention and treatment," but also advanced "the interests of the manipulative cults, including chiropractic and osteopathy; of the Abramsites, with their fantastic electronic conception; of the naturopathic cult, with its emphasis on barefoot walking in the morning dew; of colonic flushing and vegetable diet; of the antivaccinationists and antivivisectionists; of the fanatical groups that feel that their personal beliefs are more important than the good of the community."[4]

Physicians sometimes protested directly to Macfadden. An outraged West Virginia surgeon called him "a most contemptible, vicious liar" who would be "personally damned" for advertising that fasting, followed by a raw milk diet, cured syphilis. "My dear Mr. Mac Fadden," he wrote: "I hope you never get syphilis. If you do, I hope God will be kind enough not to have you bothered with doctors, so that you may have the pleasure of suffering the tortures of hell, tortures that others are certain to have that might be simple enough to read your magazine and believe it."[5]

Asserting that *Physical Culture* was not found in better homes and offices, the doctor added that he had seen it "hanging in toilets." More lighthearted was the secretary of an Indiana medical association. "Old 'Mother Wright' used to run a big successful whorehouse here, but, Bernarr, she was a piker. She would have nationalized her 'institute' and published a few magazines and covered more ground. I believe you are a lot smarter than old 'Mother Wright' even if you seem to have about the same ideas."[6]

Outraged physicians often wrote to the American Medical Association, which developed a large file of correspondence about Macfadden. Dr. Arthur Cramp, director of the AMA's department of investigation, declared that the physical culturist apparently rejected "the most axiomatic facts of medical science" and persistently blackguarded the medical profession. Recalling that Macfadden had once offered to pay any physician half the fees he obtained from a "victim" the doctor might send him, the AMA official speculated on the consequences of Macfadden's ignorance of medicine. "In cases of those individuals who are attracted by the specious claims made by Macfadden and others of his ilk, who have nothing seriously the matter with them, probably no great harm is done, except to the purse. Where, however, really competent treatment is imperative, the most serious results may be expected. Naturally, very few instances that would show the perniciousness of such doctrines as those held and practiced by men such as Macfadden ever reach the public. Large purchasers of newspaper advertising space seldom get into the news columns of the newspapers in a way that would be derogatory to them."[7]

Physical Culture's advertising pages had for many years been a haven for drugless healers, medical fakes, and frauds, according to Dr. Cramp, who cited seven examples of these advertisements that federal authorities had declared fraudulent. Had Macfadden only preached the gospel of simple diet and adequate exercise, Cramp admitted, nobody could object, except for his erotic appeal to persons "whose eyes are aroused by the flash of nakedness or whose weakened wills succumb to every new health fad." But that was not all. He flayed Macfadden for promoting manipulative cults and characterized his magazines as mainly devoted to attacking scientific medicine and discrediting medical efforts to prevent and treat disease. Instead of contributing greatly to the war on venereal disease, as claimed, Macfadden had actually hindered it by refusing to recognize that gonorrhea and syphilis were caused by bacterial parasites.[8]

The physical culturist retaliated by sending lecturers to local communities. Whenever doctors alerted the AMA, it sent them reprints of the *Hygeia* articles and quietly worked behind the scenes, but it did not publicly counter the Macfadden propaganda. As Cramp put it, "any attempt to dignify Macfadden's present tirade against the American Medical Association by replying to it would be a mistake. Any person with the intelligence of twelve years or over will see through the absurdity of the thing. The morons that take Macfadden seriously would not be convinced by anything we might publish."[9]

In December 1926, two years after the *Hygeia* essays, *Physical Culture* began a series by John L. Spivak exposing the "Medical Trust." The opening article, luridly entitled "Exposed at Last! The Medical Trust Has You at Its Mercy!" was followed in January by "The Medical Trust Has You by the Throat," in February by "Seventy Thousand Doctors Have Combined Against You," and in March by "How Doctors Get away with Murder." Outraged physicians protested to the AMA, urging a public reply, but the association kept its low profile. "Nothing would please Macfadden more," wrote Cramp, "than to have the American Medical Association take cognizance of the ridiculous series that he is now running."[10]

Macfadden's next move was to appeal directly to physicians in an effort to wean them from the influence of the AMA. Reprints of his editorial, "Doctors and Doctoring," in the June 1927 issue of *Physical Culture* and a statement of "The Physical Culture Creed," which argued that physical culture and the medical profession had much in common, were sent to physicians all over the country. Enclosed with these documents was a letter from Orr J. Elder, president of Macfadden Publications, addressed to "Dear Doctor," asking for the names of physicians sympathizing with the Physical Culture platform and practicing accordingly. "We should like to be in a position to recommend such doctors to our readers in their communities," Elder explained; "May we register you on this list?"[11]

The AMA was inundated with protests from M.D.'s, one of whom quipped that he had received his "invitation to join the intelligentsia by this morning's mail." Another suggested that Macfadden "see a nerve specialist or have his gall bladder drained."[12] To complaining physicians the association mailed out canned replies. "The Macfadden stuff is pouring in by every mail. After bedamning scientific medicine and currying favor with the cultists, he now offers to 'recommend' such physicians as will express themselves as in sympathy with the "*Physical Culture* platform." A recommendation from Macfadden is a heavy liability."[13]

While escalating his attack on the "Medical Trust," Macfadden apparently soft-pedaled his opposition to all drugs. If he were to succeed in winning over physicians to the cause of physical culture, he could not condemn drugs as he had done in the past. Further, he was promoting a research fund and hoped medical men would support it.[14]

Although Macfadden believed that doctors in nearly every state were responsible for public health laws that protected their financial interest, he disapproved of a public health plan offered by Senator Robert F. Wagner in 1940. Putting the public health in the hands of the government, he argued, was a "revolutionary and dangerous procedure" that would result in standardized and compulsory medical treatment. Political control would only worsen the "steel-like grip" of the AMA. The main objective of "the allopathic medical fraternity," he claimed, was to label as an ignorant quack the practitioner of natural, drugless methods, and he alleged that hundreds of nonmedical practitioners in New York State could not tell "when a spotter might be looking for evidence to send them to jail."[15]

In 1949, Macfadden inaugurated a brazen challenge to individuals in the medical profession. *Physical Culture* mailed out an unknown quantity of postcards headed "TELL US ABOUT THE DOCTOR," and asked the recipients to relate their experiences with doctors and nurses, including instances of mistreatment. Physicians and nurses, too, were invited to respond. Three anxious M.D.'s sent the cards to the AMA, which assured them that American doctors would not take the matter seriously.

Five years later the physical culturist aimed another blitz at physicians. By postcard he announced that he had discovered a process that would "destroy malignancy, the destructive bacteria in the blood stream," and invited recipients to a talk by "celebrated health lecturer" Veronica Hoffman, who would provide the details. Not only had the new discovery "proven successful in Leprosy, Prostatitis, two chest Inflammations, (one a T.B. diagnosis), Gonorrhea, malignant swellings in the calves and a gangrenous foot," but the malignancy was "destroyed in every case in One Treatment, even including the T.B. case." One of these cards was forwarded to the AMA, which pronounced it "an entertaining addition" to its file on Macfadden.[16] An ego trip for BM, the postcard campaign served more as a publicity stunt than a search for converts from organized medicine.

It is unlikely that the hostility of the medical establishment curtailed Macfadden's crusade to any great extent. The contemptuous attitude of orthodox physicians no doubt stimulated BM's combativeness. He sought to publicize the case of a poor man who resisted the vaccination of his child and to foster the career of an aggressive young healer who resembled the youthful Macfadden as a propagandist. In a *Liberty* editorial in 1939, he charged that the AMA leadership had always been commercially motivated and that it compelled its doctor members to "fall in line with threats of expulsion," whereas the rank and file in the profession hated its "monopolistic practices worse than the devil does holy water."[17] Although he was supported by some physicians, Macfadden appealed essentially to laymen seeking simple solutions to their physical problems.

Beginning with *Physical Culture* at the turn of the century, Macfadden had developed a wide following in his persistent campaign for proper diet and exercise and the natural healing of illnesses. He retained a hold on numerous followers, especially young men, in the cult of bodily perfection. "Body love Macfadden," as he was known by his detractors, induced countless young athletes to devote themselves to physical culture through a planned exercise program. Most of Macfadden's adherents no doubt fell within the normal range of intelligence and ability, despite the disparagement of them as morons by doctors Arthur Cramp and Morris Fishbein, both AMA spokesmen. Like the youthful Macfadden, some had undergone unfortunate experiences with doctors and drugs and had visited one physician after another without success, seeking relief or cure of maladies ranging from asthma to venereal disease. Some were fanatics for fasting, the milk diet, or the "grape cure." Among the patrons of the Physical Culture Hotel at Dansville, New York, were many simple folk who underwent treatments but also enjoyed the country air and social amenities, and they returned year after year, unaware that the hotel was not recommended by the AMA.[18]

One of the more prominent Macfadden devotees was the popular writer and reformer Upton Sinclair, who as a young man struggling with chronic indigestion and recurrent headaches, claimed to benefit from BM's advocacy of fasting and a milk diet. At the age of eighty-three, he was still praising Macfadden's methods of achieving a healthy life. "The secrets of natural living were the property of a little group of adventurous persons known as 'health cranks,'" Sinclair reminisced, "and it has been my pleasure to watch the leading ideas of these 'cranks' being rediscovered one by one by medical authority to the newspapers and the public." Another such "crank" was Floyd Starr, who applied Macfadden's principles at the Starr Commonwealth for Boys in Albion, Michigan, a home he established for maladjusted and underprivileged boys. Through the Macfadden Institute of Physical Culture and the American Institute for Physical Education, both founded by Macfadden, physical instructors and athletic directors were trained in his methods. Operators of gymnasiums and fitness centers owed much to the "Father of Physical Culture."[19] Children who attended Macfadden's schools and camps and the cadets at his Castle Heights Military Academy could not avoid the pervasive influence of one who made physical education an essential part of the curriculum.

For a younger generation of health enthusiasts, Macfadden's best remembered disciple was an Italian immigrant, Angelo Siciliano, better known as Charles Atlas, who as a teenager had read *Physical Culture* early in the century. In those years the physical culturist elaborated in his magazine what he called "dynamic tension," in which one set of muscles was exerted against another, such as an arm against an arm or a hand against a hand. Atlas adopted the system and later advertised it as his own. In 1921, as an entrant in *Physical Culture's* "World's Most Beautiful Man" contest, he was summoned to Macfadden's office, where the publisher gave him a glass of carrot juice, watched him pose in a leopard skin, and declared him the winner, handing him a check for one thousand dollars. The next year, Atlas won Macfadden's "America's Most Perfectly Developed Man" contest at Madison Square Garden and walked off with another thousand dollars. The physical culturist, having earlier described Atlas as "the living realization of my life-long battle for the body beautiful," dropped plans for any more such contests on the ground that Atlas would win every time.[20] Few Americans recall those contests, but many recognize Charles Atlas as the promoter of "dynamic tension" with advertisements displaying his superb physique with the blurb "I was a 97-pound weakling."

Probably the most important health reformer who carried on in the Macfadden tradition was J. I. Rodale, most influential of health activists during BM's later years and after. To some degree, the physical culturist was Rodale's hero. As self-made individualists who advocated the prevention of disease and were antagonists of the American Medical Association, they had common concerns, though Rodale, whose intellectual and cultural interests were wider, wrote plays and specialized in organic gardening and farming. In his published writings, he professed admiration for the physical culturist, particularly for his physical agility in old age. Rodale delighted in proclaiming that, after Macfadden, he was America's "number-one faddist."[21]

In many ways, the self-educated Macfadden was among the champions of health practices now generally accepted: attention to personal hygiene, healthful living, avoidance of restrictive clothing, and physical activity like walking in the fresh air. His enthusiasm for sunbathing would no longer be acceptable in view of knowledge that the sun's rays can cause skin cancer, although thousands of devotees still bake their bodies in the sun. In his dietary theories, he and others like Alfred McCann and Horace Fletcher, advocate of a careful diet and thorough mastication, anticipated the enormous interest today in nutrition, although Macfadden gave no hint of being a devoted follower of Fletcher, as a recent writer declares. He campaigned against white bread, and eventually bakers fortified their bread with vitamins. Milo Hastings, director of the Physical Culture Food Research Laboratory and conductor for many years of *Physical Culture*'s food department, called the advocacy of whole wheat "Plank Number One in Bernarr Macfadden's food and health platform."[22] The physical culturist undoubtedly won converts to fasting. His experiments upon himself reflected the common sense notion that the body, if given a proper chance, would eliminate poisons naturally. Fasting hastened the process. Like much of the popular literature on the subject by persons without a medical education, Macfadden's writings relied not on controlled experiments, but on anecdotal data.

His system of healing had its failures. Some of his patients benefited only partly or temporarily, and others were harmed. Inspired by BM's teachings, a cook for the Great Northern Hotel in Chicago starved to death after a two-month fast, and a man and his wife died of heart failure soon after entering Macfadden's Chicago healthatorium. After a hay fever sufferer complained that Macfadden's mail order Health Service Bureau had not helped her, a New York State medical inspector investigated, and Macfadden was fined $500 for unlawfully practicing medicine. Experiences of other dissatisfied or disillusioned patients found their way into the files of the American Medical Association.[23] Rarely admitting failure, the physical culturist exuded the confidence and dogmatism of the lay enthusiast.

Macfadden was not above misrepresentation if it advanced his causes. One of his executives considered him devious—"a little too devious for his own good." Whether carelessly or deliberately, he printed the story of a syphilitic who had deceitfully obtained from his physician an affidavit of clean health, which made it seem that the physician had personally endorsed BM's "fasting cure." When he published a picture of a supposedly cured female arthritic, poised in his arms for a waltz, he did not tell his readers that she had been lifted from her chair for the dance pose. He sometimes used without authorization the names of prominent individuals, such as Cary T. Grayson, Woodrow Wilson's physician, who was quoted as unqualifiedly agreeing with Macfadden's views on preventing venereal disease as presented in *Manhood and Marriage* and recommending the book to every mother, father, and adolescent in America.[24]

Accusations that he was a clever, money-mad schemer distressed Macfadden. "Money," he declared as early as 1906, "is of absolutely no use to me apart from the power which it brings with it. I, of course, allude to its power for good, when rightfully used." Until he donated his fortune to the Macfadden Foundation, he had to contend with the notion that he was a clever, unscrupulous operator. As his son-in-law Arthur St. Phillip remarked, "the money didn't mean a thing to him. He used it as a means toward an end: proving that health was more important than anything else." During the Great Depression, he continued to rake in money but, according to St. Phillip, "you couldn't tell it by looking at him. He and Medill Patterson (another publishing magnate of the time) would walk around looking like a couple of bums. They'd sit in the Horn and Hardart on Lexington Avenue and drink their milk or whatever and talk about health."[25]

The physical culturist was preoccupied with diet, continually experimenting and trying to discover the best combinations of food. One of his concoctions was a meal of pounded cereal, nuts, and fruits, boiled with milk and water and served with honey and cream. Usually, he went without breakfast and ate only when hungry. "The cemeteries are full of people who are slaves to the three-meal-a-day habit," he remarked. He refused to eat manufactured food products. "Candy, ice cream sodas, bakeshop pastries—I can live without these," he snorted. He was not a strict vegetarian, but he did not eat much meat. Any natural plant food appealed to him. Among his staples, consumed in vast quantities, were raw carrots, beet juice, fruit, grains, and nuts. While talking circulation with *Graphic* editor Gauvreau, he spread on a desk the contents of a great bag of walnuts.[26]

Macfadden took full credit for recognizing the importance of diet, although he was but one of a long line of food reformers in the Sylvester Graham tradition. "More than half a century has elapsed since I personally discovered the importance of diet in acquiring and maintaining normal health," he boasted in 1939. He felt vindicated by Dr. Victor G. Heiser's address to the American Association for the Advancement of Science, acknowledging that diet could cause and cure disease, and in an editorial, "After Forty Years Medical Science Discovers Diet," he announced that physicans had finally seen the light — that is, recognized Macfadden's dietetic principles.[27]

Fancy food and liquor were to be avoided. Once, sitting in Oursler's car outside a posh restaurant, he had misgivings about the food it served and asked Oursler to go in and bring back a menu, which he did. BM looked it over and said, "Nothing here for me except tomato juice, but it's time I went on a fast anyway. You go eat and I'll take a nap." And he slept in the car. One evening at the Ourslers' rambling house on Cape Cod, the publisher watched his host's elaborate ritual of serving *café diablo:* carefully measuring the coffee and adding lemon peel, cinnamon bark, and brandy, and after the lights were extinguished, touching a match to the brew, creating a spectacular burst of flame. Unimpressed, Macfadden said, "I'll take Postum."[28]

The Father of Physical Culture made an occasional concession to his own guests' drinking preferences. After an evening's entertainment he told an associate and his wife, "I know you children would like a night cap. What shall it be — Scotch?" When they accepted the offer and were served, he poured a teaspoonful of sherry into a glass of orange juice for himself and remarked with a smile, "I don't want my guests to feel that I'm not drinking with them."[29]

In his seriousness of purpose, Macfadden did not fully appreciate how eccentric he seemed to others. After a carload of Meline, a natural breakfast food he had developed, arrived at his Castle Heights Military Academy full of weevils, he is said to have remarked, "Weevils are live germ. That's great for the kids." Long before nonsmokers asserted their rights, a Macfadden associate reached for a cigarette at an executive meeting and the boss demanded to know whether someone was smoking. "I am, teacher!" the culprit responded. "You are violating my most important rule," BM warned and presciently declared that the day would arrive when people discovered that cigarettes caused cancer and heart disease. (His other objections to tobacco mixed fact and fable: it stunted growth, diminished virility, impaired appetite, digestion, vision and hearing, and contributed to nervous breakdowns.)

When he was in his late seventies, he initiated a game of follow the leader in his apartment and led his guests, willing or not, in a fast series of somersaults, to the exhaustion of all except himself. He was reported to have walked barefoot from his apartment to his office with a forty-pound bag of sand on his back. He was an enthusiastic headstander. At his office he sometimes dictated while standing on his head, and he was known to deliver "Cosmotarian" lectures in the same posture; Cosmotarianism was his short-lived attempt to link physical culture with religion. One night at a dinner party in a Sherry Netherland Hotel suite, he taught a Hollywood star how to alleviate a headache by standing on her head. Later, as they descended in the elevator, she tried it again, and he immediately joined her. Both were still upside down when the doors opened on the first floor.[30]

Such pixieish antics were intended to promote Macfadden's serious health mission. He was a prolific author. Apart from his writings in *Physical Culture* and his magazine and newspaper editorials, he wrote or edited nearly 150 books and pamphlets. Most were published before 1930, but he wrote or collaborated on at least 15 in the 1930s and 3 in the 1940s. Many were pocket-size guidebooks showing the way to physical fitness or a better sex life, dispensing advice on diet, and specific treatments for problems ranging from asthma to strengthening the eyes, the nerves, and the spine. Although he had trouble with his own teeth, he wrote about the prevention, cause, and cure of tooth troubles. He penned books on hair culture, headache, skin diseases, colds and coughs, digestive troubles, constipation, diabetes, rupture, rheumatism and tuberculosis, physical culture for the baby, sex predetermination, and the evils of tobacco. Other Macfadden writings touted fasting and walking and building "brain energy." A few of his books were translated into Spanish, French, Greek, Finnish, or Yiddish. As new editions appeared, he changed the title, perhaps partly because so many of his works had been banned from the mails.[31] Several volumes were written with others or were the product of many hands, such as his five-volume *Encyclopedia of Physical Culture* in 1911, which went into several editions. Its successor, the *Encyclopedia of Health and Physical Culture* in eight volumes, replaced the older work in 1931 and was revised in 1937, 1940, and 1942.

The most widely known among American naturopaths, Macfadden was exploited by other health cultists and lecturers like Adolphus Hohensee, who displayed a picture of himself with the Father of Physical Culture. Hohensee's advertising ran afoul of the Federal Trade Commission, which forced him to discontinue some of his claims, and after the Food and Drug Administration took him to court, he spent a year in jail. From time to time federal agencies questioned Macfadden's own health advertising, but he remained within the law.[32]

After nearly half a century of propaganda, Macfadden made no concessions to organized medicine, and the medical profession made no concessions to him. When in 1940 he proposed that homeopaths, stereopaths, naturopaths, and chiropractors be permitted to demonstrate their methods on American soldiers, the *Journal* of the American Medical Association objected to doubtful diagnoses by "incompletely and peculiarly trained cultists." If they diagnosed in their patients diseases they did not suffer, as when a common cold was called influenza, it was easy to claim a cure. The AMA was confident that the army medical corps would not be swayed by the "extravagant claims of irresponsible cultists or the distorted diatribes of Bernarr Macfadden."[33]

If BM delighted in the self-bestowed title, "Father of Physical Culture"—a recent writer has dubbed him "the impresario of physical culture"[34]—he was more than David challenging Goliath. His flourishing career as a publisher, his growing interest in public affairs, and his political ambitions absorbed more of his time and attention than ever before.

The Political Bug

LIKE WILLIAM RANDOLPH HEARST, Macfadden headed a successful publishing empire, and his newspapers exploited crime and sex. Both men were attracted to women. Both had political ambitions, although Hearst was involved in politics long before Macfadden and had considerably more influence. Both scored brain trusters, bureaucracy, regimentation, and the expanding scope of taxation. Each saw himself as a patriot combating visionary schemes of radicals and propagandized against Communist subversion. Yet there were differences: Hearst had inherited wealth, but BM earned his. Hearst was an extravagant buyer of art for his San Simeon ranch, but BM's home and office were decorated with signed photographs, portraits, or depictions of the human body, usually his own or of his children. Hearst was no health missionary, whereas Macfadden delighted in being called the Father of Physical Culture.

As a young man, and even in middle age, Macfadden had no interest in politics. His few comments on public officials almost always related to health: President McKinley, after being shot, should not have been fed solid food. Theodore Roosevelt, "the best president of the United States, barring none," had wide interests, especially in the health of his countrymen, and was a "physical culturist to the core," a "strenuous, open-air, rugged President," typical of a new generation of strong able-bodied young men in America. Had Woodrow Wilson studied physical culture, he would not have suffered a crippling stroke. "I believe I could save his life right now," Macfadden said. "It's obvious those doctors aren't doing him any good."[1]

In the early 1920s, as *True Story* provided the means, Macfadden supported the Republican party. Conventional, conservative, and strongly probusiness, he contributed to the party in power. Will Hays, chairman of the Republican National Committee (later the movie censor of the "Hays office") visited the Macfaddens at their Nyack home; and after BM gave $25,000, Hays told him that the party would not forget his patriotic interest in the country's "return to normalcy."[2]

As the physical culturist reached a wider public through *True Story*, he developed political ambitions. His tabloid newspaper, the New York *Evening Graphic*, was founded in part for political reasons. According to a Macfadden underling, the newspapers had failed to accord him the publicity he craved to enhance his political stature, so he decided to launch his own vehicle. "The *Graphic*," Fulton Oursler asserted, "was to be the magic carpet that would carry [Macfadden] to the White House." Emile Gauvreau, the *Graphic*'s editor, tried to enlist New York Mayor John F. Hylan's help in pushing BM's presidential hopes but soon learned that Hylan had no influence with Democratic party leaders, and so Tammany Hall was eager to replace him with the affable and debonair Jimmy Walker.[3]

The *Graphic* promoted Walker for mayor in 1925, as Macfadden, lowering his sights, hoped to be appointed New York City's health commissioner. When elected, Walker did not name him to that position. "Everybody knows you can live to be a hundred by following Macfadden's ideas," Jimmy quipped, "But New York wants to live the way I do. That's why I was elected. We won't last as long but we'll have more fun."[4] BM worked off his disappointment by fasting and exercising furiously for a week.

To keep Macfadden's name before the public and to gratify his pathetic craving for adulation, the *Graphic* organized testimonial banquets in his honor, at which prominent politicians mouthed flattering words. Years later, his estranged wife, Mary, wryly recollected that he enjoyed bowing to the speakers from his place at the center of the dais, as if their praise of his ideas about health were a spontaneous tribute.[5]

Macfadden's colossal ego and outward air of self-confidence masked an underlying insecurity. According to one of his daughters, his quest for personal recognition was such an obsession that he did not care what was printed about him as long as his name made print.[6] His editorials and some of his letterheads carried facsimiles of his signature or the notation "private office." Cameramen always were available for publicity shots, and his craggy face and bushy hair adorned Macfadden publications. He was surrounded by sycophants and self-seekers. Although a showman at heart, he was willing to listen to suggestions by trusted subordinates.

His board of editorial advisers, evidently weary of his corny publicity, induced him in 1927 to hire Edward L. Bernays, the public rela-
tions counselor, for several months at the princely fee of $500 a week.
Vetoing BM's proposal of walking barefooted from his office to City
Hall, Bernays planned something more grandiose: Macfadden would
make a quick trip to London for a reception by the House of Commons in recognition of his contribution to physical culture in the
United States. Bernays arranged for Sir Nicholas Grattan-Doyle, an
MP from Newcastle-on-Tyne, to give a dinner in Macfadden's honor.
In London, Macfadden spoke on the international aspects of physical
fitness at what must have been a private party rather than a public
reception, and he visited George Bernard Shaw, whose vegetarianism
and frankness about sex intrigued the American.[7] Chatting about
eating habits, health, and prudery, Shaw told him, "I see no more reason for hiding sex than for hiding the wheel on a motor car. And we're
both terrible heretics, Mr. Macfadden, when we stand for sane and
rational thinking on health and diet." After watching two reels of BM's
family movies, the author of *Mrs. Warren's Profession* observed that
they were "too moral," that Macfadden vanquished bad habits "too utterly to be convincing."[8]

Two days after returning to New York, Macfadden was escorted
by motorcycle cops to City Hall for a reception by Mayor Jimmy Walker.
It beat walking! *Graphic* editor Gauvreau, having discovered that
Daniel Webster had gone to England and visited Parliament, wrote
an account of his boss's experience in the House of Commons, which,
embellished with pictures of Webster and Macfadden, was mailed to
clergymen, senators, congressmen, and members of every state legislature.[9]

Convinced for many years that a new post in the president's cabinet, a secretary of health, was needed, Macfadden saw himself as the
logical candidate. He also saw the position as a step upward toward
the presidency, and the *Graphic* vigorously campaigned for him but
to no effect. Thus, despite his contributions to the Republican party,
he sent Gauvreau in 1928 to Judge George W. Olvaney, Tammany boss,
with an offer of enough money to secure the Democratic nomination
for governor of New York. Democratic insiders knew that Governor
Al Smith, who was expected to be the party's presidential candidate,
wished Franklin D. Roosevelt to fill his shoes at Albany. To Macfadden, Roosevelt, a crippled polio victim, lacked the physical vigor essential for a political officeholder. Naturally, BM had it.

Olvaney told Gauvreau that the publisher could not survive the

Macfadden at sixty years of age. Courtesy of Fulton Oursler, Jr.

propaganda that the medical profession would use against him, that the doctors would never forgive him.[10] The Tammany leader already knew about Macfadden's ambition and approaches to bigwigs of both major parties and understood that politicians were not physical culture enthusiasts.

> When you imagine Bernarr Macfadden as a candidate [Olvaney was quoted as saying],[11] You immediately think of the fun he'd stop you from having if he got elected. He's recognized as a crank who made the nation healthier. That's the penalty that goes with his kind of success. He will never hold public office. The voters would be afraid he would want to control their living habits, their normal impulses and natural appetites.
>
> His passion for the presidency is incurable because he's convinced he can make everybody feel better. To make matters worse for him he thinks he's got a national following to start with. He's a man with a message which already has been absorbed. He should be satisfied that he got as far as he did with it.

As a millionaire reformer, Olvaney predicted, Macfadden would persist in his quest until his money gave out. Flatterers would "take the shirt off his back," which would not be hard for him because he hated clothing—if he ever had to go naked he could "live on two-bits of cracked wheat a day." He had nothing to lose but his money, but "at the rate he's going he'll spend more of it than any man in American history who ever tried to become president."[12]

In the spring of 1928, the publisher went to Washington to talk health to politicians. He had breakfast in the speaker's room in the Capitol, visited the House and Senate chambers, and in the evening lectured in the large caucus room of the House office building. Meyer Davis's orchestra played music, and BM showed his health movies. Congressman Fiorello LaGuardia introduced the physical culturist as "this great man [who] is here to tell us the best way to get the most out of life."[13]

In June, Macfadden attended the Republican national convention in Kansas City, seeking endorsement of a cabinet-rank secretary of health. He failed, but that did not diminish his self-importance. After Hoover's nomination, he paid $50,000 for a plane to fly him to Washington to congratulate the nominee. The Democrats held their convention in Houston, and Macfadden flew there to win acceptance of his cabinet proposal, but again in vain. When Smith was nominated, the publisher flew to Albany to offer congratulations. Macfadden's idea of a national health office, which he was still proposing twelve years later, was not taken seriously.[14]

As early as April 1930, he was ready to support Hoover for reelection, but as the great depression deepened he considered other contenders for the White House. The *Graphic* picked up Congressman Loring Black's proposal that whoever was elected should be given dictatorial powers to lead a war against the depression, bolster the economy, and oust corrupt judges; and Macfadden's editorial suggested five likely dictators: Herbert Hoover, William E. Borah, Calvin Coolidge, and the Democrats John Nance Garner and Alfred E. Smith. The publisher's following of yes-men and boosters, accumulated over the years, tried to convince him that his own talents were needed, but when an organization was set up to nominate him for president in 1932 he declined the offer. He still hoped to become secretary of health.[15]

As national politics surged in his mind, Macfadden sought a wider audience than could be reached by *Physical Culture* and confession or detective magazines. He acquired newspapers in several cities. He also needed a respectable weekly journal, and *Liberty* seemed well suited. Started in 1924 by Col. Robert McCormick of the *Chicago Tribune* and Joseph Patterson of the New York *Daily News*, it had become one of the three leading weekly magazines in the United States, a competitor of the *Saturday Evening Post* and *Collier's*. As part of the McCormick-Patterson empire it won readers but lost money, reportedly about twelve million dollars over seven years. Early in 1931, Macfadden purchased *Liberty*, guaranteed 2,500,000 copies average net paid circulation for the year, and took control with the issue of April 4.[16]

Immediately after the purchase, BM telephoned Oursler, his managing editor. "Charley, I've bought *Liberty*," he announced. "You're the new editor in chief. But you'll keep on with the other magazines, too. We couldn't afford to lose you on the others." Oursler hesitated. He already supervised nine magazines: *Physical Culture, True Story, True Romances, True Detective Mysteries, True Experiences, Master Detective, Ghost Stories, Dream World,* and *Your Home.* After failing to interest the editor of *Physical Culture,* already enticed by an attractive offer from *Cosmopolitan,* the faithful Oursler accepted the job of editing the five-cent weekly with the largest single-copy sales of any magazine in the country.[17]

Oursler solicited articles from well-known people — public figures, writers, businessmen, labor leaders, and athletes. In 1932, Governor

Franklin D. Roosevelt contributed a series of articles, and for a decade *Liberty*'s galaxy of stars included Jane Addams, Eleanor Roosevelt, Harold Ickes, Herbert Hoover, Thomas Dewey, Leon Trotsky, Mohandas Gandhi, Bertrand Russell, George Bernard Shaw, H. G. Wells, Emil Ludwig, Maurice Maeterlinck, H. L. Mencken, John Erskine, Fannie Hurst, Robert Benchley, Rupert Hughes, Elmer Davis, Walter Winchell, Matthew Woll, William Green, and Jack Dempsey. Macfadden sometimes bridled at the fees Oursler paid, and he warned the editor not to play favorites in selecting authors. Let all but the top writers compete, he urged; continued use of a new author would lead to demands for higher pay, after which *Liberty* might lose him to *Collier's* or the *Saturday Evening Post*. Oursler replied that the cheaper authors could not meet *Liberty*'s standard and that underpaying contributors was risky. "We will save more money by discontinuing the magazine," he declared, "than by trying to cheat the readers."[18]

Although he allowed his chief editor a free hand in the management of *Liberty*, Macfadden wrote an editorial each week. His first, on May 2, 1931, was characteristic of his optimism and preoccupation with decency, morality, and discipline. "We want LIBERTY to be a bright spot that will bring happy moments every day," he wrote. "We want it to add to the spirit of cooperation and friendliness. We want to help all our friends to have a good time, to make life in general splendidly worth while." If he intended his magazine to be "richly laden with alluring entertainment," he nevertheless planned to cover serious problems facing the nation: prohibition, gangsterism, political greed and graft, materialism and money-making as harmful to the home, lack of parental discipline ("an appalling evil"), and youthful lack of self-control and consideration for others.[19]

BM wrote editorials in a plain style attuned to a popular audience. His opinions often were platitudes: "love is the force that makes the world go round," "you cannot buy happiness," and "those who are reared among riches have but little appreciation of its value." Throughout his writings, he sprinkled clichés like ornaments on a Christmas tree. Phrases like "a world of truth," "a crying need," "plain as the nose on your face," and "school of hard knocks" were good enough for a man with almost no formal education, and they carried the common touch.[20]

The publisher hoped to boost his political stature by reaching beyond working people to his newly acquired middle-class readers in editorials reaffirming an old-fashioned rugged American individualism. "Through my editorial page in *Liberty*," he crowed some years later, "I believe that I have more influence politically on the masses than any one individual in the United States."[21] Despite his sublime faith in himself, the sales of *Liberty* were sustained by the articles and special features for which Oursler had responsibility.

Oursler's favorable articles on Roosevelt, beginning with "Is Franklin D. Roosevelt Physically Fit to Be President?" led the New York governor to meet him in December 1931, to his decision to use *Liberty* to publicize himself, and to his first encounter with Macfadden. Shortly afterward, Louis Howe arranged for the publisher to sit on the platform with Governor Roosevelt at an outdoor Red Cross rally near Rochester. In a cunning maneuver, the physical culturist was seated next to Roosevelt. Utterly captivated by the governor's charm, Macfadden told his editor, "I think Roosevelt is the coming man. He and I see eye to eye in everything. He is an ardent devotee of physical culture and always has been."[22]

Macfadden's editorial, "The Great Political Battle," avoided recommending a candidate or party but favored repeal of prohibition, reduction of government expenses, and elimination of government interference with business. After the election of 1932, he gave his support to the president-elect and sympathized with the early New Deal measures of 1933. It cannot be proven, but it is possible, as his wife alleged, that he believed that Roosevelt's physical condition would make for a short presidential tenure, and that with money and spectacular national publicity BM could then try to convince the people that he himself was the healthy man they needed.[23]

Eleanor Roosevelt, who had lunched with him at his one-cent restaurant in August 1932, and who after the election was editing the new Macfadden magazine, *Babies—Just Babies*, promised before the inauguration to invite the publisher to the White House. Although he found it necessary to remind her of her promise, he did spend a weekend with the Roosevelts at the White House in May. Probably Macfadden hoped to persuade the president, perhaps through Eleanor's influence, to make him a secretary of health. The publisher also sent Howard Swain, the *Graphic*'s managing editor, to Jim Farley, FDR's campaign manager and postmaster general, to ask for the post of secretary of health, but Farley refused.[24]

Macfadden's relationship with the Roosevelts, never a close one, deteriorated. His deal with Mrs. Roosevelt as editor of *Babies—Just Babies* ended when embarrassed by the continuing horselaughs occasioned by the title she abandoned the project.[25] BM continued to admire Roosevelt's personality, but after a year or so condemned the New

Deal, and not merely out of pique that FDR had failed to push him for secretary of health. The New Deal was far from what he had expected, and by 1935 he was blasting away at it in passionate editorials and public statements.

Late in the summer of 1935, Macfadden announced his availability for the presidency. At a luncheon of the Republican Club of St. Louis on September 15, he declared that if offered the Republican nomination he would not refuse it. The AP dispatch to the *New York Times* was headed "Macfadden is 'Willing.'" Nearly a hundred important New Jersey businessmen and politicians, including Governor Harold G. Hoffman and a Republican national committeeman, had lunch with the publisher at his home. They heard him declare that the United States Constitution was endangered by the Roosevelt administration, and he openly offered to help finance the Republican party if it pledged support of the Constitution in the 1936 presidential campaign.[26]

BM encouraged his friends to promote him. For anyone curious at Macfadden Publications, an internal memorandum announced that the boss was "greatly interested in securing the recognition of sound principles" that would benefit the general welfare and the business interests of the country, "including his own business." A Bernarr Macfadden for President Club, with headquarters in the Graybar Building in New York, published a six-column adulatory biography. In Illinois, a few of the firm's employees and officials of paper and printing companies organized another Macfadden club. A fifty-cent booklet, *Bernarr Macfadden: Highlights of 50 Years of Service For His Country,* sprouted on the newsstands.[27]

In November, a reporter for the *New York Herald Tribune,* who visited the publisher at his office, described his qualifications: "Bernarr Macfadden, apostle of the body beautiful, healthy bathing suits and a cracked wheat diet, has heard the People's Voice, and he is not averse to doing his setting up exercises in the White House." Believing that he would "make the perfect Republican nominee in 1936," he would undertake "a cross-country marathon to spread the gospel." He was quoted as saying: "If the lightning strikes me, I'll be a willing victim. . . . If they nominate an old-line Republican, they'll be beaten worse'n last time, sure as shooting. They've just got to nominate a man who'll draw some Democratic votes, someone outside the political field. That's my chance. Of course this Republican gang like to hold everything in their hands, but I'm going to get inside them and push them the right way. It's just my duty."[28]

The reporter described BM in his large, plush, richly paneled office in the Chanin Building. Sitting behind a huge carved desk littered with manuscripts and a little pile of toothpicks was this "wiry old man" whose "small sunken eyes shone with zeal" and whose "pale sky-blue" hair formed a halo around his face, "full of authentic cracker-barrel philosopher wrinkles" matching the "careless creases of his blue suit."[29]

Macfadden said it was every businessman's duty to oppose the New Deal, that the condition of the country was worse than in 1932. He hinted that he would strongly support states' rights, governmental economy, and "annulling all fool laws," especially those encouraging "blackmailing, racketeering crooks and their legal leeches." After the publisher allowed that his magazines, which sold 15,000,000 copies every month, would help his cause because human emotion and passion were the same the world over, the interviewer contrasted the "plentiful doses of human emotion and passion" served the readers with BM's austere way of life. "I've tried all sorts of diets, vegetarianism, everything," Macfadden explained. "Now I eat like the Chinese and Japanese. And I generally fast two days a week. It has an amazing influence on your mentality and physique. Your mind clears. You have a tremendous mental power." He could solve any problem when he fasted, was in fine health and strong enough for any task. The *Herald Tribune's* report of the interview irritated the physical culturist, who nevertheless cannily promoted himself in an editorial, "Liberty's Publisher Accused of 'Muscling In' on the Republican Presidential Nomination."[30]

On February 15, 1936, he encountered some raucus heckling as he tried to speak at the annual banquet of the Advertising Club of Baltimore. He had prepared a long speech attacking the Roosevelt administration, and no sooner had he been introduced by the governor of Maryland than he heard moans, groans, and shouts of "Hurrah for Roosevelt!" The governor quieted the audience, and BM began again. More heckling and hooting. The radio broadcaster cut short his transmission. Resuming his talk, the publisher warned of enemies in the government, "secret advisers" of the president, and when he mentioned Felix Frankfurter as "listed in the Red Network" (an anti-Communist compilation that exploited the guilt-by-association technique), someone shouted "Keep politics out," which led to a round of applause. As Macfadden accused Roosevelt of deserting the Democratic platform, he was interrupted with the cry "Conditions govern platforms!" When he charged that the government was spending the people's taxes at

the rate of eighteen to twenty million dollars a day, the audience grew
so noisy that the club president pleaded for order and asked the
hecklers to leave. Nobody moved. The speaker had hardly resumed
when a "Hooray for Mr. Roosevelt!" sparked another clamor. Persist-
ing, Macfadden touched on a possible war with Japan and wildly alleged that 250,000 armed Japanese were in California and that their
fishing boats were large enough to become minelayers. At this point
the uproar was so overwhelming that the publisher was forced to end
his talk. What he had planned for forty-five minutes had lasted only
fifteen.[31]

Undaunted and eager for political combat, Macfadden wrote a
Liberty editorial proposing a potpourri of twenty-two planks for the
Republican platform, including abandonment of "the wild experiments
of fanciful and inexperienced dreamers," a balanced budget, elimination or reduction of bureaucratic expenses and "Socialistic activities"
that usurped the authority of Congress. He would repeal excessive
and discriminatory taxes and return power to the states, including the
supervision of federal relief. He would make every worker a business
partner through profit sharing, insure gainful jobs for youth, extend
old age insurance to the crippled and the helpless, and give farmers
free space for markets in thickly populated communities. He would
take the government out of business and bar the issuance of tax-free
bonds to make it easier for private businesses to raise capital. He was
for a protective tariff and stronger national defense.[32] Although he
did not lack sympathy for little people, victims of the depression, his
plainly conservative proposals reflected much of the anti-New Deal
rhetoric of the time.

The physical culturist was naïve in worldly matters. As gauged
by *Time*, the depth of his political thinking was suggested by his belief that Russia and Japan were planning to attack the United States.
His presidential ambitions led him to play both sides of the street,
and it cost him money. According to a company official, certain mid-
western Democratic politicians met him and several of his executives
in New York and offered a deal. They confided that for $100,000 he
could control a number of delegates at the Republican national convention in Cleveland who would be uncommitted on the first few
ballots and would promise to swing to Macfadden when the convention was deadlocked. When some of his incredulous associates objected, the publisher dismissed them.[33]

During the convention, BM sequestered himself in a Cleveland
hotel room, listening to the radio with an executive he had ordered

to keep him company. He was crestfallen when his name was never mentioned on the radio. Subsequently, he fired a couple of Macfadden Publications officials who had urged the political campaign as good for the company. Four years later, however, he acknowledged that his firm had spent money on his candidacy. In view of "the great financial value" of his name being prominently mentioned as a presidential candidate, he admitted that a "very small percentage" of the advertising budget had been diverted, as he put it, to promote the company. Denying that the money was spent for political purposes, he called it "a corporation publicity proposition." The Macfadden directors knew, he asserted, that it would be impossible to obtain the nomination but concluded that it "would probably be worth half a million dollars or more to the stability of the company to have the Macfadden name prominently mentioned" for the presidency.[34]

Over the years, Mary Macfadden despairingly tried to dissuade Bernarr from his political ambition, which eventually cost him almost half a million dollars, and which she traced to the machinations of Fulton Oursler who, in her presence, had patted him warmly on the back and said he belonged in the White House. She repeatedly told her husband that he could not run the country "regardless of the amount of cracked wheat he could eat or the muscles he developed." This only made him angry. As for herself, she did not want to go down in history as "the pregnant woman of the White House." Men who lived for power, she said, "wound up in such places as St. Helena. . . . Power destroys men. It destroys happiness. Let's be happy. You can be the first happy millionaire!" With a Napoleonic gesture, hand in vest, BM retorted that Napoleon "cracked up because he wasn't a physical culturist. He filled himself full of onion soup and brandy before the Battle of Waterloo. That fixed him for keeps!"[35]

After the Republicans nominated Governor Alfred M. Landon of Kansas for the presidency, Macfadden called on him and spent the night sleeping on the bare floor of an expensive Topeka hotel suite. This amused the reporters who interviewed him in the morning and apparently did not know that he habitually slept on a hard surface. In Oklahoma City, he shared a hotel room with a business associate who, retiring late, stumbled over him on the floor in the dark. "Boss, did you fall out of bed?" asked the associate. "No," said BM, "I always sleep on the floor."[36]

Macfadden became honorary chairman of a Citizens Independent Committee, which sent out pro-Landon speakers to business groups. The committee lasted only five or six weeks, owing, Macfadden claimed, to the failure of the Republican National Committee to recognize its importance. He himself made speeches in Maine, Texas, Iowa, and California, but only in Maine did he gain support and publicity for Landon. In short, he was not taken seriously either by the Republican national chairman, John D. M. Hamilton, or by the public. He would later send to former President Hoover an anti-Hamilton editorial he had penned in a blaze of anger, hoping the former president would help oust the chairman. Hoover invited Macfadden to lunch, but the outcome of their conference is unknown.[37]

Macfadden's next political foray was to seek the nomination in 1940 as United States senator from Florida. Although he was the lessee of a Miami Beach hotel, the Macfadden Deauville, he was not a resident of Florida, but his lawyers told him not to worry. Technicalities barred his running as a Republican, so he enrolled as a Democrat after calling a meeting in "Inspiration Hall" at his hotel, where two hundred people gathered. After flying to Tallahassee to qualify as one of the Democratic candidates, he began a campaign by air to arouse enthusiasm, knowing that the newspapers did not consider him a serious candidate. He flew about the state, campaigning by loudspeaker at stops in sixty-seven counties. Sound trucks blared "Boost Florida with Macfadden." His campaign manager was Joe Wiegers, the Macfadden employee who had married Helen Macfadden.[38]

The publisher ran into difficulties. He claimed that local police harassed his sound trucks and dug up old ordinances to hinder his airplane pilots; newspapers circulated "lies" about him, and phony lawsuits were trumped up against him. He was beset by special interests offering help—for a consideration—such as the man who told him, "I control the cattlemen's vote, Mr. Macfadden. I can swing 50,000 votes your way if you'll listen to my proposition." Among the other blocs he said he could have bought were the citrus growers, the fishermen, the storekeepers, even the hatcheck girls. One of his advance agents arranged a deal to win 20,000 cigar-maker votes, but BM refused to agree to it.[39]

Repeating his well-worn themes, the publisher preached against an unbalanced budget and federal extravagance, "fanatical experiments by inexperienced brain-trusters," a bureaucracy that violated the constitutional separation of powers, price fixing, and regimentation. He promised one thousand dollars to anyone who devised an old-age pension plan "that would work." He attacked the sugar act and reciprocal trade agreements as robbing Florida farmers by forcing them to compete with peon labor in Latin American countries that exported winter vegetables, avocados, and limes. As in the past, he warned of the danger of all foreign "isms." After he remarked that a government that deprived citizens of their liberties could take the joy out of life, *Time* responded, "How to put joy back: elect dynamic Bernarr Macfadden."[40]

Always one to enjoy pageantry, particularly on his behalf, he was delighted when huge crowds greeted him at the Gainesville airport and a noisy parade of students in hundreds of cars and jalopies accompanied him to the university for a speech. He claimed to be the first candidate to organize a political parade in the streets of Miami. Led by four drum majorettes, hundreds of men and women carrying signs and banners marched down Flagler Street. The candidate followed in an open car, which in turn was followed by a sixty-piece brass band and five hundred boy salesmen of *Liberty* who carried torchlights and sang "God Bless America." At Bay Front Park, the publisher addressed an audience he estimated at eight thousand, and the evening's events concluded with fireworks from a barge in the bay.[41]

BM's campaign strategy, according to his wife, was aimed at creating a springboard for his next leap toward the White House, but it was a costly failure. The incumbent, Senator Charles O. Andrews led a field of six candidates with 180,000 votes to 81,000 for Jerry Carter, the Florida railroad commissioner, and 71,000 for Macfadden; and in a runoff Andrews easily bested Carter. Macfadden attributed his defeat to the apparent manipulation of voting records in the northern part of the state. Despite the old-time politicians who regarded his campaign as a joke, the publisher pointed to his sizeable vote and said that many of his friends believed he was counted out unfairly. Had the campaign started earlier, they told him, he would have been assured of election.[42]

After his Florida failure, the physical culturist revived his advocacy of a cabinet health position. In a *Liberty* editorial he observed that Americans relied too much on healing and too little on health building. Therefore, a new cabinet post, functioning independently of the medical profession, was needed to develop a "strong and virile people"; much as one might hate the Nazis, one had to recognize the enviable German record of building physical vigor, an example that had been ignored in the English-speaking world. A health secretary, he suggested, could mold all American athletic groups into a single unit "with a view of building a nation of people that will have the same fighting spirit—the same grim determination—which gave the country its original impetus in pioneer days."[43] That such a centralizing function was totally inconsistent with his philosophy of reducing federal power over the states never occurred to Macfadden. No matter. His quaint proposal was not taken seriously.

Macfadden attended the Republican national convention in Philadelphia in 1940, where he loyally worked to win the presidential nomination for his friend Thomas E. Dewey of New York. When the convention chose Wendell Willkie, the popular and outspoken internationalist, the publisher visited the nominee at the Benjamin Franklin Hotel for a wide-ranging conference. Willkie asked about Macfadden's Alabama demonstration in youth health and asserted his own interest in health education. BM was won over. In *Liberty* editorials he pushed Willkie's candidacy, opposing a third Roosevelt term as a dangerous experiment, particularly after "nearly eight years of failure," and praising the former utility executive as a man of intelligence and character, who had grown up in a wholesome environment and had a genuine liking for people. He praised Willkie as an extraordinarily successful businessman who, if elected, would maintain constitutional government and kick out "the Communists and the Nazis on the government payroll" as well as the "wild eyed brain trusters."[44]

Temporarily overshadowed by Willkie, Dewey continued to be a Macfadden favorite. A vigorous and successful district attorney, Dewey had gained a wide reputation as a special prosecutor of crime and vice in New York, and as publisher of *True Detective Mysteries* BM had an extraordinary interest in his career. He contributed to Dewey's campaign for governor of New York State and sent joyous congratulations when he was elected. Apart from their common interest in law and order, these men had a genuine liking for each other; Macfadden addressed Dewey as "Dear Tom" in their correspondence, and Dewey called the publisher "BM." Macfadden rejoiced at his friend's nomination for the presidency in 1948. Here was a no-nonsense man of action who would dissipate the confusion caused by "school boy dreamers" of the New Deal and put an end to the inflation of the Truman years. "It would be fatal to your campaign to even 'breathe' such a thought," he wrote Dewey, "but wage increases must stop if we are to halt ruinous inflation." Like most other Republicans, BM was overconfident about the candidate's prospects. "Your election is 'in the bag,'" he exulted to his friend, whom he congratulated in advance. What Macfadden said when a victorious, grinning Harry S. Truman held up a copy of the *Chicago Tribune* with headlines screaming that Dewey had won the election was probably unprintable.[45]

While Dewey was seeking the presidency, Macfadden ran for the governorship of Florida on a platform promising to improve health standards and make the orange blossom state a world health center. He had just married Johnnie Lee [McKinney], a beautiful blonde Texas grandmother half his age who became his fourth wife, and they combined their honeymoon with a whirlwind political campaign. Taking turns with a copilot, he flew about the state in his Avion four-seater, landing long enough to make a speech before flying off to the next town. It cost him nearly $50,000, and he wound up seventh in a field of nine candidates, far behind the winner.[46]

Macfadden ardently supported Dwight Eisenhower for president in 1952, predicting that Adlai Stevenson's election would be a disaster. He dispatched nearly two thousand letters to editors across the country condemning the New Deal, which in his mind included Truman's Fair Deal. Because New Deal sympathizers had delayed "the life-saving message that the Japs were on their way" to Pearl Harbor, the New Deal was responsible for that disaster. "The New Deal gave us sentimental humanitarianism, which tries to save Korea and all the similar undependable nations, but leaves our own homes and our country indifferently defended." By "careless handling" the New Deal gave away the atomic bomb. The New Deal brought "back-breaking taxes," and Americans were now being "taxed blood-white" to arm foreign countries. During and after the campaign, Macfadden blasted the federal withholding tax as destroying initiative and ambition, the very basis of "the power that made us the world's greatest nation." To Senator Arthur Vandenberg, who was active on Ike's behalf, BM predicted that freedom from this tax would be acclaimed almost as fervently as the peace declaration after World War II. If all taxes were left to individual control, "the workers of this Nation would bring about a true adjustment in the entire field of taxation, and a fairer distribution of the burden."[47]

Eisenhower had hardly been inaugurated as president when Macfadden considered entering the race for mayor of New York City. Unable to obtain a major party nomination, he inspired the formation of an Honesty party to free the city from political greed and corruption. He set up headquarters in the Woodstock Hotel and announced that he would throw out all the politicians who had been "plundering the city these many years." He offered a grab bag of miscellaneous proposals: create a businesslike administration that would make unnecessary the city sales tax, eliminate traffic congestion, obtain double-deck subway cars, legalize gambling and use its profits for welfare, improve the schools, secure better housing and more state aid, and "purge the city of Communists."[48]

The Honesty party had difficulty rounding up signatures. The validity of its petition was challenged on the ground that signers had used the wrong election district numbers, as some numbers had been changed after the primaries. The Board of Elections then invalidated the Honesty party petition on the ground that 1,120 of the 8,306 signatures were defective. Having been discarded in this electoral shuffle, the Fighting New Yorker, as he advertised himself, finally retired from the political arena.[49] He was eighty-five years old, still supremely confident in his old-fashioned political notions, anti-Communist stance, and naïve faith that his name commanded influence with the people.

Damning the New Deal

"GOVERNMENTAL DICTATION FOR MANAGEMENT OF BUSINESS," Macfadden wired President Franklin D. Roosevelt in 1933, "would always produce dissatisfaction and altercation"; the president was "certain to lose much in prestige by unnecessarily taking part in quarrels between industry and labor." To the scrappy publisher, a rugged individualist and proponent of the survival of the fittest, it was an axiom that the government keep its hands off business; public officials lacked the expertise to direct the affairs of experienced businessmen, and costly public commissions should be abolished. The government's dealings with business, he believed, should be confined to punishing fraud and deception, capturing crooks and criminals, and protecting the public. He approved exceptional powers for the president, but only to grapple with graft and racketeering. Like many other businessmen, Macfadden misjudged the course of the New Deal, which at first he thought would cut federal expenses and reduce the national debt.[1]

In the beginning, he welcomed and generally supported the New Deal. He liked Roosevelt personally and was enthusiastic about the activism of the new president. "At last we have a real leader in Washington—unafraid, clear-headed—a great personality," he proclaimed in mid-April 1933. The extraordinary powers given him by Congress had been exerted intelligently and forcefully, and he had "already proved himself magnificently—bold, courageous, sagacious, marvelously capable." After four months BM still approved of the president and was naïvely optimistic about the New Deal. "Hurrah for Roosevelt!" he trumpeted. "Hurrah for Senator Wagner—the author of the National Recovery Bill! Hurrah for all the hard-working statesmen in Washington who have dealt the demoralizing depression such smothering blows. The war on the depression is almost won."[2]

137

As the son of impoverished farm parents, Macfadden sympathized with the depression-stricken farmers forced to sell their crops at ruinously low prices. He proposed that instead of the government buying the crops the middlemen should be required to pay whatever would guarantee the farmer a reasonable profit. Either farm prices must rise or the cost of labor fall, he asserted, and until the income of the farmer and the worker were "in proper balance" the depression would continue.[3] Although the Agricultural Adjustment Act incorporated the principle of farm subsidies, Macfadden did not seriously attack the Roosevelt farm program in its first three years.

He persistently advocated a back-to-the-land movement to alleviate unemployment. Beginning in August 1931, a dozen of his *Liberty* editorials urged government provision of subsistence homes to the starving by granting a jobless person credit to buy a modest house, farm implements, and a cow or chickens. No longer an object of charity, such a family would become self-supporting by working the land. Several times in 1931 and 1932, he sent his firm's public relations counsel to confer with senators, congressmen, and influential officials in Washington to win their support, but without result. Although he cited a successful back-to-the-land campaign in Atlanta and championed a bill in Congress to aid the return of workless men to the unworked land, he was not hopeful of success. "I hardly think anything can be accomplished with the present Congress," he wrote privately. "They are a crowd of dead ones. The efficient and capable members are held back in their activities by the mutton heads."[4]

BM's views on subsistence homesteads were similar to those of Franklin and Eleanor Roosevelt months before the presidential election. In the spring of 1932, Governor Roosevelt had discussed the matter with Harry Hopkins, Rexford Tugwell, and others, and public welfare commissioners in New York were authorized to place families on subsistence farms, although Tugwell branded the idea as the fancy of "goodhearted but impractical upper-class folk with an idealized view of going back to the soil." In October, Macfadden sent to Mrs. Roosevelt a plan for a subsistence homestead conference, which at his request she gave to her husband as the Democratic presidential candidate. As president, Roosevelt convened no such meeting; but in June 1934, BM congratulated Harry Hopkins, the Federal Emergency Relief Administrator, for the "practical constructive efforts" toward establishing a back-to-the-land program. There was more talk than action, however, and one and one-half years later Macfadden was still pushing homesteads and subsistence farming, this time to provide opportunity for American youth in addition to the Civilian Conservation Corps. Two to ten acres of land, he maintained, would supply food to feed a family through the winter: "It would not bring riches, but such a life would be an immeasurable improvement over a crowded city flat or the log huts in which our pioneer forefathers lived." Temporary governmental aid might be required for the first year or two for some of the millions who would accept the offer. To give young men and women a chance to build the homes "necessary to preserve and perpetuate this nation" was an imperative duty.[5]

Pleased with federal efforts to relieve the unemployed, Macfadden preferred job insurance to unemployment insurance. "There should be no such thing as unemployment. Every one should be insured of a job," he declared. If a worker had unemployment insurance he would grow careless and wonder why he should work when he could get an income without working. Don't hand out money, BM cautioned; the dole was a last resort because it sapped the will. "Down, down you gradually descend in the scale of life until you join the oyster and the jellyfish—spineless, spiritless, without an atom of fight left in your personality." Yet he felt compassion for the helpless. He congratulated Eleanor Roosevelt for raising money for a shelter for unemployed girls, suggested that the girls could be boarded for $1.25 or $1.50 a week, and offered to recommend a cook and a woman to run the house.[6]

In the fall of 1934, he visited Reedsville, a West Virginia mining town where Mrs. Roosevelt was working to resettle unemployed miners at a project labeled "Arthurdale." The First Lady greeted him and showed him around. Impressed, he praised her for changing the lives of desperate people and with an eye to a scoop for *Liberty* induced her to write an article about Arthurdale. She decided not to release it, however, on the advice of the manager of the federal Subsistence Homestead Division, who held that further publicity would fuel the already heated controversy over what some vocal opponents regarded as her unladylike meddling in social issues.[7]

Far more significant to Macfadden were his restaurants. Early in the century he had established a chain of physical culture restaurants in several cities to demonstrate that inexpensive wholesome food could be served without losing money. They had been profitable, their numbers had increased over the years, and by 1920 his brother-in-law, Jim Williamson, had taken charge of the thriving stock company that operated them. In the prosperous 1920s they dwindled, but in December 1931, in the depths of the depression, the Bernarr Macfadden Foundation, which in effect was himself, sponsored a penny cafeteria on

Third Avenue near Thirty-fourth Street in New York to feed the unemployed and the starving. A second penny restaurant opened its doors in June 1932 in a former *rathskeller* near Forty-third Street and Sixth Avenue, where, as Macfadden's guest in August, Eleanor Roosevelt stood up at one of the white-topped tables for a lunch of pea soup, beef stew, bread, apple pie, and milk—all for ten cents. By December, when a third restaurant was opened at 125 West Twenty-sixth Street, more than 1,500,000 New Yorkers had been fed during the course of a year. A few weeks later Macfadden claimed that the three restaurants were feeding 10,000 daily for a few cents a person and made an offer to Governor Herbert H. Lehman, who succeeded FDR in Albany, to feed a million people every day on a palatable and complete diet for $10,000. So confident was he that he was ready to sign a contract if the government furnished the buildings and equipment, and as long as prices did not rise.[8]

In the spring he arranged to open in the Negro district of Washington, D.C., a penny restaurant "exclusively for colored folks." By June, two Macfadden eateries were operating in the national capital and a fourth in New York in the Old Keen Chop House, President Roosevelt's daughter Anna Roosevelt Dall complimented him for his "splendid work," and other notables likewise praised his efforts to feed the hungry. Police Commissioner Bolan commended a food ticket committee formed to sell 25-cent food tickets, which were then sent to social welfare agencies for distribution to the poor. Because the system discouraged begging, Bolan perceived the restaurants as "a very distinct help" to his department. Macfadden, who loved the limelight, happily acknowledged the tributes. By December, after two years, five restaurants had been started in New York by the Macfadden Foundation, which offered the free services of a staff member to any city wishing to open a restaurant to feed victims of the depression. By July 1934, the foundation sponsored eight restaurants: five in New York, two in Washington, and one in Chicago. But the demand for such eating places had already declined, and the cost of operating them increased.[9]

When Macfadden learned that certain labor unions, encouraged by the New York office of the NRA, wanted to organize his restaurants as if they were higher-priced commercial establishments, his ardor cooled. Nevertheless, he conducted a demonstration in Hackensack, New Jersey, of inexpensive meals for twenty-five undernourished boys and girls, four to eight years old, obtained from local relief organizations. He recommended a national committee to investigate malnutrition among children and wrote to Eleanor Roosevelt that he wished to chair such a committee and was willing to spend several hundred thousand dollars to publicize it. His appointment, he declared, would "cause every food manufacturer to make a vitamin test of his foods." Although the First Lady replied that she would take up his suggestion, no such committee was appointed. His commitment to proper nutrition of needy children was demonstrated by his donation of 2,500 oranges at a benefit party given by the New York City police and fire departments.[10]

Macfadden persisted in championing physical fitness for American youth. While attending a conference of the Aviation Division of the Department of Commerce in 1934, he was approached by Alabama officials planning to use emergency airfields as local recreation units. He suggested that they do more: establish educational centers on these fields to promote competitive athletics and teach young men and women "the principles of American government." The Alabama Division of the American Legion cooperated with the state authorities, and Macfadden signed a contract for a "Macfadden-Legion Youth Movement." Partly because of the publisher's financial contribution, the experiment was successful. He was proud of what he called "the only substantial worth while youth movement" in the United States and hoped it would lead to a permanent national youth program.[11]

He tried to interest Roosevelt in nationalizing the project. Invited by the Roosevelts to the White House for dinner and overnight on April 29, 1935, he broached the idea, which the president appeared to endorse, appointing him to a committee to carry it out, but the publisher soon was convinced that there was no serious interest in the plan. FDR probably perceived that Macfadden would claim all the credit for a national program to strengthen American youth and undoubtedly sensed that the publisher was growing sour on his administration. Six months earlier, Macfadden had been the featured speaker at Rutgers University, where three hundred students and delegates from youth groups met as the first American Youth Congress. That his interest in young people was not limited to their physical vigor was quite obvious as he assailed government bureaucracy, urged his listeners to fight for constitutional rights, and recommended a back-to-the-land movement.[12]

In February 1938, he presented his plan for a national athletic competition to the National Youth Administration and offered to put on a demonstration in two or three states, supplying the trophies without cost to the government. He was convinced that if the country faced another war it could overcome the physical disabilities so apparent during the war of 1917–1919 only by determined action to improve the physical condition of its young people. The National Youth Administration did not accept his offer.[13]

As a successful publisher, Macfadden took a deep interest in business, and particularly in the food and publishing industries. He telegraphed the president, who was preparing a message on a food and drug bill in 1933, to consider the views of the food and drug manufacturers, wholesalers, and publishing and advertising associations, and he wrote to Eleanor Roosevelt recommending changes in the bill's wording so legitimate advertisers would not be harmed. To Macfadden, efficient, economical government meant businesslike government. In 1936, as the New Deal moved to the left, he proposed that a cabinet position be created, a secretary of business management. He was willing to apply for the job! The closest he ever got to a federal position was appointment as chairman of a large Fishery Advisory Committee set up in 1935 to advise Secretary of Commerce Daniel Roper on ways to aid the floundering American fishing industry.[14]

He blasted the income tax for restricting and hampering business. The Sixteenth Amendment was, in his opinion, one of the greatest mistakes ever made by American citizens. Admitting that the rich should pay a fair share of government expenses, he believed an inheritance tax to be the proper means of extracting their money. Wealth, when inherited, was "a curse and evil of vast consequence to those who have not earned it through hard work and sacrifice. It makes them greedy and selfish, inconsiderate and ungrateful." At death, therefore, rich men should be stripped of excess wealth acquired during life, but while alive they should be encouraged to promote their own interests. He denied that his opposition to the income tax was self-interested; his money was used solely to get his health message across. "The only kind of riches that are really worth while," he insisted, "come with dynamic, powerful health combined with the proper balance of mind, body, and soul." As he had removed himself from the multimillionaire class by giving his fortune to the Bernarr Macfadden Foundation, he had nothing to gain by advocating reduction or elimination of income taxes.[15]

Macfadden worked himself into a fury over militant labor unionism. He conceded the advantages of collective bargaining and thought unions valuable in counteracting capitalist greed. The American Federation of Labor, he admitted, had many capable officers, including President William Green, and the rank and file were good citizens.

Powerful unions, however, often dictated more arrogantly than employers, and workers had to accept the direction of organizers who thought gratitude was unimportant and had no idea of the value of cooperation. "Unionism, when it is conducted fairly and squarely, when it is intelligent and humane, is beneficent in character," the publisher declared, but when it was arrogant, greedy, "built on resentment and hate, goaded by paid agitators, the result is not unlike loosening the hordes of hell." Calling the San Francisco general strike of 1934 "a blow at the flag of our common country," he asserted that public sympathy for strikers disappeared when they "arrogantly ignore[d] the rights of the people." Labor and capital should work together. Profit sharing was a good concept, and he urged unions to demand it.[16]

Defending himself against charges that he opposed unionism, BM characteristically responded that he believed in Americanism, by which he meant that a worker had a right to join a union but also not to join. The right not to strike was as "sacred" as the right to strike. He approved "sympathetic and intelligent unionism" that raised wages and bettered living standards and he believed in limited profit sharing, but he lashed out at tactics that destroyed jobs and wrecked employers' businesses. Unwise decisions by union leaders resulted in ruinous strikes, as among the coal miners, which created a coal shortage and fostered the use of oil as a competing fuel.[17] In short, Macfadden opposed any kind of labor militancy.

Although silent when Congress passed the National Labor Relations Act, which placed federal authority behind collective bargaining, Macfadden later condemned it as promoting labor trouble and as marking the beginning of the regimentation of labor. It was a one-sided law that failed to give reasonable consideration to employers, he wrote, and it encouraged foreigners interested in the overthrow of the government to become union leaders and call strikes to foment disturbances. In its control of business and labor, the act was "fascism pure and simple," and "just another name for Hitlerism." Not only were employers' rights ignored and employees given unconstitutional privileges, but the National Labor Relations Board had acted as prosecutor, judge, and jury. In brief, the measure was "entirely foreign to our system." The Wages and Hours Law of 1938 was another "un-American threat" to business, which would add at least a million to the unemployed. This and the Wagner Act had "disheartened and disgusted employers and investors everywhere."[18]

Macfadden was enraged by the sit-down strikes organized by the CIO in the mass-production industries, beginning with the seizure of General Motors plants in Flint, Michigan, on December 31, 1936. On the second anniversary of that date he likened the conduct of many sit-down leaders to the Nazi cruelty toward the Jews. John L. Lewis's lawless "legions on the rampage" and violent pro-Communist organizers had committed viciously brutal acts. Akron, he maintained, had become "a ghost town as a result of the disorder that accompanied the efforts of Lewis and his Communistic agitators."[19]

Macfadden was a grim Communist hunter. When in 1935 the Department of Labor conducted deportation proceedings against the British Marxist John Strachey, who had been lecturing on American college campuses, only the Macfadden and Hearst publications supported the move, and after a storm of protest the department dropped the case. The Communist *New Masses* linked Macfadden and Hearst with Father Charles Coughlin and Matthew Woll as directors of a barrage against communism and observed that an editorial by "one of Mr. Macfadden's hacks" vilified Communists as "man-eating tigers" who should be strung up from the nearest lamppost by an outraged citizenry. Macfadden's editorials had amply supported the American "tories," and "for Red-baiting, for opposition to anything socially progressive and for all around viciousness, Macfadden can run rings around almost every other professional patriot in the business." His "reactionary politics" was in harmony with his "Bourbon philosophy," and he cooed to the working man with patronizing benevolence to "mask his semi-fascist attitude toward labor."[20]

Although BM was not as aggressive as Hearst in attacking left-wing college professors, he penned a wide-ranging editorial, "Communistic Agitators in Our Schools—Hang the Traitors," which was inspired by a report of Communist plans to kidnap the president and his cabinet. Macfadden disparaged local law enforcement and declared that police orders to shoot first and ask questions afterward was "good policy in this dire emergency." America's slogan should be "Death to traitors," for at any moment the nation might have to fight for its life. He was ready to risk a libel suit to exploit a story of a Chicago college girl who was said to have become promiscuous because of her belief in communism, and he gave approval to editor Oursler, who predicted that its publication would "make us a leader in the fight against Communism."[21]

The physical culturist's red baiting was most strident in 1935, when he began to take himself seriously as a political figure and when Communist membership in the United States was high, but his anticommunism persisted. In 1938, he praised the House Committee on

Un-American Activities, commonly called the Dies Committee after its chairman, Congressman Martin Dies of Texas, for having "proved beyond all possible doubt that this country is infested with traitors," supported and even encouraged by federal officials. He assailed Harry Hopkins for failing to oust "traitors" in the relief program, and he denounced the Federal Theatre Project as reeking with Communist propaganda. As nazism gravely threatened the peace of the world, he fulminated not only against red but against all followers of "European isms" in this country. Americans, he urged, should recognize the need to protect themselves from those who would undermine the American system of government. "Every hamlet, every town, every community should begin to count noses to find out definitely who want a continuance of the liberties we have been enjoying through the American system," the enemies should be labeled and a decision reached as to what should be done with them—"Deportation or a concentration camp is suggested, although Mussolini's castor oil penalty might be desirable in some cases." To Macfadden it was simply a matter of distinguishing the good guys from the bad guys. As he phrased it, "We should make a definite separation between those who are for Americanism and those who are against it." When tensions with the Soviet Union developed, he wrote to J. Edgar Hoover, asking verification of a rumor that "some units of the First Unitarian Church are now controlled by the Communists."[22] As a flag-waver, Macfadden had no peers.

His outspoken support of law and order was as much an outgrowth of his fundamental conservatism as his passionate anticommunism. He had long believed that physical culture could deter crime. Because youthful energy, if diverted into "improper channels," resulted in juvenile delinquency, society should take the responsibility for controlling it; if there were more gymnasiums there would be less need for prisons and reformatories. School athletics, he believed, not only benefited the body but also induced better reasoning power, although he never explained how this came about. He simply took it on faith that a healthy physical environment was better for youth than cramming the mind "with a vast storehouse of knowledge, a larger part of which is never used." There was only one way to cure the "crime wave" of the day: "guarantee every boy a normally developed body" and the "mental balance that comes with a perfectly adjusted human machine."[23]

The physical culturist demanded that government be more active in rooting out criminality. In 1934, after Roosevelt identified crime as a threat to American security, he congratulated the president for his interest in law enforcement. When Attorney General Homer Cummings adopted the suggestion of his friend Fulton Oursler, the editor of Liberty, and embarked on a public relations campaign for the New Deal's program of crime control, Macfadden enthusiastically approved. He had no qualms about local crackdowns. He praised the strong-arm tactics of Boss [Frank] Hague of Jersey City as showing Americans how to deal with criminals. No doubt he was pleased with H. L. Mencken's Liberty article, which took a hard line on crime and advocated death for professional criminals. Macfadden, demanding swift and certain punishment for crime, deplored what he considered the "mawkish sentimentality" of extending "sympathy for criminals," by which he meant concern for civil liberty and the rights of the accused.[24]

In 1938, Liberty awarded its first gold medal for "valor in citizenship." Its award committee, which included Attorney General Cummings and District Attorney Thomas E. Dewey, recommended that the medal be given to one Maynard Berry for his key role in sending Al Capone to Alcatraz. The next year the award went to J. Edgar Hoover, director of the Federal Bureau of Investigation, at a lavish luncheon at the Waldorf Astoria in New York. Several months later, when Hoover agreed to chair the award committee, it limited eligibility for the medal to private citizens, and Oursler offered to publicize the nominees in Liberty. In 1941, the winners were two California lumbermen who had risked their lives to capture the kidnaper of a four-year-old child, and Oursler wrote to Hoover that the award ceremony was a great success, largely owing to the presence of the head G-man and his active part in the program. Hoover wrote to Macfadden several months later, "You can justifiably feel proud of the splendid record which your publications have made during the past years, since they have come to be looked upon as outstanding mediums of furthering the cause of law and order."[25] In short, Macfadden, Oursler, Liberty, and True Detective Mysteries had a cozy relationship with the FBI.

After his early acceptance of the New Deal, Macfadden became a severe critic in 1935, and by the next year his hostility was implacable. Pump priming, he jibed, was a ridiculous slogan for "spending ourselves into prosperity." He condemned the "unparalleled waste" and "appalling inefficiency" in Washington. At a New York Board of Trade luncheon in April 1936 he accused Roosevelt of needlessly creating a new depression after having halted financial panic in the dark days of 1933, and in retrospect he lambasted the administration for its experimentation. But for the Supreme Court, he declared, the NRA would have ruined the country. Referring to FDR's sympathy for the "forgotten man," he snorted that the New Dealers "found the forgotten man all right, but it was the tax collector they sent after him." Roosevelt had cast aside Jefferson and Cleveland and embraced Tugwell and Frankfurter, "crystal-gazing philosophers" who supported communism.[26]

Macfadden came to see the New Deal programs as sheer regimentation. Sometimes he branded a program as fascistic, more often as socialistic. He could not fathom why labor leaders who welcomed government intervention in the economy failed to understand that they were taking the first step toward a foreign "ism" in the United States. The people never demanded the New Deal. It was foisted upon them by an administration that usurped the powers of the states and was experimenting with 130,000,000 people through centralized crackpot legislation. Roosevelt's plan to pack the Supreme Court was a dangerous grab for dictatorial power, and the publisher demanded its defeat.[27]

Bureaucratic government was another Macfadden theme. The New Deal had harmed the merit system far more than any previous administration, he charged. Its bureaus and commissions were new instruments of power that thwarted the liberties of the people. Nearly one-quarter of a million employees had been added to the federal payroll, providing jobs for favorites and vastly swelling the national bureaucracy. In 1938, an administration-backed reorganization bill to reshuffle federal agencies in the interest of efficiency aroused a widespread fear of a native fascism, and opponents of the president's earlier attempt to reform the Supreme Court saw the plan as another effort by Roosevelt to subvert democratic institutions. Macfadden fired off a telegram to at least one congressman predicting that a vote for the bill was a vote for dictatorship, destruction of civil service control of expenditures, and creation of a colossal political machine as effective as Stalin's in Russia. Although federal bureaucracy tragically needed reorganization, the publisher wrote, it could be done without sacrificing democracy.[28]

Macfadden deplored the payment of farm subsidies for adding to the national debt, but even more for their political effects. The Agricultural Adjustment Act of 1938, which authorized marketing quotas, acreage allotments, parity payments, and storage of crops under government auspices would regiment farmers as a unit of a vast army to carry out the orders of the federal bureaucracy. "Santa Claus has come to Washington in a big way," he observed in 1940. "Just why the farmers should be chosen for charitable consideration is not clear to anybody." In seeking farm votes, the administration had set aside about a billion dollars for farmers who complied with the requirements set by brain trusters in the Agriculture Department. Secretary Henry Wallace, BM charged, lacked experience and sound judgment, had begun the charity handouts that would continue as long as the money lasted, and was made the Democratic candidate for vice-president in 1940 because he was expected to line up the farm vote.[29]

If Macfadden felt disdain for Wallace, he was equally contemptuous of Secretary of Labor Frances Perkins and demanded her resignation. Her attitude toward strikes, he asserted, had encouraged intimidation, violence, and lawlessness, and he found it difficult to understand her "un-American love for aliens." Since she had become secretary, 200,000 aliens had entered the country by bribery and fraud, he alleged, and 4,000 criminal aliens ordered deported by the courts in 1937 had not been shipped out. Furthermore, she had failed to push for the deportation of the Communist longshoreman organizer Harry Bridges. That she was the first woman in the president's cabinet did not impress Macfadden, who declared that most of the situations handled by the Labor Department required a "masculine viewpoint."[30]

As the Roosevelt administration sedulously courted workers, farmers, and the poor in 1936, a presidential election year, the publisher of *Liberty* launched a series of tirades against it. In an editorial timed to coincide with the election, he presented a thirty-one-item indictment of the New Deal. It was a grab bag of complaints, large and small. Apart from bureaucracy, favoritism, spending, taxing, and other threadbare themes, he accused the New Deal of abusing the power given the president, passing laws infringing the Constitution and Bill of Rights, aggravating class prejudice, reducing the standard of living, undermining the private sector by competing with private business, negotiating international trade agreements at the expense of American producers and consumers, recognizing the Soviet Union, employing Socialists and Communists, and failing to deport illegal aliens.[31]

Between 1932 and 1940, Macfadden wrote 370 editorials for *Liberty*, about 94 percent of them treating public affairs. Nearly one hundred opposed the New Deal, and more than half of these were written in the five years from 1936 to 1940. Even in *True Story*, his confession magazine, he was ready to launch a flanking attack on the Roosevelt administration. He advised editor William Rapp that a particular editorial be "as non-political as possible. In other words, Gov-

ernmental Expenditures, but at the same time indirectly condemning the present administration. I will leave it to your judgment." Rapp
tersely endorsed the memo: "! Bernarr's notion of a 'non-Political
subject'!"[32]

Apart from themes of health and physical fitness, BM's editorials
revealed a clearly conservative bias. Ten essays dealt with respect for
law, eight were on crime and gangsters, and fifteen expounded his
favorite topics of patriotism, "Americanism," and anticommunism. Although Macfadden was not highly informed on world affairs, twenty
of his editorials observed conditions and events abroad and twenty-
six sounded the alarm of preparedness in a decade of international
tension, nazism in Germany, and Japanese expansionism.

Macfadden, who condoned Japanese aggression on the Asiatic
mainland, saw a Japanese threat to the United States. Having heard
that the Japanese in Hawaii and on the American west coast were
armed, he demanded as many troops in California as there were Japanese, an increase in the air force, and a powerful fleet in the Pacific.
His anti-Japanese editorials were reminiscent of his views early in the
century, when he had written in *Physical Culture* that the Japanese
had more strength and endurance per pound than any other people
in the world and that they would make war against an unprepared
United States.[33]

Even before Hitler's rise to power, Macfadden was demanding
greater military strength for the United States, especially air power.
"The average person in the United States buys his air defense every
twelve months for about the price of one admission to a motion-picture
theater," he asserted. Opposing "peace-at-any-price fanatics," he called
the neglect of American defense forces "an unspeakable national
crime." It was much better, he declared, to risk the dangers of mili-
tarism than to allow the United States to be an easy prey for warlike
nations. If war was forced on the country, "the more hell-fire we can
inject into the fight the sooner it will be over." In 1936, he demanded
a year or two of military training to build an American army of at
least a million men and a reserve force of several million. Every young
man, he believed, should have military training. If underprivileged
boys were in military service they would learn discipline and appreciation of the value of American citizenship, which would reduce
crime in the country. It was proper that American youth should do
something for the nation while building strength in their bodies.
Pacifists, who he alleged were supported by "enemies and traitors to
this country," should, on the other hand, be detected and penalized.

The more powerful the United States, the more easily it could stand aloof from war-mad nations and their glorification of wholesale killing. After Hitler's *panzers* invaded Poland in September 1939, Macfadden advocated American supremacy in the air, and when Franklin Roosevelt made his famous call for 50,000 airplanes, BM called for 100,000. "We must prepare for war up to the hilt! Every individual must be willing to make the necessary sacrifices," he demanded. Alluding to the surgeon general's statement that 40 percent of the American people were starving from malnutrition, Macfadden returned to his old theme of physical training.[34]

For half a century, he had preached the virtues, even the necessity, of physical culture. A strong people made for a strong nation, and weakness was a "crime." His marriage to Mary Williamson in 1913 had required that she be a living example of his principles. With their children, he expected, they would be a "physical culture family" whose experiences would be an object lesson to America and the world.

The Physical Culture Family

ADMIRED AS A LOVABLE, good-looking, wholesome woman and a wonderful wife, Mary Williamson Macfadden was an attractive ornament of Macfadden Publications in the early 1920s. Her frequent smiles animated her pleasant face. A certain roundness was obvious in the curves of her agile body. Her breasts and hips were ample but not overly large. To her husband, a female's well-rounded figure and good health formed an ideal combination; he was drawn to women who were plumper than the skinny figures popularized in the flapper generation. There was nothing fashionable about Mary's apparel or appearance, which gave the impression of the kindly next-door neighbor picking geraniums in her backyard. To her husband, fashion was of no interest. In the first couple of years after their marriage, she adopted his dietary habits. She no longer drank coffee or tea in the English manner but, like him, sipped honey-flavored water. She cooperated in his exercise program, just as she had done during their honeymoon days.[1]

Beyond setting an example as the ideal wife and mother in the model "physical culture family," she helped to launch the enormously successful *True Story* magazine. As the final reader of manuscripts she pored over reams of life stories, selecting the best of those not weeded out by their first readers.[2] Eventually, when her husband revised the system of readers and set up his "ministerial advisory board" to censor whatever might get him in trouble with the law, Mrs. Macfadden became superfluous and was deprived of her editorial influence.

There were other reasons for her diminished functions at Macfadden Publications. As *True Story* reaped a golden harvest in a few years, Mary believed that money had come to dominate Bernarr. He appeared to assume that the sole excuse for failure to achieve one's ambitions was a lack of wealth. "In his mind," she reminisced, "everything had come to have a price tag and you got whatever you wanted if you could afford to pay for it." Her loss of influence over her husband was traceable to the dominating presence of Fulton Oursler, who in 1922 became his supervising editor. At least Mary thought so: "My influence over Bernarr started to wane" when he accepted Oursler as "his guiding genius—the man who would never say no to him." As the Macfadden income reached a million dollars a year, she sensed a dark foreboding. She saw herself as the captive wife of a physical culture tyrant, and she wept and prayed over her "doomed marriage."[3]

In Bernarr's mind the real issue with Mary was the change in her appearance. Her attractive, athletic body had won her the title of the most perfect specimen of English womanhood and marriage to the sponsor of that contest, but she devoured pies and whipped cream and began to put on weight. Her distressed husband got her to promise that she would reduce if he hired extra house servants, yet she continued to gain, adding fifty to a hundred pounds above her normal weight. BM claimed that her heavier, fatter appearance humiliated him because he could no longer effectively draw attention to his physical culture family.[4]

Mary's physical attractiveness—or loss of it—was a matter of first importance at home as well as at business. The Macfaddens frequently entertained guests at their Nyack home west of the Hudson opposite Tarrytown and some twenty miles north of New York City. Among their friendly neighbors was a wealthy former physical culturist and Oriental cultist called Oom the Omnipotent. Bernarr and Mary remodeled and redecorated their old house, and in its fifteen rooms and sleeping porches were copious reminders of beauty and health on every wall, portraits of BM in loincloth and tensed muscles, and pictures of Mary in a daring one-piece swimsuit and the Macfadden daughters doing headstands. Behind the swinging iron entrance gates, in a small estate shaded by elms and huge maples, was a sixty-by-twenty-foot swimming pool close to the house and a well-kept tennis court, which was flooded in winter for ice skating. An array of slides, seesaws, rowing machines, chinning bars, punching bags, rings, and trapeze indicated the presence of an unusual family. Much of their land was uncultivated, although there were gardens tended by a gardener who lived in a cottage on the grounds. Macfadden himself grew strawberries and puttered among the vegetables, and each of his daughters had her own garden plot. Above the garage was a four-room school where the Macfadden girls learned their lessons from a governess.[5] But the Nyack home lacked class.

Late in 1929, Macfadden bought a much more pretentious estate in Englewood, New Jersey, only about one-fourth as far from New York City as their old home in Nyack. Their thirty-room mansion with a green tile roof and a solarium was surrounded by twenty acres of land, graced by an enormous, fifteen-foot-deep swimming pool, tennis courts, miniature golf course and putting green, and a small lake for rowing or feeding swans, mallards, or Canadian geese. Inside the house were many framed photographs of Bernarr posing in scanty exercise attire and a gymnasium with the latest strength-building devices and an electric reducing cabinet. Believing that acquired muscular strength was inheritable, Macfadden blamed parents for the physical defects of their children, and he wished to take no chances with his own family.[6]

When he turned sixty, BM had himself insured for a million dollars, his policy being underwritten by six companies. It was supposedly the largest amount of insurance ever placed on a man his age. He celebrated his sixtieth year by commissioning movies showing his physical prowess, including scenes of him running and golfing, which he had just taken up. He had been playing tennis for five years and was good enough, he said, to beat most casual players. He walked at four miles an hour. He still used dumbbells but did not recommend them for men of his age. Although he used the palatial pool outside his door, he admitted that he was not a good swimmer and confessed that all his daughters could outdistance him. But he was satisfied: "Here I am, an old man so far as age is concerned, but my body does not show it, my strength does not indicate it." To prove his fitness to the world he hired the noted sculptor George Gray Barnard to cast his entire muscular body in bronze. The process, filmed by Pathé News, was flashed across the country in forty-five hundred movie palaces. His daughters were also sculpted. Whether they liked it or not—twelve-year-old Beverly dreaded it—they submitted to being smeared with grease and coated with plaster for life-sized statues. Byrnece's, molded when she was twelve and one-half surmounted a marble base with the inscription "Dedicated to AMERICAN MOTHERHOOD." It became a companion piece to BM's statue adorning the fireplace. As one of the neighborhood children later recalled, the atmosphere at the Macfadden home was "friendly but 'different' as our parents did not make statues of us."[7]

The Physical Culture Family, which BM assiduously publicized, presented to an outsider the picture of harmony and cooperation in healthful living. Since the death in infancy of Byron in 1922 and of BM's daughter (by his second wife), Byrne, in 1926 at the age of twenty-two, the Macfadden children numbered seven, including Helen. Mary Macfadden never knew or admitted that Helen, the eldest daughter, might be the product of Macfadden's tryst with Susie Wood, but she brought up the freckled redhead as her own, and the other four girls, Byrnece, Beulah, Braunda, and Beverly, naturally accepted Helen as their older sister. At an age when she might have been in high school, Helen had a clerical job at Macfadden Publications. Privately tutored, attractive and talented, sturdy yet graceful, she became a specialty dancer in the Ziegfeld Follies, probably with the help of her father, who knew Ziegfeld. As "the eldest of the Macfadden Venuses" she also led a dozen chorus girls in weekly physical culture drills. Eventually she wrote articles on health and beauty for *Physical Culture*. According to Fern Matson, BM's executive secretary, who was also her dear friend, Helen was closer to Macfadden than the other children.[8]

As the Macfadden children grew up the sedulously cultivated image of a happy, healthy family belied festering tensions in the household. Bernarr let his wife arrange the children's schooling after they had outgrown the tutelage of a governess. Contrary to his wishes, she refused to send them to the Englewood public school because it enrolled black children, and he resented the costly expenditures for the girls' private schooling. He wanted to send a son to a military academy he controlled, but when Mary placed the boy in another private school he refused to pay the tuition. Only after she sued him for the money did he pay to avoid adverse publicity.[9]

Bernarr and Mary argued over the physical training of their children. He claimed that his wife undermined his health crusade by depriving him of honor in his own home, degraded his efforts to inculcate physical culture concepts into their children, opposed entering them in swimming races, and ordered the governesses to deceive him. Whereas he wanted his daughters to be all-around athletes and expert dancers as well as cultivated singers and good pianists, Mary retorted that he used his family as guinea pigs, that he craved publicity and hero worship and tried to force them to yield to his "eccentric notions." Her two older daughters, Byrnece and Beulah, were subjected to a strict physical culture regimen whenever Macfadden was present to supervise. Because none of their friends lived like this, they had few playmates. The girls were too often in the company of older people and by 1930, when they were seventeen and fifteen, BM finally recognized their need to associate with children their own age, and he sanctioned plans to fix them up with carefully selected dates at parties. He regarded Byrnece, who attended the Semple School in New York, as irresponsible, undisciplined, and lacking in physical vitality. When she planned to marry he wrote her, "To meet with my approval you should have at least three months vigorous training, six months would be better . . . walk five miles daily, gradually increase to ten." She should spend at least an hour a day swimming, dancing, and otherwise strengthening her body. "Your father's only desire is for your future happiness," he professed, "and if you start wrong now, you may never be diverted to the road that makes life truly worth living."[10]

Byrnece did not choose that road. Despite her father's solicitude, and contrary to the ever-present smiling publicity photos, she regarded Macfadden as a tyrant, a fearful foreboding figure. She once appealed to him on behalf of her sisters, but he rejected her overture. As she later recalled, nobody could argue with him and succeed. His word was law, and she hated his Spartan life. In August 1931, at seventeen—although the news account gave her age as nineteen—she was liberated by marrying Louis I. Muckerman, an investment broker. Less than five years later, after Muckerman's death, she married George R. Metaxa, a New York City entertainer, but this union was unfortunate and short-lived.[11]

Beulah, Mary's second daughter, studied at Mrs. Dow's School in Briarcliff Manor, New York, and some time afterward developed a severe drinking problem. When Macfadden sent her to stay with the wife of his west coast representative she consorted with movie stars and showed up drunk every night until her hostess shipped her back east. The news got out, to the great embarrassment of her father. Beulah never overcame her alcoholism, spent the last years of her life at the Macfadden health hotel in Dansville, and was only forty-six when she died.[12]

Mary's third daughter, Braunda, was a plump and buxom girl with a persistent weight problem. As her part-time governess wrote to Macfadden, she was "a walking challenge to all your Physical Culture ideals." At Mrs. Dow's School she was put on a special diet prescribed by a nutritionist at Macfadden's Physical Culture Institute Of Nutrition. After attending the Dwight School in Englewood, and when she was not quite twenty, she married L. Arthur ("Sandy") St. Phillip, a young Newark lawyer, in the sun room at the Macfadden estate. She was unattended and given away by her mother, an odd circumstance, for as Byrnece remembered it, Braunda was Macfadden's favorite daughter, yet he was not present at the wedding. The St. Phillips settled next door to the Macfaddens in Englewood, and Sandy joined Macfadden Publications. Braunda remained overweight, perhaps because she did not take physical culture very seriously. Some years afterward, at a party in Macfadden's Fifth Avenue apartment, she and Sandy furtively drank beer and hid the cans under a bed. She died of a heart attack at the age of forty-eight.[13]

Beverly, the youngest daughter, occasionally attended the Dwight School but so irregularly that the school has no record of her. A lovable child, she had personality problems. When she was thirteen her frustrated part-time governess, who was also a writer, informed Macfadden that she had rather work twelve hours a day on an editorial job than deal with some of Beverly's emotions and social attitudes: "She is an engaging little rascal and bright as a silver dollar but she is pretty much of a hoodlum still, if I may say so, and her principal object in life seems [to be] to get somebody to spend large amounts of money on things suitable only for a chorus girl of nineteen with a rich sugar daddy on the string." Macfadden agreed with the governess that Beverly was too much influenced by her mother in her independence and spending proclivities.[14]

The youngest Macfadden children were the boys, Berwyn and Brewster, neither of whom had the slightest interest in emulating their father as a health reformer. Preoccupied with business and personal interests and his quarrels with Mary, BM failed to create a warm and loving relationship with them. In 1937 in a lawsuit with his estranged wife, with whom their sons were living, Macfadden won the right to select their summer camp and to take them to his New York office on the assumption that they should familiarize themselves with the publishing firm whose stock they would inherit. Berwyn, after graduating from the Hun Preparatory School, attended Columbia, was drafted during the Second World War and later became a photographer. When he was nineteen, apparently overheated by a family quarrel, he barged into the inner office at Macfadden Publications, whacked his father about the head, and gave him a black eye. It was said that eventually Berwyn became an alcoholic. Brewster was, in Macfadden's opinion, the best athlete in the family. An expert swimmer at the Lawrenceville School and at Yale, he left college just prior to being called to active duty by the navy. After the war he eventually settled on a career in the insurance business.[15]

Macfadden and his five daughters. Courtesy of Fulton Oursler, Jr.

By the early 1930s the already strained relations between Bernarr and Mary Macfadden worsened. The housekeeper, a Mrs. Craig, evidently took orders from BM and counteracted Mary's wishes as they struggled for control of Byrnece, Beulah, and Braunda. Mrs. Craig cooperated with Mrs. Marjorie Greenbie, wife of the writer Sydney Greenbie and herself a writer, employed by Macfadden as a part-time governess and social adviser to the girls. But her functions were never quite clear. As a sort of go-between, Mrs. Greenbie was trapped in the web of a deteriorating marriage. While keeping on good terms with Mrs. Macfadden, she reported loyally to her boss that his wife ran up bills he had not authorized, and she managed to take over from his wife the handling of educational and social arrangements for the daughters. For a rich man, Macfadden was niggardly when it came to education expenses, and if he recognized that Mrs. Greenbie was a well-bred and educated lady, he undervalued her literary talent. While using her as an adviser and social arranger, he neglected to give her work as an editor or writer. "I'm not ready," she protested, "to sell my personal services for casual driblets of money like a poor governess out of a job."[16]

Mrs. Greenbie told Macfadden that the more she saw of his family the more convinced she was that it took much more than physical culture to make a happy home life. She doubted whether making his daughters into first-rate athletes would enable them to be good wives. As she contemplated the "mental and spiritual vaccuums" [sic] in the Macfadden family, she found none of the essential emotional bonds of a healthy home life—"no affection, no instinctive loyalty, no fund, apparently, of happy childhood memories." The girls, she observed, were endowed with fine qualities but barely endured one another and, it seemed, mainly wanted to keep as far apart as possible.[17]

Bernarr and Mary had long clashed over differing life styles and deepening mutual suspicions. Considering it a waste of money, he refused to buy jewelry for her. If he viewed her as extravagant, she saw him as a cheapskate when it came to personal adornment. Once, while living in Nyack, they had bickered so intensely that livid with rage they struggled for the possession of a revolver he kept in a secret drawer. Another time he became so exasperated that he brought home a trainer to accompany him on long walks. Mary objected to the trainer in their home, so Bernarr stormed out of the house to live in the woods for several days. While the Macfaddens were in Europe in 1930 they wrangled so bitterly that she returned ahead of him to their Englewood estate, and thereafter they lived under the same roof but in separate bedrooms. Several months later, amid mutual accusations of infidelity, he threatened her with a chair, and she flung a metal razor box in his face, cutting a lip and breaking two teeth. He claimed that she was trying to kill him. She claimed self-defense.[18]

In April 1932, they decided to separate. Their agreement set up a trust fund of 2,500 shares of Macfadden Publications stock as a basis of an income for Mary of $15,000 a year. At the end of the first year, however, she complained that she had received only $10,330 and filed suit for an accounting, charging that by controlling the corporation BM had prevented payment of adequate dividends, which left her impoverished and heavily in debt. Macfadden attributed the failure to pay in full to "financial reverses" and in the summer of 1933 counterattacked by filing suit for divorce, claiming that his wife was an adulteress and a noisy, boisterous, drunken, and unfit mother. He sought custody of the children. He alleged that Mary had been intimate with a certain Baron Rosencranz, a Swedish nobleman, and he later named a West Point cadet as another co-respondent. Mrs. Macfadden denied the allegations and countersued, charging that he, not she, was the adulterer. She alleged that he had been unfaithful while at his Physical Culture Hotel in Dansville, where she had seen the hotel's female physical culture director leaving his room at a late hour.[19]

The publisher, who was living in Hackensack, New Jersey, asserted that his wife ridiculed his efforts to impart physical culture to their children, discouraged them from exercising and permitted them "to smoke and drink in swanky speakeasies." Mrs. Macfadden, who continued to live with the children at the Englewood estate, contradicted him and declared that he forced his physical culture on the children against their wills.[20] Judging from the available evidence, she accurately gauged their reactions to his stern and humorless dictates.

On June 20, 1934, Macfadden withdrew his divorce action and agreed to abide by the terms of the 1932 separation agreement, which meant paying arrears of $13,568. If the Macfadden Publications dividends failed to earn the stipulated $15,000 annually, he was now bound to pay the difference. From the annual income, $7,000 would be deducted to pay for maintenance and upkeep of the Englewood home. Satisfied, his wife dropped her suit.[21]

It is difficult to believe that Mary Macfadden had been ignorant of her husband's relations with other women during these years of turmoil, but in any event, he acted discreetly and avoided publicity in these private affairs. It was not until March 1934 that the newspapers reported a suit against him involving another woman. A Boston cafeteria manager, Soitir C. Adams, sued him for $100,000 for alienating the affections of his wife, Abbie Reinhardt Adams. Mr. Adams charged that Macfadden had seduced his wife in his Battle Creek sanitarium, where she was employed as a nurse. Mrs. Adams testified that she had left her husband and been intimate with Macfadden because she liked him better. Now a masseuse in Joplin, Missouri, she told the court that she had "enjoyed Macfadden's hikes, talks about nature, money, and 'technique.'" The physical culturist denied Adams's accusations, and a jury of seven men and five women cleared him of alienating Abby's affections.[22]

Mary Macfadden, having long presumed that Fulton Oursler's magnetic influence on her husband adversely affected their marital life, sparked a controversy with BM's chief editor in 1936 and 1937. Aware that he often was in the middle between the battling Macfaddens, the editor was equally conscious of Mary's conviction that he held hypnotic power over her husband. Referring to a photo of Ber-

narr standing on his head, she told Oursler that "he would still be
standing on his head, except for me. I put him on his feet." This was
"funny but not true," the editor recorded. In the middle of the night
on March 13, 1936, Governor Hoffman of New Jersey came to Oursler's
rooms in the Waldorf Astoria bearing an accusation of complicity in
the murder of the Lindberghs' baby. "I have a letter," he explained,
"pointing out that you were the mastermind who inspired the crime
in order to get the Jafsie articles for *Liberty*. The person who wrote
this letter and who wrote very bitterly about you was Mrs. Mary
Macfadden."[23]

When Macfadden learned of the incident he wrote Oursler, "You
would think there is a limit to the perfidy of some people, but apparently this party has gone far beyond the limit and then some and
I would consider it a big favor if she were properly penalized regardless of the publicity." If her actions were publicized, her ability to
harm anybody by her "scandalous tongue" would be terminated.[24] Thus
encouraged, Oursler sued Mrs. Macfadden for libel, asking $150,000
in damages. His complaint quoted from the letter to Governor Hoffman:

> This Fulton Oursler came into our employment about 14 or 15
> years ago with only about $50 to his name, but with an abundance
> of shrewdness through his former work as a magician and hypnotist
> and was soon able to influence Macfadden in nearly every action.
> He played upon Mr. Macfadden's love of publicity, and through his
> cleverness in this line was able to attract much publicity to my hus-
> band for which he is now held in the highest regard and esteem by
> Mr. Macfadden.[25]

The letter expressed the belief that Oursler had conceived and
conspired with Gaston B. Means and others the plan to kidnap the
Lindbergh child, without intent to kill or harm it, as a way to achieve
publicity for Oursler and Macfadden and "great financial gain" for all
the participants. "I feel sure," the letter continued

> that it was Oursler's intention, with his great influence over Mr. Mac-
> fadden to pay any large or fabulous reward for the child's return, as
> a grand gesture which would appeal to the public and prove Mr. Mac-
> fadden as a great philanthropist, a desire which is almost an obses-
> sion with my husband to be known as such and am sure he would

have gladly paid any price to gain this good public opinion, all of which Fulton Oursler knew, so Oursler had a double motive for the crime, the great publicity for Mr. Macfadden which would insure him of the permanent gratitude of my husband, also be the recipient of the large reward paid by Mr. Macfadden."[26]

Oursler vehemently denounced the statements as entirely false and intended to injure his reputation. His complaint quoted from a letter Mrs. Macfadden had written to Governor Hoffman's secretary, describing the editor as "one of the cleverest charlatans I have had the displeasure to meet," who "had much to do with causing me mental anguish because of his strong and wicked influence upon my husband."[27]

In response, Mrs. Macfadden's lawyers denied that she had written to Governor Hoffman. The letter in question, they asserted, was a forgery some blackmailer had crafted to embarrass her. They admitted, however, that she had penned two letters to the governor's secretary setting forth her suspicions that Oursler was involved in the Lindbergh case. One of her attorneys added that in spite of her request for confidentiality the governor had turned over these letters to Oursler.[28]

Embarrassed by the glare of publicity and the need to prove that the letter to Hoffman had actually been written by Mary Macfadden, Oursler grew uneasy. His lawyer, prominent civil liberties attorney Arthur Garfield Hays, maneuvered to convince Mary Macfadden's lawyer that she had no case against either Macfadden or the editor and to suggest that if the letters in question were forgeries the suit be terminated. Despite Mrs. Macfadden's admission that she had, in fact, written to the governor's secretary, a relieved Oursler decided to drop the case.[29] Who the forger was, if indeed the letter to the governor was a forgery, is a mystery to this day.

Another reason for Mary Macfadden's dislike of Oursler was his membership on the board of the Bernarr Macfadden Foundation, which BM had established in 1931 with an endowment of $5,000,000. In typically grandiose fashion, the publisher envisioned the foundation as advancing the well-being of all mankind. It subsidized his health projects, mainly sanatoriums, schools, and camps that emphasized physical culture. Considering the climate of opinion in the 1930s, it is remarkable that the foundation's charter banned discrimination because of age, sex, race or color, nationality, or creed. On the original board of directors, in addition to BM and Oursler, were Orr J. Elder, Haydock Miller (Macfadden's cousin), Lee Ellmaker, Meyer Dworkin,

Edwin Doty, Susie Wood, and Joseph Schultz, all important associates in Macfadden Publications.[30]

Evidently unable to persuade her husband to admit that he had used her money to set up the foundation, Mary sued him in 1936 for breach of contract, charging that he had transferred five million dollars to the foundation to strip her of her half-interest in the wealth they had accumulated as partners in sixteen years of health promotion. Her suit specifically named Oursler among those who had created the foundation "actually as a dummy and conduit for the purpose of holding and receiving assets" that really belonged jointly to her and her husband. In October 1914, she alleged, she and Bernarr had made an agreement that during their lives they would be partners in publishing books, magazines, and periodicals, and operating health resorts to expound "their personal precept of physical culture." By organizing the foundation, BM had broken his contract, inasmuch as the new entity deprived her of control over her assets in their partnership.[31]

Mary did not succeed in breaking up the foundation, and her strained relations with Bernarr grew steadily worse in the 1930s. She felt that he continued to betray her, whereas he no longer regarded her as physically fit. In fact, she had undergone a hysterectomy and surgery for hernia and pelvic damage resulting from childbirth. She developed a tendency toward bronchial asthma and, according to her physician, pronounced psychosomatic disturbances traceable to menopause.[32]

In January 1943, eleven years after their separation agreement, Macfadden filed in Miami for a divorce, charging extreme cruelty and a violent and ungovernable temper. Mary denied the cruelty accusation, derided his health and physical culture programs as "crackpot," and complained that he used their children as "guinea pigs in carrying out his experiments on health, sex and social conduct." He later amended his complaint against her, alleging that she had humiliated him by failing to keep her body beautiful, trim, and healthy.[33]

Meanwhile, disagreements over the children and quarrels over money fanned the flames of their hostility. Mary had accused him of threatening her: "With my money and power I will show you what I'll do to you." He doggedly fought her in court. Finally, after three years he obtained the divorce. His marriage of thirty-three years came to an official end on January 9, 1946. Mary sought a reversal, but the Florida Supreme Court affirmed the divorce in May. Eight years later she again tried to void the divorce and again failed.[34]

During these years of turmoil the physical culturist was ever more absorbed in the affairs of the Bernarr Macfadden Foundation. He had established it, he affirmed, to quiet a frequent criticism that his sole ambition was to make money. The public could now view him as the disinterested humanitarian he had long claimed to be. He had, in fact, anticipated one of the foundation's objectives, education for physical fitness, when in 1928 he purchased the Castle Heights Military Academy in Lebanon, Tennessee. Located in the foothills of the Cumberland Mountains, its 225-acre campus contained substantial buildings, gymnasium, large indoor swimming pool, athletic fields, and tennis courts. The school, which required its boys to participate in sports every day and maintained an R.O.T.C. unit, was later subsidized by the foundation.[35]

For the projects that interested Macfadden the foundation supplied the money. In 1932 it fostered a "diet marathon" at the Grand Central Palace in New York. Twelve men and twelve women were divided into three groups, and for thirty days one group was to subsist entirely on whole wheat, the second on white flour products, and the third on water alone. Macfadden, who maintained that a family could live healthfully on a bushel of wheat a month, hoped to confront the Great Depression with evidence that every hungry person in the country could be well nourished indefinitely without burdening private charity or public relief.[36]

BM arranged in 1939 for his foundation to take over the Loomis Sanatorium, which had been treating tuberculosis patients for nearly seventy years on 750 acres at Liberty, New York, and was on the verge of financial collapse. Macfadden did not expect to operate it for profit, but he hoped that it would be a practical vindication of his cure for TB: fresh air, careful diet control, and moderate exercise. To secure patients, he offered six months of free treatment to one person from each state of the union and a special low rate for "moderately advanced" cases.[37]

The foundation subsidized several schools, including an elementary school for undernourished slum children in Hackensack, where Macfadden was living. With a staff of six, including a physical instructor, it embodied the physical culturist's hope that it would be a model for similar schools throughout the nation. More elaborate was the Bernarr Macfadden School on thirty-six wooded acres in Briarcliff Manor, New York, a posh community where boys and girls from wealthier homes could progress from kindergarten to the sixth grade according to BM's ideas. The school advertised outdoor activities, corrective exercises, wholesome diet, arts and crafts, music, dancing, and hobbies to encourage self-expression. In the 1930s the foundation maintained at Tarrytown, New York, a coeducational summer camp and a school for children four to fourteen that promised to convert them from "emaciated, often unsocial-minded children, through well balanced nourishing food, scientific physical training, good schooling, intelligently and individually administered, into clean-minded, sports-loving boys and girls and good citizens." The Macfadden schools lost money, and only one was still operating when the foundation reported that it had spent $3,000,000 of its $5,000,000 endowment.[38]

Most important to Macfadden was a health resort and hotel in western New York that had been erected in 1883 by Dr. James Caleb Jackson, whose ideas had been similar to Macfadden's — bodily imbalances produce illnesses, which could be corrected by exercises, good diet, rest, and fresh air. The hotel had been a mecca for Victorian health enthusiasts but declined in the twentieth century. It came under new management, sheltered disabled soldiers after World War I, and later was taken over by a medical association whose stockholders lost their shirts. In 1929, Macfadden assumed several mortgages on the financially ailing institution, hired new personnel, and lowered the rates to attract more people. The solid four-story brick building and outlying cottages on sixty acres of wooded hillside overlooking the Genesee valley soon were full of paying guests, most of them readers of Physical Culture, which continually advertised the facilities in glowing terms. Macfadden renamed the resort the Physical Culture Hotel, installed a nude statue of himself in the lounge, held a physical culture convention there in 1932, and gave control of the institution to the Bernarr Macfadden Foundation.[39]

From the moment Macfadden stepped out of an amphibian plane at the Dansville airport on March 15, 1929, that quiet village was bathed in the spotlight of publicity. He walked to his holdings on the hill and vowed to "rebuild bodies ravaged by improper living and the use of medicine." At a welcoming dinner sponsored by the Genesee Country Association, he visualized the region as a future healthful playground, a center of athletics and horse racing. The physical culturist often celebrated his birthdays in Dansville with a party or dinner dance and, in time, paying guests from coast to coast watched him blow out candles and joined in eating wheat germ cake, while, probably unknown to him, the liquid refreshments were spiked. His showmanship did not exclude the people of Dansville, and on one birthday he held hands with a five-year-old girl on the skating rink on Main

Street. When he was in town, he often strolled about and talked with the townsfolk.[40]

Every summer, the Physical Culture Hotel received more than 200—mostly paying—guests. Macfadden sent special invitations to leading politicians. For these privileged individuals, he offered golf, tennis, swimming, and tours of the countryside. Celebrities such as Fred Allen were welcomed. Most of the guests, of course, were patients suffering from a wide variety of illnesses, who took Swedish massages, underwent alcohol, salt, ice, and oil rubs, partook of various baths—Molière, Steam and Electric Cabinet, Nauheim, Sitz, Brine, Aix, Scotch douches, and "packs and fomentations." Apart from the hydropathic treatments, exercise classes were conducted at eleven o'clock every morning, with patients performing the routines while seated in chairs. There were early morning hikes and later in the day, sunbaths. As the law required, a licensed physician was on the premises, but Macfadden saw to it that he sympathized with the methods of physical culture, including fasts. Meals were in accordance with Macfadden's teachings on food. However rigorous the routine, it was neither grim nor Spartan, and the physical culturist tried to make life at the spa enjoyable. Walks in the woods, riding, sports, swimming, and dancing were encouraged. Two or three dances were held every week. There was much singing and even a singing class, for Macfadden recognized that using the voice was mentally therapeutic and imparted a feeling of well-being. Gradually the hotel lost much of its sanitarium atmosphere and mellowed as a plush recreation resort.[41]

The physical culturist's group hikes to Dansville from New York City, a distance of 325 miles, won him national publicity. Newspaper reporters filed amusing copy with their editors, and photographers snapped pictures at the start, along the route, and at the finish. In May 1935, forty-eight men and women converged on Broadway at Sixty-fourth Street, near Macfadden's headquarters, where a squinting Mayor Fiorello La Guardia waved a pistol, which misfired, to start them off. A crowd of two hundred surrounded the energetic entrants from all over the United States, ranging from a nineteen-year-old girl from Memphis, Tennessee, to eighty-three-year-old Louis Kossuth Worthington of Bucks County, Pennsylvania. Ed Skinner, fifty-six, a circus acrobat from Lancaster, Ohio, and Ida Wolf, a fifty-four-year-old Detroit grandmother, joined many younger walkers. For nourishment en route a five-ton truck, loaded with 600 pounds of cereal and 300 pounds of raisins, brown sugar, and salt, accompanied the hikers. The participants were allowed a bowl of cracked wheat cereal and milk three times a day, and they bought fruit along the route. Macfadden wanted to prove that his walkers' diet increased their energy despite the exercise. On the New Jersey side of the George Washington Bridge the elderly Worthington dropped out, and the party gradually dwindled as it plodded on. The heaviest walker, weighing 183 pounds, was permitted to ride to Dover, halfway across New Jersey. At the Parsippany Presbyterian Church Macfadden—not a regular churchgoer—delivered a Sunday sermon before taking a plane to Washington for a conference. Rejoining the "bunion derby," Macfadden led the group into Stroudsburg, Pennsylvania. They had covered 88 miles, averaging 22 miles a day. As the "cracked wheat derby" made its way through Scranton, two hikers wearing only shorts were jailed for indecent exposure but were freed under orders to leave town within twenty-four hours. When things got dull, a plump torch singer banged on a piano, hauled by a trailer, and led the hikers in song:

> Cracked wheat our diet,
> Keeps tummies quiet,
> As we sing our song;
> Footsore and weary,
> Still we are cheery,
> As the miles roll along.

On the twelfth day the group left Corning, New York, and lunched at Bath on cracked wheat, raisins, and honey, but sixteen hikers ate meat, their first since Paterson. Eventually, on May 17, thirty-eight members of the "dietitians' derby" marched into Dansville, where they were welcomed by Mayor Charles Lemen. One triumphant walker, a sixty-nine-year-old lumber dealer from Memphis, Tennessee, claimed to have won $5,000 on bets.[42]

For several years, the hikes were an annual ritual. Beyond the physical effects of sustained walking, overnight rests at stopovers and wholesome meals, the walkers contemplated the beauty of the verdant hills and valleys, the cooling streams, the bursts of floral bloom along the way. One hiker considered the journey "a wonderful outlet for accumulated energy of a sexual nature for me, a healthy man of twenty-five, unmarried, trying to live a clean continent life." Another noticed many budding romances as the group developed a camaraderie, and he admitted getting "a great kick from seeing them holding hands."[43]

In 1936, with Mayor La Guardia again present at the start, Macfadden advanced with another group up the west shore of the Hudson to Albany, westward along the Mohawk valley and on to Dansville by way of Syracuse, Auburn, and Geneva. Of the seventy-four who had set out from New York, fifty-six made it to their Holy Grail. The next year, correspondent-commentator Floyd Gibbons fired the starting gun, and lightweight boxer Tony Canzoneri and artist James Montgomery Flagg were among those giving their blessing to the third annual "health and rejuvenation walk." Following a route south of the Catskills and along the southern tier counties of New York, fifty bedraggled men and women out of the original sixty-three finally slogged into Danvsille in a downpour. Macfadden, having left the hikers to participate in school exercises in Hackensack, was not among the finishers. The most ambitious health walk was a 617-mile journey from Philadelphia to Dansville, then through the Finger Lakes district towns to Paterson, New Jersey, and on to the New York World's Fair from June 3 to July 7, 1939. Macfadden joined the group at Dansville, walked 550 miles, and announced at the end that he "felt fine."[44] He was seventy-one years old, sponsor of an elaborate exhibit at the World's Fair, proud of his army of faithful followers, serenely confident, yet a lonely man.

He could not say he "felt fine" about his wife and family. "You need a home with a sweetheart in it, and with happy voices resounding through its rooms, glad of your homecoming," he had written in a *True Story* editorial.[45] A home was life's richest reward, he had preached, yet he now lived alone in New York City or Hackensack, begrudging Mary Macfadden the upkeep of the Englewood home, and he saw his children slipping away from his control, abandoning the precepts of physical culture. To make matters worse, he had to deal with the increasingly precarious position of Macfadden Publications.

Macfadden Ousted

ON THE SURFACE Macfadden Publications seemed to be healthy during the 1930s, but the Great Depression took its toll. "We are making Herculean efforts to keep our heads above the water and weather the storm," the publisher remarked late in 1931 after enforcing strict economy in every department. Wide fluctuations in the circulation of *Liberty* made him and his associates jittery. *Collier's* and the *Saturday Evening Post*, the magazine's competitors, had larger circulations, but *Liberty* always led in newsstand sales. When *Liberty*'s sales slumped, the circulation department blamed the editors, and the editorial department blamed the circulation staff. Macfadden agreed to fix the quota of subscriptions at one-half million to stabilize newsstand sales.[1]

With circulation one-half million less than when Macfadden had bought the magazine, Fulton Oursler as editor was finding it hard to attract good authors. In 1935, he reported to his boss that Faith Baldwin, who had once sold a novel to Macfadden Publications for $5,000, had contracted to write two serials for the *Saturday Evening Post* for $50,000 each. He implied that BM should pay his authors more, but the publisher's response was discouraging: "Apparently we discovered Faith Baldwin. As far as I can see it is our duty to continue the discovery procedure. If we can find enough of these good writers, maybe we can keep the price down to where we can afford to buy their manuscripts."[2]

Macfadden claimed to see "stupendous" difficulties in making *Liberty* a financial success and was not ready to throw good money after bad, nor was he willing to offend conservative readers by publishing information that would displease them. When Oursler suggested printing the results of the magazine's poll strongly supporting the Roosevelt administration, Macfadden feared the withdrawal of advertisers who had supported his anti-New Deal editorials.[3]

By March 1938, *Liberty's* condition had improved despite the publisher's apprehensions. Its net paid circulation even reached an all-time high of 2,850,000, more than 150,000 higher than its previous record as a Macfadden publication, and Harold A. Wise, the advertising director, announced that its net paid circulation guarantee would be increased to 2,500,000. Perhaps more than anything else, its three articles by Emil Ludwig on Franklin Roosevelt boosted the magazine's newsstand sales.[4]

Liberty's rejuvenation was a bright spot in a bleak picture. It was not enough to counter the sagging fortunes of the company, which began to run in the red to the tune of $200,000 in 1938. The order went out to slash expenses. Budgets were reduced, and on Oursler's report of these actions Macfadden wrote "Good Job!" Yet the firm continued to lose money, and in 1940, at BM's suggestion, Oursler, Wise, Orr J. Elder (Macfadden's long-time associate and second in command), and Haydock Miller (director, vice-president, and Macfadden's cousin) met every week as a steering committee to make recommendations to the boss. Even so, the firm lost more than half a million dollars that year. *True Story,* the company's dependable money-maker, was in trouble. Its higher price of 15 cents a copy had not prevented it from outselling its competitors on the newsstands, but in the late thirties, in spite of expensive newspaper and radio advertising, its sales advantage steadily dwindled. Other Macfadden magazines told the same story, which was summarized in a long staff memorandum to Macfadden on November 11, 1940. In that year, two million more copies of the firm's magazines had been printed than in 1935, yet their net sale was smaller by 1,500,000 copies; newsdealers were returning 3,600,000 more copies than in 1935. All the costs of publication had risen; paper, machinery, artwork, manuscripts, editorial and production, newsstand arrangements, advertising and shipping expenses had increased by $1,676,000. The staff called for further retrenchment and urged BM to authorize a single person to manage Macfadden Publications, but existing records do not show whether he did so.[5]

Frauds were committed in the wholesaling of *True Story* and *Liberty.* The former falsified its sales by an average of 76,697 copies, the latter by 21,185. When sales of *True Story* lost out to cheaper competitors, Macfadden offered contests and lavish bonuses to distributors for keeping up sales quotas, which made it more profitable for them to "eat," or destroy, rather than return unsold copies. Those guilty of circulation padding were never officially ferreted out, but O. J. Elder's son believed that Oursler and Macfadden were responsible for it.[6]

Since 1932, the company had paid no dividends on its common stock and was deeply in arrears on its preferred. Macfadden was beleaguered by protests from stockholders. When the firm failed to pay the bills of suppliers they tried to force the company into bankruptcy, threatening to bring criminal charges against Macfadden unless he turned over 72 percent of his stock to them. It was alleged that he had taken kickbacks from the suppliers and when this became known a group of stockholders filed suit against him and the company.[7]

BM's interests and activities, particularly since 1935, gradually alienated top executives of the company and led to grumblings of dissatisfaction among some stockholders. He had diverted corporate funds to his health projects, the Castle Heights Military Academy in Tennessee, the Macfadden-Deauville Hotel in Miami Beach, and various personal enterprises to such an extent that several key officials, including kindly, fair-minded O. J. Elder, a vice-president, came to view him as a business liability. Moreover, as Macfadden ventured into politics he was seen as neglecting the affairs of Macfadden Publications. Among those who believed this was Joseph Schultz, the firm's legal counsel, who saw no point in spending corporate money to further the boss's public career.

In 1937, Carroll Rheinstrom, the efficient advertising manager of *True Story*, told Elder that he was thinking of leaving the company, and Elder took him to Macfadden's apartment for a private interview. "I want you to be president," BM told Rheinstrom. "I'm going to get rid of Elder." Rheinstrom replied that if he became president he must have complete authority, that he was (unlike Elder) unwilling to be overruled even by Macfadden. Although the publisher agreed orally, he subsequently procrastinated, offered excuses, and finally failed to produce a contract, so Rheinstrom left Macfadden Publications to join a Philadelphia advertising agency.[8]

It is possible, though it was never proved, that Macfadden's sex life got him into difficulties with his directors. About thirty years after he left the company, a lurid story was told to Fulton Oursler, Jr., son of the faithful chief editor, that Mary Macfadden suspected BM of seeing other women and that he often took unexplained trips. She hired detectives to follow him, according to the informant, and they photographed him with assorted young women in cities across the land. The pictures, said the source, were made available to the board of directors. Although the younger Oursler was unable to obtain confirmation of the story, one former Macfadden executive remarked to him that he would not be surprised to learn it was true.[9]

In April and May 1940, three suits were filed in federal court in New York charging Macfadden with a series of criminal offenses and seeking an accounting of the $1,400,000 assets of Macfadden Publications. The first was instituted on April 22 by Leon S. Brach, who owned one hundred shares of the company's preferred stock. Two days later, one Norman Cohen brought similar charges, and on May 22 Samuel and Rose Mann, owners of 117 shares of common and 50 shares of preferred stock, filed suit, listing as additional defendants Haydock Miller and Harold Wise, who were both officers and directors of the company. To the satisfaction of these complainants, the cases were combined. The plaintiffs charged that Macfadden had always treated the corporation as a personal holding company and "completely disregarded the rights of the remaining stockholders," that he owed the firm more than $400,000 arising from a private agreement that was wrongfully cancelled by the corporation, that he influenced the corporation to pay $125,000 to the owner of the Macfadden-Deauville Hotel for his personal use from 1936 to 1939, and that he caused the corporation to spend $100,000 in advertising his personal ventures. The publisher was also accused of placing his personal employees on the corporation's payroll to the extent of at least $100,000, of causing the payment of $25,000 to the Castle Heights Military Academy to his personal benefit, and of wrongfully receiving over $250,000 in royalty rights from the corporation. Since 1936, the complaint charged, he had been compensated $50,000 a year although his services were not worth that much because he had not spent all his time on corporation affairs. He had neglected to perform his duties as an officer and director, and thus was responsible for squandering the firm's property. Furthermore, he was blamed for having spent more than $250,000 of the corporation's money in seeking the nomination by the Republican party as a candidate for president of the United States. In brief, beyond concealing by devious consolidations the nearly three-million-dollar deficit expenditures of the *Evening Graphic,* Macfadden was accused of applying nearly $900,000 of the corporation's money for his personal and political expenses and paying himself a salary far above the value of his services.[10]

What appeared on the surface to be the initiative of four stockholders was really part of a conspiracy to oust Macfadden. Cohen, who launched his suit two days after Brach, had bought his stock only three days before Brach's action, and an unknown number of stockholders formed a "protective committee" to coordinate their moves. The legal mastermind of the conspirators probably was Joseph Schultz, whom BM had fired as company lawyer some time before Brach's suit. Schultz had kept a record of BM's real estate deals and remarked, "I can prove that he's taken several hundred thousand dollars from the company." As Joe Wiegers, Macfadden's son-in-law and public relations man put it, "It was common knowledge that Schultz headed the *coup* which ousted the old man." Elder, Wise, and Meyer Dworkin, the company's comptroller, all of whom were unsentimental, business-minded executives, were involved in the cabal.[11]

Macfadden was bewildered by the sudden gathering of storm clouds. From the beginning, he denied the charges. Although he held a majority of the corporation's stock, he did not seem to realize that a public corporation could not be controlled like a medieval fief, and he conducted his personal ventures with little regard for the nuances of corporation law. He was, at the time of the suit, hoping to become a United States senator from Florida, and he labeled the Brach case as a trumped up effort to injure him in his campaign. "Nothing else but political animosity," he declared, "could cause such a suit to be brought after four years of silence."[12]

In their answer to Brach's complaint, Macfadden's lawyers denied virtually all the allegations and pointed out that because BM's actions had been accepted and approved at stockholders' meetings, the complainants should have known of them at the time they occurred. These attorneys put up a stout defense. In July, the judge denied the plaintiff's motion to be permitted to take testimony and have documentary evidence produced, and later that summer the litigants reached an agreement for an out of court settlement. On February 27, 1941, Macfadden and the disgruntled stockholders worked out terms of their settlement, and after a court-appointed referee held hearings open to all the stockholders, the court approved the terms on September 2.

Macfadden had been forced out. Husky, square-jawed Elder, with thirty-seven years' experience in the company, was promoted to president; Harold Wise, director and key advertising and sales official, became vice-president in charge of advertising. Both Elder and Wise had protested directly to Macfadden his questionable use of company funds. Fulton Oursler, BM's loyal supervising editor, who apparently was extremely unnerved by the allegation that his boss was taking kickbacks, was named a vice-president and editorial director but soon retired. Haydock Miller, director and vice-president, became secretary, and Joe

Schultz was reinstated as the corporation lawyer. The only new name was Charles H. Shattuck, the treasurer.[13]

A complete account of what had happened never reached the public, and the stockholders heard a cosmetic report from Elder at a special meeting on November 25. While the terms of the settlement were being discussed, Elder recounted, Macfadden "decided to retire from the publishing business and to dispose of his stock holdings of the Macfadden Foundation. Being desirous that the interests of the other stockholders be thoroughly protected, he felt that the future management of the business could best be entrusted to certain executives who had been associated with him in the conduct of the business for many years and who were thoroughly experienced in the affairs of the company and qualified to deal with the numerous problems the company was then facing."[14]

The terms were lenient because the real purpose of the suit had been achieved outside the courtroom; if BM would retire as president and chairman of the board, the plaintiffs would not try to throw him in jail.[15]

Publicly, Macfadden declared that he had decided to step down. It was as if there had been no pressure upon him: "Having reached the age of 73 years and finding that my Foundation Enterprises are demanding more and more of my time and attention, I have decided to relinquish control of Macfadden Publications, Inc." In fact, he was angered and deeply hurt. He felt betrayed by his long-term associates. With his son-in-law Joe Wiegers, he walked in silence down Fifth Avenue unable or unwilling to unburden himself. He later asserted that he would have fought the charges instead of accepting the settlement, had he known the attitude of the officials who took control of the company. He noted that the stockholders' suit represented only one-tenth of 1 percent of the outstanding stock of the company, implying that other stockholders were satisfied with his leadership of the firm. He denied taking financial advantage of the stockholders and stressed the fact that he had cut his own salary from $50,000 to $33,750. In twenty years of publishing, he asserted, he could have drawn five million dollars in salaries, "which is twenty to forty times the amount that was falsely claimed that the company lost due to faults on my part." He compared his salary with the half-million Hearst was making and the $200,000 earned by the president of the Warren Publishing Company, a much smaller firm than Macfadden Publications. "It is indeed deplorable," he brooded, "that I have to defend myself against

executives who, at present, control the Macfadden Organization."[16]
BM could not fathom their true motives. That he ran his enterprises autocratically never occurred to him. He saw nothing wrong in his magazines' devotion of much free space to advertising his health projects, and his company's footing the bills for his personal airplanes and press agents. Indeed, in prosperous times nobody complained of his freewheeling, free-spending methods; during the depression, as income plummeted and competitors cut into sales, his activities were bound to cause criticism. He admitted that his publications had paid some of the expense of his quest for the presidency in 1935–1936, but he stoutly maintained that Macfadden Publications benefited from the publicity he generated.[17]

As Macfadden faced his critics to work out a settlement, he offered to sell all his stock in the company and all the stock held by the Macfadden Foundation to the new management group, the very people who had served him for years. The offer was accepted, and he then resigned. Four printing and paper supply firms acted as bankers and advanced the money for 22,162 shares of 6 percent cumulative preferred stock, and Macfadden agreed to pay back to the company $300,000.[18]

As part of the settlement, BM consented not to compete directly with the reorganized Macfadden Publications for five years. He did some free-lancing for several of the cheaper magazines and wrote a syndicated column for a number of newspapers until 1943, when he bought back *Physical Culture*, which the new management had renamed *Beauty and Health* but suspended in June 1942. He reissued it in pocket size as *Bernarr Macfadden's Health Review*. The survivor of his favorite publication, it offered no threat to the company he had dominated so long, and it continued to promote his health interests by advocating "not merely muscles but health." At the end of his period of noncompetition with Macfadden Publications, he had ambitious plans for a new company in which his sons Berwyn and Brewster, both in their early twenties, would be associated. His contemplated publishing empire would include detective, love story, and radio magazines. The dream never materialized, although he continued to publish the *Health Review*, restoring its former title *Physical Culture* until at least November 1947. In 1953, he was still publishing it as *Bernarr Macfadden's Vitalized Physical Culture*.[19]

Apart from writing and publishing, Macfadden was preoccupied with the properties of the Macfadden Foundation, now ten years old. In the summer of 1941, he accompanied forty-eight health hikers for

a few miles near the end of their long trek to the Physical Culture
Hotel in Dansville, New York. He visited this flourishing health spa
from time to time, often to generate publicity for himself, but he did
not spend long periods there. Elsewhere he had troubles. The Loomis
Sanatorium for tubercular patients in Liberty, New York, which the
foundation had rehabilitated to the tune of nearly $90,000, was faced
with an attempt by Sullivan County to take it over for a fraction of
the foundation's investment. In Miami Beach, the Macfadden-
Deauville Hotel, a resort that Macfadden had acquired on a thirty-
three-year lease in 1935, was occupied by the United States Army late
in 1942, and after it was returned BM had difficulties with the owner,
the Deauville Corporation, guided by Lucy Cotton Thomas, former
musical comedy star and a business woman.[20]

Over the years, Macfadden had spent nearly half a million dollars
refurbishing the hotel, erecting a third story, and adding nearly a hundred rooms, and after a few years of heavy losses put the resort on
a paying basis. He had agreed to pay the lessor 15 percent of the income from renting out concessions, but unfortunately his lawyer had
neglected to insert the word "rental" in the lease. Taking advantage
of this omission, the Deauville Corporation sued Macfadden, demanding 50 percent of the gross income of the hotel and alleging that he
owed half a million dollars in arrears on rent. The physical culturist
complained that Lucy Thomas, "wife of a fake Russian prince," was
seeking "by treachery and probably by perjured evidence to rob us of
this lease." The Florida trial court ruled against him, however, and
the ruling was upheld on appeal. Desperately casting about for a dependable lawyer to help save his investment, he eventually found one
to his liking, almost by accident. He read in the Pismo Beach (California) *American Vegetarian* about the acquittal of a client defended
by one Harry Gilgulin, a wiry little man who was also a vegetarian
health enthusiast. On the strength of that performance, BM hired Gilgulin. The new attorney was shrewd and resourceful. He asked where
the lease had been drawn, and when Macfadden replied "in New York"
he pointed out that only New York law applied and that the lawyers
had no right to argue the case under Florida law. He then went to
Florida and induced Macfadden's Florida lawyers to move that the proceedings be vacated, which they did, and the case was dropped. Nevertheless, in spite of this brilliant maneuver, the publisher was not in
the clear. The hotel was costly to maintain, and in 1949, unable to
meet his financial obligations, Macfadden lost control of the Deauville, a total investment for him of one million dollars. About one

year later, the resort was acquired by E. M. Loewe, the Boston theater chain operator.[21]

In the years since he was forced out of Macfadden Publications, the physical culturist kept his eyes on public affairs, and although he no longer had *Liberty* as a mouthpiece, he remained firmly attached to the Republican party. He admired Thomas E. Dewey and offered to help elect the dapper district attorney as governor of New York in 1942. Contributing $500 to the cause, he pinned his hopes on Dewey as a possible president: "If you can win this fight with a big lead, you are bound to be drafted for the presidency at the next election—whether or not you want it. And God only knows we need a change!" After Dewey's election, a delighted Macfadden congratulated the former racket buster, asserting with his usual aggressiveness, "I have been fighting a racket for 50 years. It is so powerfully installed that I am inclined to give up at times." He was referring, of course, to the American Medical Association. When six years later the Republicans renominated Dewey—he had been overwhelmed by Roosevelt in 1944 —an elated Macfadden expected an end to Democratic control of the White House. On FDR's death in 1945, Harry Truman had succeeded to the presidency and sponsored the Fair Deal, which BM detested as much as the New Deal; but by 1948 it was widely believed that "Give 'em hell Harry" would be defeated. "You have a terrific job before you," Macfadden wrote the New York governor, "to bring order out of the chaotic confusion brought on by school boy dreamers associated with the 'new deal.'" He assured Dewey that he would be expected to check the ruinous inflation brought on by too-frequent wage increases, to halt foreign entanglements, and to keep the country out of war.[22]

If politics aroused the physical culturist from time to time, health continued to be his consuming passion. He was proud of his physical condition and never shunned personal publicity. On his seventy-fifth birthday he stood on his head for newspaper photographers and lectured reporters on the advantages of physical perfection. He sponsored ostentatious banquets at his Physical Culture Hotel in Dansville or, until he lost it, his Deauville resort in Miami Beach and invited prominent people to acknowledge and help celebrate his youthful vigor. As always, food and diet drew his attention. When he learned of a Texas wheat with a high phosphorus content, he sent a sample to Eleanor Roosevelt, asserting that it eliminated the need for vitamins and minerals.[23]

He was convinced that physical culture was essential for Amer-

Macfadden celebrates his seventy-fifth birthday. Courtesy of Johnnie Lee Macfadden and with the permission of Wide World Photos.

ica's survival in a strife-torn world. Alluding, as he often did, to the sturdy American pioneers, he declared that Americans lacked their ancestors' vitality and endurance, and he predicted that unless they made sacrifices their way of life would soon disappear. It was not enough to train soldiers, he warned early in 1941; the entire nation, competing with totalitarian regimes in a world controlled by brute force, should be prepared to meet Hitler's legions in a possible war. Ten days before the Japanese attack on Pearl Harbor, he wrote to Eleanor Roosevelt urging a federal subsidy for prizes to be awarded in championship games in every American village, town, and city. It might cost the government a few million dollars, he admitted, but it would benefit the country immeasurably by promoting health building through athletics. The First Lady replied that the government would not be justified in paying for the prizes. After Pearl Harbor he repeated the proposal, but she curtly responded that she had not changed her mind. Macfadden was undeterred. Ten weeks before the end of the war in Europe, he broached a similar plan to Governor Dewey, still the Republican party's bright hope for the future.[24]

After V-J Day in 1945, President Truman, who had long believed in a prepared soldier-citizenry, recommended universal training to Congress. Keenly interested, Macfadden sought an interview with the president on the subject of Americans' physical fitness, particularly on "what is not being done for youth in this country." He did not meet Truman but telegraphed congratulations to the president for his interest in building national health. "Hope you don't pass all responsibility over to allopathic physicians. They are responsible for millions of 4F's," he wrote, suggesting the appointment of lay commissioners "like Barney Baruch" and Rollie Bevans, the army football coach, and even medical advisers "where needed." A year later, he wrote to Truman's secretary, again commending the president's concern over the nation's health and observing that on the newsreels the Russians showed a vitality deplorably lacking in the United States. During the Second World War, he asserted, the men classified as 4F should have been "regimented and trained until they were in class 'A.'" That they were left to shift for themselves was a national disgrace, and unless America faced up to the danger another war would be disastrous for the country. On learning of the army's program to encourage voluntary enlistments, Macfadden wrote to the White House criticizing the failure of the War Department to stress the army's value in training for athletic careers such as boxing, wrestling, and teaching physical culture. He favored the appointment of Gene Tunney, former heavyweight boxing champion, to promote sports in the United States, and he continued to deplore the physical weakness of Americans, predicting that without radical measures to interest the people in health building "our American system of government will be headed for the scrap heap." He appealed to President Truman to tell the world that the United States "takes up Physical Culture for the honest purpose of national health and security, and not for any ulterior motive of international 'bully-ho,'" and he again urged upon Truman a miniature Olympics program.[25] He failed, however, to obtain an appointment with the president, who was careful to keep his distance from the publicity-hungry health promoter.

Despite his contempt for the Fair Deal, Macfadden approved certain of Truman's specific actions. When the president ordered the millers to turn a larger part of their wheat kernel into flour to help avert starvation abroad in 1946, he praised the order, not for its humanity but because it made inroads on the market for bleached white flour and whiskey. After Truman vetoed a bill as ineffective in restricting labor strikes, BM sent him a copy of a newspaper editorial entitled "Mr. Truman's Shoes Don't Fit," and commented, "most men's shoes are too small for them—even if yours are too large—keep them—and GROW! We have faith in you to do something better for all of us than the bill you have vetoed. I'm from Missouri too!"[26]

The physical culturist planned to publish a series of articles on the health of Governor Dewey, General Eisenhower, and Truman, but the president did not cooperate. Knowing that Truman was in the habit of taking morning walks, he inquired about accompanying the president on one of them but was informed that those walks were unscheduled and unpublicized.[27] The American public was thus deprived of homilies on health, and probably much more, by two high-spirited, nationally prominent native Missourians of humble origin, one of them perhaps facing the camera in bare feet.

In his later years, Macfadden was described as the Father of Physical Culture by his devotees. The title originated at a "golden Jubilee convention of physical culture and naturopathy" in 1947, during which six hundred enthusiasts heard him praised for his "unselfish service to mankind" and named "Father of Physical Culture and Apostle of Health."[28] Other health reformers in the land, to say nothing of those elsewhere in the world, might consider it extravagant homage and presumptuous of BM to accept the title, but he gloried in it. It seemed for him a fitting reward for a lifetime of tireless and single-minded advocacy.

After his retirement from Macfadden Publications, he not only revived *Physical Culture*, wrote articles, corresponded with well-known personages, and lectured on health topics, but also introduced Cosmotarianism. This fanciful new faith, which he developed with the help of George Schubel, a former clergyman, linked physical culture with religion. Speaking to 2,000 listeners in Carnegie Hall on "The Joyous Life—How to Live It," he explained that Cosmotarianism provided a religion through happiness "on a whole-grain thesis." Its cardinal tenet was that if man cherished his God-given body it would automatically lead to the Kingdom of Heaven. Although Macfadden conducted a Cosmotarian Science Institute and correspondence courses, his new faith failed to take hold. In addressing the American Naturopathic Association in Chicago, he offended members of established religions by calling his movement a new religion, and Cosmotarianism collapsed within six months.[29]

Religion had to be in accord with nature, Macfadden believed. He had no sense of sin. The honest promptings of one's physical nature, which others might call the temptations of the body, were frustrated by organized religion, he held. When he studied the Bible, it was to discover a religious sanction for physical culture and to show that Jesus and his apostles were the original physical culturists. Church attendance itself was often unnatural. According to Mary Macfadden, he often remarked that Christ talked to the multitudes out in the open. He did not "coop them up in a stuffy church where they couldn't breathe." As a farm boy in Illinois, starved for love and affection, Bernarr had been forced to attend Sunday School and memorize the Bible, and he came to see churches as restrictive and otherwise unsympathetic to human problems.[30] "I may know but little of the religion of theology [he wrote at the age of 33]. It is too deep for me—too much beyond me—but I know much of the religion of life, and health, and truth, and I know that if there is a hell in the future world, a special place must be kept at a white heat for the inhuman specimens of mankind who are murdering our boys by wholesale in their attempts to stamp indecency on every display of the human body."[31]

Macfadden denied that he was irreligious, yet he resisted the traditional religious creeds, and he did not worry about life beyond the grave. In the early twentieth century, his teaching vibrated to the beat of the social gospel. "There is within me," he had written in 1908, "a deep, even intense reverence for that Christianity which brings strength and light and truth into the life of any individual." As a married man, he rarely attended church, although he sent his children to Sunday School to give them enough religious education to enable them to make their own choices. In an article entitled "Bring the Churches to the People," he argued that it was the minister's duty to make his church attractive. If Macfadden were a clergyman he would show sympathetic understanding of the difficulties of everyone in his flock, and he would talk freely of love, romance, and marriage.[32]

For the "Father of Physical Culture" love, romance, and marriage were more than topics of talk. He became intimate with a woman he had met at a Cosmotarian meeting in Steinway Hall in New York. His letters to her, she recalled, were full of devotion and affection.

She spent many a weekend with him, lived for three weeks in his apartment while he was ill in December 1947, and was living with him for a week before he left for Florida in the following spring. Shocked, angered, and heartbroken, for he had given no hint of it, she learned of Macfadden's marriage to Johnnie Lee McKinney.[33]

Life with Johnnie Lee

MACFADDEN BECAME FASCINATED with airplanes and air travel in the 1920s. His first trip by air was in a hydroplane that flew around the Woolworth Building in New York. With an eye to publicity in 1928, he arranged to be flown from both the Republican and Democratic national conventions to be the first one to congratulate presidential nominees Herbert Hoover and Alfred E. Smith. In March 1929, he took delivery of his first plane, a standard Loening Cyclone C-2-C amphibian, which he christened *Miss True Story*, but he flew as a passenger until, at the age of sixty-two, with 20-20 vision and youthful muscular coordination, he qualified for a license to fly and bought a Lockheed Altair monoplane. Although beyond the usual age limit for pilots, he was not the oldest flier to get a license; a seventy-six-year-old Briton had recently qualified to be a pilot.[1]

Glorying in his new hobby, the publisher felt a magic charm in soaring above the clouds. He later claimed that he had determined to fly earlier in the century when he had seen one of the Wright brothers zoom into the air. On his first solo flight of any length, from Newark to Falmouth, Massachusetts, he flew at 4,000 feet wearing summer clothing and was shivering when he landed. It was, he remembered, the poorest landing he ever made. On several flights to a farm he bought in Vermont he put down safely in a large field near Brattleboro. By 1935, he had traveled 300,000 miles in aircraft, more than 50,000 of these as his own pilot.

His enthusiasm outweighed his ability, however. Knowing nothing about navigation, he was a poor pilot. He followed landmarks, often tilting his plane so that he could spot them. On a flight over Long Island, one of his passengers got down on her knees and prayed. He bobbed up and down through the clouds, sighting rivers, railroad tracks, and other landmarks. One of his executives who accompanied him on a flight from Cape Cod to New York told of a harrowing experience in a two-seater Stinson biplane that took off in a fog. Although visibility was zero, Macfadden shrugged off his passenger's apprehension as the plane dipped so low that it brushed the treetops. After flying nearly an hour, Macfadden landed at Newport, Rhode Island, where the frightened passenger promptly bought railroad tickets to New York.

Because BM flew without regard to weather or landing conditions, he cracked up five times over a ten-year period, but with no injuries and only minor damage. While on a speaking tour for Alf Landon in 1936, his plane plowed through two fences as he attempted a takeoff from Stinson Field in San Antonio. The next month, his plane overturned at the Falmouth, Massachusetts, airport, but he and his passengers proceeded unhurt to a Thanksgiving dinner with the Ourslers at "Sandalwood." Two years later, he was met by his daughter Beverly after his plane nosed over while landing at Westfield, Massachusetts.[2]

Undaunted, a jaunty Macfadden continued to fly, and in 1948 he campaigned by plane in a spectacular but unsuccessful effort to become governor of Florida. This political foray was unique: a campaign by air that at the same time was a honeymoon with a beautiful blonde bride who was half his age. There is good reason to believe that he chose to marry her as a way of showing that he was still virile and could project a youthful image.[3]

The blonde was Johnnie Lee, born on August 20, 1904, to Roy A. and Hattie Frances Dean McKinney of Waco, Texas. On the marriage certificate her name is spelled "Jonnie" because a Macfadden public relations man persuaded them that it would look more feminine, though in later years, with her husband's agreement, she reverted to Johnnie. She had become interested in diet at the tender age of six, preferring carrots and raw fruit to heavy Southern meals of meat and gravy. At sixteen, her favorite magazine was *Physical Culture*, and she predicted that some day she would marry its publisher, her ideal man.[4]

A girl with superabundant energy and a strong sex drive, she attended a Dallas finishing school; and while at Texas Women's College at Fort Worth, she spent more time advising classmates about beauty and boys than studying. At nineteen, she married William C. Holt, a wealthy oilman who, she said, "brought in the biggest gusher in Breckenridge, Texas." He was much older than she, their marriage was unhappy, and they separated before his early death. She brought up their children, Carol Ann and Jack, and made a living by teaching composition and diction and counseling people with personal problems. Sallying forth from bases in Hollywood, Chicago, and later New York, she built a dual career as interior decorator and sex and health lecturer, offering a creed of Cosmo-Dynamics, which concentrated on personal magnetism, love, and youthfulness. She taught women how to prevent wrinkles and how to gain an inner peace that would radiate through their outer beauty. Among her most successful lectures were her Sunday afternoon sessions in a room at Carnegie Hall, where men and women came to absorb her prescriptions for health, love, and peace of mind.[5]

In 1948 an old friend, a sports lover and ice skater, then employed in the advertising department of Macfadden Publications, told the publisher about her. The fascinated Macfadden immediately telephoned her New York apartment and demanded that she break a date to have dinner with him. Although she declined his peremptory invitation, he called her again the next morning, his voice dripping with honey, and they arranged to meet at his office in the French Building on Fifth Avenue. She was ushered past gawking editors and secretaries to the inner sanctum, where he was sitting behind a huge carved mahogany desk. He was surrounded by walls bedecked with autographed photos of Bernard Shaw, Winston Churchill, Eleanor Roosevelt, screen stars Jean Harlow, Clark Gable, Joan Crawford, and many others, and a cabinet full of trophies. When the publisher rose, Johnnie Lee was surprised that he was less than 5 feet, 7 inches in height, whereas his pictures gave the impression of a tall, even large man. He grasped her hand with a painful clasp and pulled her close to his chest. "I can't believe you are 44 years old," he exclaimed. "You look like you're in your twenties." He led her to the window and appraised her in the bright sunlight, like a Kentucky connoisseur inspecting a horse. "Your eyes are beautiful, like pools of brown velvet . . . your complexion is flawless, not a wrinkle . . . perfect teeth . . . no fillings." Then he whirled her around and pinched her bottom, announcing "fine muscle tone, fine muscle tone, but still feminine and soft to the touch."[6]

Looking at his watch, he marched her out of the office, his arms about her waist, and headed for the exit, to the gasps of open-mouthed office workers. While walking up Fifth Avenue, he explained his mission to spread his message of health and natural methods of healing. He saw her as a perfect example of a woman who lived by his principles and showered her with compliments. Then, noticing her high heels, he said firmly, "those heels must go."

They entered the elegant dining room of the New York Athletic Club. Before being seated he again pinched Johnnie Lee's buttocks, something he would do repeatedly over the years. She had never before been pinched on her fanny and she did not like it, yet, enthralled by his "sex magnetism," she did not resist. He ordered the same dinner for two: a "health cocktail" of vegetable juice, brewer's yeast and a touch of *piña colada*; a finely seasoned hamburger with baked potato, onions, and baby carrots; a fruit and almond dessert; with a honey-sweetened health tea. As they ate he patted her and squeezed her hand in his. She was thrilled, like a school kid on a hot date.

They held hands as he walked her home. Once inside her apartment, he grabbed her around the waist, lifted, and twirled her around, and exclaimed that he was going to marry her. His dominant will astonished her, but before she could open her mouth he smothered her with passionate kisses, pulled her down on a chaise, unbuttoned her blouse and kissed her neck, her chest, and breasts. He unzipped his pants, and out popped "the most exquisite sex organ I had ever seen on a man." Startled and fearing rape, she pulled herself free, shouted that she was unaccustomed to such unbridled passion, gathered up his coat and hat, and shoved him out of the apartment.

Macfadden telephoned to apologize for offending her. Still distraught over his wild animal passion, torn between caution and sympathy for a man whose principles she admired, she accepted his apology but made him promise to control himself. She was strongly attracted to him but at the same time repelled by his domineering manner and unbridled sexuality.

The following evening Macfadden surged into her apartment, his arms laden with paper packages from which he proceeded to pour onto the floor cascades of almonds, raisins, dates, figs, and soybeans. Johnnie Lee broke into laughter. This was his substitute for a box of chocolates. As they sampled the goodies he informed her that she would have to do without two items lying on her grand piano: a three-pound box of chocolates Walter Huston had given her, and a large framed picture of the actor, inscribed to her with "all my love." Seizing and pounding the frame, Macfadden roared, "This wolf must go—and all the other wolves that might be howling at your door, because you are all mine, Johnnie Lee, and I'm going to marry you. Now get that through your head." Taken aback, she retrieved the portrait and reproved him for his jealous outburst. Suddenly his demeanor changed, and he was an almost docile, sweet-talking suitor, proclaiming his love and admitting jealousy of any rivals. She told him she liked serene—

not tempestuous—relationships and for years had cultivated self-control. His immature and boisterous behavior was foreign to her nature. Moving closer, Bernarr took her hands in his, got down on his knees, promised no more such scenes, and again insisted that he would marry her. When she asked him to leave, he talked her into having another dinner with him.

Johnnie Lee discovered that the physical culturist, in some ways, put her at ease. For the first time in her life, she was not criticized for her addiction to health foods. She enjoyed holding hands with him and appreciated his attention, but she played for time. Resisting his repeated insistence on marriage, she told him of her writings and lectures on health, metaphysics, and the occult. This gave him an opening. "I'm flying down to my hotel, the Macfadden-Deauville in Miami Beach," he volunteered. "Why don't you fly down with me and do a series of lectures at the hotel on how to stay young and healthy through the years?" When she replied that she had to finish a decorating job and needed money to put her son through college, he offered her twice what she would earn if she agreed to come with him. She thought it over and decided to go, not with him but a week later.[7]

Taking off in Macfadden's private plane in the midst of a March snowstorm, she pondered her immediate future: lecturing on health and sex, and possible marriage, though she still did not know whether to take seriously his profession of love and insistent wooing. From the Miami airport, a chauffeured limousine took her to the Macfadden-Deauville, where clerks, bellboys, and maids stared at her as she registered and was shown to her room. Macfadden had left an order that she come to his office, and as she entered she beheld at their secretarial desks half a dozen voluptuous girls clad in bikinis and bras, their full, luscious breasts, almost bared to the nipples, bobbing up and down to the rhythm of their typewriting. The physical culturist pranced out of his private office, lifted and whirled her around, and proudly showed her his wall-to-wall pictures, his shelves of trophies, medals, and scrolls of honor. "Let's get into our bathing suits," he chirped, "and take a long walk on the beach and swim, and after your lecture tonight we will have another walk in the moonlight." She agreed, and on entering her room to change, discovered a bouquet of pink roses and a basket of fruit with a note: "Welcome to your new life, Johnnie Lee. Remember there are many surprises in store for you and a whole new life with me. All my love, Bernarr Macfadden."[8]

They walked silently on the sand, their physical closeness and mutual admiration substituting for conversation. Squeezing her hand as they returned to the hotel, he kissed her and reminded her to be at the lecture hall promptly at eight o'clock. That evening he introduced her as "the true miracle woman of the 20th Century," young-looking at age forty-four and "a living example of my techniques." Her talk described four requisites for health and well-being: faith in oneself or a higher power; intense desire to achieve one's dreams or ambitions; perseverance; and study to perfect one's talents. When finished she shook hands with appreciative listeners, and Macfadden glowed with pride.[9]

That night, Bernarr and Johnnie Lee walked hand in hand along the beach in the bright moonlight, the quiet waves softly lapping the shore. "It is destiny, Johnnie Lee, that we are together," he declared. "You were meant for me." As her mind flashed back to her girlhood prediction that she would some day marry Macfadden, he drew her close, sat beside her on a gentle dune, took off his shoes and asked her to do the same. When she hesitated he slid his hand down her leg, removed her shoes and impressed on her the importance of walking in bare feet: "The magnetic currents in the earth," he theorized, "could go right into your feet and up through your body, giving energy, strength and renewal to all of your cells." The physical culture lesson over, he grew softly romantic, in sharp contrast to his previous outburst of crude sexuality. Now he tenderly declared his love and caressed her face and neck. Despite her awareness of his strange changes in mood, Johnnie Lee nestled in his arms, enfolded by a "strange mysterious force." Suddenly, their embrace was interrupted by a bellboy's announcement of an important long-distance telephone call for Macfadden. They separated and she returned to her room.

During the night she was awakened when the door to the adjoining suite opened and Bernarr Macfadden, naked, was silhouetted against the bright light of his room. Startled, she jumped up, turned on her light and screamed at him to leave, but he did not move. While she stood, hands on hips, in the middle of her bed, he sweet-talked her again, eying her lacy, see-through pink nightgown. She pleaded that they should talk over their relationship in the morning. Suddenly he withdrew and slammed the door.

At seven in the morning he cheerfully telephoned her to join him at his cabaña on the beach. It was as if nothing unusual had happened. She accepted, and they walked the beach, returning to a breakfast of fruit and grains. Nothing further was said about his nocturnal intrusion. A few days later, he tried again to talk Johnnie Lee into marrying him. She had been warned many times that he was not fair in his relations with women, and so she determined to resist his sexual advances, much to his annoyance. After a week she told him he was too uncontrolled, overbearing, and unpredictable. She packed her clothing and flew back to New York.

Macfadden phoned her as often as two or three times a day, professing his love and begging her to return. She told him she needed time for seclusion and spiritual guidance. After a week of contemplation, fasting, and prayer, she sensed a revelation that part of her destiny was to marry Macfadden. Relieved of tension and uncertainty, she telephoned him that she would marry him. "I knew you would," he responded. "Catch the next plane for Miami."

Back at the Macfadden-Deauville Hotel, she was surrounded by swarms of reporters and publicity men probing for every intimate detail of her personal life. How long had she known Macfadden? Why would a forty-four-year-old woman marry a man twice her age? Could she have a satisfying sex life with him? On and on. Every day before their marriage Bernarr brought into her suite a postal mailbag weighted down by newspapers from far and near. "See, Carrot Top," he announced as he flung the bundle toward her, "The world now knows I love you . . . and from what the reporters have said to me, they love you, too." He reveled in a riot of publicity poses. Cameramen snapped him standing on his head, doing handsprings, embracing Johnnie Lee, sitting with her on a bicycle, and lifting her over his head.

On the wedding day, April 23, 1948, the bride wore a pale pink gown with V-neck and long sleeves. Pinned to her shining curls was a tiny hat with small tea roses and lilies of the valley sewn in. Her bouquet of roses, baby's breath, honeysuckle, and lilacs was a gift from Bernarr, who appeared in a white linen suit and black tie. A specially built golden Cadillac with uniformed chauffeur whisked them from the hotel to the Miami Beach Community Church, where cheering spectators behind picket fences threw rose petals at them. Five hundred guests watched the couple walk down the aisle. Suddenly, a woman leading a large white goat with a bow tied around its neck forced her way past the hired security guards at the door. According to Johnnie Lee, the woman had regularly sold goat's milk to Macfadden and was determined to assure him of a continuing supply of the precious liquid, but the *New York Times* reported that she had often been seen leading the goat in downtown Miami and that she shouted in the church, "This is against the holy word! It is illegal." Once he overcame his momentary anger at the disturbance, the groom joined the onlookers in a burst of laughter. A burly policeman nabbed the

Macfadden and Johnnie Lee three days before their marriage. Courtesy of Johnnie Lee Macfadden.

goat woman and shepherded her and the animal out of the building. In the wedding ceremony, the word "obey" was omitted. Macfadden was deeply moved, and tears streamed down his face, which reassured the bride that she was indeed, as he told her, the love of his life. Afterward, their golden chariot carried them back to the Deauville.[10]

At the portico of the hotel, another throng greeted the newlyweds as they made their way to the reception in the ballroom, crowded with relatives, friends, fans, and reporters. Johnnie Lee was delighted with the whole wheat, carrot, and honey wedding cake, topped with raisins, almonds, and pecans, and, to her pleasure, containing no preservatives. Bending tolerantly to custom, Bernarr permitted the serving of pink champagne, but for himself and close companions there was apple juice.[11]

Macfadden was ill at ease in what he called a "social hullabaloo." Perhaps because he was so awkward at it, he intensely disliked small talk and idle chatter. If the topic of discussion was not health food, exercise, natural healing, sex, or politics, he lost interest and became silent. Turning away from a lively conversation among friends, he whirled about with Johnnie Lee for their first dance to the strains of a five-piece band. She discovered that he loved dancing. His son Brewster, to his annoyance, cut in on them, and Johnnie Lee sensed his jealousy of anyone who dared to share his interest in her. It was not long before the newlyweds retired to a honeymoon suite penthouse. Surrounding them were flowers, fruit, gourmet goodies, lavish gifts of silver, paintings, and ceramics, and a mountain of letters and telegrams from all over the country and abroad, many in response to the wide media coverage of the most interesting romance of 1948.

Johnnie Lee knew that her husband was highly sexed; she rationalized his egoism by reflecting that many geniuses were egoists — and she regarded him as a genius. While he was taking a shower the phone rang, and she asked who was calling. A sharp female voice replied "Wouldn't you like to know! So this is your bridal night. Well, maybe he married you, but he is mine, *mine*. I'll never give him up. Tell lover-boy Macfadden HIS ROSEBUD called to wish him sleepless nights!" When Bernarr emerged from the shower, his appalled wife repeated the message. He blanched but quickly recovered. "Darling, I know I love *you* and chose you to be my bride," he declared. "You'll get used to this in time." He attributed the call to some crackpot and assured her that people in the public eye were subject to all kinds of harassment.

There was a knock at the door, and Macfadden admitted a maid laden with sheets and light blankets. Grinning, she asked how to make up the honeymoon bed. Johnnie Lee saw that the large bed was already made up and was perplexed at the maid's obvious giggling over what she called the bridal bed. "Go right ahead," Bernarr laughingly directed. "Make up our bridal bed on the floor."

"Does you really want it for one or two?"

"Well, we're going to start off our marriage right, so make it up on the floor for two."

Johnnie Lee's puzzlement turned to annoyance as her eyes shifted to the soft and inviting bed. After the maid left, Bernarr purred, "Now, now, honey, it's all for health's sake" and held forth on the desirability of sleeping on a hard surface. A bed sinks in the middle, he explained, cramping the spine and preventing proper circulation of the blood. "When you sleep on a hard surface like the floor, the blood is allowed to flow freely into its natural magnetic rhythm, the bloodstream is feeding, healing and repairing and recharging new cells and tissues. . . . This amazing organized network within the body was given by God to man and woman as his greatest master creation." This impressed his wife, whose health ideas paralleled his. She melted in his arms as he pulled her down to that firm, hard floor, whispering love-talk into her receptive ear.

At seven in the morning, Macfadden kissed her, stroked her face and hair, and remarked that love and sex were nature's tranquilizers. He suggested a nude swim, and they scampered like children down to the beach, where they abandoned their bathrobes and frolicked in the ocean waves. He splashed her and dove under her, pinching her backside as he surfaced. Wading to the shore, they slipped on their robes and jogged for a mile along the beach. When they stopped he told her to dress carefully for the reporters who would be present for the important news he would disclose that day. He would not reveal it to her.

The ballroom was packed with correspondents and photographers with flashing cameras. Macfadden announced that he was running for the governorship of Florida and, glancing proudly at his wife, said she would campaign for him at his side. Disconcerted at this disclosure, she could only bow and smile. It was another of his many decisions without consulting her.

They flew by private plane, barnstorming all over Florida. He called for higher ethical standards for politicians and emphasized improved health standards for a state well known as a recreational playground. Much to Johnnie Lee's relief, he lost. As she learned, he was obsessed

Campaigning for the governorship of Florida. Courtesy of Johnnie Lee Macfadden.

with politics and angrily assailed the "unscrupulous, money-driven,
power-obsessed, drinking, smoking" politicos but never told her the
details of his own political dabbling. When the campaign ended, he
rushed off with his wife to New York, brushing aside her plea to extend their honeymoon in Florida.

Macfadden's New York apartment had no curtains, no rugs, no
beds. In the words of a *New Yorker* profile, it bore "a marked resem-
blance to the cell of an especially negligent monk."[12] Its tenant slept
on the floor with an old army blanket around him.

Before they had boarded their plane for the north, Bernarr had proposed that they live apart, each of them maintaining a separate apart-

ment in the city. By telephoning each other before making a date, he assured her, neither would intrude upon the other's privacy. She was astounded. What sort of marriage was this? She protested against this weird arrangement but Macfadden was not to be denied. "Darling," he persisted, "it is because I want our marriage to last that you will keep your own apartment and I will have mine, and we will have all the excitement and romance of constant surprises in courtship." He shoved into her hands a document he had drawn up, specifying that they were to have the freedom of their own apartments but must call each other before visiting. He demanded that they both sign it. Not daring to tough it out with him, she reluctantly placed her signature on a plan that admirably suited her husband's convenience.[13]

In her New York apartment—where Helmsley's Park Lane Hotel now stands—36 Central Park South, she opened the stack of letters that had mounted in her absence. Many contained warnings about Macfadden's quirks. Most upsetting to her were those characterizing him as promiscuous, stingy with money, at least as far as women were concerned, and obsessed with his own ideas and plans. Not a few seemed to be from females he had jilted. Some were vindictive, blaming him for disloyalty and criticizing her for marrying such a shameless wretch. She crumpled to the floor and dissolved in tears. As was her habit, she talked to herself, trying to overcome her despondency by acknowledging that everyone had weaknesses. While she was gaining control of her emotion, the telephone rang. It was Macfadden's familiar voice: "This is your lover-boy. How about a date tonight? And would you like to spend the night with me at my apartment?"

They had dinner together at the New York Athletic Club, his favorite place, and walked to his apartment. After a penetrating gaze into her eyes he told her that, although he expected to live long, should anything happen to him he wanted her to carry on his health crusade. "I sincerely feel that God sent you into my life for this purpose," he affirmed. Then, with a sexy glance, he found another purpose: "As a virile man I need *you*, Johnnie Lee. You are an exciting companion, amazingly spontaneous, warm and understanding." She yielded. They passed the evening in mutual fulfillment, and she fell asleep in his embrace.

In the morning he awakened before his wife, walked to his office and phoned her to come over for a surprise. She hastened to BM's inner office and was thrilled to see a handsome lady's desk, on which stood a basket of fruit with a pink and gold label:

Johnnie Lee Macfadden's
Desk
We All Love You

Bernarr swung her around, kissed her, and announced that the office was hers, too. Then, cryptically, he remarked that she should rest for a few days. Puzzled, she sensed that he was testing her, that he was not sure she could live up to the terms of the contract they had signed.

Happy that Macfadden had chosen her over the many women who had chased after him, she returned to her apartment to ponder BM's system of being "free but married," with freedom to come and go as she wished. To please him she abandoned the decorating part of her career, but whenever she broached her yearning for a home, a place she could decorate for them both, he refused to listen. They had their separate apartments in New York, their Miami Beach resort, and the Physical Culture Hotel in Dansville; weren't they enough? Her protest that the hotels did not afford true privacy, and her suggestion that they buy a little farmhouse, only irritated him. Although they looked at a town house near Sutton Place, Bernarr resisted buying it, and when she asked to know why, he flew into a rage. From then on, she avoided mentioning a home.

Marriage to Macfadden posed other problems for Johnnie Lee. In his entirely undecorated bachelor apartment, she helped to cook dinner four times a week, but it was not served in her accustomed style. As they sat at the table the hamburger was still on the skillet, the milk in the bottle, the salt in its box, and a double handful of raw vegetables was scattered on the tabletop. She tried to spruce up Bernarr's appearance and give his old clothing to the Salvation Army, but without much success. So indifferent was he to clothes that on one occasion a stranger in his office lobby tossed him an overcoat and said, "Hang that up, will you, uncle?" and the office staff took up a collection to buy the boss a new suit for Christmas.[14]

Although the physical culturist neglected his attire, he zealously cultivated the image of youth and vitality. He kept his body in tip-top shape and terrified his wife with a new attention-getting interest, parachute jumping. It began in 1949, when he celebrated his eighty-first birthday by dropping from a small plane and touching ground safely before a crowd of spectators near his health hotel in Dansville, "the most talked about jump since the cow jumped over the moon." He wore a business suit, tennis shoes, football helmet, and a baseball catcher's knee and shin guards. As his pilot recollected, Macfadden quickly opened the door and, without warning, took a header out "as if he had suddenly remembered an appointment." He narrowly missed a stand of pines, gliding over a shed and landed on his feet in a stubbly field. Unhurt and in excellent spirits, he was embraced for the cameramen by a smiling Johnnie Lee.[15]

For several years, he celebrated birthdays by parachuting. For his eighty-third he intended to jump into the Hudson near the George Washington Bridge, but New York City police aircraft shooed him off to the north. He dropped from a Stinson monoplane some 1,500 feet above the river and drifted down near Alpine, opposite Yonkers. A gust of wind caught him and nearly tossed him against the rocky Palisades before he hit the water, back first, only twenty-five feet from the New Jersey shore. Wearing a ski suit, helmet, and life belt, he freed himself from his entangling parachute and as he was fished out of the water boasted "I feel like twenty-five." He transferred from the rescue boat to a yacht that brought him to Manhattan, and he later entertained reporters at his Park Avenue apartment.[16]

Living up to the terms of her marriage contract, Johnnie Lee refrained from questioning her husband about his personal activities yet made a point of telling him where she was going, in whose company, and under what circumstances. He told her nothing about his doings, but he was persistently inquisitive about her, especially after she enrolled in Anthony Norvell's series of lectures at Carnegie Hall on the occult, astrology, and life after death. One night, after the lecture, a well-dressed man followed her along her route home. Sensing that he was trailing her, she turned, confronted him, and boldly invited him into Rumpelmayer's cafe for a frank discussion. He admitted that he was a detective, hired by Macfadden to follow her, and said that the publisher had already spent $16,000 in spy money. Fed up with Macfadden's accusations of failure to report truthfully and even "falling for" his wife, the detective revealed to her that he intended to quit.[17]

It was probably late in 1950 when Johnnie Lee entered Bernarr's apartment in the afternoon, using the key he had given her when they were married. Expecting him to be napping, she discovered him in bed with a woman she had never seen, both of them naked. He hastily shielded his penis with his pants and ordered the other woman to leave. She dressed frantically and darted out the door. Johnnie Lee, who had been persuaded that her husband loved no other woman, was shocked and humiliated, and she sobbed uncontrollably while Mac-

Johnnie Lee greets Macfadden after his parachute jump at age eighty-one.
Courtesy of Johnnie Lee Macfadden.

fadden tried to explain his predicament. "I love only you, Johnnie Lee,"
he affirmed. "This woman is in love with me, but I have never been
in love with her." For years she had wanted him to marry her, but instead he had married Johnnie Lee—"*you*, my beloved one. . . . Now
please don't cry." He slipped his arm around her and persuaded her
to take a long walk in Central Park. Neither said a word. When they
eventually arrived at her apartment, he wanted to spend the night
making love, but she refused to let him stay, protesting that she could
not be in a loving mood after seeing him in bed with another woman.
He was incensed, and they quarreled bitterly. She accused him not
only of infidelity but of having her shadowed. "That's a lie!" he
screamed. "Now I *know*," she yelled, "you are deadly suspicious of me

because you yourself have been betraying our marriage vows. I even signed that stupid marriage contract to please *you*. I never wanted separate apartments!" He snatched his hat in anger and stalked out.[18]

Late in the night, he returned and pleaded at her door to let him in. She was awakened from a fantastic dream of nearly nude Macfadden surrounded and caressed by beautiful maidens in transparent gowns offering him lush fruit on a golden platter. Fascinated by his magnetism and male sexuality, she admitted him. He stood in the doorway offering her roses, baby's breath, and a basket of fruit, and as she accepted these tokens of appeasement, he suddenly gathered her up in a burst of passion and carried her to bed.

The next morning, as they lay entwined, his first words on awakening were, "Darling, we are flying to California tomorrow. I'm going to look at a hotel and health spa that Conrad Hilton bought and does not know what to do with." Resolving to blot from her mind the painful scene of Macfadden's lovemaking to another female, Johnnie Lee prepared herself for California, where as a child she had once lived with her family and had loved it. Now she imagined settling in the far west with Bernarr, making the home she so ardently craved.

The Macfaddens occupied a small bungalow behind the main building of the Beverly Hills Hotel until in the spring of 1951 Bernarr announced excitedly that Hilton had sold him the Arrowhead Springs Hotel and Spa in the beautiful San Fernando Valley. He described its setting close to the mountains with a thrilling vista of the valley below, told her that Indian tribes once traveled for miles to use the healing waters of bubbling springs and made mud packs for the sick to extract poisons from their bodies. Two inspired Macfaddens then stepped into a chauffeur-driven Cadillac limousine for the fifty-mile drive to the east. Once at the Arrowhead Springs, he conferred with Hilton to complete the details of their deal, while she enjoyed the panorama of mountain scenery from the window of their suite and was escorted about the spa, its springs, pools, baths, and steam rooms a beehive of orderly activity. On the second floor, she saw the rooms that her husband intended to use for massages, exercises, dance classes, and songfests. She observed the kitchen, where she asked for and was served a concoction of celery hearts, carrot, parsley, spinach, brewer's yeast, lecithin, and *piña colada*.[19]

Along a little path from the main hotel surrounded by lush wild flowers was a small cottage that Macfadden had furnished for Johnnie Lee, who convinced herself that, after all, he really did love her. Packed in barrels were a complete table setting of initialed, gold-rimmed

Haviland china and handsome crystal goblets. Bernarr would not tell her when he had bought these expensive gifts. It was part of his pattern: he did not discuss his personal affairs with her, nor did he reveal his inner thoughts. Communication with his wife was limited to his experiences in health methods and plans for health projects. His reticence made it hard for Johnnie Lee to cope with his inner conflicts, his mood changes, his jealousies and suspicions, and his unpredictable outbursts, but she rationalized her feelings by dwelling on his achievements in natural healing and his championing of pure food. With all his eccentricities, he was, she believed, a sincere humanitarian, divinely inspired and dedicated to help the sick and the suffering.[20]

When she received her personal mail, she was in the habit of slitting open the ends of all envelopes before commencing to read. One day Macfadden's personal mail was somehow mixed with hers, and she inadvertently opened one of his letters. It was a shocker:

My beloved Bernarr sexpot:

When are you coming back to N.Y. and my arms? *You know* what is *twitching*, and longing for you to be in! Darling, you *promised* me when you left N.Y. you would only be gone a little while. Now it has been 2 months. When are you going to leave her, my love, and come back to my eager arms?

All yours,
Rosebud

Johnnie Lee sank into a chair. Betrayed again! But then she reasoned that if Bernarr had really cared about this woman he would not have left New York, that she was trying to get him back by breaking up his marriage. This was the same designing female who had insultingly phoned her on her wedding night, whom she caught in sexual embrace at Macfadden's apartment, and who, playing on his suspicions, planted the seeds of doubt about his wife, inducing him to set a detective on her trail.

Suddenly, Macfadden bounded in and announced that he had to fly to New York on urgent business. Fearing to antagonize him, Johnnie Lee asked no questions and did not reproach him. She packed his suitcase and kissed him as he departed. Alone again, overwhelmed with conflicting emotions of love and disappointment, assurance and doubt, she resolved to keep herself occupied. She led morning songfests and health walks and lectured in the hotel auditorium on health, beauty, and the solving of emotional problems.

Meanwhile, Bernarr wrote and telephoned her every day, but neither knew what was on the other's mind. When he rejoined her at the cottage, he informed her that he was returning the hotel to Hilton and decreed that they fly to New York the next day. The fact was that he had sunk $100,000 in a losing venture. The Alberts Arrowhead Corporation, of which he was the sole stockholder, filed for bankruptcy listing $76,265 in debts against assets of $46,170, and Hilton resumed operation of the hotel. As one of a great chain of San Bernardino Valley health resorts that Macfadden envisioned, its business potential, as in so many of his grandiose undertakings, was far below his expectations.[21]

Without explaining why they were leaving the Arrowhead Springs, Bernarr took his zippered duffel bag and sauntered out of the cottage to a path ascending the mountain. Johnnie Lee, her curiosity aroused, followed, watched him stop, open his bag, take out a small shovel, and start to dig. Remembering that once before he had buried money and was angry when she had discovered him, she inched closer to find out whether he was burying again or digging up money to take to New York. He spotted her, flew into a rage, and demanded that she leave. She refused. Swinging the shovel, he raced toward her, but she scampered down the mountain to the safety of the cottage. When he reached the door, his mood had changed. He hugged and kissed her as if nothing had happened, but she merely smiled, concealing her determination to discover what might be in his duffel.[22]

That night, as Bernarr was sleeping on the floor with the bag close to his body, she crept alongside him and stealthily unzipped it. Using a tiny flashlight she saw rows of neatly packed bills ranging in denomination from a thousand to ten thousand dollars. She zipped up the bag and crawled back to bed, pondering her husband's obsession with burying treasure. She recalled his displeasure when she had wanted a fur coat. "I'm not buying you a fur coat to make you even lovelier than you look now," he had told her. "Why should I make you look more bewitching when men already look at you so much? One day you are going to be one of the richest women in America, because you will outlive me and inherit all my buried money, which goes into millions."

Macfadden was secretive and niggardly about money. He never allowed Johnnie Lee to write a check or share a bank account with him. He had offered to give her two columns in *Physical Culture* and make her beauty editor, with a drawing account of $500 a month, but he let her pay for personal expenses, including the rent on her apartment at 36 Central Park South.

Back in New York, they returned to their separate apartments and resumed their contractual dating. To prove his virility, Bernarr tried to induce Johnnie Lee to feign pregnancy by strapping a pillow to her waist. His plan was secretly to adopt a baby nine months later. His former wife Mary charged him, somewhat later, with announcing in the papers that he was expecting a "blessed event." "This I gotta see," she would say. But Johnnie Lee refused to cooperate. One Sunday evening, while she and Macfadden were visiting an old business associate, Walter Winchell broadcast a "flash" on the radio that she was pregnant. "She's not pregnant," said the Father of Physical Culture. "I would like to have another child but Johnnie Lee doesn't want to."[23]

At the age of fifty, she was far from eager for a living treasure but remained curious about buried treasure. One day, Bernarr drove her in their station wagon to an isolated wooded area about seven miles from the city for a hike in the country. He parked the car, reached for his little duffel bag, and set off with his wife. After some four miles he stopped, embraced her, and instructed her to sit on a nearby rock and wait for him. He strode off, and in the distance she saw him halt, take his shovel from the bag and dig a hole in the ground. According to her account, he took a metal box from the bag, placed it in the hole, and covered it with earth, jumping on it to pack it down and then scattering leaves and twigs on the surface. Waving to Johnnie Lee, he shouted, "This is for you." He rejoined her, and they returned to the city. Despite what she believed was a mystical bond that held them in mutual attraction, she did not dare to question him. She had a premonition that he would never return for his hidden hoard, and so she tried to retain in her mind the exact spot between two trees where it was buried.[24]

For his eighty-fourth birthday he suggested to her a joint parachute jump over the Seine at Paris. She had been anxious at each of his previous jumps, had never overcome her nervousness about flying with him, and now feared that he was stretching his luck. "Well, honey, if you love me we'll die together," he pleaded, but when he proposed that she wear red tights with MACFADDEN in large white letters across her bottom, she drew the line. She had no intention of exposing her buttocks, labeled or not, to the Parisians as she descended to earth. Bernarr flew into a tantrum at her refusal to cooperate. Expecting him to cool off in his usual way by telephone or a visit to her apartment with a floral peace offering, she left his Park Avenue penthouse. When she returned it was empty; Macfadden had left for France. He jumped alone, and the news pictures showed him surrounded by Parisian girls.[25]

After his escapade in France, his relations with Johnnie Lee grew more tense. He became more possessive of her, even to the point of inducing her to leave her apartment and move in with him in the penthouse. He accused her of admitting a lover through a window at night and sought to rehire the detective who had shadowed her, but the detective warned her to expect more jealous accusations and confided that he had seen Macfadden taking long walks with another woman. Already prepared for a showdown with her husband, Johnnie Lee caught him in bed with another woman. Betrayed again. She came to believe that he went to bed with nearly every girl to whom he was attracted. She confronted him, and they quarreled as never before. Finally, she told him she was considering a separation.[26]

His spirit collapsed like a pricked balloon. He begged her not to leave him and for the first time admitted that the other woman had importuned him to leave Johnnie Lee. When he had failed to respond to her demands, he said, the other woman had campaigned to discredit Johnnie Lee with false accusations but the other woman was willing to settle for one million dollars. Johnnie Lee was relieved in having finally forced a confession from Bernarr, but she was already aware that the breach between them was too wide to heal.[27]

She returned to her apartment and decided to leave Macfadden, recognizing that his uncontrollable sexuality and mercurial emotions prevented him from remaining loyal to any one woman. His promiscuity and lack of candor could not be squared with her commitment and fidelity. Whatever he may have written in his publications, marriage was to Bernarr an ego trip, a means to an end, and not the partnership of equals he had promised his second and third wives. He expected Johnnie Lee, his beautiful blonde plaything, to do his bidding, and the fact that she shared his beliefs in natural healing and wholesome foods served to enhance his narcissistic needs. Recognizing this, she filed suit for a legal separation, which she obtained in 1954.[28]

Macfadden was required to pay alimony of $1,500 a month, but after a few months he stopped paying, and he sought, unsuccessfully, an annulment of the marriage on the grounds that Johnnie Lee had misrepresented herself as financially responsible and had failed to live up to her promise to make him a home and be mother to his children. The law caught up with him in December 1954, when he was arrested in his room at the Hotel Earle in Jersey City and taken to the Hudson County jail because he could not make bail. He had been adjudged in contempt of the New York Supreme Court in two cases: for failing to pay $1,500 in alimony arrears and $5,000 in counsel fees to Johnnie Lee, and for failing to make up deficits of $3,315 in the trust he had created for his third wife, Mary. In a statement to reporters he claimed that the New York courts refused to believe that his finances had been depleted by back taxes and alimony to two wives. "This," he lamented, "is my worst Christmas in 80 years." Despite a plea to his old friend Jack Dempsey, former world heavyweight boxing champion, to help raise $10,000, he spent several days in jail until the Bernarr Macfadden Foundation put up bail. His only income at the time seems to have been $2,000 a month from an annuity, nearly all of which was eaten up by meeting judgments and back taxes. To former Governor Thomas Dewey, he fretted that he was "driven to the wall by two gold-digging women who apparently are being aided to the limit by the New York Courts and by doublecrossing and incompetent lawyers to defend me."[29]

After his release from jail, and pressed by the authorities for further payments amounting to $6,500, Macfadden kept a step ahead of the sheriff and fled to Niagara Falls in Canada. "Well, Bee, we sure have troubles, don't we," he told a hostess from his Dansville hotel whom he invited to dinner.[30] Meanwhile, the *Genesee Country Express* waggishly described the situation: "While the aged romeo sits it out in the plush Sheraton-Brock Hotel . . . his lawyers spread all the way from Geneseo to New York via Canandaigua are trying their best to keep the paws of his onetime sweetie Johnnie Lee . . . off what's left of his $24,000 per annum—after said lawyers get through cutting themselves in for their share."[31]

Macfadden returned to Jersey City, where four months after his Christmas in jail he was again arrested. On Johnnie Lee's charge that he owed her $4,000 for support plus $5,000 counsel fees, he was taken into custody on April 18. He asked permission to spend the night in his room at the Hotel Earle, which was denied, and in default of $20,000 bail he was again slapped into the Hudson County jail. Johnnie Lee later asserted that she had not approved of jailing him but that her aggressive attorney had caused it for the sake of publicity.[32] How Macfadden was released is not known, but probably his foundation once more supplied the bail money. In June, his annulment action against Johnnie Lee was blocked until he paid back alimony and counsel fees of some $7,000; but because he could not pay, his case was thrown out of court.

Overwhelmed by debts, he lived alone in a small suite at his obscure Jersey City hotel. "Jesse, I have so much trouble, so much trouble," he sighed to a physician and associate of thirty-five years, as he ran his fingers through his wiry hair. Fulton Oursler's son Will described him as "a kind of prisoner in that hotel room, with few friends and little to do, alone there with his tangled, fuzzy memories of grandeur, when he was the head of a group of magazines worth more than $30,000,000." When his daughter Byrnece came to see him, he held on to her hand and revealed his loneliness.[33]

Almost until the twilight of his life, Macfadden remained in remarkable physical condition. He weighed about 142 pounds, and the symmetry of his upper body seemed to offset his five-foot-six stature. His chest was strong and large, his shoulders and arms well formed, his abdominal muscles powerful, all kept in tip-top shape by regular exercise. Disdaining dentists, he had trouble with his teeth, his only chronic ailment, and when he had a toothache he bit or chewed on a piece of hard wood. He hoped to reach one hundred twenty-five, but in his mid-eighties he began to feel the effects of age. His acute 20-20 eyesight started to fail, and he used a small magnifying glass when nobody could see him. His legs troubled him, and his body slowed down. He had spells of depression but rejected a suggestion that he see a psychiatrist.[34]

For much of his life he had harbored a paranoic fear of being poisoned. Occasionally he persuaded his third wife to act as his food taster. He fired a maid after accusing her of trying to poison him. He suspected that the American Medical Association was hiring spies to poison the wells at his Englewood estate, and his family drank buttermilk while he had the water analyzed. He even hired private detectives to ferret out the phantom perpetrators. It was said that he kept "a stable of 'private eyes' in comfort for years." While married to Johnnie Lee, he imagined murder plots, insisted on locking doors, and tossed away any food he considered tainted. Once he dumped a dozen eggs down an incinerator chute, claiming that poison had been injected into them with a hypodermic needle.[35]

Nor was he trusting in other matters. He hired a detective to shadow Johnnie Lee because he suspected her of having affairs with other men. With her, as with Mary, he was stingy in providing money. Having an inordinate fear of robbery, he habitually wore a moneybelt, or kept his bills stuffed in various pockets, or attached a steel chain to the wallet in his pants pocket. As he grew wealthier and older he became more suspicious of swindlers and burglars. He hid money under a rug, in books, in vases, even in kitchenware, and often forgot where he had stashed it.[36]

Fantastic stories of his buried treasure passed from mouth to mouth. Based on her conversations with him, Johnnie Lee believed that he buried cash mainly to prevent his assets from being tied up in lawsuits. Although he kept some of it in a safety vault, he convinced Johnnie Lee that he had buried about four million dollars in various hiding places around the country so that he would always be near ready cash if he needed it. When she suggested that he place these bills in a vault, he told her to mind her own business: "Just don't go sneaking around after me. . . . I know what I'm doing. Some day before I die I'll give you a map, but I'm not going to die for another 50 years, so don't get anxious," snapped the physical culturist, then in his eighties. He would not tell her whether he really had a map, and she was unable to uncover his caches. One hiding place was supposed to be somewhere in the Palisades above the Hudson, another three thousand miles away, near Los Angeles. Most persistent were stories of his treasure buried on the 11,600-foot bluff behind the Physical Culture Hotel in Dansville where, according to one account, Macfadden was believed to have interred a tin pail containing half a million dollars. A slightly different version was given by a hotel employee who had glimpsed the physical culturist climbing the hill with a shovel and what seemed to be a child's lunchbox. Later, when Macfadden was seen sitting here and there on that Dansville hillside, people began to speculate that there might be several caches of buried money.[37]

Nobody has found any of Macfadden's hidden treasure. Meyer Dworkin, a publishing associate of many years, was asked about the rumor that BM buried his money or had satchels full of it and was seen shoveling; he heatedly responded "Absolute nonsense!" Another Macfadden Publications executive, affirming that the boss was pretty tight with his money, snorted, "I don't believe he buried a damn thing." In June 1960, a bulldozer operator clearing a wooded lot near Jericho and Hicksville, Long Island, which Johnnie Lee understood had once been owned by Macfadden, unearthed a green metal 50-calibre ammunition box containing $89,000 in $10, $20, $50 and $100 bills, neatly wrapped in plastic and brown paper packages secured by rubber bands. The police said it had been in the ground for several years. On the assumption that this money had been buried by her husband, Johnnie Lee laid claim to it, but on January 3, 1964, Nassau County Judge

Paul Widlitz dismissed her claim, and the treasure was divided between the bulldozer operator and the owner of the property where it was found.[38] Despite the evidence, or lack of it, tales of Macfadden's buried hoard persist.

In his last years, BM was burdened with mounting troubles and lost his zest for life. His former wife Mary, collaborating with one-time *Graphic* editor Emile Gauvreau, published a book that highlighted his shortcomings and deflated his pretensions. Described as "raffish," "uninhibited," and "merciless," this lengthy memoir was highly embarrassing to him. The protracted marital litigation, his financial distress, and the humiliation at being clapped into jail preyed on his mind. In the words of Ed Bodin, a Macfadden associate since 1948 and vice-president of the Macfadden Foundation, BM "went to pieces after that jail thing last April. Something broke in Macfadden. I saw it in his eyes." Although he smiled and danced for photographers when released from jail, he became bitter. The rebukes of his critics, which had not bothered him in the past, were harder to bear. Discouraged at public indifference to his health teachings, partly owing to his lack of standing with many physicians, the American Medical Association and the American Physical Education Association, Macfadden lamented, "People today do not want to be helped and if I had to do it all over again I would have kept the money" [instead of endowing a foundation]. He had devoted a lifetime to promoting healthful living, but he now wearily admitted that the young preferred to risk illness and death than spoil their pleasure by taking up physical culture.[39]

Early in October 1955, Macfadden suffered a digestive disorder, which he tried to cure by fasting for three days. The manager of the Hotel Earle found him unconscious on October 7 and called the police, who summoned an ambulance. Semiconscious and too weak to object—at any earlier time he would have resisted hospitalization—he was rushed to the Jersey City Medical Center, where his malady was diagnosed as jaundice, complicated by his fast. Dehydrated and helpless, the physical culturist was probed and tested, catheterized and X-rayed, and fed intravenously by a medical team. His attending physician suspected a "duct stone" as the cause of the deepening jaundice, but in view of the patient's critical condition, did not risk exploratory surgery.[40]

Meanwhile, Johnnie Lee, while lecturing at a Los Angeles hotel, was interrupted by an urgent telephone call from a friend and former Macfadden associate in New York, who informed her that Bernarr was seriously ill and calling out her name. Following a conscientious impulse to be at his side, this tender and loving woman took the next plane east, but it was too late. Macfadden had expired less than an hour after her arrival in New York. His last words were, "Please, Johnnie Lee, please forgive me."[41]

Macfadden died on October 12. Funeral arrangements were made at the Larchmont home of his eldest daughter, Helen Macfadden Wiegers. About two hundred mourners filed into the Frank Campbell funeral chapel on Madison Avenue at 81st Street in Manhattan. The Reverend Herbert C. Willenberg, pastor of the Presbyterian Church of Teaneck, New Jersey, officiated, and Rabbi Max Felshin, a director of the Macfadden Foundation and an old friend, delivered the eulogy. Both Mary and Johnnie Lee Macfadden attended with their children, as did some of BM's fellow Masons.[42] The health crusader was buried in the family plot in Woodlawn Cemetery in the Bronx. If one visits the grave site today one will see his unique headstone, a tall upright slab, topped by a relief bust of Macfadden's head and neck, with bow tie, against a circular background. Beneath it are the words:

BERNARR
MACFADDEN
1868   1955

FATHER
OF
PHYSICAL
CULTURE

The physical culturist and millionaire publisher died poor. His assets were reported as worth less than $5,000. As Ed Bodin told reporters, "The lush days are gone. They've hit rock bottom."[43]

In his will, drawn up in 1953, Macfadden left a thousand dollars to each of five nieces, a nephew, and two cousins, and a thousand to be shared equally between another niece and her husband. One-half of the remainder of the estate he willed to his two sons, five daughters, and one granddaughter, and the other half to the Bernarr Macfadden Foundation. He made no provision for his wife, Johnnie Lee, "for the reason that she has unjustifiably abandoned me and has left my home without my consent, and has failed and refused to return to me and my home."[44] Although Johnnie Lee heard that on his deathbed he had begged forgiveness for his behavior toward her, he was determined until his final illness to deprive her of an inheritance. By then it was too late.

In the years that followed, Johnnie Lee managed to survive by selling health and beauty preparations and by counseling troubled people, some of whom were hooked on alcohol or drugs, and by investing her earnings. Today her tiny, cluttered New York City apartment contains a wall of books, including a set of *Macfadden's Encyclopedia of Physical Culture*, several boxes of publicity photographs, a memoir of her life with BM, and a handsome oil portrait of him set conspicuously on the wall facing her clients.

The publisher's third wife, Mary, from whom he had obtained a divorce in 1946, continued to live alone at the Macfadden mansion in Englewood, New Jersey, and kept in shape by strenuous jogging. She sued to have her former husband's estate pay for maintenance and taxes; and after the suit was upheld on appeal in 1958, the Macfadden Foundation, which was supplying her with barely enough money to live on, tried in vain to force her into a nursing home so that it could sell the property. Two local associations tried to buy all or part of the land for a nature preserve but failed. Lonely and rather reclusive, diabetic, and becoming blind, Mary was eventually taken care of by an Irish couple. She died in 1969 at age seventy-seven and was survived by her adopted daughter Helen, daughters Byrnece and Beverly, sons Berwyn and Brewster, ten grandchildren, and eleven great-grandchildren. Her estate was declared insolvent. So badly had the half-century-old mansion deteriorated during her last years that the foundation hired a caretaker to live in it until, to the dismay of Englewood conservationists, it sold the property in 1972.[45]

Bernarr Macfadden's lifetime crusade was not carried on by his children, despite his high hopes for the "Physical Culture Family," nor was the Bernarr Macfadden Foundation, a New York corporation of which he was the guiding spirit, effective in perpetuating his memory. When he died, the assets of the foundation's original $5,000,000 were said to have dwindled to less than $500,000, and a little more than twenty years later they amounted to only a few thousand dollars. The foundation went bankrupt, turned over its paltry assets to creditors, and by 1978 was out of business.[46]

"I Love Life"

UNTIL HIS MIDDLE EIGHTIES, Macfadden hoped to inspire in others his zest for life. He preached optimism and avoidance of self-pity, worry, and anger: a hopeful spirit would contribute to health. On the inside of a Christmas card to employees at Macfadden Publications, he inscribed the words and music of "I Love Life," and on the cover a characteristic message:

Life should be wonderful
but we must love life to
receive the glorious rewards it
can bring
I send you herewith a verse
of my favorite song. May
it help to make your
Christmas More Merry
and bring you added
Happiness throughout the
New Year

Bernarr Macfadden

His employees were not exactly thrilled to receive it. They had been expecting a Christmas bonus.[2]

Like his expressions, Macfadden's costume reflected his feeling about life. Indifferent to clothing styles, he often looked like a bum. Not appearance but comfort was his rule. Once he defied a theater manager who tried to eject him from an orchestra seat for removing his jacket on a hot summer evening. He sometimes wore sneakers with an opera cape. He never fussed about missing buttons. Most of the suits he was wearing in 1950 had been bought thirty years earlier, and he resisted his wife's efforts to spruce him up. She discovered that he had two prized garments: a frayed vest and an old pair of leather mesh shoes through which, he believed, the earth's magnetic force could penetrate. His other shoes lasted for many years because he so seldom wore them. At eighty-three, he padded about in glovelike shoes especially made with a slot for each toe. "It makes me feel comfortable like I'm walking barefooted," he said.[3] Barefoot walks were a Macfadden specialty. A story was told of BM striding along a Florida beach, barefoot, unshaven, and wearing old clothing. He stopped to admire an attractive beachfront house with a "For Sale" sign on the lawn and walked around the property. An alarmed woman rushed from the house and warned him to leave or she would call the police.

"But this place is for sale. I was only looking it over."

"Don't be ridiculous. This place is only for a millionaire."

"Well, I'm a millionaire, and I'd like to buy it."[4]

To some who knew him, Macfadden was an enigma. Public relations expert Edward L. Bernays called him "unfathomable." Fulton Oursler, his managing editor for twenty-one years, found him to be a package of paradoxes. "Nothing that I have ever read of Macfadden, including that which I have written myself, has ever captured him, or caged him in words," wrote Oursler. "Everyone has told of his fads and how he made them pay, but nowhere is his kindly naïveté, his deep suspicion of his fellowman, his openhearted generosity in large matters and pinchpenny habits in small, his natural humility and almost supernatural egotism, all blended into the surprising and wholly convincing character that he unvaryingly showed himself to me." Macfadden told his editor why he held no grudges: life was too short for hate; besides, it was bad for one's health.[5] A ferocious attacker of prudery, he was uncomfortable and even offended by smutty stories. A tasteless egotist, he had his modest moments. Impulsive and self-righteous, he usually accepted the judgment of those he trusted. Fundamentally serious, he could be lighthearted and playful, even humorous, as in this reply to a *Physical Culture* reader:

> Q. I have severe attacks of cramps every Sunday after preaching. Never have an attack; only on Sunday after preaching. Can you advise me in the matter?
>
> A. One thing is certain—either your Sunday dinner is too heavy or the sermon. We would advise you to experiment with both of them and cut out the one that causes the cramps.[6]

Sometimes BM was compassionate and gentle. He personally doubled the pay of an unfortunate and desperate Macfadden Publications artist. His third wife melted to him when he was tender, and his fourth wife, who described him as passionate and occasionally violent, yet always tender, believed he knew the secret of making a woman feel utterly feminine. She rolled around with him on the floor and joined him in laughter, which, he explained, was the most natural and beneficial exercise for starting the day. Had he not been so tender yet exciting, had she not been so in love with him, she could not have tolerated his eccentricities — or so she later recalled. Laughing easily, he also recommended smiling to foster contentment and "sooth the soul that may have been scourged with sorrow."[7]

At other times, Macfadden lost his temper and burst into a tempestuous rage. His capricious disposition baffled his wives, as when Johnnie Lee discovered him in bed with another woman and his embarrassment and anger suddenly gave way to a disarming humility as he begged forgiveness. Although Oursler, his faithful subordinate, considered him mild and eager to be friendly, he was combative when aroused, and never more so than in the early years of his health crusade. "I am proud of the enemies I have made," he bragged in 1906, and he expected to make thousands more in the future.[8]

In one respect, he was completely consistent: he had full confidence in his naturopathic notions, and he was genuinely interested in people's physical well-being. "He would always talk about your health," said his son-in-law, Joe Wiegers. At Macfadden Publications, he sponsored a regular exercise program staffed with a full-time health consultant and offered free treatment for ailing employees at his Dansville hotel. If judged by the practice of his philosophy of health, he was the soul of sincerity, even if to his detractors he was a charlatan.[9]

Intuitive and sharply intelligent, Macfadden could penetrate like an arrow to the core of a problem. His native shrewdness was apparent to those who knew him well and who made generous allowance for his inelegance and eccentricity. Aware of his educational limitations, he surrounded himself with capable lieutenants who, by flattery, bolstered his self-image. When told that his susceptibility to adulation was his most dangerous weakness, he responded that flattery steamed him up to do things.[10]

BM was inordinately concerned with his image, with the way he appeared rather than with the way he felt. Through his foundation he offered $1,000 for the best three-act play on his life, of which he would be the sole judge. He was a narcissist whose relationships with people, except Fulton Oursler, were characterized by self-centeredness, coupled with feelings of inferiority that made him overly dependent on the admiration or flattery of others.[11] He attracted yes-men. Striving for power and control, he exploited most of those closest to him. His relations with women were manipulative, and he could not tolerate rivals. Underneath his often charming and solicitous behavior lurked a certain ruthlessness that gave rise to mercurial outbursts of temper. His bleak childhood, with a father often drunk and a mother who abandoned him first to an orphan school, then to distant relatives, and his exploitation by a stingy, unforgiving taskmaster on an Illinois farm probably led to fantasies of power, omniscience, and body-love to compensate for the deprivation and frustration of his first ten years. Deprived of sustained love, he became a husband and father who was neither loving nor accepting, but domineering. The longest of his four marriages was consciously and essentially an experiment in physical culture, and it failed.

In 1929, two biographies and an account of Macfadden's family were published. All were authorized by him and, as H. L. Mencken noted, they did not "spare the goose grease." The Baltimore editor could recall "no more passionate anointing of a living man," and he descanted on BM's "vast and cocksure ignorance" and posturing as "an authority upon the crimes of modern medicine without knowing anything more about the human body than any other gymnast."[12]

Macfadden was used to criticism and ridicule, and his response could be crude, as in his condemnation of the Society for the Suppression of Vice, or quaint, as when he was queried about his fitness for politics. Claiming that ninety-nine out of every one hundred intelligent Americans would not refuse a chance to become president if offered to them, he declared, "Christ was crucified for His teachings. Socrates was condemned to death for the same reason. Lincoln was vilified most unmercifully previous to his nomination. Not that I should be classed with any of these renowned characters, but a lowly crusader like myself can take comfort in the thought that the punishment might have been more severe."[13]

Many people looked upon Macfadden with contempt. Some despised him for his tasteless showmanship and self-promotion, as in a four-page illustrated brochure bearing the title:

BERNARR MACFADDEN
BENEFACTOR OF HUMANITY
A LIFETIME OF ACHIEVEMENT[14]

Orville Allen, editor of the newspaper in Dansville, where BM's health hotel was situated, adjudged him a shrewd businessman and an interesting conversationalist but "about 90 per cent phony." Macfadden's greatest failures, Allen reminisced, came when he let his vanity stand in the way of his better judgment, which happened more often as he "slipped down the other side of life's highway." When chasing publicity he was "almost obnoxious." The publisher George Delacorte described him as a somewhat insincere headline hunter with an eye for capable subordinates; he "enjoyed their ass-licking," did not bear grudges, and was quite a good listener.[15]

In his business dealings, he was unsentimental. Friendship and goodwill were "okay when it is to our business interest," he advised his circulation department. "In Chicago and New York we have been turning double somersaults to favor dealers in these cities, and I think our attitude should change. Either they make good or out they go." A shift to the American News Company in Chicago or New York, he wrote, was worth considering, perhaps as a favor to get that company to handle and push all the Macfadden magazines on their stands. As the journalist Alva Johnston observed in 1941, "only a business genius of the highest order could have so many profitable eccentricities and income paying follies."[16]

Macfadden regretted that he was not an effective speaker, especially as he liked to preside at banquets. All his life he tried to overcome the lack of resonance in his voice and the flat twang of the Ozarks which resembled the speech of W. C. Fields. By mooing, growling, and roaring as a form of exercise, often in deserted subway cars, he tried to acquire a more forceful and varied speaking style. He was conscious that his sporadic formal schooling had lasted only three years, and in ordinary conversation he blundered into phrases like "buying a pork in a poke," "the flea in the ointment," and "a laughing stork." It is difficult to evaluate his feeble attempts at oratorical humor because Oursler probably touched up his speeches, but in a talk to a Macfadden-Deauville audience the words he used seem genuinely his own. "Kissing a person whose lips are not alive with the stimulation of blood circulation," he affirmed, "is like kissing a tub of butter."[17]

Macfadden took no interest in genteel culture. Lacking aesthetic sensitivity, he enjoyed painting and sculpture only if they depicted the human body and the less clothing the better. Although he was articulate about public affairs, his sense of history was molded by the simple nostalgic image of America's pioneers. Antiquity held little interest for him. While in Europe he was not attracted to its historic cathedrals. "Dead things," he said, "have no lure for me." He was ignorant of literature, although he once admitted to admiring Dickens without explaining why. He distrusted bookworms and could not understand why his valued editor Fulton Oursler would waste so much time reading Shakespeare. If the Bard were living today, Oursler declared, he would be rich from royalties and author's percentages from theatrical performances all over the world. That impressed BM, who had the last word: "I know something about Shakespeare that you don't. To have accomplished all that he must have kept himself in wonderful physical condition. Shakespeare was a great physical culturist." Macfadden's regard for George Bernard Shaw derived from their common interest in health and their battle against prudes. As early as 1908, *Physical Culture* reprinted part of a Shaw article on American prudery, and both men loathed Anthony Comstock, whom Shaw labeled "the celebrated Purity Witch Doctor." BM and the playwright shared for many years an interest in vegetarianism, vitality, and longevity, yet, according to Mary Macfadden her husband neither read Shaw's plays nor spoke of his literary accomplishments.[18]

The publisher's interest in drama was limited to simple, happy plays that ended well for the good guys and badly for the villains. "Personally, I am not fond of the drama," he wrote in 1909. "Somehow I have always felt that there are enough tragedies in life without adding to them by torturing one's self with the tribulations through which the characters of an ordinary drama are dragged." To help out a longtime friend, he put up a thousand dollars in 1928 to sustain a Greenwich Village production of Upton Sinclair's *Singing Jailbirds*. He attended a performance and relished the "wonderful piece of acting," but because he saw no need for a pro-labor play in prosperous times he thought it would be a financial flop. "According to our present mode of living, with working men securing the luxuries that only rich men could enjoy a few years ago," he wrote Sinclair, "it would be difficult to arouse interest in heart-rending, soul-tearing drama such as you have presented." He was unwilling to make another contribution to bring the play to an uptown theater.[19]

Macfadden's taste in music ran to popular tunes, and he liked to dance and sing. His favorite song was "I Love Life." He had no ear for tonal qualities and admitted that serious music was "all right for those that like it. If they want to hear a lot of noise, that's *their* business." When asked what he thought of Beethoven, Bach, Brahms, and Wagner, he smiled, shook his head and chirped, "They're all right for those that like them." At the opera he was bored. "Nobody can like this sort of thing. Anyone who says so is posing," he told one of his editors. To his wife's annoyance he talked over the music. His interest was in the physical aspects of a performance. Animated conductors appealed to him because they were vigorously exercising their back and shoulders, and he judged the great tenor Enrico Caruso as overweight and in sad physical shape.[20]

Listening to music, watching dramas, and reading literary classics were too sedentary and confining for one whose entire life was geared to the perfection of the human body. Macfadden considered himself a man of action. Books conveying the wisdom and knowledge of the ages would never die, he asserted, but "the greatest lessons of life come not from reading but from doing." Life was a continuing athletic contest. To arouse enthusiasm and broaden one's abilities, he recommended hobbies, but his own hobbies were entirely physical: exercise, especially walking, flying a plane, and parachuting. When told that he worked too hard as a publisher, he insisted that he enjoyed it in all its detail. "Work," he said, "is my swimming pool, and I love splashing around in it."[21]

Macfadden was unable to loaf. Urged to take a vacation and get a change of scene, he responded that a long hike would do him good — say, a walk from New York to Chicago, over the mountains by way of Pittsburgh. He was uncomfortable amid idle conversation but swept up in the spirit of struggle and achievement. Nor could he condone an eat, drink, and be merry philosophy, as indicated by his disapproval of a quotation of Edna St. Vincent Millay:

> My candle burns at both ends;
> It will not last the night;
> But ah, my foes, and oh, my friends —
> It gives a lovely light![22]

BM visualized himself as a innovator and a leader. He was not a joiner, not a follower. He did not often attend church and had no affiliation with any religious organization. In 1924 he became a Mason, but apparently that was his only fraternal association. He organized gymnastic societies and hiking groups and is said to have founded in 1903 the Polar Bear Club, which still sponsors winter swims in the icy waters off Coney Island. Although not an expert swimmer like his wife Mary or his children, he encouraged his employees to participate in swimming. A reformer by temperament who was bored by management routines, he delighted in ostentatious promotional schemes and assigned administrative tasks to subordinates. He had real organizational ability but he neglected to foster systematically many of the health projects he initiated. His physical fitness and walking clubs, most of his health homes and his penny restaurants were ephemeral.[23]

Although he had the temperament of a fighter, he eventually learned to appreciate that people could honestly differ in opinions, but he was not, as Oursler contended, a "stern advocate of tolerance." Having friends and colleagues of various religious persuasions, he expressed no religious or racial bigotry in his public statements, but in an office memo in 1934 he confided his concern that "a certain race was back of the Communistic activities in Russia" and intended to foster communism in every country.[24] He could only have meant Jews. Four years later he privately expressed a prejudice quite prevalent in the United States of the 1930s:

> On numerous occasions I have referred to the Jewish question, and somehow or other I cannot help but feel that the time is near at hand when this should be brought out in the open more forcibly.
>
> The Jews who are attacking the American system ought to be informed in a very effective manner of the nature of this disastrous blunder on their part.[25]

Apparently, Macfadden associated Jews, or certain Jews, with Communists or with New Dealers he regarded as Communist sympathizers. Although there is no direct evidence, he may also have believed that pressure for the admission of more Jewish refugees from Nazism to the United States would undermine the immigration laws. Moreover, his support of law and order and working relationship with J. Edgar Hoover indicate that he could not sympathize with civil libertarians, Jewish or otherwise.

Early in 1954, Macfadden received two anonymous handwritten letters asserting that the Soviet Union had perfected an odorless chemical, a biological warfare agent, that could destroy all life, and that the Soviet government planned to spread the poison in Spain, North Africa, Japan, the Aleutian Islands, and Alaska. The writer offered to provide particulars if Macfadden inserted this notice in the *Washington Post:*

Brown envelope containing chemical formula lost in lobby of
Hotel Washington. Large reward. Tel. St. 3-6296

At the behest of the Macfadden Foundation, the *Post* published
the advertisement, and BM forwarded copies of the two letters to the
FBI. After a yearlong investigation, involving the CIA, Army intelligence, the State Department, and other agencies, the FBI closed the
case for lack of evidence. The physical culturist could not understand
why the letters had been addressed to him. He had no acquaintances
with ties to the Soviet Union, and he knew nobody living behind the
Iron Curtain. That the letters had been sent to him because of his
well-known interest in health was his only conclusion. It is more likely
that the anonymous author was an unbalanced alarmist or a practical
joker. Macfadden had so often received anonymous crank letters that
he did not retain them in his files.[26]

Probably the most colorful publisher in twentieth-century America, he influenced the course of popular journalism. His magazines
were the first to cultivate a readership among the masses, who found
in *Physical Culture, True Story, True Detective Mysteries,* and other
Macfadden publications entertainment, inspiration, and information, and he was among the first to use photographs as magazine illustrations.[27] To countless people, young and old, in the first half of
the century his name was well remembered. He reached a vast audience as publisher of periodicals with a total circulation estimated at
35,000,000 to 40,000,000 a year when the population of the United
States was a little more than half of what it is today. His bold publication of photographs of nearly naked men and women evoked many
imitations and broadened American attitudes toward the display of
the human body in magazines, newspapers, and posters. What was
shocking in the 1920s became tame in the 1940s. Proud of his sexuality, unrelenting in attacking prudery, and outspokenly optimistic
about life's opportunities, he understood the romantic yearnings of
urban working girls and the demand of young men for tales of crime,
detectives, and derring-do. His tabloid newspaper, the *Graphic,* drew
denunciations and attracted lawsuits, but its large circulation, as the
rival *News* and *Mirror* also learned, proved that sex and sensation
sold newspapers.

Publishing enabled Macfadden to carry his health message across
the land and beyond. Through more than one hundred health books
and *Physical Culture,* his personal instrument for nearly half a century, he touched many lives. His teachings about nutrition and, later,

the value of vitamins were ahead of his time, as he anticipated the wide popular interest in natural foods and healthful living so evident today. His long-distance hikes and flamboyant promotions attracted national attention. His schools, camps, and health resorts flourished, and he inspired a younger generation of muscle men. To some disciples, he seemed almost a god or a guru of devoted adherents. Letters poured into his office thanking him for strengthened bodies, reduced weight, or clearer complexions. Unsolicited testimonials came from readers in every state of the Union, many parts of Europe, and even the British colonies.[28]

Many of Macfadden's medical beliefs were mistaken. His concept of disease was simplistic. His cures for cancer, tuberculosis, and venereal diseases, to name a few, were demonstrably inadequate and, as his AMA critics pointed out, based on uncontrolled experiences. His rabid opposition to vaccination continued long after it became standard medical practice. Finally, his excessive faith in fasting probably hastened his death at the age of eighty-seven.

In some ways, however, his techniques have been vindicated. After World War II the Baruch Committee on Physical Medicine, a special committee of Congress created as a result of physical disabilities incurred in the war, conducted a study of naturopathic treatment and upheld hydrotherapy, the use of light, heat, cold, and exercise programs, including mechanical devices, for physical and occupational therapy.[29] Today, postoperative treatment includes deep breathing and exercise; physical therapy is widely prescribed by physicians; and hiking, running, and jogging (whatever its disadvantages), and bicycling are popular. Health spas and physical fitness centers are part of the urban and suburban scene.

During much of his life, Macfadden faced legal difficulties, which was natural for a controversial publisher, but which also resulted from his personal conduct, real or alleged. In 1909, a year after his conviction for sending "licentious" material in the mail, he was sued by a young woman whose picture he had printed as proof of the desirability of a luxuriant head of hair. She won a judgment of $3,198 on her claim that he had used her photograph in advertisements without her consent. That same year, he was jailed in Hudson County, New Jersey, to await trial on a charge by a Hoboken teenage girl that she had been the victim of a "certain offense," but the case never came to court, and Macfadden later claimed that he had forced retractions from newspapers that reported the story. In 1930, in a suit by a woman who contended that he had paid her only $2,500 of a $15,000 debt, his attorney charged that she sought to embarrass the defendant and the plaintiff's daughter as part of a scheme to blackmail them. In later years, he was deeply enmeshed in legal disputes with his third and fourth wives, and at the age of seventy was sued for alienating the affections of a married woman, but he was cleared.[30]

Macfadden was highly sexed and proud of his masculinity. As he confessed to his hostess-yoga instructor at his Dansville hotel, the allure of women was his greatest weakness. His health consultant, Paul Veatch, recalled that BM changed managers at Dansville because of the probing criticism of "flattering women" in his New York office. He hired women who pleased him, but he found ways of getting rid of them if they smoked or if they powdered and rouged their faces. His roving eye extended beyond his inner, private office. Orr J. Elder's son remembered that it was impossible for his father "to keep any young office girls around with Macfadden."[31] The publisher's weakness for women was an important factor in his separation and divorce from Mary and his separation from Johnnie Lee. Although Mary was quoted as saying that he had many illegitimate children, there is no evidence, other than his daughter Helen, of his fathering a brood of bastards.

The physical culturist's sex life violated his publicly stated principle that sexual indulgence should be moderated at middle age. "After the age of forty-five or fifty," he wrote at the age of sixty-eight, "a man will find it the safest plan to exercise extreme moderation" of sexual activity. Overindulgence, he asserted, often weakened the lungs, heart, kidneys, and even the brain: "No man can be mentally capable and efficient who is continually draining his vitality by sexual excesses." He thought women's bodies could endure more sexual abuse than men's, but he condemned the use of women as sexual objects. Macfadden, obviously, did not drain his own vitality. Even in his eighties he put sex ahead of other considerations. According to Johnnie Lee, he believed that the joyous fulfillment of a loving relationship brought supreme delight, and that spontaneous enjoyment of sex was essential to health and happiness. Almost to the end he acted on that belief. In the words of a Dansville editor, he "probably had more to do with making the United States sex-conscious than any other single individual of the time."[32]

One of a long line of health reformers, and not above exaggerating his importance, Bernarr Macfadden affected the social fabric of twentieth-century America. He was a muscular muckraker who not only championed sexuality and sex education, but promoted the display of beautiful bodies, assailed prudery, condemned the wearing of restrictive garments, and fostered physical culture. In his crusade for health he was derided by traditional physicians as an ignorant and dangerous quack, but was gratefully remembered by many whom he had helped by his prescription of exercise, diet, and natural healing. To some observers he was simply an amusing eccentric who would do anything to win publicity; yet such feats as parachute jumping in his eighties served not merely to feed his ego but to prove that the body, if properly cared for, retained its youthful fitness. Macfadden set trends in journalism as a publisher of mass magazines and news-papers that exploited romance, sex, and crime. To businessmen he embodied the old-fashioned virtues and stubborn self-assurance of free enterprise promoters. An incarnation of the rags-to-riches theme, the little strongman from Missouri who became a millionaire New Yorker naïvely dreamed of restoring the rugged qualities of early American pioneers and never tired of preaching that his countrymen had to be physically strong if the United States were to survive in a violent world.

Abbreviations
Notes
Bibliography
Index

Abbreviations

AMA	American Medical Association, Chicago, Illinois
FBI	Federal Bureau of Investigation, Washington, D.C.
FDRL	Franklin D. Roosevelt Library, Hyde Park, New York
FULA	Fordham University Library Annex, Bronx, New York
KLUO	Knight Library, University of Oregon, Eugene, Oregon
LLIU	Lilly Library, Indiana University, Bloomington, Indiana
PC	*Physical Culture*
RLUR	Rush Rhees Library, University of Rochester, Rochester, New York

Notes

1. OUT OF THE OZARKS

1. William H. Taft, "Bernarr Macfadden," *Missouri Historical Review*, Oct. 1968, 83; Ethel Johnston Chilton, "Bernarr Macfadden Ties with Local Families Are Remembered," *Doniphan Prospect News* [Mo.], Oct. 20, 1955, 1; Clement Wood, *Bernarr Macfadden, A Study in Success* (New York: Lewis Copeland, 1929), 191–94; Rose Fulton Cramer, *Wayne County, Missouri* (Cape Girardeau, Mo.: Ramfre Press, 1972), 569.

2. This and the following three paragraphs are based on Cramer, *Wayne County*, 122, 140, 190, 199, 229, 238–39, 256, 267, 342–43; *Goodspeed's History of Southeast Missouri*, (1888; reprint; Cape Girardeau, Mo.: Ramfre Press, 1955), 503; Lucien Carr, *Missouri, A Bone of Contention* (Boston: Houghton-Mifflin, 1888), 358–59; WPA Federal Writers' Project, American Guide Series, *Missouri, A Guide to the "Show Me" State* (New York: Duell, Sloan and Pearce, 1941), 68, 427; William E. Parrish, *Turbulent Partnership, Missouri and the Union, 1861–1865* (Columbia: Univ. of Missouri Press, 1963), 195; idem, *A History of Missouri*, vol. 3, 1860 to 1875 (Columbia: Univ. of Missouri Press, 1973), 191; Paul C. Nagel, *Missouri, A Bicentennial History* (New York: W. W. Norton, 1977), 74–75; Frederic A. Culmer, *A New History of Missouri* (Mexico, Mo.: McIntyre Publishing, 1938), map opposite 352.

3. Cramer, *Wayne County*, 340, 378; United States Census, 1840, manuscript schedules, Jefferson Township, Wayne County, Mo., 232; Taft, "Bernarr Macfadden," 73; Iron County, Mo., Record of Wills, 1856–88, 24–25, County Court House, Ironton, Mo.

4. Chilton, "Bernarr Macfadden Ties," *Doniphan Prospect News* [Mo.], Oct. 20, 1955; Cramer, *Wayne County*, 122; Robert Lewis Taylor, "Physical Culture," pt. 1, *New Yorker*, Oct. 14, 1950, 47.

5. Wood, *Bernarr Macfadden*, 27; Chilton, "Bernarr Macfadden Ties"; Cramer, *Wayne County*, 124.

6. *Iron County Register* [Ironton, Mo.], Sept. 19, 26, 1867. The newspaper erroneously stated Mary's name as "Molly." The manuscript schedule of the United States Census, 1870, Benton Township, Wayne County, Mo., gave her name as Mary. It has proved impossible to identify conclusively the given names of the girl's parents, but from a study of the Miller families listed for Iron County and other indications I believe that George and Mary are the probable parents.

7. United States Census, 1870, manuscript schedules, Benton Township, Wayne

County, Mo., family group number 72. The census, taken in June or July 1870, listed "May" as one month old; it also listed "Adolphus," i.e., Bernard Adolphus McFadden. The complete absence of family records makes it necessary to rely heavily on incomplete and often inaccurate census and property records and on secondary sources.

8. Wood, *Bernarr Macfadden*, 28–29; Cramer, *Wayne County*, 568; Taylor, "Physical Culture," pt. 1, 47; Iron County Circuit Court Records, 3 (1870–1874), 358, 390, 393, 400; St. Francois County Circuit Court Records, 7 (1870–1873), 384, 389, 405, 419, and 8 (1873–1877), 17, 18, 20, 22, 24, 25, 46, 49, Missouri State Archives, Jefferson City, Mo.

9. Wood, *Bernarr Macfadden*, 29–30.

10. Ibid., 30–31.

11. Ibid., 32; Taylor, "Physical Culture," pt. 1, 47.

12. Bernarr Macfadden, "A Great National Disgrace," *Liberty*, Nov. 4, 1933, 3.

13. Taylor, "Physical Culture," pt. 1, 48.

14. *Liberty*, Aug. 3, 1940, 4; Taft, "Bernarr Macfadden," 73, 74; Wood, *Bernarr Macfadden*, 132.

15. Taylor, "Physical Culture," pt. 1, 48–49.

16. Wood, *Bernarr Macfadden*, 33–34; Cramer, *Wayne County*, 568.

17. Taylor, "Physical Culture," pt. 1, 49; Wood, *Bernarr Macfadden*, 36–37, 194.

18. Wood, *Bernarr Macfadden*, 39–40; Taylor, "Physical Culture," pt. 1, 50; Taft, "Bernarr Macfadden," 75; Mary Macfadden and Emile Gauvreau, *Dumbbells and Carrot Strips, The Story of Bernarr Macfadden* (New York: Henry Holt, 1953), 51; *PC*, Apr. 1933, 14.

19. Taylor, "Physical Culture," pt. 1, 50–51; Wood, *Bernarr Macfadden*, 38, 41; Emile Gauvreau, *My Last Million Readers* (New York: E. P. Dutton, 1941), 122.

20. Taylor, "Physical Culture," pt. 1, 50–51; *PC*, Apr. 1933, 14; Wood, *Bernarr Macfadden*, 41–42.

21. Taylor, "Physical Culture," pt. 2, *New Yorker*, Oct. 21, 1950, 39; Wood, *Bernarr Macfadden*, 42–43. In *Gould's St. Louis Directory* for 1883, 1884, and 1885 (cited in Taft, "Bernarr Macfadden," 76) Macfadden is listed as a clerk.

22. *PC*, June 1899, 108; Oct. 1899, 232–33; Aug. 1901, 206. Wood, *Bernarr Macfadden*, 45; Taft, "Bernarr Macfadden," 75; Taylor, "Physical Culture," pt. 2, 39.

23. Harvey Green, *Fit for America: Health, Fitness, Sport and American Society*, paperback ed. (Baltimore: Johns Hopkins Univ. Press, 1988), 98–99, 186–92, 199–201, 205; James C. Whorton, *Crusaders for Fitness: The History of American Health Reformers* (Princeton: Princeton Univ. Press, 1982), 274–82.

24. *PC*, Apr. 1933, 20, 73, 75; Taylor, "Physical Culture," pt. 2, 39; Wood, *Bernarr Macfadden*, 47, 76, 77.

25. *PC*, May 1933, 14–15.

26. Taylor, "Physical Culture," pt. 2, 39; William Blaikie, *How to Get Strong and How to Stay So* (New York: Harper, 1884), passim; Green, *Fit for America*, 202; Fulton Oursler, *The True Story of Bernarr Macfadden* (New York: Lewis Copeland, 1929), 64; Wood, *Bernarr Macfadden*, 58–59.

27. *PC*, May 1933, 15–16; June 1933, 15–16. Taylor, "Physical Culture," pt. 2, 39–40, 42; Taft, "Bernarr Macfadden," 76–77. The quotation about the *McCune Brick* is from Macfadden and Gauvreau, *Dumbbells*, 51.

28. *PC*, June 1933, 93; July 1933, 15. Taylor, "Physical Culture," pt. 2, 42; Taft, "Bernarr Macfadden," 77.

29. *PC*, June 1933, 93–94; July 1933, 14–16. Taylor, "Physical Culture," pt. 2, 42, 44.

30. *PC*, June 1933, 16; Taylor, "Physical Culture," pt. 2, 44; Taft, "Bernarr Macfadden," 78; Wood, *Bernarr Macfadden*, 64–65; Macfadden and Gauvreau, *Dumbbells*, 52–53.

31. *PC*, July 1933, 15, 18, 88; Aug. 1933, 17. Oursler, *True Story*, 73–74; Taylor, "Physical Culture," pt. 2, 44–45.

32. *PC*, Aug. 1933, 18; Taylor, "Physical Culture," pt. 2, 45–47; Taft, "Bernarr Macfadden," 49; Frances S. Stadelman to the author, June 11, 1984. Mrs. Stadelman's mother knew Macfadden when he taught at the Bunker Hill Academy.

33. Taft, "Bernarr Macfadden," 79, citing Frances S. Stadelman's letter to him, Feb. 27, 1967; Taylor, "Physical Culture," pt. 2, 46.

34. Taylor, "Physical Culture," pt. 2, 45–46.

35. *PC*, Sept. 1933, 42–43; Taft, "Bernarr Macfadden," 80–81, citing *Sedalia Bazoo* [Mo.], Apr. 30, 1893.

36. *PC*, Aug. 1933, 18, 82; Taft, "Bernarr Macfadden," 81.

37. Green, *Fit for America*, 6–9.

38. Ibid., 10; Whorton, *Crusaders for Fitness*, 38–61.

39. Wharton, *Crusaders for Fitness*, 46–49, 63–65, 96–102, 127–30, 135–36, 271; Christopher Gian-Curso, ed., *Eternal Health Truths* (New York: n. p., 1960), 7–9, 13, 87–105, 114–23; Jane B. Donegan, *'Hydropathic Highway to Health': Women and Water Cure in Antebellum America* (New York: Greenwood Press, 1986), 20–21.

40. Donegan, *'Hydropathic Highway,'* xiii–xiv, 27–34; Green, *Fit for America*, 54–76; Whorton, *Crusaders for Fitness*, 24–25, 136–39.

41. Donegan, *'Hydropathic Highway,'* 149.

42. *PC*, Sept. 1933, 79; Taft, "Bernarr Macfadden," 81–82.

2. LAUNCHING A CRUSADE

1. *PC*, Oct. 1933, 39; Wood, *Bernarr Macfadden*, 73; Taylor, "Physical Culture," pt. 2, 47; Alva Johnston, "The Great Macfadden," *Saturday Evening Post*, June 21, 1941, 11.

2. Vera Caspary, *The Secrets of Grown-ups* (New York: McGraw Hill, 1979), 89.

3. *PC*, Oct. 1933, 101; Wood, *Bernarr Macfadden*, 75–79; Oursler, *True Story*, 88–89; Taylor, "Physical Culture," pt. 2, 47; Johnston, "Great Macfadden," 11; Ben Yagoda, "The True Story of Bernarr Macfadden," *American Heritage*, Dec. 1981, 23.

4. Taylor, "Physical Culture," pt. 2, 44; Macfadden and Gauvreau, *Dumbbells*, 56–57; Taft, "Bernarr Macfadden," 71. Exactly when Macfadden changed his name is not known. According to the *Dictionary of American Biography*, Supplement 5, 452, he probably did so in 1893, but other evidence suggests 1895 or 1896. Mary Macfadden (*Dumbbells*, 56) asserted that he had been impressed with the promotion of Mack trucks as powerful machines and thus changed the *Mc* to *Mac*, but this is erroneous because the Mack truck was not produced until 1905. *Time*, Feb. 14, 1927, 30, reported a legend that the name change originated in a typographical error on one of his magazine covers. This is quite doubtful. The name change occurred before Macfadden started *Physical Culture* in 1899.

5. Taylor, "Physical Culture," pt. 2, 47–48; *PC*, Oct. 1933, 103; Wood, *Bernarr Macfadden*, 80–81.

6. Taylor, "Physical Culture," pt. 2, 48; Wood, *Bernarr Macfadden*, 81–82; *PC*, Oct. 1899, 232–38.

7. Wood, *Bernarr Macfadden*, 82–83, 95; Fulton Oursler, "Bernarr Macfadden—His Life and Work," *PC*, Jan. 1929, 145; Bernarr Macfadden, *Macfadden's New Hair Culture*, 3d ed. (New York: Physical Culture Publishing, 1901).

8. *PC*, Oct. 1933, 17, 98; Taylor, "Physical Culture," pt. 2, 48; Wood, *Bernarr Macfadden*, 83–84.

9. Wood, *Bernarr Macfadden*, 84–86; Annie Riley Hale, *"These Cults," An Analysis of the Foibles of Dr. Morris Fishbein's "Medical Follies" and an Indictment of Medical Practice in General* (New York: National Health Foundation, 1926), 142; Taylor, "Physical Culture," pt. 2, 48, 49; Bernarr Macfadden to Thomas E. Dewey, Apr. 20, 1953, Dewey Papers, RLUR; *PC*, Oct. 1905, 382–83, and Mar. 1902, supplement D.

10. George B. Davis, interview with the author, June 10, 1982; Taft, "Bernarr Macfadden," 87–88; Clifford J. Waugh, "Bernarr Macfadden: The Muscular Prophet" (Ph.D. diss., SUNY Buffalo, 1979), 173.

11. Wood, *Bernarr Macfadden*, 88; Bernarr Macfadden, *A Strenuous Lover, A Romance of Natural Love's Vast Power: Original Story by Bernarr Macfadden; Revised with the Assistance of John R. Coryell* (New York: Physical Culture Publishing, 1904).

12. E.g., *PC*, Aug. 1899, 163.

13. Ibid., May 1900, 81; May 1901, 83; Nov. 1904, 419, 536–37; Jan. 1905, 627–28, Nov. 1909, 405–09. See also Bernarr Macfadden, *Coughs, Colds and Catarrh* (New York: Macfadden Publications, 1926), 2.

14. *PC*, Dec. 1901, 128–31, 138–39; Feb. 1902, 230; Apr. 1902, 18–20, 43; May 1902, 100; Oct. 1902, 49; Nov. 1902, 11; Jan. 1903, 24; Apr. 1904, 309; Aug. 1904, 187; Feb. 1905, 49. *New York Evening Graphic*, May 18, 1925; Oursler, *True Story*, 37.

15. *PC*, Aug. 1899, 168; Sept. 1906, 292.

16. Ibid., July 1911, 5; Aug. 1911, 113.

17. Waugh, "Bernarr Macfadden," 138; *PC*, Aug. 1906, 196, 198; July 1907, 4.

18. Ibid., Jan. 1903, 67–68; Apr. 1903, 340; June 1903, 181; Dec. 1903, 529–33; Apr. 1904, 302; June 1904, 456; Nov. 1904, 428–32; Waugh, "Bernarr Macfadden," 113, 181; Oursler, *True Story*, 123, 125.

19. Morris Fishbein, *Medical Follies, An Analysis of the Foibles of Some Healing Cults* (New York: Boni and Liveright, 1925), 179; James Harvey Young, *The Toadstool Millionaires, A Social History of Patent Medicines in America before Federal Regulation* (Princeton: Princeton Univ. Press, 1961), 205; Frank Presbrey, *The History and Development of Advertising* (Garden City, N.Y.: Doubleday, Doran, 1929), 531–32; Edward Bok, *The Americanization of Edward Bok* (Charles Scribner's Sons, 1921), 340; *PC*, Sept. 1905, 315.

20. *PC*, Feb. 1903, 96; July 1903, 70–71, 134–38; Jan. 1904, 33–34, 40, 201–3; Dec. 1905, 529; Mar. 1906, 342–43; Apr. 1906, 454; May 1906, 454, 498; July 1907, 5.

21. Ibid., Mar. 1900, 253; June 1904, 523. See examples in advertising sections, 1901, 1905, and for Page System of Hygiene, Sept. 1908. Young, *Toadstool Millionaires*, 206–8; Morris Fishbein, *A History of the American Medical Association* (Philadelphia: Saunders, 1947), 112–13, 115, 161–63, 168–69, 198–99; Waugh, "Bernarr Macfadden," 122–23.

22. *PC*, Aug. 1899, 163; Feb. 1900, 36; Apr. 1900, 36; Dec. 1900, 130; Apr. 1902, 44; Dec. 1902, 190; July 1911, 6. Oursler, *True Story*, 117–18.

23. Alexander Markovich, "The Publishing Empire of Bernarr Macfadden" (M.A. thesis, Univ. of Missouri, Columbia, 1958), 52, 59; Oursler, *True Story*, 118; *PC*, Dec. 1905, 482; Sept. and Nov. 1911.

24. Waugh, "Bernarr Macfadden," 27–30; Macfadden and Gauvreau, *Dumbbells*, 145–46; Oursler, *True Story*, 189; *PC*, Sept. 1905, 260.

25. Oursler, "Bernarr Macfadden," 145; *PC*, Jan. 1906, 116.

26. *PC*, July 1901, 180–81.

27. Johnston, "Great Macfadden," June 21, 1941, 10, 11; Bernarr Macfadden, *Strength from Eating: How and What to Eat and Drink to Develop the Highest Degree of Health and Strength* (New York: Physical Culture Publishing, 1901), 132; Macfadden and Gauvreau, *Dumbbells*, 33; *PC*, Nov. 1900, 86; Dec. 1900, 86; Jan. 1901, 160; Feb. 1903, 154; Dec. 1909, 540.

28. George Rosen, *A History of Public Health* (New York: MD Publications, 1958), 405–7; Elmer V. McCollum, *A History of Nutrition* (Boston: Houghton-Mifflin, 1957), 201, 420–21; *PC*, Apr. 1905, 287; Whorton, *Crusaders for Fitness*, 298.

29. *PC*, July 1906, 112; Oct. 1906, 331–33.

30. Ibid., Sept. 1905, 296–97; Oct. 1907, 212; July 1908, 3. See also Dec. 1911, 552.

31. Ibid., May 1902, 97–98, 100; July 1903, 92; July 1906, 3; June 1908, 363–64; Apr. 1911, 393–94; Sept. 1912, 309. Bernarr Macfadden, *The Miracle of Milk: How to Use the Milk Diet Scientifically at Home* (New York: Macfadden Publications, 1923), 5; *PC*, May 1909, 302.

32. *PC*, Apr. 1902, editorial supp. B–C; May 1902, 102; Sept. 1902, 347; July 1903, 98; July 1905, 63; Oursler, *True Story*, 199–200; Harria Gray, "Physical Culture Restaurant," *PC*, Mar. 1903, 206–9; Oct. 1904, 381; Sept. 1907, 145; Dec. 1909, 7a (advertisement).

33. Johnston, "Great Macfadden," 10; Oursler, *True Story*, 143; *PC*, Feb. 1907, 108; Bernarr Macfadden, *Fasting for Health: A Complete Guide on How, When and Why to Use the Fasting Cure* (New York: Macfadden Book Company, 1935), 63.

34. Oursler, *True Story*, 148.

35. *PC*, Aug. 1907, 72–73; Sept. 1911, 233–38; Upton Sinclair, *The Fasting Cure* (Pasadena, Calif.: published by author, 1911), 22, 29; Bernarr Macfadden to Upton Sinclair, Mar. 27, 1930, Sinclair Papers, LLIU.

36. *PC*, Aug. 1905, 120; Mar. 1902, supps., E, F; July 1912, 1; Bernarr Macfadden, *Building of Vital Power: Deep Breathing and a Complete System for Strengthening the Heart, Lungs, Stomach and all the Great Vital Organs* (New York: Physical Culture Publishing, 1904), 65.

37. Macfadden and Gauvreau, *Dumbbells*, 203–4; Bernarr Macfadden, *The Virile Powers of Superb Manhood: How Developed, How Lost, How Regained* (New York: Physical Culture Publishing, 1900), 11; Bernarr Macfadden, *Marriage a Lifelong Honeymoon: Life's Greatest Pleasures Secured by Observing the Highest Human Instincts* (New York: Physical Culture Publishing, 1903), 142–43.

38. Macfadden and Gauvreau, *Dumbbells*, 100; *PC*, May 1906, 551; Macfadden, *Marriage*, 149.

39. *PC*, Apr. 1899, 37; Macfadden, *Marriage*, 55, 98, 212, 219, 221, 227–28.

40. Bryan Strong, "Ideas of the Early Sex Education Movement in America, 1890–1920," *History of Education Quarterly*, Autumn 1972, 137, 141–44, 153; Bernarr Macfadden, *Man's Sex Life* (New York: Macfadden Book Company, 1936), passim.

41. *PC*, May 1907, 314; Macfadden, *Marriage*, 87, 91; Bernarr Macfadden and Marion Malcolm, *Health—Beauty—Sexuality from Girlhood to Womanhood* (New York: Physical Culture Publishing, 1904), 9, 37.

42. Macfadden, *Man's Sex Life*, 2; Macfadden and Malcolm, *Health—Beauty—Sexuality*, 51, 69, 110–12, 116.

43. Macfadden and Malcolm, *Health—Beauty—Sexuality*, 51, 69, 110–12, 116.

44. Ibid., 14, 171–72, 175, 176.

45. Macfadden, *Marriage*, 106, 109–12; *PC*, Aug. 1902, 285–86; Oursler, *True Story*, 131.

46. *PC,* Sept. 1910, 221; May 1911, 497–98; June 1920, 13.

47. Ibid., Sept. 1910, 221, 222; Jan. 1911, 7.

48. Ibid., July 1903, 94–95; Oct. 1914, 291–96; Bernarr Macfadden, *Macfadden's Physical Training: An Illustrated System of Exercise for the Development of Health, Strength and Beauty* (New York: Macfadden Company, 1900); Macfadden and Gauvreau, *Dumbbells,* 227.

49. *PC,* Nov. 1901, 90; Dec. 1901, 108; Jan. 1905, 559; July 1906, 110; Apr. 1909, 255–56. Waugh, "Bernarr Macfadden," 46–47.

50. Macfadden, *Marriage,* 89; Whorton, *Crusaders for Fitness,* 281–82; *PC,* Sept. 1899, 199; Aug. 1904, 106–7; May 1906, 552; Dec. 1906, 557, 561. B. A. McFadden [Bernarr Macfadden], *The Athlete's Conquest, The Romance of an Athlete,* rev. ed. (New York: Physical Culture Publishing, 1901), 6–7; Waugh, "Bernarr Macfadden," 55; Bernarr Macfadden editorial, *Liberty,* May 18, 1940.

51. Whorton, *Crusaders for Fitness,* 287–89; G. Stanley Hall, "Some Relations Between Physical and Mental Training," in *Proceedings of the American Association for the Advancement of Physical Education,* Ninth annual meeting, no. 2, 1894, 37; Macfadden and Gauvreau, *Dumbbells,* 201.

52. *PC,* Nov. 1904, 417; Sept. 1908, 194.

53. Ibid., Apr. 1902, 45; Sept. 1908, 194. For foreign armies see Jan., Mar., Apr., and May 1902.

54. Ibid., Apr. 1902, editorial supp. A; July 1909, 2. Whorton, *Crusaders for Fitness,* 147.

55. *PC,* Dec. 1901, 137; Jan. 1902, 157–61; Feb. 1902, 236.

56. Ibid., Sept. 1904, 284; Apr. 1905, 247; Apr. 1908, 247; July 1908 (advertisement); July 1910, 3–4; Oct. 1915, 77. Waugh, "Bernarr Macfadden," 145–46.

57. Mabel Lee, *A History of Physical Education and Sports in the U.S.A.* (New York: John Wiley and Sons, 1983), 269; Whorton, *Crusaders for Fitness,* 282–84; *New York Times,* Apr. 9, 14, 1911 and Jan. 14, 15, 1912.

3. NUDITY, PRUDERY, AND THE LAW

1. *Liberty,* Dec. 3, 1938, 3; *PC,* Mar. 1902, 290; May 1902, 90; June 1902, 163–64; July 1902, 230; Nov. 1902, 122, 347.

2. *PC,* Feb. 1901, 198; Feb. 1902, 236; Apr. 1904, 291; May 1904, 428; Nov. 1904, 477; Mar. 1905, 160; Jan. 1906, 73.

3. Ibid., Mar. 1901, 250; Apr. 1901, 8–9; Nov. 1902 (advertisement); Oct. 1904, 291–96.

4. Oursler, *True Story,* 182–83; Waugh, "Bernarr Macfadden," 140; *PC,* Jan. 1901, 155–57; Oct. 1911, 343.

5. *PC,* Aug. 1902, supp.; Oursler, *True Story,* 186; Wood, *Bernarr Macfadden,* 106.

6. *PC,* Jan. 1903, 72; July 1903, 93. Macfadden toyed with a weekly magazine, *The Cry for Justice,* selling at two cents a copy and featuring editorials on achieving success in life. It failed. *PC,* Nov. 1902, 123; Jan. 1903, 71.

7. Gauvreau, *My Last Million Readers,* 95; *PC,* July 1899, 152; Apr. 1900, 35–36; Oct. 1900, 131. Apparently, Macfadden placated Cromie because *Physical Culture* (May 1900, 77) carried an article by him.

8. Oswald Garrison Villard, "Sex, Art, Truth and Magazines," *Atlantic Monthly,* Mar. 1926, 394; Macfadden and Gauvreau, *Dumbbells,* 289; *PC,* Jan. 1901, 155; Oct. 1901, 37; Feb. 1903, 150, 151.

9. *PC*, Apr. 1899, 37; Dec. 1903, 497. *New York Times*, Aug. 6, 1911; Harry Kemp to David Howatt, June 2, 1905, Howatt Papers, LLIU; Taft, "Bernarr Macfadden," 88; Macfadden and Gauvreau, *Dumbbells*, 279–80.

10. *New York Times*, June 21, 1926; Waugh, "Bernarr Macfadden," 73; Harry Kemp, *Trampling on Life, An Autobiographical Narrative* (Garden City, N.Y.: Garden City Publishing, 1922), 164, 167. Kemp substituted the name Barton for Macfadden.

11. *PC*, June 1904 (advertisement); Jan. 1905, 638; Feb. 1905, 4; Apr. 1905, 217, 284–85; May 1905, 326–30; June 1905, 417–19; July 1905, 33–35; Jan. 1906, 53–55. *New York Times*, June 21, 1926, which erroneously refers to Byrne as a son; Oursler, *True Story*, 203; Caspary, *Secrets of Grown-ups*, 97.

12. *PC*, Dec. 1903, 547; Apr. 1904, 344. Johnston, "Great Macfadden," 9.

13. *New York Times*, Oct. 2, 1905.

14. Ibid., Oct. 6, 1905.

15. Ibid., Oct. 7, 8, 1905.

16. Quoted in Heywood Broun and Margaret Leech, *Anthony Comstock: Roundsman of the Lord* (New York: Albert and Charles Boni, 1927), 237.

17. *New York Times*, Oct. 10, 1905; *PC*, Dec. 1905, 575.

18. Waugh, "Bernarr Macfadden," 90–91; *PC*, June 1906, 584; *New York Times*, Feb. 5, 1927.

19. *PC*, Dec. 1905, 561–63.

20. Ibid., Aug. 1903, 177–79; Nov. 1904, 446–48; June 1905, 471–73. Jamesburg *Record* [N.J.], Mar. 10, 1905, quoted in WPA Federal Writers' Project, American Guide Series, *Monroe Township, Middlesex County, New Jersey, 1838–1938* (n.p.: Monroe Township Committee, 1938), 79; Waugh, "Bernarr Macfadden," 39, 64.

21. WPA Federal Writers' Project, *Monroe Township*, 80; *PC*, June 1905, 471, 473.

22. *PC*, Aug. 1906, 217.

23. Waugh, "Bernarr Macfadden," 71; Upton Sinclair, *Autobiography of Upton Sinclair* (New York: Harcourt, Brace and World, 1962), 159; WPA Federal Writers' Project, *Monroe Township*, 81.

24. Oswald Garrison Villard, *Sex, Art, Truth and Magazines* (Boston: Atlantic Monthly, 1926), 18–19; Macfadden and Gauvreau, *Dumbbells*, 118.

25. Waugh, "Bernarr Macfadden," 66, 70; Mae Weitzner telephone interview with the author, Apr. 16, 1982. (One of the girls was Mrs. Weitzner at the age of nine or ten.) Harry Kemp to David Howatt, June 2, 1905, Howatt Papers, LLIU.

26. Kemp, *Trampling on Life*, 166, 175, 185; Waugh, "Bernarr Macfadden," 66; *New Brunswick Daily Home News* [N.J.], Nov. 7, 1914; *PC*, June 1940, 39; Macfadden and Gauvreau, *Dumbbells*, 118–19; Harry Kemp to David Howatt, May 5, 19, 1905, Howatt Papers, LLIU. Using fictitious names, Kemp penned an amusing description of Physical Culture City in his *Trampling on Life*.

27. Kemp, *Trampling on Life*, 167; Waugh, "Bernarr Macfadden," 74; Mae Weitzner interview, Apr. 16, 1982.

28. Macfadden and Gauvreau, *Dumbbells*, 178, 183, 230.

29. Waugh, "Bernarr Macfadden," 73; Kemp, *Trampling on Life*, 169.

30. Oursler, *True Story*, 191–92.

31. Waugh, "Bernarr Macfadden," 3, 98–101; Bernarr Macfadden Plaintiff in Error vs. United States of America Defendant in Error, United States District Court for the District of New Jersey, Proceedings no. 236 (1909), 5 microfilm, Federal Building, Trenton, N.J.

32. Bernarr Macfadden, *Is It a Crime to Expose a Crime?* pamphlet bound with *Physical Culture*, Dec. 1907, 11–12; Bernarr Macfadden, *The Macfadden Prosecution:*

A Curious Story of Wrong and Oppression Under the Postal Laws (Battle Creek, Mich: n.p., 1908), 1.

33. Oursler, *True Story*, 192, 193; Macfadden, *Macfadden Prosecution*, 2; Macfadden, *Is It a Crime to Expose a Crime?* 13.

34. *PC*, Jan. 1908, 2, 6; Jan. 1910, 1-2. *New Brunswick Daily Home News*, Jan. 19, 1909.

35. *PC*, Feb. 1908, 74-75, 108, 121-24; Mar. 1908, 75-80, 141-42, 191-93, 241-43, 309-10; Feb. 1909, 99. Oursler, *True Story*, 195; Waugh, "Bernarr Macfadden," 103, 106.

36. *PC*, Jan. 1910, 1, 133; Oursler, *True Story*, 195; Johnston, "Great Macfadden," 98; *New York Times*, Nov. 18, 1909; L. B. Nichols, memorandum for Mr. Tolson, Jan. 5, 1940, Bernarr Macfadden File, no. 62-33905, sec. 1, Federal Bureau of Investigation, Washington, D.C.; Macfadden and Gauvreau, *Dumbbells*, 119; *Congressional Record*, 76th Cong., 1st sess., Mar. 8, 1939, vol. 84, 2440, and app., 948; Taylor, "Physical Culture," pt. 2, 5.

37. Macfadden, *Macfadden Prosecution*, 3; *PC*, June 1908, n.p.; Mar. 1909, 176-77; A. R. Simpier to Clifford J. Waugh, May 22, 1973, quoted in Waugh, "Bernarr Macfadden," 75-76; Oursler, *True Story*, 193.

38. *PC*, Feb. 1908, 73; Apr. 1908, 257-58; Feb. 1909, 97.

39. Ibid., Aug. 1907, 109-10, 112; Sept. 1907, 161-62; Mar. 1908, 202. Oursler, *True Story*, 202; Gerald Carson, *Cornflake Crusade* (New York: Rinehart, 1957), 186.

40. Macfadden and Gauvreau, *Dumbbells*, 226-27; Carson, *Cornflake Crusade*, 186.

41. Oursler, *True Story*, 202; Wood, *Bernarr Macfadden*, 114; Macfadden and Gauvreau, *Dumbbells*, 178, 181-86, 229; Waugh, "Bernarr Macfadden," 141-42; *PC*, Oct. 1911, 344.

42. Wood, *Bernarr Macfadden*, 286-90. The final printing was in 1942.

43. Macfadden and Gauvreau, *Dumbbells*, 204-06; Waugh, "Bernarr Macfadden," 168-69; *PC*, Aug. 1912, 117. Jesse Gehman, later an associate of the health crusader, claimed that Macfadden had referred to his sudden trip abroad as an "exile" and confided the reasons for it. Gehman, however, refused to divulge them (Waugh, "Bernarr Macfadden," 169).

4. THE PERFECT WOMAN

1. Macfadden and Gauvreau, *Dumbbells*, 19-20, 44; Oursler, *True Story*, 203-5. Macfadden never wrote anything more than the sketchiest outline of the events of 1913-1914, including the early months of his marriage, and he barely mentioned his wife. The only detailed account of the early relationship of Macfadden and Mary Williamson is *Dumbbells and Carrot Strips*, written many years later with the collaboration of Emile Gauvreau, who had edited Macfadden's *New York Evening Graphic*. This chapter, therefore, rests essentially upon Mary's assertions as reworked by Gauvreau, and the reader must allow for the bias of an alienated wife.

2. Macfadden and Gauvreau, *Dumbbells*, 3-5, 13, 41, 44; Grace Perkins [Oursler], *Chats with the Macfadden Family* (New York: Lewis Copeland, 1929), 5-7.

3. [Censored] to J. Edgar Hoover, date deleted but the letter probably was received May 22, 1964, Bernarr Macfadden File, FBI, no. 62-33905, sec. 1. Macfadden and Gauvreau, *Dumbbells*, 19.

4. Macfadden and Gauvreau, *Dumbbells*, 4.

5. Ibid., 3, 4, 42.
6. Ibid., 5.
7. Ibid., 16–19.
8. Ibid., 24–25, 27, 66.
9. Entry of June 29, 1913, ibid., 99.
10. Macfadden and Gauvreau, *Dumbbells*, 10, 30.
11. Ibid., 74–75.
12. Ibid., 42.
13. Diary entry, June 29, 1913, ibid., 97–98.
14. Macfadden and Gauvreau, *Dumbbells*, 112, 116.
15. Ibid., 117.
16. Ibid., 114–15, 120–21.
17. Ibid., 121.
18. Ibid., 130–31.
19. Ibid., 123.
20. Ibid., 124.
21. This and the following paragraph are based on Macfadden and Gauvreau, *Dumbbells*, 127–29.
22. This and the following two paragraphs are based on Macfadden and Gauvreau, *Dumbbells*, 132–40.
23. This and the following paragraph are based on Macfadden and Gauvreau, *Dumbbells*, 139–43.
24. Ibid., 143–48; Perkins, *Chats*, 4; *PC*, Sept. 1934, 17.
25. Macfadden and Gauvreau, *Dumbbells*, 151–58; Perkins, *Chats*, 15; *PC*, Sept. 1934, 17.
26. Macfadden and Gauvreau, *Dumbbells*, 158–59, 164.
27. Ibid., 162, 169, 171; Perkins, *Chats*, 15–16; *PC*, Sept. 1934, 17.
28. Macfadden and Gauvreau, *Dumbbells*, 162–69, 172–73; *New York Times*, Oct. 9, 1914; *PC*, Sept. 1934, 97.
29. Macfadden and Gauvreau, *Dumbbells*, 177–79; *PC*, Sept. 1943, 98.
30. This and the following two paragraphs are based on Macfadden and Gauvreau, *Dumbbells*, 179–81, 184–91.
31. Ibid., 191–96.
32. This and the following three paragraphs are based on Macfadden and Gauvreau, *Dumbbells*, 193, 197–204, 212–17.
33. Ibid., 224, 247; Perkins, *Chats*, 36–37; *PC*, Sept. 1934, 99.
34. Macfadden and Gauvreau, *Dumbbells*, 247–48; Physical Culture Corporation, undated letter addressed "Dear Doctor," enclosed with Dr. Helena T. Ratterman to editor, *Journal of the American Medical Association*, Mar. 25, 1922, Macfadden File, AMA; Arthur J. Cramp to Dr. H. A. Peck, Mar. 14, 1922, and to Dr. Helena T. Ratterman, Mar. 29, 1922, Macfadden File, AMA.
35. Macfadden and Gauvreau, *Dumbbells*, 278; Wood, *Bernarr Macfadden*, 129.
36. This and the following four paragraphs are based on Macfadden and Gauvreau, *Dumbbells*, 330–41.
37. Fulton Oursler, *Behold This Dreamer! An Autobiography by Fulton Oursler* (Boston: Little, Brown, 1964), 173–74.
38. Macfadden and Gauvreau, *Dumbbells*, 341, 344–45, 355–58; Waugh, "Bernarr Macfadden," 219, citing Bernarr Macfadden vs. Mary Macfadden, 10, 47, 145.
39. Macfadden and Gauvreau, *Dumbbells*, 356–58, 394.

40. Elsa Weinberg Branden, interview with the author, Mar. 4, 1982; Wood, *Bernarr Macfadden*, 143; *PC*, 1939–1940, passim; *Macfadden Wholesaler*, May 1937, 8, owned by Beulah Keenan; advertisement in *Liberty*, Apr. 22, 1939; S. O. Shapiro, interview with the author, Mar. 23, 1982; Tom Holloway, interview with the author, Mar. 26, 1982.

41. "Exploiting the Health Interest," 3, *Hygeia*, Dec. 1924, 748; *New York Times*, June 21, 1926; Macfadden and Gauvreau, *Dumbbells*, 320; Caspary, *Secrets of Grown-ups*, 98–100.

42. Caspary, *Secrets of Grown-Ups*, 98–99.

5. CONFESSIONS MAKE MILLIONS

1. Elsa Weinberg Branden, interview with the author, Mar. 23, 1982; Beatrice Lubitz Cole, interview with the author, Sept. 21, 1982; Gauvreau, *My Last Million Readers*, 102–3.

2. Carroll Rheinstrom, interview with the author, Sept. 21, 1983; Cole interview (see n. 1); Johnston, "Great Macfadden," 20–21.

3. George B. Davis, interview with the author, June 10, 1982; S. O. Shapiro, interview with the author, Apr. 27, 1982. An art department veteran later said it was common knowledge that Macfadden employed spies. (Tom Holloway, interview with the author, Mar. 26, 1982.)

4. Oursler, *Behold This Dreamer*, 182, 191.

5. Caspary, *Secrets of Grown-ups*, 90–91.

6. Gauvreau, *My Last Million Readers*, 101; Oursler, *Behold This Dreamer*, viii; Will Oursler, *Family Story* (New York: Funk and Wagnalls, 1963), 43.

7. Oursler, *Behold This Dreamer*, 146–47, 164; Macfadden and Gauvreau, *Dumbbells*, 222, 232–33.

8. Oursler, *Behold This Dreamer*, 165; Will Oursler, *Family Story*, 34.

9. Oursler, *Behold This Dreamer*, 166.

10. Ibid., 174; Fulton Oursler (Jr.), interview with the author, Aug. 18, 1982. The boss recognized his value to the company and soon was paying him $25,000 a year (Oursler, *Behold This Dreamer*, 100).

11. Oursler, *Behold This Dreamer*, 184; Lester Cohen, *The New York Graphic, The World's Zaniest Newspaper* (Philadelphia: Chilton Books, 1964), 5.

12. Will Oursler, *Family Story*, 42, 43; Beatrice Lubitz Cole, interview with the author, Sept. 21, 1982; Tom Holloway, interview with the author, Mar. 26, 1982; S. O. Shapiro, interview with the author, March 23, 1982.

13. Fulton Oursler (Jr.), in Oursler, *Behold This Dreamer*, 303–4, 306; Will Oursler, *Family Story*, 119–20.

14. Macfadden and Gauvreau, *Dumbbells*, 218, 219.

15. Bernarr Macfadden vs. Mary Macfadden, Special Master's Report, case no. 77430, Chancery in circuit court in and for Dade County, Fla., Oct. 29, 1945, 5. (Transcript furnished by Richard P. Brinker, clerk, circuit court, Feb. 20, 1985); Waugh, "Bernarr Macfadden," 177; *PC*, Sept. 1934, 92; Harland Manchester, "True Stories," *Scribner's Magazine*, Aug. 1938, 25; Robert Lewis Taylor, "Physical Culture," pt. 3, *New Yorker*, Oct. 28, 1950, 42.

16. Harold B. Hersey, *Pulpwood Editor* (New York: Frederick A. Stokes, 1937), 205–6; Macfadden and Gauvreau, *Dumbbells*, 228.

17. Oursler, *True Story*, 24, 207, 216.

18. Hersey, *Pulpwood Editor*, 218–19, 223, 225–27.

19. Markovich, "Publishing Empire," 72; Waugh, "Bernarr Macfadden," 178–79; *True Story Magazine as a Great Moral Force*, ([New York]: Macfadden Publications, n.d.); Frederick Lewis Allen, *Only Yesterday, An Informal History of the Nineteen-Twenties* (New York: Blue Ribbon Books, 1931), 98. During the depression of the 1930s *True Story* sold for fifteen cents.

20. Oursler, *Behold This Dreamer*, 170–71; Hersey, *Pulpwood Editor*, 223–24.

21. The undated text of this telegram is in Oursler, *True Story*, 227–28.

22. Hersey, *Pulpwood Editor*, 216–17; Oursler, *Behold This Dreamer*, 174–75, 230; Cohen, *New York Graphic*, 79; Johnston, "Great Macfadden," 21.

23. Cohen, *New York Graphic*, 220–22.

24. Oursler, *True Story*, 233–35; examples in *True Story*, Nov. 1934, Mar. 1935; Markovich, "Publishing Empire," 82.

25. *True Story*, Nov. 1934, 46–47; July 1935, 24–25.

26. Oursler, *True Story*, 224–25; Hersey, *Pulpwood Editor*, 214.

27. [True Story Magazine], *The American Economic Revolution*, 2 vols. (New York: True Story, 1930–1931), 2:54. The chapters in this work are reprints of full-page public relations statements in newspapers and magazines.

28. [True Story], *How To Get People Excited* (New York: True Story, 1937), 14.

29. *True Story*, Nov. 1934, passim, and Apr. 1935, 13, 158; Johnston, "Great Macfadden," 20.

30. For this paragraph, see *True Story*, Feb., Mar., Apr., July, Sept., and Oct. 1935.

31. *PC*, March 1929, 118; *True Story*, Mar., Apr., Sept., and Oct. 1935; Markovich, "Publishing Empire," 72; "A Colorful Publishing Career," *Printer's Ink*, Oct. 21, 1955, 82; Johnston, "Great Macfadden," 21.

32. William Jourdan Rapp to Fulton Oursler, office memo., Nov. 16 [1926], William Jourdan Rapp Papers, KLUO.

33. William Jourdan Rapp to Bernarr Macfadden, June 28, 1928, confidential memo.: Readjustment of Salary; Rapp to Fulton Oursler, office memos. May 27, 1935, Aug. 24, 1936; Rapp to Haydock Miller, (vice-president of Macfadden Publications and Bernarr's cousin), Feb. 11, 1935, all in Rapp Papers, KLUO; Manchester, "True Stories," 27, 28.

34. William Jourdan Rapp to Haydock Miller, office memo., Feb. 11, 1935, Rapp Papers, KLUO; Theodore Peterson, *Magazines in the Twentieth Century*, 2d ed., (Urbana: Univ. of Illinois Press, 1964), 299.

35. Hersey, *Pulpwood Editor*, 227; Peterson, *Magazines in the Twentieth Century*, 85; [Macfadden Publications], *Statistical and Financial Analysis of Macfadden Publications* (New York: Macfadden Publications, 1929), 11; Beulah Keenan (widow of Phil Keenan, sales manager of Macfadden Publications), interview with the author, Apr. 15, 1982.

36. Peterson, *Magazines in the Twentieth Century*, 299–300; [Macfadden Publications], *Statistical and Financial Analysis*, 8–9; Macfadden and Gauvreau, *Dumbbells*, 399.

37. [Macfadden Publications], *Statistical and Financial Analysis*, 12; Will Oursler, *Family Story*, 49; Hersey, *Pulpwood Editor*, 190–91; Phil Keenan, Macfadden Publications in-house announcement, Apr. 2, 1931, owned by Beulah Keenan; *Newsweek*, Dec. 14, 1935.

38. Will Oursler, *Family Story*, 43–44; Macfadden and Gauvreau, *Dumbbells*, 295–96.

39. Caspary, *Secrets of Grown-ups*, 92, 101.

40. [Macfadden Publications], *Statistical and Financial Analysis*, 12, 77.

41. Bernarr Macfadden editorial, *True Detective Mysteries*, May 1939; Oursler, *Behold This Dreamer*, 251; [Macfadden Publications], *Statistical and Financial Analysis*, 10, 17.

42. Macfadden editorial, *True Detective Mysteries*, May 1939.

43. J. Edgar Hoover to John Shuttleworth, and J. Edgar Hoover to Bernarr Macfadden, Mar. 27, 1939, Bernarr Macfadden File, FBI, no. 94-3-4-30.

44. Markovich, "Publishing Empire," 74–75; Fulton Oursler, "Bernarr Macfadden—His Life and Work," *PC*, April 1929, 144–45; William Jourdan Rapp to Mrs. [Susie] Wood, office memo., Jan. 12, 1926, Rapp Papers, KLUO; Rapp to Fulton Oursler, office memo., Nov. 16 [1926], Rapp Papers, KLUO; Macfadden and Gauvreau, *Dumbbells*, 349–50; Wood, *Bernarr Macfadden*, 121; *Macfadden Retailer*, Dec. 1929, 2, and *Macfadden Wholesaler*, Jan. 1937, owned by Beulah Keenan; *Your Faith*, Apr. 1939, Oursler Papers, FULA; George B. Davis, announcement, Dec. 20, 1939, owned by Beulah Keenan.

45. Oursler, *Behold This Dreamer*, 372; Joseph P. Lash, *Eleanor and Franklin, The Story of Their Relationship Based on Eleanor Roosevelt's Private Papers* (New York: W. W. Norton, 1971), 355, 373; Bernarr Macfadden to Eleanor Roosevelt, May 1, 1933, Eleanor Roosevelt Papers, FDRL; Macfadden and Gauvreau, *Dumbbells*, 299–300.

46. Oursler, *Behold This Dreamer*, 194; Macfadden and Gauvreau, *Dumbbells*, 260, 276; Will Oursler, *Family Story*, 44, 46.

47. *Tide*, Oct. 1, 1939, 38; June 1, 1940, 14. [Macfadden Publications], *Statistical and Financial Analysis*, 24; Harrison B. Summers, ed., *A Thirty-year History of Programs Carried on Radio Networks in the United States, 1926–1956* (New York: Arno Press, 1971), 17, 39, 45, 53, 61, 69, 77, 95; John Dunning, *Tune in Yesterday: The Ultimate Encyclopedia of Old-time Radio, 1925–1976* (Englewood Cliffs, N.J.: Prentice-Hall, 1976), 242, 243, 615–16; (*Collier's*, *Literary Digest*, and *Time* also sponsored radio programs). S. O. Shapiro, interview with the author, Apr. 27, 1982; *Macfadden Retailer*, Dec. 1929, 4, owned by Beulah Keenan.

48. *PC*, Oct. 1915, 16a; Dec. 1915, 65–68; Jan. 1916, 118; Oct. 1919, 92. Macfadden and Gauvreau, *Dumbbells*, 241–45; Grace Perkins [Oursler], *Chats*, 205, 208; George B. Davis, interview with the author, June 10, 1982; Bernarr Macfadden to Upton Sinclair, Mar. 3, 1931, Sinclair Papers, LLIU.

49. Peterson, *Magazines in the Twentieth Century*, 256; Taylor, "Physical Culture," pt. 1, 39. Few houses were erected in the suburban development. Macfadden refused to pay assessments on the improvements, claiming that they were excessive, and the city of Hackensack auctioned the property in 1934 (*New York Times*, Apr. 2, 7, 1934).

6. THE "PORNO-GRAPHIC"

1. S. O. Shapiro, former Macfadden associate, to the author, Nov. 5, 1984; John Stuart, "Bernarr Macfadden from Pornography to Politics," *New Masses*, May 19, 1936, 8; *Newsweek*, June 29, 1935, 28; *Time*, Sept. 21, 1936, 45; Johnston, "Great Macfadden," 91; Allene Talmey, "Millions from Dumb-bells," *Outlook and Independent*, June 4, 1930, 164.

2. Frank Mallen, *Sauce for the Gander* (White Plains, N.Y.: Baldwin Books, 1954), 3; *PC*, Oct. 1934, 41, 100–101.

3. *New York Evening Graphic* (hereafter cited as *Graphic*), Sept. 17, 22, 1924.

4. Macfadden and Gauvreau, *Dumbbells*, 302; Cohen, *New York Graphic*, 205, 227-28; *Graphic*, Sept. 13, 1924.

5. Bernarr Macfadden, "A Crusading Newspaper," *Graphic*, Sept. 17, 1924. See also the first issue, Sept. 15, 1924.

6. Oursler, *Behold This Dreamer*, 204, 205; Macfadden and Gauvreau, *Dumbbells*, 367.

7. Macfadden and Gauvreau, *Dumbbells*, 368-75; Cohen, *New York Graphic*, 4, 18-19, 26; *Time*, Oct. 6, 1941, 66; Gauvreau, *My Last Million Readers*, 100-103; Wood, *Bernarr Macfadden*, 124-25.

8. Oursler, *Behold This Dreamer*, 207-8, 224; Edward L. Bernays, interview with the author, May 25, 1982; Cohen, however, claimed (*Graphic*, 3) that feature editor John W. Vandercook lost his job after a disagreement with Oursler. Herbert Hoover, then secretary of commerce, filed Gauvreau's telegram without replying. (Emile Gauvreau to Herbert Hoover, Sept. 8, 1924, Herbert Hoover Papers, Herbert Hoover Presidential Library, West Branch, Iowa.)

9. John A. Gambling, telephone conversation with the author, 1983.

10. Cohen, *New York Graphic*, 2-12; Mallen, *Sauce for the Gander*, 147-58.

11. Gauvreau, *My Last Million Readers*, 122; Talmey, "Millions from Dumb-bells," 166 for quotation on Winchell's gossip; Mallen, *Sauce for the Gander*, 147-86; Markovich, "Publishing Empire," 97-98.

12. *Graphic*, Jan. 1, 1932.

13. Simon Michael Bessie, *Jazz Journalism, The Story of the Tabloid Newspapers* (New York: Russell and Russell, 1969), 192; *Graphic*, Jan. 1, 1932; Markovich, "Publishing Empire," 101-2, citing personal communication from Ed Bodin, who by 1956 had become president of the Macfadden Foundation.

14. Mallen, *Sauce for the Gander*, 158-63.

15. *Graphic*, Sept. 26, 27, Oct. 17, 1924.

16. Bessie, *Jazz Journalism*, 202; Oursler, *True Story*, 245-46, for the Macfadden quotation; *Time*, Feb. 14, 1927, 30; Aben Kandel, "A Tabloid a Day," *Forum*, Mar. 1927, 383; H. L. Mencken, "An American Idealist," *American Mercury*, May 1930, 125.

17. Oswald Garrison Villard, "I—Tabloid Offenses," *Forum*, Apr. 1927, 487; Johnston, "Great Macfadden," 91; Cohen, *New York Graphic*, 6, for Macfadden's advice to his staff (see also Oursler, *True Story*, 245-46); Frank Luther Mott, *American Journalism, A History: 1690-1960*, 3d ed. (New York: Macmillan, 1962), 670; "Mr. Macfadden Defines News," *New Republic*, Oct. 8, 1924.

18. *Graphic*, Oct. 2, 1924; Mar. 20, 1930; May 19, July 20, Sept. 29, 1931 (Sports final ed.).

19. Ibid., Sept. 17, 20, 1924.

20. Ibid., May 2, July 29, Oct. 12, 1931.

21. Ibid., Sept. 18, 1924; Mar. 20, July 22, 1931; Apr. 6, 1932.

22. *Newsweek*, June 29, 1935, 28; *Graphic*, Mar. 2, 3, 5, 1932; *New York Times*, May 13, 1932.

23. *New York Times*, July 4, 1927; John L. Spivak, "The Rise and Fall of a Tabloid," *American Mercury*, July 1934, 308.

24. Bessie, *Jazz Journalism*, 197-98; Spivak, "Rise and Fall of a Tabloid," 311. Reproductions of this composite picture are in Mallen, *Sauce for the Gander*, following p. 36, and Cohen, *New York Graphic*, following p. 54.

25. Mallen, *Sauce for the Gander*, 119-20; Bessie, *Jazz Journalism*, 198 (see reproductions in Mallen, following p. 36, and Cohen, following p. 54); *New York Times*,

Feb. 5, 8, 6, 1927; Henry F. Pringle, "Another American Phenomenon Bernarr Mac-fadden—Publisher and Physical Culturist," *World's Work*, Oct. 1928, 666.

26. Mallen, *Sauce for the Gander*, 32; Cohen, *New York Graphic*, 102. Reproductions of this composite are in Mallen, following p. 36, and Cohen, following p. 54.

27. *Graphic*, Jan. 23, 1932. A *Daily News* photographer had violated the prison rule by attaching a camera to his ankle and surreptitiously photographing the execution of Ruth Snyder and Judd Gray on Jan. 13, 1928 (Mott, *American Journalism*, 671).

28. *Graphic*, Jan. 23, 1932.

29. Ibid., June 23, 1932. See also *PC*, Oct. 1934, 101.

30. Gauvreau, *My Last Million Readers*, 131.

31. Cohen, *New York Graphic*, 14–15, 18, 20, 47, 67, 75, 76, 77, 81; Spivak, "Rise and Fall of a Tabloid," 312–13; Gauvreau, *My Last Million Readers*, 108. The Madison Square Garden event was on Mar. 16, 1925.

32. Gauvreau, *My Last Million Readers*, 123; *Graphic*, passim.

33. *Graphic*, July 21, 1921; Feb. 20, Sept. 23, 1924; Oct. 11, 1928; Nov. 15, 1928; June 4, 14, 18, 24, 1929; Mar. 12, 1930; July 28, 1931. The *Graphic* adopted Macfadden's mania for physical culture in such fiction as "My Victory over Dope" (Bessie, *Jazz Journalism*, 193).

34. Pringle, "Another American Phenomenon," 659; *Graphic*, Sept. 18, 30, 1924; June 21, 1929; Mar. 4, 18, 1930; Mar. 11, May 4, 1931; Jan. 12, 22, 1932. Macfadden favored birth control as one way to perpetuate a "vital race of people." *Graphic*, Apr. 1931. He gave money to support Margaret Sanger's work to control births among tenement women (Macfadden and Gauvreau, *Dumbbells*, 231).

35. *Graphic*, June 9, 1931.

36. Ibid., June 6, 12, 1929; Mar. 17, Apr. 16, May 28, 1931; Jan. 29, Mar. 11, May 12, June 15, July 6, 1932. Macfadden's editorial on Oct. 1, 1928, was entitled "Shameful Neglect of Victims of Legal Blunders." As early as Sept. 16, 1924, a *Graphic* headline screamed "Poor Boy, Facing Noose, Cries Must I Die When Rich Killers Get Life." *Graphic*, Oct. 2, 1931; *Liberty*, July 28, Aug. 18, 1934; *Graphic*, Sept. 30, Oct. 16, 1924; Nov. 5, 1928; Jan. 13, Mar. 1, May 10, 1932.

37. *Graphic*, June 7, 1929; Mar. 7, 20, 1930; Mar. 20, 31, 1931; Jan. 27, Apr. 29, 1932. Thomas Dixon, *A Dreamer in Portugal* (New York: Covici-Friede, 1934), 34.

38. "Macfadden and Successors" File, Office of North Dansville Town Historian, Town Hall, Dansville, N.Y.; *Graphic*, Mar. 31, 1931; Dixon, *Dreamer in Portugal*, 34.

39. Fulton Oursler (Jr.), in Oursler, *Behold This Dreamer*, 262; *Graphic*, Mar. 7, 1931.

40. Dixon, *Dreamer in Portugal*, 55–60, 144.

41. Gauvreau, *My Last Million Readers*, 126.

42. Cohen, *New York Graphic*, 132–33; Gauvreau, *My Last Million Readers*, 113; *New York Times*, Feb. 11, July 2, 1927; July 2, 8, 1932. The Atlantic City and Carroll suits were dropped years later. (Spivak, "Rise and Fall of a Tabloid," 311.)

43. *Graphic*, June 4, 8, 1929; Mar. 9, 1931; Oursler, *Behold This Dreamer*, 224–27; Talmey, "Millions from Dumb-bells," 196; *Graphic*, Jan. 11, 1932.

44. Bessie, *Jazz Journalism*, 206–7.

45. Gauvreau, *My Last Million Readers*, 112–13.

46. Ibid., 104, 108; Markovich, "Publishing Empire," 97; John K. Winkler, *William Randolph Hearst, A New Appraisal* (New York: Hastings House, 1955), 208; Bessie, *Jazz Journalism*, 185, 202, 206; *New York Times*, July 2, 8, 1932.

47. The other Macfadden tabloids were the *Philadelphia Daily News, Detroit Daily*

News, Automotive Investment News, and [New York] *Daily Investment News;* his full-size papers were the *New Haven Times-Union, Lansing Capital News,* [Wyandotte] *Daily Record, Mount Pleasant Daily Times,* and [Greenville] *Daily News.* Markovich, "Publishing Empire," 105; Gauvreau, *My Last Million Readers,* 133; *New York Times,* July 8, 1929. Gauvreau, who was also a *Graphic* executive and a stockholder in Macfadden Publications, did not blame Macfadden, who had treated him fairly and enabled him to save considerable money (*My Last Million Readers,* 134).

48. Johnston, "Great Macfadden," 91; Oursler, *Behold This Dreamer,* 227; Markovich, "Publishing Empire," 106, citing communication from Ed Bodin. Meyer Dworkin, the *Graphic's* comptroller for many years, explaining the $11,000,000 figure (Cohen, *New York Graphic,* 219). The *New York Times,* Oct. 22, 1926, reported that the new plant involved $4,000,000. Cohen, *New York Graphic,* 231, 232; *New York Times,* June 9, July 8, 1932. After the Graphic's demise, none of Macfadden's other newspapers remained except two small ones in Michigan.

49. Bernarr Macfadden to Arthur Garfield Hays, May 24, 1940, copy, Oursler Scrapbook, "F. O. Personal, 1940, 3," Oursler Papers, FULA; *PC,* Oct. 1934, 101–2; Pringle, "Another American Phenomenon," 660; Bessie, *Jazz Journalism,* 203; Oursler, *Behold This Dreamer,* 226–27.

50. "Perhaps the Public Has Been Maligned," *Christian Century,* July 20, 1932, 901.

7. "THE FATHER OF PHYSICAL CULTURE"

1. Dr. Eugene L. Fisk to Frank Munsey, Feb. 8, 1924, copy in Bernarr Macfadden File, AMA, Chicago.

2. Arthur J. Cramp to Col. W. E. Elwell, Jan. 27, 1911, Bernarr Macfadden File, AMA. Similar replies were sent to James Mullenbach, Aug. 11, 1911; Dr. Lester L. Betts, July 24, 1912; Dr. Vincent Shepherd, Oct. 14, 1914; Dr. E. O. Daniels, Dec. 27, 1915; Dr. J. U. Paullin, Jan. 28, 1916; Dr. Harvey Wiley, Director of Bureau of Foods, Sanitation and Health, *Good Housekeeping Magazine,* May 25, 1916; and Dr. G. W. States, July 13, 1917, Bernarr Macfadden File, AMA. The articles were in the *American Journal of Clinical Medicine,* vol. 17, no. 10, Oct. 1910, and the *Kentucky Medical Journal,* vol. 10, no. 7, Apr. 1, 1912.

3. *PC,* Mar. 1911, 266.

4. Fishbein, *Medical Follies,* 175–77. The AMA articles were: "Exploiting the Health Interest. I. Type of Advertising that Makes 'Physical Culture' Commercially Profitable," *Hygeia,* Nov. 1924, 678–83, and "Exploiting the Health Interest. II. Type of Literature on Which 'Physical Culturists' and Macfaddenists Thrive," *Hygeia,* Dec. 1924, 744–48.

5. Dr. D. B. Ealy to Bernarr Macfadden, Dec. 14, 1926, copy, Macfadden File, AMA.

6. Secretary of the Grant County Medical Association, Marion, Ind., to Bernarr Macfadden, Apr. 8, 1927, quoted in Waugh, "Bernarr Macfadden," 162. The anonymous secretary wrote on behalf of the association's members. For the AMA's contemptuous comment on Macfadden's recommendations of a two-week fast followed by a raw milk diet to cleanse the blood stream, see "Macfadden Says 'I Told You So' about Syphilis," *Journal of the American Medical Association,* vol. 88, no. 15, Apr. 10, 1937, 1266.

7. Dr. Arthur J. Cramp to Dr. D. E. Harding of the Mayo Clinic, Apr. 1, 1924, Macfadden File, AMA.

8. "Exploiting the Health Interest. II," *Hygeia*, Dec. 1924, 744–48. Quotation is on 748.

9. Dr. Arthur J. Cramp to Dr. H. J. McLaren, Dec. 10, 1926, and to Dr. W. O. LaMotte, Dec. 21, 1926, Macfadden File, AMA.

10. Dr. Arthur J. Cramp to Dr. Albert J. Harris, Feb. 3, 1937, Macfadden File, AMA.

11. Elder's letter, dated Aug. 26, 1927, and accompanying documents attached to Dr. C. A. Ringle to AMA, Sept. 16, 1927, Macfadden File, AMA.

12. Dr. Millard H. Foster to AMA, Aug. 31, 1927, and Dr. Elizabeth C. Mallon to editor *AMA Journal*, Sept. 16, 1927, Macfadden File, AMA.

13. E.g., Dr. Arthur J. Cramp to Dr. Erwin J. Gottsch, Sept. 7, 1927, Macfadden File, AMA.

14. Dr. Mazyck P. Ravenel, editor in chief, *American Journal of Public Health*, to Dr. Arthur J. Cramp, Oct. 15, 1931, and Cramp to Ravenel, Oct. 20, 1931, Macfadden File, AMA.

15. Bernarr Macfadden, "Remove Commercialism From Public Health," *Liberty*, Feb. 3, 1940, 4; Bernarr Macfadden to Thomas E. Dewey, Nov. 18, 1947, Dewey Papers, RLUR.

16. Oliver F. Field of the AMA's Bureau of Investigation to Dr. Adam P. Leighton, Apr. 14, 1929, Macfadden File, AMA; postcard signed Bernarr Macfadden, enclosed with Dr. Warren G. Kauder to AMA, June 10, 1954, and Field to Kauder, Aug. 2, 1954, Macfadden File, AMA.

17. Bernarr Macfadden to Fulton Oursler, office memo., Nov. 3, 1938, Oursler Scrapbook, Oursler Papers, FULA; Bernarr Macfadden, "We Endorse the President's Health Crusade," *Liberty*, Feb. 4, 1939, 3.

18. Dr. Jack R. Linden to Clifford J. Waugh, May 14, 1973, Waugh, "Bernarr Macfadden," 248. Bliss O. Halling to Dr. L. A. Ruhl, May 5, 1943; Paul C. Barton, director of the AMA Bureau of Investigation, to Dr. G. C. Hedrick, Jr., Oct. 1, 1940; Bliss O. Halling to Dr. G. M. De Woody, June 29, 1935; and Dr. Arthur J. Cramp to Dr. E. R. Schoolfield, May 10, 1937; all in Macfadden File, AMA.

19. Sinclair, *Autobiography*, 73, 87, 125, 137, 140–41, 158–60, 232, 237, 313 (quotation on 158–59); *PC*, Nov. 1940, 69–70; Johnnie Lee Macfadden, interview with the author, Sept. 22, 1981; Vic Boff, operator of a fitness center in Brooklyn, N.Y., telephone conversation with the author, Sept. 29, 1981.

20. Waugh, "Bernarr Macfadden," 45–46, citing advertisements in *PC* in 1900, 1903, and 1906; Charles Gaines and George Butler, *Yours in Perfect Manhood, Charles Atlas* (New York: Simon and Schuster, 1982), 57–59.

21. Carlton Jackson, *J. I. Rodale, Apostle of Nonconformity* (New York: Pyramid Books, 1974), 29.

22. *PC*, July 1940, 87; Donald J. Mrozek, *Sport and American Mentality, 1880–1910* (Knoxville: Univ. of Tennessee Press, 1983), 92.

23. Waugh, "Bernarr Macfadden," 213, 233–35, 250; "Macfadden and a Starvation Death," *Journal of the American Medical Association*, Jan. 10, 1925, 136; Dr. Arthur J. Cramp to Dr. Fred H. Krug, May 2, 1919; Dr. David C. Hall to AMA, Dec. 12, 1912 and Feb. 8, 1913, and accompanying documents; Bliss O. Halling to Morris Fishbein, Nov. 12, 1943; all in the Macfadden File, AMA.

24. Macfadden executive who requested anonymity, interview with the author, Sept. 21, 1983; Harry G. Mitchell, "Fasting and Diet Cured Me of a Terrible Blood Disease," *PC*, Dec. 1926, 36–37, 70, 72; C. E. Papadopoulos, M.D., to Whom it May Concern, Sept. 30, 1926, Macfadden File, AMA; Miss Sidney Lloyd, hostess and yoga in-

structor at Macfadden's Dansville hotel, interview with Clifford J. Waugh, Oct. 7, 1973, Waugh, "Bernarr Macfadden," 231–32; Cary T. Grayson to Dr. George H. Simmons, Dec. 28, 1920, and to Physical Culture Corporation, Jan. 10, 1921, copy, and leaflet advertising *Manhood and Marriage*, issued by the Physical Culture Corporation, Macfadden File, AMA.

25. *PC*, Oct. 1906, 378; *Evening Record* [Hackensack; Bergen County, N.J.], Mar. 28, 1972.

26. Fulton Oursler, Scrapbook, "Personal 1924," entry for June 5, Oursler Papers, FULA; Barry Good to Clifford J. Waugh, Mar. 23, 1973 in Waugh, "Bernarr Macfadden," 59; Wood, *Bernarr Macfadden*, 134; Gauvreau, *My Last Million Readers*, 135.

27. *Liberty*, Sept. 2, 1939, 4.

28. Oursler, *Behold This Dreamer*, 306–7.

29. Dorothy Sherrill to Clifford J. Waugh, Apr. 11, 1973 in Waugh, "Bernarr Macfadden," 187.

30. George B. Davis, Macfadden executive, interview with the author, June 10, 1982; S. O. Shapiro, Macfadden executive, interview with Clifford J. Waugh, July 1, 1972, in Waugh, "Bernarr Macfadden," 245; *PC*, Feb. 1902, 236; Oct. 1903, 336; Beulah Keenan, interview with the author, Mar. 26, 1982; Taylor, "Physical Culture," pt. 1, 39; *Dictionary of American Biography*, supp. 5, 454; Fulton Oursler, "The Most Unforgettable Character I've Met," *Reader's Digest*, July 1951, 82.

31. Taft, "Bernarr Macfadden," 82. Taft noted that the Library of Congress had more than sixty Macfadden books and pamphlets, and that the London Library in England had more than sixty volumes.

32. James Harvey Young, *The Medical Messiahs: A Social History of Health Quackery in Twentieth Century America* (Princeton: Princeton Univ. Press, 1967), 347; *Dictionary of American Biography*, supp. 5, 453.

33. Bernarr Macfadden, "War–Health–Doctors," *Liberty*, Nov. 30, 1940, 4; "Macfadden Discusses Army Medical Service," *Journal of the American Medical Association*, Nov. 30, 1940, 1890.

34. Harold Aspiz, "Sexuality and the Pseudo-Sciences," in *Pseudo-Science and Society in Nineteenth Century America*, edited by Arthur Wrobel (Lexington: Univ. Press of Kentucky, 1987), 149.

8. THE POLITICAL BUG

1. *PC*, Mar. 1902, supp. p. F; Feb. 1907, 107; Aug. 1904, 189. Macfadden and Gauvreau, *Dumbbells*, 351.

2. Macfadden and Gauvreau, *Dumbbells*, 350–51.

3. Ed Zoty, interview with Clifford J. Waugh, Mar. 26, 1973 in Waugh, "Bernarr Macfadden," 191; Will Oursler, *Family Story*, 57; Cohen, *New York Graphic*, 54, 73.

4. Macfadden and Gauvreau, *Dumbbells*, 380.

5. Ibid., 379.

6. Byrnece Macfadden Muckerman, interview with Clifford J. Waugh, Apr. 21, 1973 in Waugh, "Bernarr Macfadden," 240.

7. Edward L. Bernays, interview with the author, May 25, 1982; Edward L. Bernays, *Biography of an Idea: Memoirs of Public Relations Counsel, Edward L. Bernays* (New York: Simon and Schuster, 1965), 359–61. The record of debates in the House of Commons does not mention an address by Macfadden. There is no reference either

to the address or to Sir Nicholas's dinner in the London *Times* during the two weeks the American was in London. The events must have been off the record, and Macfadden must have been disappointed by the absence of local publicity.

8. Wood, *Bernarr Macfadden*, 160–61. Johnnie Lee Macfadden recalled that Shaw visited her husband when he came to the United States and that the two men "sat up all night trading stories, comparing muscles and congratulating each other on having found the secret of everlasting youth" (Johnnie Lee Macfadden, *Barefoot in Eden: The Macfadden Plan for Health, Charm and Long-Lasting Youth* [Englewood Cliffs, N.J.: Prentice-Hall, 1962], 191).

9. Gauvreau, *My Last Million Readers*, 130; Wood, *Bernarr Macfadden*, 156–63, 167–70; *PC*, Feb. 1928, 33, 96. In 1839, Webster visited the houses of Commons and Lords but did not make a speech there. Harold D. Moser, former editor of *The Papers of Daniel Webster*, to the author, Dec. 11, 1984.

10. Gauvreau, *My Last Million Readers*, 110–11.

11. Macfadden and Gauvreau, *Dumbbells*, 398.

12. Ibid.

13. Wood, *Bernarr Macfadden*, 179.

14. Ibid., 189–90; Macfadden and Gauvreau, *Dumbbells*, 398; Macfadden, "BERNARR MACFADDEN WANTS TO BE SECRETARY OF HEALTH," *Liberty*, Aug. 3, 1940, 4.

15. S. N. Baruch to George Ackerson, executive secretary to President Hoover, Apr. 24, 1930, Herbert Hoover Presidential Library, West Branch, Iowa; *Graphic*, May 6, 1932; Markovich, "Publishing Empire," 112.

16. Peterson, *Magazines in the Twentieth Century*, 80; S. O. Shapiro, acting head of Circulation Department, Bulletin to Representatives, Apr. 9, 1931, owned by Beulah Keenan; Phil Keenan, assistant sales manager, memo. to wholesalers, Apr. 13, 1931, owned by Beulah Keenan.

17. Will Oursler, *Family Story*, 154; Fulton Oursler, *Behold This Dreamer*, 267–68.

18. Bernarr Macfadden to Fulton Oursler, office memo., Nov. 23, 1931, and Fulton Oursler to Bernarr Macfadden, office memo., Nov. 20, 1931, Oursler Scrapbook, Oursler Papers, FULA.

19. Bernarr Macfadden to Sydney Greenbie, Oct. 7, 1932, Sydney Greenbie Papers, Special Collections Div., KLUO. (For Oursler's full command of *Liberty*, see Will Oursler, *Family Story*, 154.) *Liberty*, May 2, 1931, 4.

20. *Liberty*, June 20, 1931, 4; July 11, 1931, 4; Oct. 10, 1931, 4; Nov. 3, 1934, 4; Dec. 3, 1938, 4.

21. Bernarr Macfadden to Thomas E. Dewey, June 26, 1940, Dewey Papers, RLUR. Dewey was then district attorney of New York County.

22. Oursler, *Behold This Dreamer*, 269, 370–71 (quotation on 371).

23. *Liberty*, Nov. 12, 1932, 3; Macfadden and Gauvreau, *Dumbbells*, 300.

24. Bernarr Macfadden to Eleanor Roosevelt, May 1, 1933, postscript, Eleanor Roosevelt to Bernarr Macfadden, May 5, 1933, and Macfadden to Eleanor Roosevelt, May 22, 1933, Eleanor Roosevelt Papers, FDRL; Macfadden and Gauvreau, *Dumbbells*, 299–300; Cohen, *New York Graphic*, 209.

25. Bernarr Macfadden to Eleanor Roosevelt, May 1, 1933, and Eleanor Roosevelt to Macfadden, May 5, 1933, Eleanor Roosevelt Papers, FDRL.

26. *New York Times*, Sept. 17, Oct. 29, 1935.

27. Guy L. Harrington to All Executives, office memo., Nov. 19, 1935, Oursler scrapbook, "Personal, 1935, vol. 2," Oursler Papers, FULA; *Liberty*, Mar. 28, 1936, 4;

microfilm of undated biographical sketch, Ewing Y. Mitchell Papers, folder 3938, Joint Collection, Univ. of Missouri Western Historical Manuscripts Collection and State Historical Society Manuscripts, Univ. of Missouri Library, Columbia; Taft, "Bernarr Macfadden," 85; *Newsweek,* Dec. 14, 1935.

28. *New York Herald Tribune,* Nov. 1, 1935.

29. Ibid.

30. Ibid; *Time,* Nov. 1, 1935, 61; *Newsweek,* Dec. 14, 1935, 36–37; *Liberty,* Dec. 14, 1935, 4–5.

31. *New York Times,* Feb. 16, 1936; Bernarr Macfadden, "Some New Dealers Can't Take It," *Liberty,* Mar. 28, 1936, 4.

32. Bernarr Macfadden, "Various Planks Suggested for the Republican Platform," *Liberty,* June 13, 1936, 4.

33. *Time,* Sept. 21, 1936, 45; statement to the author by a former Macfadden executive who requested anonymity, Mar. 23, 1982.

34. Former executive's statement to the author (see n. 33, above). Probably Macfadden spent more than $100,000 because the arrangers expected their cut. Bernarr Macfadden, typescript, "PERSONAL—ABOUT BERNARR MACFADDEN," accompanying his letter to Arthur Garfield Hays, May 20, 1940, "F. O. Personal, 1940," and Bernarr Macfadden to Arthur Garfield Hays, May 24, 1940, copy, Oursler Papers, FULA.

35. Macfadden and Gauvreau, *Dumbbells,* 308–9, 241.

36. Taylor, "Physical Culture," pt. 1, 45; former Macfadden executive, interview with the author, Apr. 27, 1982.

37. Bernarr Macfadden, "The Ghastly Blunders of the Republican Campaign Managers," *Liberty,* Jan. 2, 1937, 4; Bernarr Macfadden, "The Poor Old Republican Party," *Liberty,* Sept. 17, 1938, 3; Bernarr Macfadden to Herbert Hoover, Oct. 6, 1938, Herbert Hoover Presidential Library. The letter is endorsed "Harry ask him to lunch—H," and "O.K. for Lunch Friday Oct. 14th *1 PM,* IR."

38. *Liberty,* Aug. 24, 1940, 51; *New York Times,* Mar. 24, 1940; Waugh, "Bernarr Macfadden," 198. At Macfadden Publications the suspicion that Helen Macfadden was Susie Wood's daughter was widely held.

39. *Liberty,* Aug. 24, 1940, 51; George B. Davis, interview with the author, June 10, 1982.

40. *Liberty,* Apr. 27, 1940, 4; Aug. 24, 1940, 50. Macfadden and Gauvreau, *Dumbbells,* 309; *Time,* May 6, 1940, 21.

41. *Liberty,* Aug. 24, 1940, 52.

42. Macfadden and Gauvreau, *Dumbbells,* 309; Bernarr Macfadden to Ewing Y. Mitchell, May 24, 1940, Joint Collection, Univ. of Missouri Western Historical Manuscripts Collection and State Historical Society Manuscripts, Columbia; Bernarr Macfadden, "Another Way to Save the Nation," *Liberty,* Aug. 10, 1940, 4.

43. "BERNARR MACFADDEN WANTS TO BE SECRETARY OF HEALTH," *Liberty,* Aug. 3, 1940, 4.

44. Bernarr Macfadden to Thomas E. Dewey, Jan. 29, Apr. 12, June 26, 1940; and Dewey to Macfadden, Apr. 12, July 19, 1940, Dewey Papers, RLUR. In 1938, Dewey had been grateful for Macfadden's support in his unsuccessful gubernatorial campaign (Dewey to Macfadden, Nov. 3, Dec. 28, 1938, Dewey Papers, RLUR). Bernarr Macfadden, "The Man Behind the Miracle," *Liberty,* Aug. 10, 1940, 21–22; *Liberty,* Nov. 2, 1940, 4; Bernarr Macfadden, "We Can Win with Willkie," *Liberty,* Nov. 9, 1940, 3.

45. Bernarr Macfadden to Thomas E. Dewey, Nov. 8, 1942, Dewey Papers, RLUR. (For Macfadden's support of Dewey's campaign, see his letters to Dewey, Aug. 27 and

Oct. 15, 1942, and to Herbert Brownell, Oct. 13, 1942. See also Dewey's letters to Macfadden, Aug. 31, Oct. 17, 1942, Dewey Papers, RLUR.) Bernarr Macfadden to Thomas E. Dewey, July 16, Oct. 29, 1948, May 19, 1950, Dewey Papers, RLUR.

46. Johnnie Lee Macfadden, *Barefoot in Eden*, 54–55; Taft, "Bernarr Macfadden," 85; *Dictionary of American Biography*, supp. 5, 453.

47. *New York Times*, Aug. 17, 1952; Bernarr Macfadden to Thomas E. Dewey, Sept. 5, Nov. 26, 1952; and Bernarr Macfadden to "Editor," Oct. 22, 1952, Dewey Papers, RLUR; Bernarr Macfadden to Arthur H. Vandenberg, Jr., Dec. 11, 1952, Dwight D. Eisenhower Library, Abilene, Kans. See also Macfadden to Vandenberg, Dec. 1, 1952, Dwight D. Eisenhower Library.

48. Bernarr Macfadden to Thomas E. Dewey, Mar. 27, Apr. 20, 1953, Dewey Papers, RLUR. *New York Times*, July 21, 1953.

49. *New York Times*, Sept. 30, Oct. 3, Oct. 9, Oct. 14, 1953; photocopy of special edition of *Evening Graphic*, n.d., entitled "Macfadden for Mayor," Dwight D. Eisenhower Library, Abilene, Kans.

9. DAMNING THE NEW DEAL

1. Bernarr Macfadden to Franklin D. Roosevelt, telegram, Nov. 6, 1933, Franklin D. Roosevelt Papers, FDRL; Bernarr Macfadden, "Governmental Competition in Private Business," *Liberty*, Jan. 28, 1933, 4; idem, "Our New President Should Have a Free Hand," *Liberty*, Feb. 4, 1933, 3; idem, "Only Dictatorial Powers Can Save Us," *Liberty*, Mar. 25, 1933, 4; idem, "They Say This Is Inflation, But—," *Liberty*, Mar. 4, 1933, 4.

2. Bernarr Macfadden, "The New Deal Is Here—God Be Praised," *Liberty*, Apr. 22, 1933, 3; idem, "The Depression Is Staggering," *Liberty*, Aug. 5, 1933, 4. Macfadden favored the National Recovery Administration only as an emergency body, considering a permanent NRA an unconstitutional assumption of powers that belonged to the states ("The Permanency of the NRA," [*Liberty*, Apr. 21, 1934]).

3. Bernarr Macfadden, "We Accept the Challenge," *Liberty*, Mar. 11, 1933, 4; idem, "Wages and the Depression," *Liberty*, Apr. 15, 1933, 4.

4. *Liberty*, Sept. 12, 1931; Dec. 24, 1932. Edith R. Lumsden to Sydney Greenbie, Feb. 9, 1932, Sydney Greenbie Papers, Special Collections Div., KLUO; Bernarr Macfadden to Sydney Greenbie, Mar. 17, 1932, Greenbie Papers.

5. Rexford G. Tugwell, *The Brains Trust* (New York: Viking Press, 1968), 177–79; Bernarr Macfadden to Eleanor Roosevelt, Oct. 10, 1933, Eleanor Roosevelt Papers, FDRL; *Liberty*, June 30, 1934, 4; Jan. 11, 1936, 3.

6. Bernarr Macfadden, "Job Insurance Far Better than Unemployment Insurance," *Liberty*, Aug. 11, 1934, 4. (See also his "Job Insurance Will Save the Nation from Ruin," *Liberty*, Dec. 1, 1934, 4.) "The Dole—a Great Calamity," *Liberty*, July 29, 1933, 4. Although appreciating his interest in her girls' shelter, the First Lady replied that the accommodations were not dormitories but a place for rest and simple refreshment. Bernarr Macfadden to Eleanor Roosevelt, June 1, 1933, and Eleanor Roosevelt to Bernarr Macfadden, June 16, 1933, Eleanor Roosevelt Papers, FDRL.

7. Bernarr Macfadden to Eleanor Roosevelt, Oct. 17, Nov. 13, 1934; Eleanor Roosevelt to Bernarr Macfadden, Nov. 1, 1934; and Eleanor Roosevelt's secretary to Bernarr Macfadden, Dec. 11, 1934, Eleanor Roosevelt Papers, FDRL.

8. Macfadden and Gauvreau, *Dumbbells*, 224; *New York Times*, June 22, Aug. 5, Dec. 15, 1932; Feb. 4, 1933.

9. Bernarr Macfadden to Eleanor Roosevelt, May 22, 1933, Eleanor Roosevelt

Papers, FDRL; *New York Times,* June 22, Dec. 24, 1933; July 12, 1934. For the first half of 1936, the restaurants showed a small deficit of $5,610.40. *Time,* Sept. 21, 1936, 45.

10. *New York Times,* July 12, 1934; Bernarr Macfadden to Eleanor Roosevelt, Nov. 20, 1934, May 24, 1935, and Eleanor Roosevelt to Bernarr Macfadden, May 27, 1935, Eleanor Roosevelt Papers, FDRL; *New York Times,* Dec. 23, 1939.

11. *Bernarr Macfadden: Highlights of Fifty Years Service for His Country* (n.p., n.d., unpaged publicity booklet, probably 1935).

12. Eleanor Roosevelt to Bernarr Macfadden, Mar. 13, 1935; Macfadden to Eleanor Roosevelt, Mar. 18, 1935; Mrs. J. M. Helm to Macfadden, Mar. 23, 1935; Macfadden to Mrs. Helm, telegram, Apr. 29, 1935; Macfadden to Marvin H. McIntyre, undated telegram attached to Macfadden to Eleanor Roosevelt, June 28, 1935; Macfadden to Eleanor Roosevelt, Jan. 13, 25, 1928, Eleanor Roosevelt Papers, FDRL; *New York Times,* Oct. 26, 1934.

13. Bernarr Macfadden to the National Youth Administration, Feb. 9, 1938, Eleanor Roosevelt Papers, FDRL; Bernarr Macfadden, "Intelligence—the Greatest Need of the Democracies," *Liberty,* Oct. 28, 1939, 4–5.

14. Bernarr Macfadden to Franklin D. Roosevelt, telegram, May 1, 1933, Franklin D. Roosevelt Papers, FDRL; Bernarr Macfadden to Eleanor Roosevelt, Nov. 29, 1933, Eleanor Roosevelt Papers, FDRL; Bernarr Macfadden, "A New Cabinet Position—Secretary of Business Management," *Liberty,* May 30, 1936, 3; *New York Times,* Mar. 25, 1935.

15. *Liberty,* Feb. 22, 1936, 4; Bernarr Macfadden, "When Wealth Brings Disaster," *Liberty,* July 1, 1933, 3. For the Foundation, see chap. 10.

16. *Liberty,* Nov. 11, 1933, 3; Nov. 18, 1933, 4; Apr. 28, 1934, 4; Mar. 9, 1935, 4. Bernarr Macfadden, "Brutal, Murderous Strikes—Who Is to Blame," *Liberty,* Sept. 1, 1934, 4; *Liberty,* June 3, 1933, 4; July 6, 1935, 3.

17. *Liberty,* June 3, 1933, 4; Feb. 16, 1935, 4; June 3, 1939, 4.

18. Ibid., Nov. 17, 1937, 4; May 7, 1938, 4; July 16, 1938, 4; Aug. 20, 1938, 3; Nov. 25, 1939, 4.

19. Ibid., Dec. 31, 1938, 3.

20. Rodney P. Carlisle, *Hearst and the New Deal, The Progressive as Reactionary* (New York: Garland Publishing, 1979), 182; *New Masses,* Feb. 5, 1935; John Stuart, "Bernarr Macfadden: From Pornography to Politics," *New Masses,* May 9, 1936, 10, 11.

21. *Liberty,* Feb. 2, 1935, 4; Fulton Oursler to Bernarr Macfadden, office memo., June 25, 1935, Oursler Scrapbook, Oursler Papers, FULA. Oursler's memo. was endorsed by Macfadden: "O.K. Your run for it."

22. Bernarr Macfadden, "Throw Out the Foreign Traitors," *Liberty,* Nov. 26, 1938, 3; Bernarr Macfadden, "We Are with the President in His Fight Against Spies," *Liberty,* Jan. 14, 1939, 4; Bernarr Macfadden to J. Edgar Hoover, Apr. 30, 1947, Bernarr Macfadden File, FBI, 60–33905, sec. 1.

23. *PC,* Feb. 1906, 141–43; Bernarr Macfadden, "The Gigantic Cost of Crime," *Liberty,* Apr. 5, 1941, 4.

24. Kenneth O'Reilly, "A New Deal for the FBI: The Roosevelt Administration, Crime Control, and National Security," *Journal of American History,* Dec. 1982, 643; Bernarr Macfadden, "Enforce the Laws or Get Out," *Liberty,* July 21, 1934, 4; H. L. Mencken, "What to Do with Criminals," *Liberty,* July 28, 1934, 7–9.

25. J. Edgar Hoover to Bernarr Macfadden, May 3, 1939, and Frederick L. Collins, secretary of the Committee of Awards to Clyde Tolson of the FBI, Nov. 24, 1939, Bernarr Macfadden File, FBI no. 94–3–4–30, Bernarr Macfadden to Louis B. Nichols, Dec. 30, 1940, and Fulton Oursler to J. Edgar Hoover, Jan. 8, 1941, Bernarr Macfadden File, FBI.

(See also Senator W. Warren Barbour of New Jersey to Bernarr Macfadden, July 11, 1939, commending *Liberty* for effectively furthering the work of the FBI, Bernarr Macfadden File, FBI.) J. Edgar Hoover to Bernarr Macfadden, Jan. 3, 1940, Bernarr Macfadden File, FBI.

26. *Liberty*, Mar. 21, 1936, 4; Apr. 18, 1936, 4; *New York Times*, Apr. 9, 1936.

27. Bernarr Macfadden, "Do the Workers All Want Government Jobs?" *Liberty*, June 25, 1938, 3; Bernarr Macfadden, "At One Time There Were States' Rights," *Liberty*, Feb. 18, 1939, 4. (See also *Liberty*, Nov. 7, 1936, 4, and Dec. 17, 1938, 4.) Bernarr Macfadden to ———? [1937], HM2973, Huntington Library, San Marino, Calif.

28. Bernarr Macfadden, "I Indict the New Deal for . . . ," *Liberty*, Nov. 7, 1936, 4; Bernarr Macfadden to C. Jasper Bell, telegram, Mar. 25, 1938, Charles Jasper Bell Papers, Joint Collection, Univ. of Missouri Western Historical Manuscripts Collection and State Historical Society Manuscripts, Univ. of Missouri Library, Columbia.

29. Bernarr Macfadden, "Our Farmers Will Now Be Instructed Like School Boys," *Liberty*, Apr. 2, 1938, 3; Bernarr Macfadden, "Playing the Farmers for Suckers," *Liberty*, May 25, 1940, 4; Bernarr Macfadden, "Henry Wallace, the Fair-Haired Dreamer," *Liberty*, Oct. 5, 1940, 4.

30. Bernarr Macfadden, "A Nation-wide Demand for the Resignation of Madam Perkins," *Liberty*, Oct. 22, 1938, 4. See also his editorial, "Americanism—Open Declaration Demanded," *Liberty*, July 27, 1940, 3.

31. Bernarr Macfadden, "I Indict the New Deal for . . . ," *Liberty*, Nov. 7, 1936, 4.

32. Bernarr Macfadden to William Jourdan Rapp, office memo., Apr. 2, 1940, Rapp Papers, KLUO.

33. Bernarr Macfadden, "Only Dictatorial Powers Can Save Us," *Liberty*, Mar. 25, 1933, 4; Bernarr Macfadden, "Forcing Japan into the Hell of Another War," *Liberty*, Jan. 26, 1935, 4; Bernarr Macfadden, "War! War! An Open Letter to President Roosevelt," *Liberty*, May 16, 1936, 4–5; *PC*, Feb. 1907, 105; Apr. 1908, 211–13.

34. *Liberty*, Feb. 13, 1932, 4; Oct. 21, 1933, 4; Dec. 12, 1936, 4; Nov. 13, 1937, 4; Sept. 16, 1939, 4; June 22, 1940, 4.

10. THE PHYSICAL CULTURE FAMILY

1. George B. Davis, interview with the author, June 10, 1982; Edward L. Bernays, interview with the author, May 25, 1982; Macfadden and Gauvreau, *Dumbbells*, 66; Bernarr Macfadden vs. Mary Macfadden, Proceedings before Hon. John C. Grambling, Special Master's Report, Chancery Case no. 77430–A, circuit court in and for Dade County, Fla., 1943–1946 (transcript furnished by Richard P. Brinker, clerk, circuit court, Feb. 20, 1985), 79; Waugh, "Bernarr Macfadden," 217.

2. Macfadden and Gauvreau, *Dumbbells*, 234, 368.

3. Ibid., 375, 376, 289.

4. Bernarr Macfadden vs. Mary Macfadden, Proceedings, 26, 28, 78, 85; idem, Special Master's Report, Chancery Case no. 77430, Circuit Court in and for Dade County, Fla., Oct. 29, 1945, 4; Talmey, "Millions from Dumb-bells," 165; Beulah Keenan, interview with the author, Apr. 15, 1982.

5. Perkins, *Chats*, 69–73; Caspary, *Secrets of Grown-ups*, 91.

6. Title deed, Nov. 7, 1929, Deed book 1619, 119, Bergen County Clerk's Office, Registry Div., Hackensack, N.J. (Macfadden and Gauvreau, *Dumbbells*, erroneously state the year as 1927.) Mrs. George R. Leslie, Jr., to the author, undated but postmarked

May 3, 1983; *Evening Record*, [Hackensack, Bergen County, N.J.] Mar. 28, 1972; *PC*, Oct. 1919, 39; Julia Flitner Lamb, in an interview with the author on Jan. 6, 1982, stated that the property, half a century later, with only half its former acreage, was on the market for $4,000,000.

7. *New York Times*, Apr. 7, 1928; *PC*, Jan. 1928, 37, 94; Wood, *Bernarr Macfadden*, 137–38, 145; Mrs. George R. Leslie to the author, postmarked May 3, 1983.

8. Wood, *Bernarr Macfadden*, 143; Fern Matson Wiegers to the author, Feb. 20, 1985.

9. Bernarr Macfadden vs. Mary Macfadden, Proceedings, 65, 134, 143, 146, 176.

10. Ibid., 29–30, 45–46; Marjorie Greenbie to John ———, Dec. 11, 1930, and Bernarr Macfadden to Marjorie Greenbie, telegram, Jan. 19, 1931, Sydney Greenbie Papers, Special Collections Division, KLUO; *New York Times*, Aug. 13, 1931; Bernarr Macfadden to Byrnece Macfadden, undated (1931), quoted in Waugh, "Bernarr Macfadden," 220.

11. Byrnece Macfadden Muckerman, interview with Clifford J. Waugh, Apr. 21, 1973, quoted in Waugh, "Bernarr Macfadden," 220; *New York Times*, Apr. 12, Aug. 13, 1931. Apparently, she wished to forget the marriage to Metaxa and she dropped his name (Clifford J. Waugh to the author, June 26, 1982).

12. George B. Davis, interview with the author, June 10, 1982; *New York Times*, Dec. 2, 1981.

13. Marjorie Greenbie to Bernarr Macfadden, office memo., Mar. 12, 1931; Doris Laura Flick, principal, to Bernarr Macfadden, Jan. 5, 1931; Marjorie Greenbie to Bernarr Macfadden, telegram [n.d.] and a copy of the diet, Greenbie Papers, KLUO; *New York Times*, June 7, 1936; Byrnece Macfadden Muckerman, interview with Clifford J. Waugh, Apr. 21, 1973, in Waugh, "Bernarr Macfadden," 219; *Evening Record* [Hackensack, Bergen County, N.J.], Mar. 28, 1972; Beulah Keenan, interview with the author, Apr. 15, 1982; Arthur St. Phillip, interview with Clifford J. Waugh, Mar. 21, 1973, in Waugh, "Bernarr Macfadden," 219–20.

14. Marjorie Greenbie to Bernarr Macfadden, Jan. 9, 1931, Greenbie Papers, KLUO; Julia Flitner Lamb, interview with the author, Jan. 6, 1982; Marjorie Greenbie to Bernarr Macfadden, office memo., Mar. 12, 1931 (for quotation) and Bernarr Macfadden to [Marjorie] Greenbie, telegram, Mar. 14, 1931, Greenbie Papers, KLUO. Beverly was the only Macfadden daughter to attend college. At twenty, she married Roland Hebert, a druggist, and lived for a time in Holyoke, Massachusetts. Bernarr Macfadden vs. Mary Macfadden, Proceedings, 146; Beulah Keenan, interview with the author, Apr. 15, 1982.

15. Bernarr Macfadden vs. Mary Macfadden, Proceedings, 10, 47, 65, 145; *New York Times*, June 6, 1937; *Evening Record*, June 9, 1937; Johnnie Lee Macfadden, interview with the author, May 29, 1984; Waugh, "Bernarr Macfadden," 227, citing *New Brunswick Daily Home News* [N.J.], Oct. 7, 1954; the Rev. David Krampitz to the author, phone conversation, Mar. 23, 1985; information supplied, June 18, 1982, by a former acquaintance of Brewster Macfadden.

16. Marjorie Greenbie to Bernarr Macfadden, Mar. 12, 1931, and Mar. 20, 1931 (telegram); Jan. 19, 1931; Mar. 10, 1931. Doris Laura Flick to Bernarr Macfadden, Jan. 5, 1931; Bernarr Macfadden to Doris Laura Flick, Jan. 7, 1931; all in Greenbie Papers, KLUO.

17. Marjorie Greenbie to Bernarr Macfadden, Mar. 12, 1931, Greenbie Papers, KLUO.

18. Bernarr Macfadden vs. Mary Macfadden, Proceedings, 4–18, 33, 75–77, 116–17, 161, and Bernarr Macfadden vs. Mary Macfadden, Special Master's Report, 3, 6, 7.

19. *Evening Record*, May 10, 1933; *New York Times*, May 10, Nov. 21, 1933; Mary

Macfadden to Marjorie Greenbie, Aug. 30, 1933, Greenbie Papers, KLUO; *Evening Record,* June 30, 1934.

20. *Evening Record,* Nov. 20, 1933; *New York Times,* Nov. 21, 1933.

21. *Evening Record,* June 20, 1934; *New York Times,* June 21, 1934; *Newsweek,* June 29, 1935, 28.

22. *Evening Record,* Mar. 26, 1934; Feb. 21, 1938. *New York Times,* Mar. 25, 1934; Feb. 22, 1938; Waugh, "Bernarr Macfadden," 205.

23. Oursler, *Behold This Dreamer,* 171, 330–31; Fulton Oursler to Bernarr Macfadden, office memo., Mar. 13, 1936, Oursler Scrapbook, Oursler Papers, FULA. "Jafsie" was John F. Condon, a publicity-seeking go-between in efforts to locate the kidnapped child.

24. Bernarr Macfadden to Fulton Oursler, office memo., Mar. 17, 1936, Oursler Scrapbook, Oursler Papers, FULA.

25. *Editor and Publisher,* Jan. 16, 1937, 38. Mary Macfadden's reference to Oursler's "former work" is erroneous. He was only an amateur magician. His complaint against Mary Macfadden, June 1936, is in the Oursler Papers, FULA.

26. *Editor and Publisher,* Jan. 16, 1937, 38.

27. Oursler's complaint against Mary Macfadden, June 1936, and Mary Macfadden to R. W. Lagay, Feb. 10 [1936], both in Oursler Scrapbook, Oursler Papers, FULA.

28. *Time,* Feb. 1, 1937, 36–37. See also *Editor and Publisher,* Jan. 16, 1937, 38.

29. Arthur Garfield Hays to Bernarr Macfadden, personal, Feb. 8, 1937, copy, Oursler Scrapbook, "Personal, 1937, vol. 1," Oursler Papers, FULA; statement by Fulton Oursler, Jr., Oursler, *Behold This Dreamer,* 331.

30. At the same time, Macfadden set aside $1,500,000 as a bequest for his dependents. *Editor and Publisher,* Oct. 3, 1941, 14. *New York Times,* Sept. 25, 1931; *PC,* Feb. 1932, 89. Oursler resigned from the foundation's board in 1949 (Fulton Oursler to Bernarr Macfadden, Oct. 30, 1949, Oursler Scrapbook, Oursler Papers, FULA.)

31. Garfield and Seligson [Mary Macfadden's lawyers] to Fulton Oursler, May 14, 1937, Oursler Scrapbook, "Personal, 1937, vol. 1," Oursler Papers, FULA; *New York Times,* May 16, 1936.

32. Bernarr Macfadden vs. Mary Macfadden, Proceedings, 148; Waugh, "Bernarr Macfadden," 217.

33. *New York Times,* Jan. 30, June 23, 1943; Feb. 8, 1945.

34. Mary Macfadden to R. W. Lagay, Feb. 10 [1936], Oursler Scrapbook, Oursler Papers, FULA; *New York Times,* Jan. 10, 1946; June 10, 1954.

35. Bernarr Macfadden, "Intelligence—The Greatest Need of the Democracies," *Liberty,* Oct. 28, 1939; *PC,* July 1928, 56; advertisement inside the front cover of *Liberty,* Aug. 1935. Exact date torn off copy in New York Public Library.

36. *New York Times,* May 22, 1932.

37. Bernarr Macfadden, "Good News for Tuberculosis Victims," *Liberty,* Oct. 21, 1939; publicity material dated May 23, 1939, and related letters, sent by E. A. Meyerding and Paul Barton of the American Medical Association, June 14, 1939, Macfadden File, AMA.

38. Bernarr Macfadden to Eleanor Roosevelt, May 24, 1935, June 7, 1937, Eleanor Roosevelt Papers, FDRL; *PC,* Sept. 1939, advertisement, 73; advertisement of Macfadden Foundation facilities, accompanying Bernarr Macfadden to Dwight D. Eisenhower, June 5, 1953, File no. 1–L "M," July 1953, Dwight D. Eisenhower Papers, Dwight D. Eisenhower Library, Abilene, Kans.; [Dansville, N.Y.] *Genesee Country Express,* Mar. 2, 1955.

39. *Rochester Democrat and Chronicle,* Oct. 5, 1958, May 22, 1977; Vaugn Polmenter, "Caches in the Hillside. Did Bernarr Macfadden Bury a Fortune Near His Dansville Resort?" *Upstate Magazine* (Sunday supp. to *Rochester Democrat and Chronicle*) Dec. 12, 1982, 40, 41; *Dansville Express,* May 3, 1929; *PC,* Nov. 1934.

40. Wilfred J. Rauber (North Dansville town historian), draft of article for *Genesee Country Express,* Aug. 8–15, 1968, 6, file B–5–b, Town Hall, Dansville, N.Y.; unidentified clipping, July 6, 1929, owned by Wilfred J. Rauber; Wilfred J. Rauber, interview with the author, June 20, 1983.

41. For example, Bernarr Macfadden to Thomas E. Dewey, June 16, 1941, Sept. 15, 1942, Dewey Papers, RLUR; unidentified clipping and note by Wilfred J. Rauber, Town Hall, Dansville, N.Y.; Grace Perkins [Oursler], *Chats,* 210–11; *PC,* Nov. 1934, 97, 99; Waugh, "Bernarr Macfadden," 184–85.

42. Wilfred J. Rauber, draft of article for *Genesee Country Express,* 11; *Newsweek,* May 18, 1935, 17; *New York Times,* May 5, 8, 10, 18, 1935.

43. Robert Wake, "There's Rejuvenation in Walking," *Liberty,* Jan. 13, 1940.

44. *New York Times,* May 17, 1936; *Macfadden Wholesaler,* May 1937, 2, and June 1937, 3, owned by Beulah Keenan; *New York Times,* July 8, 1939.

45. Bernarr Macfadden, "The One Thing That Matters," *True Story,* Oct. 1935, 16.

11. MACFADDEN OUSTED

1. Bernarr Macfadden to Upton Sinclair, Dec. 1, 1931, Sinclair Papers, LLIU; Oursler, *Behold This Dreamer,* 348; Guy Harrington to Bernarr Macfadden, office memo., Mar. 5, 1935, Oursler Scrapbook, Oursler Papers, FULA.

2. Oursler, *Behold This Dreamer,* 319–20.

3. Bernarr Macfadden to Fulton Oursler, office memo., Sept. 16, 1936, Oursler Scrapbook, Oursler Papers, FULA. The circulation director reported in Mar. 1935 that criticism of a Macfadden editorial, "Shackled Business," had resulted in a loss of customers, and he stressed the importance to the magazine of its editorials. S. O. Shapiro to Bernarr Macfadden, office memo., Mar. 29, 1935, copy, Oursler Scrapbook, Oursler Papers, FULA.

4. Harold A. Wise to Fulton Oursler, Mar. 8, 1938, and H. A. Wise announcement, Mar. 31, 1938, Oursler Scrapbook, Oursler Papers, FULA; Oursler, *Behold This Dreamer,* 353, 357.

5. Gorman Loss to Fulton Oursler, office memo., Jan. 30, 1939, and Fulton Oursler to Bernarr Macfadden, Feb. 19, 1939, Oursler Scrapbook, "Personal, 1939," vol. 1, Oursler Papers, FULA; Haydock Miller to Bernarr Macfadden office memos., April 30, May 28, 1940, Oursler Scrapbook, "F. O. Personal, 1940," vol. 2, Oursler Papers, FULA; Peterson, *Magazines in the Twentieth Century,* 258; O. J. Elder, report at special meeting of stockholders, Nov. 25, 1941, in Macfadden Publications *Report to Stockholders for the Year Ended August 31, 1941,* 10–11; Unsigned five-page memo. to Bernarr Macfadden, Nov. 11, 1940, copy, Oursler Scrapbook, "F. O. Current, 1940," vol. 1, Oursler Papers, FULA.

6. *Tide,* June 15, 1941, 58; *Time,* May 12, 1941, 61; Peterson, *Magazines in the Twentieth Century,* 28; Waugh, "Bernarr Macfadden," 208. After Macfadden resigned, the new management admitted the facts and voluntarily made full refunds.

7. *Standard Corporation Records: Dividend Payments in 1938* (New York: Standard Statistics Co., 1939), 58; ibid. for 1939 (New York, 1940), 74; *1941 Annual Dividend Record* (New York: Standard and Poor's Corp., 1942); *Moody's Manual of Invest-*

ments, 1939, 677, and 1942, 699, cited by Waugh, "Bernarr Macfadden," 208; Robert Ernst interviews with a former Macfadden executive who wished not to be identified, Apr. 27, 1982, and with Carroll Rheinstrom, Sept. 21, 1983. In Aug. 1941, the corporate deficit was recorded as $2,725,353. *Moody's Industrials 1942* (New York: Moody's Investor's Service), 1264.

8. Waugh, "Bernarr Macfadden," 201-2, citing interview with O. J. Elder, Jr., Oct. 4, 1973; Irving B. Simon to Clifford J. Waugh, Feb. 28, 1973, and Mrs. Joseph Schultz to Waugh, Dec. 25, 1972, cited in Waugh, "Bernarr Macfadden," 202; Carroll Rheinstrom, interview with the author, Sept. 21, 1983.

9. Fulton Oursler (Jr.), untitled MS., 139, owned by Fulton Oursler (Jr.).

10. *New York Times*, April 23, 1940; Waugh, "Bernarr Macfadden," 209. (The case was entitled Leon S. Brach vs. Macfadden Publications Incorporated and Bernarr Macfadden, and dated Apr. 22, 1940. It is available at the Federal Archives and Record Center, Bayonne, N.J., as File no. FRC 272946, Case no. civ. 8–322, Archives Box, 472.) Summary of complaint, taken from defendant's brief, ibid; Waugh, "Bernarr Macfadden," 209-210.

11. George T. Delacorte, interview with the author, May 31, 1984; Waugh, "Bernarr Macfadden," 210, citing Carroll Rheinstrom to Waugh, Aug. 15, 1972, and interviews with Joseph Wiegers, June 20, 1973, Arthur St. Phillip, Mar. 7, 1973, and Mrs. Milo Hastings, Feb. 7, 1973.

12. *New York Times*, Apr. 24, 1940.

13. Answer to complaint, by Hays, St. John, Abramson, and Schulman, Aug. 14, 1940, in Leon S. Brach vs. Macfadden Publications and Bernarr Macfadden, and other documents in the Brach case, which was eventually dismissed on Sept. 5, 1941; Waugh, "Bernarr Macfadden," 209-11; *Tide*, Mar. 15, 1941, 12-13; Fulton Oursler, Jr., untitled MS, 142, in his possession.

14. Macfadden Publications, *Report to Stockholders for the Year ended August 31, 1941*, 9.

15. Waugh, "Bernarr Macfadden," 210-11, citing interview with Ed Bodin, Aug. 8, 1972.

16. *New York Times*, Feb. 28, 1941; Joseph Wiegers to Clifford J. Waugh, June 29, 1972, cited by Waugh, "Bernarr Macfadden," 211; carbon copy of undated letter by Macfadden, which he did not send, Oursler Scrapbook, "Current, Jan.–Mar. 1951," Oursler Papers, FULA. This letter is located next to his letter to Oursler dated Feb. 9, 1951.

17. Johnston, "Great Macfadden," 92.

18. Macfadden Publications, *Report to Stockholders*, 1941, 9; *Tide*, Mar. 15, 1941, 12-13; Leon S. Brach vs. Macfadden Publications Incorporated and Bernarr Macfadden; *New York Times*, Aug. 29, 1941; Waugh, "Bernarr Macfadden," 210.

19. Bernarr Macfadden to Eleanor Roosevelt, Oct. 1, 1941, Eleanor Roosevelt Papers, FDRL; Peterson, *Magazines in the Twentieth Century*, 258; Will Oursler to Fulton Oursler, "Thursday," [November 1942], Oursler Papers, FULA; *Bernarr Macfadden's Latest Detective Magazine* appeared for several months in 1947.

20. *Genesee Country Express and Advertiser* [Dansville, N.Y.], June 19, 1941; Bernarr Macfadden to Eleanor Roosevelt, July 1, 1941, Eleanor Roosevelt Papers, FDRL; Bernarr Macfadden to Thomas E. Dewey, Nov. 8, 1942, Dewey Papers, RLUR; *Newsweek*, June 29, 1935, 27; L. B. Nichols, memo. for Mr. Tolson, Feb. 9, 1944, Macfadden File, FBI, no. 62–33905, sec. 1.

21. *Miami Herald*, June 2, 1949; Harry Gilgulin, interviews with the author, May 12, 1983, and Mar. 21, 1984; Bernarr Macfadden to J. Edgar Hoover, Mar. 3, 1944, Bernarr Macfadden File, FBI, no. 62–33905; *American Vegetarian* [Pismo Beach, Calif.]

[July 1946]; Waugh, "Bernarr Macfadden," 223, citing *Miami Herald*, June 2, 1949; *New York Times*, July 2, 1959.

22. Bernarr Macfadden to Herbert Brownell, Oct. 13, 1942, copy, Dewey Papers, RLUR; Bernarr Macfadden to Thomas E. Dewey, Oct. 15, Nov. 8, 1942; July 16, 1948, ibid.

23. *New York Times*, Oct. 13, 1955; Waugh, "Bernarr Macfadden," 213-14; Bernarr Macfadden to Eleanor Roosevelt, Dec. 14, 1944, [Malvina C. Thompson] to Bernarr Macfadden, Dec. 14, 1944, and Bernarr Macfadden to Malvina Thompson, Jan. 17, 1945, Eleanor Roosevelt Papers, FDRL.

24. Bernarr Macfadden, "Entire Nation Must Train to Avoid Enslavement," *Liberty*, Jan. 18, 1941, 4; Bernarr Macfadden to Eleanor Roosevelt, Nov. 27, Dec. 11, (telegram), and Dec. 17, 1941, Eleanor Roosevelt Papers, FDRL; Bernarr Macfadden to Thomas E. Dewey, Feb. 21, 1945, Dewey Papers, RLUR.

25. Harry S. Truman, *Memoirs by Harry S. Truman* (Garden City, N.Y.: Doubleday, 1955-1956), 1, 510; Bernarr Macfadden to William D. Hassett, Oct. 31, 1945, President's Personal File, Harry S. Truman Papers, Harry S. Truman Library, Independence, Mo.; Bernarr Macfadden to Harry S. Truman, Dec. 4, 1945 (telegram), Truman Papers; Bernarr Macfadden to Charles G. Ross, secretary to the president, Sept. 21, 1946, Truman Papers; Bernarr Macfadden to Harry S. Truman, attention of Brigadier General Wallace H. Graham, Nov. 7, 1946, Truman Papers; Bernarr Macfadden to Harry S. Truman, Jan. 18, 1947, Truman Papers; Bernarr Macfadden to Thomas E. Dewey, Nov. 18, 1947, Dec. 1, 1947, Dewey Papers, RLUR; Bernarr Macfadden to Charles Ross, Nov. 29, 1948 and to Matthew J. Connolly, Dec. 21, 1948, President's Personal File, Truman Papers.

26. Bernarr Macfadden to Harry S. Truman, Mar. 30, 1946, Truman Papers. (For Truman's action, see *New York Times*, Feb. 7, 1946.) Bernarr Macfadden to Harry S. Truman, June 15, 1946, Truman Papers.

27. Bernarr Macfadden [or his representative] to Sergeant J. P. Leveritt, White House, Oct. 6, 1947 (telegram), incomplete photocopy, endorsed "File (ignore) (CGR)," Truman Papers; Eben A. Ayers (assistant to Charles Ross) to Ed Bodin (Promotion Department, Bernarr Macfadden Foundation), Dec. 28, 1948, ibid.

28. Col. William H. Rankin, undated [1947] telegram to Thomas E. Dewey, Dewey Papers, RLUR. Compare scroll presented by Freedom for Health to Macfadden, Aug. 16, 1952, photocopy accompanying Charles J. Oringer to Harry S. Truman, Aug. 12, 1952, Official File, Truman Papers.

29. Waugh, "Bernarr Macfadden," 215, citing interview with Jesse Mercer Gehman, Apr. 26, 1973. Gehman was a physician and long-time associate of Macfadden.

30. Macfadden and Gauvreau, *Dumbbells*, 271, 288-89; *PC*, June 1905, 419; Wood, *Bernarr Macfadden*, 41.

31. *PC*, Aug. 1901, 228.

32. Ibid., Mar. 1908, 143b; Wood, *Bernarr Macfadden*, 264; *Your Faith*, Apr. 1939, 1-3.

33. Irene King to Fulton Oursler, May 20, 1948, Oursler Scrapbook, "Current—April–May 1948," Oursler Papers, FULA.

12. LIFE WITH JOHNNIE LEE

1. *Graphic*, June 18, 1928; *PC*, Dec. 1934, 27, 63-64; photocopy of page of unidentified publication, office of the historian of the Town of North Dansville, Dansville, N.Y.; *New York Times*, July 19, 1931; Johnnie Lee Macfadden, *Barefoot in Eden*, 53-54.

2. Bernarr Macfadden, "The Thrill of Flying," *Liberty,* Sept. 9, 1933, 4; Bernarr Macfadden, "Lost in the Sky," *Liberty,* Oct. 5, 1940, 43–44; *PC,* Jan. 1935, 41, 84; Feb. 1935, 85–86. George B. Davis, interview with the author, June 11, 1982; S. O. Shapiro, interview with the author, Apr. 27, 1932; Waugh, "Bernarr Macfadden," 190; *Graphic,* Feb. 22, 1932; Johnston, "Great Macfadden," 92; *New York Times,* Oct. 11, Nov. 27, 1936, Dec. 27, 1938.

3. Waugh, "Bernarr Macfadden," 220–21, citing Arthur St. Phillip, Macfadden's son-in-law, to Waugh, Mar. 21, 1973, and Waugh's interview with Macfadden's daughter Byrnece, Apr. 21, 1973.

4. Florida marriage certificate, Apr. 23, 1948, owned by Johnnie Lee Macfadden; Johnnie Lee Macfadden, interview with the author, May 18, 1984; Johnnie Lee Macfadden, *Barefoot in Eden,* 4; Johnnie Lee Macfadden, MS memoir of her life with Bernarr Macfadden (hereafter cited as Johnnie Lee Macfadden memoir).

5. Johnnie Lee Macfadden, interview with the author, May 1, 1984; Taylor, "Physical Culture," pt. 1, 42; Johnnie Lee Macfadden, *Barefoot in Eden,* 14–15.

6. This and the following five paragraphs are based on the Johnnie Lee Macfadden memoir, 2–21, 25–29.

7. Ibid., 29–31; Taylor, "Physical Culture," pt. 1, 42.

8. Johnnie Lee Macfadden, *Barefoot in Eden,* 29; Johnnie Lee Macfadden memoir, 35–38.

9. This and the following five paragraphs are based on the Johnnie Lee Macfadden memoir, 39–50, 54–57.

10. Ibid., 59–62; *Miami Herald,* Apr. 23, 1948; *New York Times,* Apr. 24, 1948.

11. This and the following seven paragraphs are based on the Johnnie Lee Macfadden memoir, 63–78, 80–81.

12. Taylor, "Physical Culture," pt. 1, 44.

13. According to Johnnie Lee, he told her that he had gotten the idea from Fannie Hurst, who had such an arrangement with her husband. This and the following five paragraphs are based on the Johnnie Lee Macfadden memoir, 82–97.

14. Taylor, "Physical Culture," pt. 1, 45.

15. Waugh, "Bernarr Macfadden," 222, citing undated article in the *Rochester Democrat and Chronicle;* Taylor, "Physical Culture," pt. 1, 42.

16. *New York Times,* Aug. 27, 1951; *Evening Record* [Hackensack, Bergen County, N.J.], Aug. 27, 1951. The two accounts differ in several details.

17. Johnnie Lee Macfadden memoir, 98–103.

18. This and the following three paragraphs are based on the Johnnie Lee Macfadden memoir, 104–14.

19. Ibid., 115–19; Bernarr Macfadden to Thomas E. Dewey, May 19, 1950, Dewey Papers, RLUR.

20. This and the following three paragraphs are based on the Johnnie Lee Macfadden memoir, 120–27.

21. *New York Times,* Feb. 7, 1951; Waugh, "Bernarr Macfadden," 223.

22. This and the following two paragraphs are based on the Johnnie Lee Macfadden memoir, 127–32.

23. Johnnie Lee Macfadden, interview with the author, Sept. 10, 1984. (She claimed that Ed Bodin, Macfadden's public relations man, originated the scheme.) Macfadden and Gauvreau, *Dumbbells,* 207; former Macfadden executive who asked not to be identified, interview with the author, Oct. 19, 1982.

24. Johnnie Lee Macfadden memoir, 133–35.

25. Johnnie Lee Macfadden, *Barefoot in Eden*, 211–15; Johnnie Lee Macfadden, interview with Clifford J. Waugh, Feb. 6, 1973, Waugh, "Bernarr Macfadden," 225. In 1954, Macfadden planned to parachute into the Great Salt Lake, but the Utah Aeronautics Commission refused its permission on the ground that his stunt would not promote its policy of aerial safety (*New York Times*, Mar. 11, 1954).

26. Johnnie Lee Macfadden memoir, 135–37; Johnnie Lee Macfadden, interview with the author, May 1, 1984.

27. Johnnie Lee Macfadden memoir, 137–38.

28. *Miami Herald*, Nov. 19, 1952; Taft, "Bernarr Macfadden," 88.

29. *Genesee Country Express* [Dansville, N.Y.], Mar. 2, 1955; *New York Times*, Dec. 25, 1954, June 5, 25, 1955; *St. Louis Post-Dispatch*, Dec. 26, 1954; Taft, "Bernarr Macfadden," 88; Bernarr Macfadden to Thomas E. Dewey, Jan. 18, 1955, Dewey Papers, RLUR.

30. Waugh, "Bernarr Macfadden," 228, citing the Racine [Wisconsin] *Journal-Times*, Jan. 26, 1955.

31. *Genesee Country Express* [Dansville, N.Y.], Mar. 2, 1955.

32. *New York Times*, Apr. 19, 1955; Johnnie Lee Macfadden, interview with the author, Apr. 20, 1985.

33. Jesse Mercer Gehman, eulogy article, *Morning Call* [Paterson, N.J.], Dec. 2, 1955; Will Oursler, *Family Story*, 285; Byrnece Macfadden Muckerman, interview with Clifford J. Waugh, Apr. 21, 1973, Waugh, "Bernarr Macfadden," 284–85.

34. Macfadden and Gauvreau, *Dumbbells*, 36, 51, 337; Waugh, "Bernarr Macfadden," 224, 227, citing interviews with Byrnece Macfadden Muckerman, Apr. 21, 1973, Joseph Wiegers, June 6, 1973, and Ed Bodin, Aug. 8, 1972.

35. Macfadden and Gauvreau, *Dumbbells*, 65, 390; Johnnie Lee Macfadden, *Barefoot in Eden*, 208–10.

36. Macfadden and Gauvreau, *Dumbbells*, 91; Johnnie Lee Macfadden, *Barefoot in Eden*, 62–63, 65.

37. Johnnie Lee Macfadden, *Barefoot in Eden*, 66–70; *Genesee Country Express* [Dansville, N.Y.], Apr. 26, 1956; *Upstate Magazine*, Sunday supp. of *Rochester Democrat and Chronicle*, Dec. 12, 1982, 41.

38. Cohen, *New York Graphic*, 232; George B. Davis, interview with the author, June 10, 1982; *Newsday* [Garden City, N.Y.], June 3, 4, 1960; Samuel J. Rozzi, Nassau County Police Commissioner, to the author, June 21, 1983; Stephen J. Fox Plaintiff vs. Police Department of Nassau County, Fred J. Gouse, Johnnie Lee Macfadden and American Millwork Co. Defendants, Index no. 9783, (1962), Nassau County Supreme Court, Judgment Liber, microfilm 392, 322–27, county clerk's office, Mineola, N.Y. All the papers in the case except the final judgment of the court were consumed in a warehouse fire about 1980. Johnnie Lee Macfadden's account of the finding of this cache (*Barefoot in Eden*, 70) erroneously states the date as 1961.

39. The book, *Dumbbells and Carrot Strips*, was reviewed in the *New York Times*, Apr. 26, 1953. Obituary article, *Rochester Times-Union*, Oct. 13, 1955; Jesse Mercer Gehman, eulogy article, *Morning Call* [Paterson, N.J.], Dec. 2, 1955; Markovich, "Publishing Empire," 122, citing interview with Felix May, editor of *Physical Culture*, n.d.; *Genesee Country Express* [Dansville, N.Y.], Mar. 2, 1955.

40. Markovich, "Publishing Empire," 123, citing Ed Bodin, personal communication, n.d.; *New York Times*, Oct. 10, 11, and 13, 1955; Waugh, "Bernarr Macfadden," 229, citing Dr. Charles A. Landshoff, Official Medical Report, Jersey City Medical Center, Jersey City, N.J.

41. Johnnie Lee Macfadden memoir, 141-42.

42. Handwritten note, n.d., "Macfadden and Successors" File, office of North Dansville Town historian, Town Hall, Dansville, N.Y.; Taft, "Bernarr Macfadden," 89; Johnnie Lee Macfadden, interview with the author, May 4, 1982.

43. Chicago Daily Tribune, Oct. 13, 1955; Daily American Republican [Poplar Bluff, Mo.], Oct. 13, 1955; Miami Herald, Jan. 1, 1955; Chicago Daily News, Oct. 13, 1955.

44. Bernarr Macfadden's will, dated Mar. 12, 1953, now located at the Hudson County Court House, Jersey City, N.J.

45. Evening Record [Hackensack, Bergen County, N.J.], Nov. 28, 1969, Mar. 28, 1972; Campbell Norsgaard, a former neighbor, telephone conversation with the author, Dec. 30, 1981; Julia Flitner Lamb, a former young neighbor who had attended school with Beverly Macfadden, interview with the author, Jan. 6, 1982.

46. Obituary article, Chicago Daily News, Oct. 13, 1955; Irwin Small, C.P.A., to State of New York, Department of Law, Nov. 29, 1982, re: Bernarr Macfadden Foundation, ID 001625, year ending Dec. 1981. This letter, with pertinent income tax forms, is in the department's files, World Trade Center, New York, N.Y.

13. "I LOVE LIFE"

1. Bernarr Macfadden, Health for the Family (New York: Macfadden Publications, 1929), 46-48; Christmas card owned by Beulah Keenan.

2. Tom Holloway, Macfadden artist, interview with the author, Mar. 26, 1982.

3. PC, June 1930, 30-31; Cohen, New York Graphic, 221; Taylor, "Physical Culture," pt. 1, 46; "Health Expert Macfadden to Lecture with Sniffles," Pittsburgh Press, Dec. 11, 1951.

4. He did buy it, according to Fulton Oursler, "Most Unforgettable Character," 78-79.

5. Bernays, Biography of an Idea, 359; Oursler, Behold This Dreamer, 168; Oursler, "Most Unforgettable Character," 78.

6. PC, April 1902, 17.

7. Tom Holloway, interview with the author, Mar. 26, 1982; Macfadden and Gauvreau, Dumbbells, 74, 82; Johnnie Lee Macfadden, Barefoot in Eden, 59, 73, 77; True Story, Nov. 1943, 16.

8. Oursler, True Story, 28; PC, June 1906, 646-47.

9. Joseph Wiegers, interview with Clifford J. Waugh, June 29, 1972, Waugh, "Bernarr Macfadden," 16; Barry Good (health consultant for Macfadden Publications employees and health instructor at the Physical Culture Hotel in Dansville) to Waugh, Mar. 30, 1973, ibid., 243-44; Irving B. Simon (production manager for True Story, Liberty and other Macfadden magazines) to Waugh, Feb. 28, 1972, ibid.

10. George T. Delacorte, interview with the author, May 31, 1984; Macfadden and Gauvreau, Dumbbells, 308.

11. New York Times, Aug. 18, 1951. For narcissism, see Otto F. Kernberg, Borderline Conditions and Pathological Narcissism (New York: J. Aronson, 1975); Heinz Kohut, The Analysis of Self: A Systematic Approach to Psychoanalytic Treatment of Narcissistic Personality Disorders (New York: International Universities Press, 1971); and Alexander Lowen, Narcissism, Denial of the True Self (New York: Macmillan, 1983).

12. Mencken, "An American Idealist," 124.

13. *Liberty*, Dec. 14, 1935, 5.

14. This undated brochure is in the office of the North Dansville town historian, Town Hall, Dansville, N.Y.

15. Orville Allen in *Genesee Country Express* [Dansville, N.Y.], undated (but after 1965) clipping, office of town historian, Dansville, N.Y.; George T. Delacorte, interview with the author, May 31, 1984.

16. Bernarr Macfadden, memo. to Phil Keenan, Sept. 5, 1939, copy owned by Beulah Keenan; Johnston, "Great Macfadden," 9.

17. Markovich, "Publishing Empire," 22–23; Macfadden and Gauvreau, *Dumbbells*, 8, 23, 51, 305; Waugh, "Bernarr Macfadden," 213; George T. Delacorte, in an interview with the author, May 31, 1984, contended that Oursler wrote all of Macfadden's speeches and even his articles. This is an exaggeration. For the quotation on kissing, see Waugh, "Bernarr Macfadden," 213–14.

18. *PC*, Aug. 1934, 54; Cohen, *New York Graphic*, 221; Johnston, "Great Macfadden," 93; Oursler, *Behold This Dreamer*, 168–69; *PC*, Feb. 1908, 105; Macfadden and Gauvreau, *Dumbbells*, 70.

19. *PC*, Apr. 1909, 253; Bernarr Macfadden to Fulton Oursler, undated, Fulton Oursler Memorial Collection, Georgetown Univ. Library, Washington, D.C.; Sinclair, *Autobiography*, 232; Bernarr Macfadden to Upton Sinclair, Dec. 14, 1928, Sinclair Papers, LLIU; Upton Sinclair to Fulton Oursler, Dec. 8, 1928, and Oursler to Sinclair, Dec. 17, 1928, Fulton Oursler Memorial Collection, Georgetown Univ. Library.

20. Macfadden and Gauvreau, *Dumbbells*, 277, 235; Wood, *Bernarr Macfadden*, 292; Cohen, *New York Graphic*, 221.

21. Wood, *Bernarr Macfadden*, 241; *PC*, Jan. 1905, 669; *True Story*, Feb. 1935, 16. The occasion of the swimming pool remark was a dinner on his sixtieth birthday in 1928 (Wood, *Bernarr Macfadden*, 149).

22. Fulton Oursler, "Bernarr Macfadden—His Life and Work," *PC*, Sept. 1928, 93, 97.

23. Fulton Oursler, Scrapbook, "Personal 1924," entry for June 16, 1924, and Fulton Oursler to Perry Githens, Sept. 12, 1940, "F. O. Personal, 1940, 3," Oursler Papers, FULA; *Sportswise Magazine*, Sept.–Oct. 1984, 32; Harry Kemp to David Howatt, May 19, 1905, Howatt Papers, LLIU; Waugh, "Bernarr Macfadden," 235.

24. Oursler, "Bernarr Macfadden—His Life and Work," 92–93; Bernarr Macfadden to Fulton Oursler, office memo., July 12, 1934, Oursler Scrapbook, "Mr. Oursler Current 1934 vol. 1," Oursler Papers, FULA.

25. Bernarr Macfadden to Fulton Oursler, July 29, 1938, Oursler Scrapbook, Oursler Papers, FULA.

26. The letters, dated Jan. 24 and Feb. 6, 1954, are in the Bernarr Macfadden File, FBI, no. 62–33905, sec. 1. This file includes pertinent documents: L. Whitson to W. A. Branigan, FBI office memo., Feb. 24, 1955; an FBI internal memo. dated April 2, 1954; a special delivery letter from Edward Bodin, vice-president of the Bernarr Macfadden Foundation, to the *Washington Post*, Jan. 27, 1954; and John Grant to the Bernarr Macfadden Foundation, Feb. 2, 1954; Bernarr Macfadden, interview with FBI agent, n.d., and teletype message from FBI agent Kelly in New York to FBI headquarters, Apr. 9, 1954; FBI report, Sept. 21, 1954. For the reference to the numerous anonymous crank letters, see SAC, New York, office memo. to director, Jan. 24, 1955, also in the Bernarr Macfadden File, ibid.

27. "A Colorful Publishing Career," *Printer's Ink*, Oct. 21, 1955, 82.

28. Jesse Mercer Gehman, interview with Clifford J. Waugh, Nov. 21, 1972, Waugh,

"Bernarr Macfadden," 247; Harry Good to Waugh, Mar. 30, 1973, ibid; Wood, *Bernarr Macfadden*, 6; "Macfadden's Family," *Time*, Sept. 21, 1936, 44–46. Early letters of appreciation can be found in the issues of *Physical Culture* for 1900 and 1901.

29. Baruch Committee on Physical Medicine, *Annual Report*, Apr. 1, 1945, to Dec. 31, 1946, 146–48 (New York, 1947), and Jan. 1, 1948, to June 30, 1949, 139–41 (Chicago, 1949 or 1950).

30. *New York Times*, Dec. 3, 1909; Villard, *Sex, Art, Truth and Magazines*, 18; *PC*, Mar. 1909, 179; *New York Times*, Feb. 15, 1930, Feb. 22, 1938; *Evening Record* [Hackensack, Bergen County, N.J.], Feb. 21, 1938.

31. Miss Sidney Lloyd, interview with Clifford J. Waugh, Oct. 7, 1973, Waugh, "Bernarr Macfadden," 205; Paul Veatch to Waugh, May 5, 1973, ibid; Macfadden executive who wished to remain anonymous, interview with the author, Mar. 23, 1982; Orr J. Elder, Jr., interview with Clifford J. Waugh, Oct. 4, 1973, Waugh, "Bernarr Macfadden," 204.

32. Macfadden, *Man's Sex Life* (New York: Macfadden Book Company, 1936), 61, 13–15; Johnnie Lee Macfadden, *Barefoot in Eden*, 136; Orville Allen in *Genesee Country Express* [Dansville, N.Y.], undated clipping, but after 1965.

Bibliography

UNPUBLISHED SOURCES

Charles Jasper Bell Papers. Joint Collection, Univ. of Missouri Western Historical Manuscripts Collection and State Historical Society Manuscripts, Univ. of Missouri Library, Columbia, Mo.

Bergen County, N.J. Title deed, Nov. 7, 1929, Deed book, 1619, 119, Bergen county clerk's office, Registry Division, Hackensack, N.J.

Thomas E. Dewey Papers. Rush Rhees Library, University of Rochester, Rochester, N.Y.

Dwight D. Eisenhower Papers. Dwight D. Eisenhower Library, Abilene, Kans.

Sydney Greenbie Papers. Special Collections Division, Knight Library, Univ. of Oregon, Eugene, Oreg.

Herbert Hoover Papers. Herbert Hoover Presidential Library, West Branch, Iowa.

David Howatt Papers. Lilly Library, Indiana Univ., Bloomington, Ind.

Iron County [Mo.] Circuit Court Records. Vol. 3, 1870–1874, Missouri State Archives, Jefferson City, Mo.

Iron County [Mo.] Record of Wills, 1856–1888. County Court House, Ironton, Mo.

"Macfadden and Successors" File. Office of North Dansville town historian, Town Hall, Dansville, N.Y.

Bernarr Macfadden File. American Medical Association, Chicago.

Bernarr Macfadden File. Federal Bureau of Investigation, Washington, D.C.

Bernarr Macfadden to ——? [1937], HM2973. Huntington Library, San Marino, Calif.

Bernarr Macfadden's will. Mar. 3, 1953, Hudson County Court House, Jersey City, N.J.

Macfadden, Johnnie Lee. Unpublished memoir in her possession.

Markovich, Alexander. "The Publishing Empire of Bernarr Macfadden." M.A. thesis, Univ. of Missouri, Columbia, 1958.

Ewing Y. Mitchell Papers. Joint Collection, Univ. of Missouri Western Historical Manuscripts Collection and State Historical Society Manuscripts, Univ. of Missouri Library, Columbia, Mo.

Fulton Oursler Memorial Collection. Georgetown Univ. Library, Washington, D.C.

Fulton Oursler Papers. Fordham Univ. Library Annex, Bronx, N.Y.

Oursler, Fulton, (Jr.). untitled MS in his possession.

William Jourdan Rapp Papers. Special Collections Division, Knight Library, Univ. of Oregon, Eugene.

Rauber, Wilfred J. MS draft of article for *Genesee Country Express*, file B–5–b, Town Hall, Dansville, N.Y.

Eleanor Roosevelt Papers. Franklin D. Roosevelt Library, Hyde Park, N.Y.

Franklin D. Roosevelt Papers. Franklin D. Roosevelt Library, Hyde Park, N.Y.

St. Francois County [Mo.] Circuit Court Records. Vols. 7 and 8, 1870–1877, Missouri State Archives, Jefferson City, Mo.

Upton Sinclair Papers. Lilly Library, Indiana Univ., Bloomington.

Harry S. Truman Papers. Harry S. Truman Library, Independence, Mo.

Stadelman, Frances S. Letter to author, June 11, 1984.

United States Census 1840. Manuscript schedules, Jefferson Township, Wayne County, Mo.

United States Census 1870. Manuscript schedules, Benton Township, Wayne County, Mo.

Waugh, Clifford J. "Bernarr Macfadden: The Muscular Prophet." Ph.D. diss., SUNY Buffalo, 1979.

SELECTED COURT DOCUMENTS

Leon S. Brach vs. Macfadden Publications Incorporated and Bernarr Macfadden. File no. FRC272946, Case no. civ. 8–322, archives box 472, Federal Archives and Record Center, Bayonne, N.J., Apr. 22, 1940.

Stephen J. Fox Plaintiff vs. Police Department of Nassau County, Fred J. Gouse, Johnnie Lee Macfadden, and American Millwork Co. Defendants. Index no. 9783, (1962), Nassau County Supreme Court, Judgment Liber, county clerk's office, Mineola, N.Y., 1962. Microfilm 392, 322–27.

Bernarr Macfadden vs. Mary Macfadden. Proceedings before Hon. John C. Grambling, Special Master, Chancery Case no. 77430–A, circuit court in and for Dade County, Fla., 1943–1946.

Bernarr Macfadden vs. Mary Macfadden. Special Master's Report, Chancery Case no. 77430, circuit court in and for Dade County, Fla., Oct. 29, 1945.

Bernarr Macfadden Plaintiff in Error vs. United States of America Defendant in Error. United States District Court for the District of New Jersey, Proceedings no. 236, 5, Federal Building, Trenton, N.J., 1969. Microfilm.

ARTICLES IN PERIODICALS

"Bernarr Macfadden Foundation Takes over a Sanatorium for Tuberculosis." *Journal of the American Medical Association*, vol. 13, no. 2, July 8, 1939.

"The Big Muscle Boys: The Apotheosis of Brawn as a Goal of Health." *Hygeia*, vol. 3, no. 4, Apr. 1925.

"The Big Muscle Boys: More Exponents of Mail Order Physical Culture." *Hygeia*, vol. 3, no. 5, May 1925.

Burnham, John C. "The Progressive Era Revolution in American Attitudes Towards Sex." *Journal of American History*, vol. 69, no. 4, Mar. 1973.

"A Colorful Publishing Career," *Printer's Ink*, Oct. 21, 1955.

Congressional Record. 76th Cong., 1st sess., Mar. 8, 1939. Vol. 84, 2440, and app. 948.

Dykstra, David L. "The Medical Profession and Patent and Proprietary Medicines during the Nineteenth Century." *Bulletin of the History of Medicine*, vol. 29, no. 5, Sept.–Oct. 1955.

"Exploiting the Health Interest. I. Type of Advertising that Makes 'Physical Culture' Commercially Profitable," *Hygeia*, vol. 2, no. 11, Nov. 1924.

"Exploiting the Health Interest. II. Type of Literature on Which 'Physical Culturists' and Macfaddenists Thrive." *Hygeia*, vol. 2, no. 12, Dec. 1924.

Garrett, Oliver H. P. "Another True Story." *New Yorker*, Sept. 19, 1925.

Gerber, George. "The Social Role of the Confession Magazine." *Social Problems*, vol. 6, no. 1, Summer 1958.

Gray, Harria. "Physical Culture Restaurant," *Physical Culture*. Mar. 1903.

Hall, G. Stanley. "Some Relations Between Physical and Mental Training." In *Proceedings of the American Association for the Advancement of Physical Education*. Ninth annual meeting, no. 2, 1894.

Johnston, Alva. "The Great Macfadden." *Saturday Evening Post*, June 21, 28, 1941.

Kandel, Aben. "A Tabloid a Day." *Forum*, Mar. 1927.

Macfadden, Bernarr. "Americanism—Open Declaration Demanded." *Liberty*, July 27, 1940.

_____. "Another Way to Save the Nation." *Liberty*, Aug. 10, 1940.

_____. "At One Time There Were States' Rights." *Liberty*, Feb. 18, 1939.

_____. "Bernarr Macfadden Wants to Be Secretary of Health." *Liberty*, Aug. 3, 1940.

_____. "Brutal, Murderous Strikes—Who Is to Blame." *Liberty*, Sept. 1, 1934.

_____. "Celebrating Fifty Years of Physical Culture." *Physical Culture*, Mar.–Oct. 1933.

_____. "A Crusading Newspaper." *New York Evening Graphic*, Sept. 17, 1924.

_____. "The Depression Is Staggering." *Liberty*, Aug. 5, 1933.

_____. "Do the Workers All Want Government Jobs?" *Liberty*, June 25, 1938.

_____. "The Dole—a Great Calamity." *Liberty*, July 29, 1933.

_____. "Enforce the Laws or Get Out." *Liberty*, July 21, 1934.

———. "Entire Nation Must Train to Avoid Enslavement." *Liberty,* Jan. 18, 1941.

———. "Forcing Japan into the Hell of Another War." *Liberty,* Jan. 26, 1935.

———. "The Ghastly Blunders of the Republican Campaign Managers." *Liberty,* Jan. 2, 1937.

———. "The Gigantic Cost of Crime." *Liberty,* Apr. 5, 1941.

———. "Good News for Tuberculosis Victims." *Liberty,* Oct. 21, 1939.

———. "Governmental Competition in Private Business." *Liberty,* Jan. 28, 1933.

———. "Henry Wallace, the Fair-Haired Dreamer." *Liberty,* Oct. 5, 1940.

———. "I Indict the New Deal for . . . ." *Liberty,* Nov. 7, 1936.

———. "Intelligence—the Greatest Need of the Democracies." *Liberty,* Oct. 28, 1939.

———. "Job Insurance Will Save the Nation from Ruin." *Liberty,* Dec. 1, 1934.

———. "Lost in the Sky." *Liberty,* Oct. 5, 1940.

———. "The Man Behind the Miracle." *Liberty,* Aug. 10, 1940.

———. "A Nation-wide Demand for the Resignation of Madam Perkins." *Liberty,* Oct. 22, 1938.

———. "A New Cabinet Position—Secretary of Business Management." *Liberty,* May 30, 1936.

———. "The New Deal Is Here—God Be Praised." *Liberty,* Apr. 22, 1933.

———. "The One Thing That Matters." *True Story,* Oct. 1935.

———. "Only Dictatorial Powers Can Save Us." *Liberty,* Mar. 25, 1933.

———. "Our Farmers Will Now Be Instructed Like School Boys." *Liberty,* Apr. 2, 1938.

———. "Our New President Should Have a Free Hand." *Liberty,* Feb. 4, 1933.

———. "The Permanency of the NRA." *Liberty,* Apr. 21, 1934.

———. "Playing the Farmers for Suckers." *Liberty,* May 25, 1940.

———. "The Poor Old Republican Party." *Liberty,* Sept. 17, 1938.

———. "Remove Commercialism from Public Health." *Liberty,* Feb. 3, 1940.

———. "Some New Dealers Can't Take It." *Liberty,* Mar. 28, 1936.

———. "They Say This Is Inflation, But—." *Liberty,* Mar. 4, 1933.

———. "The Thrill of Flying." *Liberty,* Sept. 9, 1933.

———. "Throw Out the Foreign Traitors." *Liberty,* Nov. 26, 1938.

———. "Various Planks Suggested for the Republican Platform." *Liberty,* June 13, 1936.

———. "Wages and the Depression." *Liberty,* Apr. 15, 1933.

———. "War—Health—Doctors." *Liberty,* Nov. 30, 1940.

———. "War! War! An Open Letter to President Roosevelt." *Liberty,* May 16, 1936.

———. "We Accept the Challenge." *Liberty,* Mar. 11, 1933.

———. "We Are with the President in His Fight Against Spies." *Liberty,* Jan. 14, 1939.

———. "We Can Win with Willkie." *Liberty,* Nov. 9, 1940.

_____. "We Endorse the President's Health Crusade." *Liberty*, Feb. 4, 1939.

_____. "When Wealth Brings Disaster." *Liberty*, July 1, 1933.

"Macfadden and a Starvation Death." *Journal of the American Medical Association*, vol. 84, no. 2, Jan. 10, 1925.

"Macfadden as Educator." *Outlook and Independent*, Nov. 14, 1928.

"Macfadden Says 'I Told You So' about Syphilis." *Journal of the American Medical Association*, vol. 88, no. 15, Apr. 10, 1937, 1266.

"Mr. Macfadden Defines News." *New Republic*, Oct. 8, 1924.

"Mr. Macfadden Discusses Army Medical Service." *Journal of the American Medical Association*, vol. 115, no. 22, Nov. 30, 1940.

Manchester, Harland. "True Stories." *Scribner's Magazine*, Aug. 1938.

Mencken, H. L. "An American Idealist." *American Mercury*, May 1930.

_____. "What to Do with Criminals." *Liberty*, July 28, 1934.

Mitchell, Harry G. "Fasting and Diet Cured Me of a Terrible Blood Disease." *Physical Culture*, Dec. 1926.

O'Reilly, Kenneth. "A New Deal for the FBI: The Roosevelt Administration, Crime Control, and National Security." *Journal of American History*, vol. 69, no. 3, Dec. 1982.

Oursler, Fulton. "Bernarr Macfadden—His Life and Work." *Physical Culture*, Sept. 1928–May 1929. Each issue contains a "chapter."

Oursler, Fulton. "The Most Unforgettable Character I've Met." *Reader's Digest*, July 1951.

"Perhaps the Public Has Been Maligned." *Christian Century*, July 20, 1932, 901.

Pringle, Henry F. "Another American Phenomenon Bernarr Macfadden—Publisher and Physical Culturist." *World's Work*, Oct. 1928.

Spivak, John L. "The Rise and Fall of a Tabloid." *American Mercury*, July 1934.

Strong, Bryan. "Ideas of the Early Sex Education Movement in America, 1890–1920." *History of Education Quarterly*, vol. 12, no. 2, Summer 1972.

Stuart, John. "Bernarr Macfadden: From Pornography to Politics." *New Masses*, May 9, 1936.

Swerling, Jo. "The Picture Papers Win." *Nation*, Oct. 21, 1925.

Taft, William H. "Bernarr Macfadden." *Missouri Historical Review*, vol. 63, no. 1, Oct. 1968.

Talmey, Allene. "Millions from Dumb-bells." *Outlook and Independent*, June 4, 1930.

Taylor, Robert Lewis. "Physical Culture." Pts. 1, 2, 3, *New Yorker*, Oct. 14, 21, 28, 1950.

Villard, Oswald Garrison. "I—Tabloid Offenses." *Forum*, Apr. 1927.

_____. "Sex, Art, Truth and Magazines." *Atlantic Monthly*, March 1926.

Wake, Robert. "There's Rejuvenation in Walking." *Liberty*, Jan. 13, 1940.

Weyrauch, Martin. "II—The Why of Tabloids." *Forum*, March 1927.

Yagoda, Ben. "The True Story of Bernarr Macfadden." *American Heritage*, Dec. 1981.

In addition, I have consulted and cited the following periodicals, with an asterisk indicating those cited extensively: *Editor and Publisher, Liberty,* * *Macfadden Retailer, Macfadden Wholesaler, Newsweek, Physical Culture,* * *Sportswise, Tide, Time, True Detective Mysteries, True Story,* * and *Your Faith.*

NEWSPAPERS

American Vegetarian [Pismo Beach, Calif.], July 1946.
Chicago Daily News, Oct. 13, 1955.
Chicago Daily Tribune, Oct. 13, 1955.
Daily American Republican [Poplar Bluff, Mo.], Oct. 13, 1955.
Dansville Express [N.Y.], May 3, 1929.
Doniphan Prospect News [Mo.], Oct. 20, 1955.
Evening Record [Hackensack, Bergen County, N.J.], various issues.
Genesee Country Express [Dansville, N.Y.], Mar. 2, 1955; Apr. 26, 1956.
Genesee Country Express and Advertiser, June 19, 1941.
Graphic. See New York Evening Graphic.
Iron County Register [Ironton, Mo.], Sept. 19, 26, 1867.
Miami Herald, Jan. 21, 1947; Apr. 23, 1948; June 2, 1949; Nov. 19, 1952; Jan. 1, 1955.
Morning Call [Paterson, N.J.], Dec. 2, 1955.
New Brunswick Daily Home News [N.J.], Nov. 7, 1914.
Newsday [Garden City, N.Y.], June 3, 4, 1960.
New York Evening Graphic, 1924–1932.
New York Herald Tribune, various issues.
New York Times, various issues.
Pittsburgh Press, Dec. 11, 1951.
Rochester Democrat and Chronicle, Oct. 5, 1958; May 22, 1977; and Sunday supp., *Upstate Magazine,* Dec. 12, 1982.
Rochester Times-Union, Oct. 13, 1955.
St. Louis Post-Dispatch, Dec. 26, 1954.
The World [New York], 1905–1907.

BOOKS AND PAMPHLETS

Allen, Frederick Lewis. *Only Yesterday, An Informal History of the Nineteen-Twenties.* New York: Blue Ribbon Books, 1931.
Aspiz, Harold, "Sexuality and the Pseudo-Sciences." In *Pseudo-Science and Society in Nineteenth Century America,* edited by Arthur Wrobel. Lexington: Univ. Press of Kentucky, 1987.
Baruch Committee on Physical Medicine. *Annual Report,* Apr. 1, 1945 to Dec. 31, 1946 [New York, 1947], and Jan. 1, 1948 to June 30, 1949 [Chi-

cago, 1949 or 1950). Apparently, these reports were published by the committee itself.

Bernarr Macfadden: Highlights of Fifty Years Service for His Country. N.p., n.d., probably 1935.

Bernays, Edward L. Biography of an Idea: Memoirs of Public Relations Counsel, Edward L. Bernays. New York: Simon and Schuster, 1965.

Bessie, Simon Michael. Jazz Journalism, The Story of the Tabloid Newspapers. 1938. Reprint. New York: Russell and Russell, 1969.

Blaikie, William. How to Get Strong and How to Stay So. New York: Harper, 1884.

Bok, Edward. The Americanization of Edward Bok. New York: Charles Scribner's Sons, 1931.

Broun, Heywood, and Margaret Leech. Anthony Comstock: Roundsman of the Lord. New York: Albert and Charles Boni, 1927.

Burnham, John C. How Superstition Won and Science Lost: Popularizing Science and Health in the United States. New Brunswick, N.J.: Rutgers Univ. Press, 1987.

Carlisle, Rodney P. Hearst and the New Deal, The Progressive as Reactionary. New York: Garland, 1979.

Carr, Lucien. Missouri, A Bone of Contention. Boston: Houghton-Mifflin, 1888.

Carson, Gerald. Cornflake Crusade. New York: Rinehart, 1957.

Caspary, Vera. The Secrets of Grown-ups. New York: McGraw Hill, 1979.

Cohen, Lester. The New York Graphic, The World's Zaniest Newspaper. Philadelphia: Chilton Books, 1964.

Cramer, Rose Fulton. Wayne County, Missouri. Cape Girardeau, Mo.: Ramfre Press, 1972.

Culmer, Frederic A. A New History of Missouri. Mexico, Mo.: McIntyre Publishing, 1938.

Dixon, Thomas. A Dreamer in Portugal. New York: Convici-Friede, 1934.

Donegan, Jane B. 'Hydropathic Highway to Health': Women and Water-Cure in Antebellum America. New York: Greenwood Press, 1986.

Dunning, John. Tune in Yesterday: The Ultimate Encyclopedia of Old-time Radio, 1925–1976. Englewood Cliffs, N.J.: Prentice-Hall, 1976.

Fishbein, Morris. A History of the American Medical Association. Philadelphia: Saunders, 1947.

——. Medical Follies, An Analysis of the Foibles of Some Healing Cults. New York: Boni and Liveright, 1925.

Fletcher, Horace D. The A. B. –Z of Our Own Nutrition. New York: Frederick A. Stokes, 1903.

Gaines, Charles, and George Butler. Yours in Perfect Manhood, Charles Atlas. New York: Simon and Schuster, 1982.

Gauvreau, Emile. My Last Million Readers. New York: E. P. Dutton, 1941.

Gian-Curso, Christopher, ed. Eternal Health Truths. New York: n.p., 1960.

Goodspeed's History of Southeast Missouri. 1888. Reprint. Cape Girardeau, Mo.: Ramfre Press, 1955.

Green, Harvey. *Fit for America: Health, Fitness, Sport and American Society.* Paperback ed. Baltimore: Johns Hopkins Univ. Press, 1988.

Hale, Annie Riley, *"These Cults": An Analysis of the Foibles of Dr. Morris Fishbein's "Medical Follies" and an Indictment of Medical Practice in General.* New York: National Health Foundation, 1926.

Haley, Bruce. *The Healthy Body and Victorian Culture.* Cambridge, Mass.: Harvard Univ. Press, 1978.

Hersey, Harold B. *Pulpwood Editor.* New York: Frederick A. Stokes, 1937.

Hunt, William R. *Body Love: The Amazing Career of Bernarr Macfadden.* Bowling Green, Ohio: Bowling Green State Univ. Popular Press, 1989.

Jackson, Carlton. *J. I. Rodale, Apostle of Nonconformity.* New York: Pyramid Books, 1974.

Kemp, Harry. *Tramping on Life, An Autobiographical Narrative.* Garden City, N.Y.: Garden City Publishing, 1922.

Kernberg, Otto F. *Borderline Conditions and Pathological Narcissism.* New York: J. Aronson, 1975.

Kohut, Heinz. *The Analysis of Self: A Systematic Approach to Psychoanalytic Treatment of Narcissistic Personality Disorders.* New York: International Universities Press, 1971.

Lash, Joseph P. *Eleanor and Franklin: The Story of Their Relationship, Based on Eleanor Roosevelt's Private Papers.* New York: W. W. Norton, 1971.

Lee, Alfred McClung. *The Daily Newspaper in America: The Evolution of a Social Instrument.* New York: Macmillan, 1947.

Lee, Mabel. *A History of Physical Education and Sports in the U.S.A.* New York: John Wiley and Sons, 1983.

Lowen, Alexander. *Narcissism, Denial of the True Self.* New York: Macmillan, 1983.

McCollum, Elmer V. *A History of Nutrition.* Boston: Houghton-Mifflin, 1957.

Macfadden, Bernarr. *The Athlete's Conquest, The Romance of an Athlete.* Rev. ed. New York: Physical Culture Publishing, 1901.

————. *Building of Vital Power: Deep Breathing and a Complete System for Strengthening the Heart, Lungs, Stomach and All the Great Vital Organs.* New York: Physical Culture Publishing, 1904.

————. *Coughs, Colds and Catarrh.* New York: Macfadden Publications, 1926.

————. *Fasting for Health: A Complete Guide on How, When and Why to Use the Fasting Cure.* New York: Macfadden Book Company, 1935.

————. *Health for the Family.* New York: Macfadden Publications, 1929.

————. *Is It a Crime to Expose a Crime?* Pamphlet bound with *Physical Culture,* Dec. 1907.

————. *Macfadden's Encyclopedia of Physical Culture.* 5 vols. New York: Physical Culture Publishing, 1911–1912.

——. *Macfadden's New Hair Culture.* 3d ed. New York: Physical Culture Publishing, 1901.

——. *Macfadden's Physical Training: An Illustrated System of Exercises for the Development of Health, Strength and Beauty.* New York: Macfadden Company, 1900.

——. *The Macfadden Prosecution: A Curious Story of Wrong and Oppression under the Postal Laws.* Battle Creek, Mich.: n.p., 1908.

——. *Manhood and Marriage.* New York: Physical Culture Publishing, 1916.

——. *Man's Sex Life.* New York: Macfadden Book Company, 1936.

——. *Marriage a Lifelong Honeymoon: Life's Greatest Pleasures Secured by Observing the Highest Human Instincts.* New York: Physical Culture Publishing, 1903.

——. *The Miracle of Milk: How to Use the Milk Diet Scientifically at Home.* New York: Macfadden Publications, 1923.

——. *Plain Speech on a Public Insult: Bernarr Macfadden Replies to the Atlantic Monthly.* New York: Macfadden Publications, 1926.

——. *Strength from Eating: How and What to Eat and Drink to Develop the Highest Degree of Health and Strength.* New York: Physical Culture Publishing, 1901.

——. *A Strenuous Lover: A Romance of Natural Love's Vast Power.* Original story by Bernarr Macfadden; revised with the assistance of John R. Coryell. New York: Physical Culture Publishing, 1904.

——. *The Virile Powers of Superb Manhood: How Developed, How Lost, How Regained.* New York: Physical Culture Publishing, 1900.

——, and Marion Malcolm. *Health—Beauty—Sexuality from Girlhood to Womanhood.* New York: Physical Culture Publishing, 1904.

Macfadden, Johnnie Lee. *Barefoot in Eden: The Macfadden Plan for Health, Charm and Long-Lasting Youth.* Englewood Cliffs, N.J.: Prentice-Hall, 1962.

Macfadden, Mary, and Emile Gauvreau. *Dumbbells and Carrot Strips, The Story of Bernarr Macfadden.* New York: Henry Holt, 1953.

[Macfadden Publications]. *Report to Stockholders for the Year ended August 31, 1941.* New York: 1941.

[Macfadden Publications]. *Statistical and Financial Analysis of Macfadden Publications.* New York: Macfadden Publications, 1929.

Mallen, Frank. *Sauce for the Gander.* White Plains, N.Y.: Baldwin Books, 1954.

Moody's Industrials. New York: Moody's Investor's Service, 1942.

Mott, Frank Luther. *American Journalism, A History: 1690–1960.* 3d ed. New York: Macmillan, 1962.

——. *A History of American Magazines.* Vol. 4. Cambridge, Mass.: Belknap Press, 1957.

Mrozek, Donald J. *Sport and American Mentality, 1880–1910.* Knoxville: Univ. of Tennessee Press, 1983.

Nagel, Paul C. *Missouri, A Bicentennial History.* New York: W. W. Norton, 1977.

Oursler, Fulton. *Behold This Dreamer! An Autobiography by Fulton Oursler.* Boston: Little, Brown, 1964.

————. *The True Story of Bernarr Macfadden.* New York: Lewis Copeland, 1929.

Oursler, Will. *Family Story.* New York: Funk and Wagnalls, 1963.

Parrish, William E. *A History of Missouri.* Vol. 3, 1860 to 1875. Columbia: Univ. of Missouri Press, 1973.

————. *Turbulent Partnership, Missouri and the Union, 1861–1865.* Columbia: Univ. of Missouri Press, 1963.

Perkins, Grace [Grace Perkins Oursler]. *Chats with the Macfadden Family.* New York: Lewis Copeland, 1929.

Peterson, Theodore. *Magazines in the Twentieth Century.* 2d ed. Urbana: Univ. of Illinois Press, 1964.

Presbrey, Frank S. *The History and Development of Advertising.* Garden City, N.Y.: Doubleday, Doran, 1929.

Rosen, George. *A History of Public Health.* New York: MD Publications, 1958.

Sinclair, Upton. *Autobiography of Upton Sinclair.* New York: Harcourt, Brace and World, 1962.

————. *The Fasting Cure.* Pasadena, Calif.: author, 1911.

[Standard and Poor's Corporation]. *1941 Annual Dividend Record.* New York: Standard and Poor's, 1942.

[Standard Statistics Company]. *Standard Corporation Records: Dividend Payments in 1938.* New York: Standard Statistics Company, 1939; also for 1939 (New York, 1940).

Summers, Harrison B., ed. *A Thirty-year History of Programs Carried on Radio Networks in the United States, 1926–1956.* New York: Arno Press, 1971.

[True Story Magazine]. *The American Economic Revolution.* 2 vols. New York: True Story, 1930–1931.

————. *How to Get People Excited.* New York: True Story, 1937.

True Story Magazine as a Great Moral Force, n.p. [New York]: Macfadden Publications, n.d.

Truman, Harry S. *Memoirs by Harry S. Truman.* 2 vols. Garden City, N.Y.: Doubleday, 1955–1956.

Tugwell, Rexford G. *The Brains Trust.* New York: Viking Press, 1968.

Villard, Oswald Garrison. *Sex, Art, Truth and Magazines.* Boston: Atlantic Monthly, 1926. (Pamphlet reprint of article in *Atlantic Monthly,* Mar. 1926.)

Whorton, James C. *Crusaders for Fitness: The History of American Health Reformers.* Princeton: Princeton Univ. Press, 1982.

Winkler, John K. *William Randolph Hearst, A New Appraisal.* New York: Hastings House, 1955.

Wood, Clement. *Bernarr Macfadden, A Study in Success.* New York: Lewis Copeland, 1929.

WPA Federal Writers' Project. *Missouri; A Guide to the "Show Me" State.* American Guide Series. New York: Duell, Sloan and Pearce, 1941.

WPA Federal Writers' Project. *Monroe Township, Middlesex County, New Jersey, 1838–1938.* American Guide Series. n.p.: Monroe Township Committee, 1938.

Young, James Harvey. *The Medical Messiahs: A Social History of Health Quackery in Twentieth Century America.* Princeton: Princeton Univ. Press, 1967.

————. *The Toadstool Millionaires: A Social History of Patent Medicines in America before Federal Regulation.* Princeton: Princeton Univ. Press, 1961.

Index